C. S. L. Davies was born in 1936. Educated at St. Paul's School and Wadham College, Oxford, he then did research on Tudor history under Lawrence Stone. He taught at Glasgow University. Since 1963 he has been Fellow and Tutor in Modern History at Wadham. He has published

THE PALADIN HISTORY OF ENGLAND

General Editor: Lord Blake

Advisory Editor: Cameron Hazlehurst

C. S. L. DAVIES

Peace, Print and Protestantism 1450–1558

PALADIN
GRAFTON BOOKS
A Division of the Collins Publishing Group

LONDON GLASGOW
TORONTO SYDNEY AUCKLAND

Paladin
Grafton Books
A Division of the Collins Publishing Group
8 Grafton Street, London W1X 3LA

Published in Paladin Books 1977
Reprinted 1982, 1984, 1988, 1990

First published in Great Britain by
Hart-Davis, MacGibbon Ltd 1977

Copyright © C. S. L. Davies 1976, 1984, 1986

A CIP catalogue record for this book
is available from the British Library

ISBN 0-586-08266-2

Printed and bound in Great Britain by
Collins, Glasgow

Set in Ehrhardt

For
PHILIP WHITTING
Magistro Optimo

ACKNOWLEDGEMENTS

Thanks to the General Editors, Lord Blake and Cameron Hazlehurst, for suggesting and guiding this book; to Peter Sommer and Susan Hill of Paladin Books; to Peter Lewis, Peter Clark, Kathleen Davies and Christopher Harrison for patiently and critically reading the text; to Roger Schofield for allowing citation from his (lamentably) unpublished thesis; to the Cambridge University Press and the journal *Economica* for the use of material upon which two graphs in the appendix were based; H. L. Gray, J. P. Cooper and the *Economic History Review*; and C. D. Ross, T. B. Pugh and the *Bulletin of the Institute of Historical Research*; to a stream of typists, most notably Miss Marja Naatanen and Mrs Joan Morrall, for patiently struggling with my writing. Too many influences combine in a general book of this kind to mention them individually. The dedication records one of the earliest and most far-reaching.

Publication in paperback has made possible the correction of errors detected by vigilant friends, most notably John Hadwin and Paul Slack; further errors were corrected in the 1984 reprint (my thanks to David Palliser and Penry Williams).

FOREWORD

by Robert Blake

History does not consist of a body of received opinion handed down by authority from the historiographical equivalent of the heights of Mount Sinai. It is a subject full of vigour, controversy, life – and sometimes strife. One of the purposes of the Paladin History of England is to convey not only what the authors believe to have happened but also why; to discuss evidence as well as facts; to give an idea and an evaluation of the controversies which surround so many episodes and interpretations of the past.

The last twenty years have seen important changes in the approach to history and to historical questions. There has also been much painstaking research which throws new light on old problems and brings new problems into the field of discussion. Little of all this has so far got through to the general reader because it has been, naturally, confined to specialist journals and monographs. A real need exists for a series of volumes to inform the wide public interested in the history of England, and this is what the Paladin volumes are intended to meet.

All history is in one sense contemporary history. These volumes inevitably and rightly reflect to some extent the outlook of those who, whatever their own age, are writing in the 1980s. But there are in any decade a wide variety of attitudes and schools of thought. The authors of this series are not chosen to represent a particular body of doctrine; conservative, liberal, Marxist – or whatever. They are scholars who are deeply involved in the historical questions of their particular fields, and who believe that it is possible to put across something of the challenges, puzzles and excitements of their theme to a large audience in a form which is readable, intelligible and concise.

All historical writing must in some measure be arbitrary as to dates and selective as to area. The dates chosen in this series do not depart far from convention but perhaps just enough to encourage both author and reader to take a fresh view. The decision to make this a history of England, rather than Britain, is quite deliberate. It does not mean omission of the important repercussions of events in Scotland, Ireland, Wales or the countries which later constituted the Empire and the Commonwealth; rather a recognition that, whether for good or ill, the English have been the dominant nation in what Tennyson called 'our rough island-story', and that a widening of the scope would lead to diffuseness and confusion.

Historical writing also has to be selective as to themes. Each author uses his own judgement here, but, although politics, ideas, art and literature must always be central features in any work of general history, economic background, social structure, demography, scientific and technical developments are no less important and must be given proper weight.

All sorts of reasons can be given for reading history, but the best of them has always seemed to me sheer pleasure. It is my hope as editor of this series that this enjoyment will be communicated to a large number of people who might otherwise perhaps have never experienced it.

CONTENTS

CONTENTS

INTRODUCTION

Readers of history – especially of introductory works of this sort – should beware of neat formulations. Human experience is too many-sided, too ragged, to be summed up in a trite phrase; the age of this, the century of that. Any account of the history of a nation over a century necessarily involves selection, simplification, and concentration on certain themes; the alternative is a mish-mash of uncoordinated information. I do not, therefore, claim that the three themes I have singled out offer a complete explanation of the period; still less, that they offer the only explanation; only that the creation of a real, if precarious, internal peace, the revolution in the dissemination of knowledge and information made possible by the printing press, and the appearance of a radical new religious consciousness, are three of the most striking developments of the period. And these must be set in the context of economic change; of growing national wealth, on the one hand, of growing population on the other. We cannot tell which grew faster overall; but what does seem clear is that the distribution of wealth was increasingly polarized, that the better-off got richer, and the poor poorer. The problem of poverty and destitution cast an ever-darkening shadow on the national life, to reach its culmination in the famine and mortality of the 1550s.

Any division into periods is arbitrary. That said, a good case can be made out for the dates adopted here. 1450 as a starting date at least gets away from the unwarranted importance often attached to the accession of Henry VII in 1485. It pitches us into the middle of events, rather before the outbreak of the Wars of the Roses; and there is a distinct need to understand the causes of the Wars of the Roses if we are to understand the subsequent political recovery. Tudor historians often exaggerate the tendencies to disorder in the fifteenth century; and that in turn leads them to exaggerate the statesmanship required to re-establish stability, by Edward IV or by Henry VII. More generally, the early Tudor period makes a good deal more sense studied against its fifteenth-century background rather than treated as the back-drop to the Elizabethan period. Perhaps the terminal date, the accession of Elizabeth I, is rather less satisfactory. The first dozen years of Elizabeth's reign were in many ways a continuation of the period of change and uncertainty which had marked English history since the death of Henry VIII; and there would be a good case for continuing the period to 1569 or 1570. Nevertheless, one has to stop somewhere; and slicing through Elizabeth's reign would create more problems than it solves.

The period chosen might suggest that the theme of the book should be the transition from 'medieval' to 'modern'. I have resisted the temptation. Indeed, I have tried not to use the word 'medieval' at all, except in quotations from other historians. The period saw important, long-ranging changes. But I cannot accept the implied assumption that the years from AD 1000 (or even earlier) to about 1500 possessed special unifying 'medieval' characteristics which mark them off as a distinct entity; nor do I believe that the changes which took place in the years around 1500 were decisively more important than those which took place in, say, the 'scientific revolution' of the seventeenth century. Some historians have tackled the problem by pushing the key date forward in time, or, more commonly, backward. The 'Renaissance' is liable to infinite recession. But the assumption remains that there was a single decisive period of change; and it is an unwarranted one. Many historians who recognize this, nevertheless, continue to use the traditional classification, justifying themselves purely in terms of convenience. But words have a subtle way of determining one's cast of thought; and this is a dangerous proceeding. Too soon we find ourselves back to a sterile debate on whether such and such a development was 'medieval' or 'modern'.

A good deal of the book is taken up with political history; politics, after all, supply the essential dimension of movement.

Economic and social change is, especially at this period, very long-term, very gradual. Political events cannot, therefore, be explained purely in terms of changes in the social structure, in the relative strength of classes and so on. Social structure determined the broad limits of political life; but within those limits the actual course of events was affected by unpredictable features. England was, after all, a functioning monarchy; and the different personalities of successive kings, the chance of whether or not an early death produced a royal minority, obviously mattered.

It is comforting to think that all this is irrelevant in the long run; but that is an unproven assumption, and a naïve one. Political events, after all, help to determine social structure; history is not a one-way process. I shall argue, for instance, that long-term trends made Protestantism possible in England, but by no means inevitable; that Henry VIII's decision to break with Rome was not the inevitable result of the clash of royal and papal power, but was largely determined by Henry's matrimonial difficulties; and that it is by no means certain that Queen Mary, had she lived longer, might not have been successful in permanently re-establishing England as a Catholic country. Of course, Protestantism might have succeeded without state support; but the result would have been a very different Protestantism to that with which we are familiar. Or again, the Elizabethan age owed an enormous amount to the 'accidental' factor of the queen's longevity. If the queen had died in the 1560s or 1570s the country would almost certainly have dissolved into a bitter succession war, and that in turn would have dangerously polarized religious feeling, with incalculable results. History is much more than the lives of great men. But it would be absurd to underestimate the importance of chance in a world in which –

> The cease of majesty
> Dies not alone, but like a gulf doth draw
> What's near it with it; it is a massy wheel
> Fix'd on the summit of the highest mount,
> To whose huge spokes ten thousand lesser things
> Are mortised and adjoined.*

Wadham College
Oxford 1975

* *Hamlet*, act 3, scene 3.

Chapter One

THE LIFE OF A SOCIETY

ECONOMY AND SOCIAL STRUCTURE

England was rather off the beaten track for fifteenth-century tourists, and few foreign accounts have survived. The French, naturally, studied their aggressive neighbours closely; the English were said to have killed more Christians in a hundred years than all the other nations in Europe (which means that, at intervals, their kings had been invading France since 1339), to be a mortal danger to all their neighbours, and to kill their own kings. Other observers could afford to be more detached. They agreed that the English were an exceptionally passionate and demonstrative people, a nice indication of how national stereotypes change over the centuries. The men were quick to anger and violent, and the women remarkably free with their favours (though in this the visitors may have been misled by superficial impressions, since 'to take a kiss in England is the equivalent of shaking hands elsewhere'). The prosperity of the country was noted; a 'little sea-girt garden', thought a Czech, who had nowhere seen more beautiful churches 'all covered . . . with lead and tin and adorned in a truly wonderful fashion'; and he had never heard better music.

The only discordant note came from an Italian diplomat (and later pope), Aeneas Sylvius, who once had the misfortune to return overland from Scotland. Hospitably entertained in a Northumbrian farmhouse he was surprised to find that at nightfall the men withdrew to a fortified tower. The women stayed behind, since the Scots would do them no harm; 'they do not count outrage a wrong.' Two of the women promptly offered to sleep with him, according to custom, but he refused, through fear of having his throat cut while in a state of mortal sin; and in fact the night passed peacefully, a reward, he believed for his virtuous resistance to temptation. Allowance must be made for literary exaggeration; but even Sylvius, once he got to Newcastle, found himself in civilized country, and commended the usual tourist round of London Bridge, the goldsmiths' shops and the tomb of Thomas Becket at Canterbury.

Sylvius would have made himself understood in Latin – the international language of the church and of education; though there can have been little similarity between the language of the fashionable Italian humanist and the rough-and-ready North-umbrian priest. Knowledge of Latin marked off the educated from the general mass; 'illiterate' meant incompetent in Latin. Up to about a hundred years before there had been a further linguistic complication: the upper classes had normally spoken French. But this had begun to change from about 1350 (nicely symbolized by the success of Chaucer before a court audience in the 1370s), and in 1422 the London brewers justified keeping their records in English because Henry v's official use of the language had given it social cachet. Of course, English itself was very far from being a unified language. When a Kentishwoman was asked by a group of London merchants for 'eggs' she excused herself for not understanding French, and communication between, say, a Yorkshireman and a man from Somerset must have been almost impossible. Nevertheless, the fact that even the aristocracy now spoke something similar to the language of the people indicated a new sense of national unity and self-consciousness.

This was probably, in part at least, the result of the long and sporadic war with France. Curiously, if the English had been more successful in arms, the result would have been to make England itself an irritating and touchy appendage to the greater kingdom; English kings would have become first and foremost kings of France. The glory of spectacular victories, under Edward III in the fourteenth century, and again under Henry v (1413–22), and perhaps even more the frustration of subsequent defeats, had made the English touchily proud and condescending towards foreigners. 'Whenever they see a handsome foreigner, they say, "he looks like an Englishman".' More often, visitors complained of being beaten up for no apparent reason. Anti-Italian riots were common in London, mainly for economic reasons, and a long poem, the *Libelle of Englyshe Polycye*, written in about 1436, advocated a policy of aggressive economic nationalism.

But we must not exaggerate these nationalistic tendencies. England was riven by sectional interest; economic rivalry between towns, and between town and country (about the competition of sweated rural labour), were far more immediate issues for most English artisans than were the malpractices of foreign merchants. More generally, hatred between northerners and southerners was intense, and played its part in politics. London in 1461 closed its gates to the queen's northern army for fear of spoil 'for the people in the north rob and steal and be appointed to pillage'; while a southern chronicle thought that Richard III's distribution of land to northerners bulked high among his sins, 'to the disgrace of all the people in the south'. Nationalism in the modern sense was not the determinant of foreign policy; national interest bulked less large (in spite of the *Libelle*) than national honour, and national honour depended on the personal honour of the king. The war with France was discussed almost entirely in terms of the king's noble quarrel and 'very right' to the French crown.

England impressed foreigners as a rich country with fertile soil and good natural resources (tin, lead, above all, wool), and an abundance of fine building and expensive furnishings. One starry-eyed Venetian thought that the smallest inn-keepers had silver plate. To be fair, visitors other than the unfortunate Sylvius rarely saw the highland areas. England's prosperity was largely due to peace. Unlike the French the English were spared the ravages of invading (or defending) soldiers except in the far north; they were spared, too, paying taxes for a large army. The civil wars of the fifteenth century hardly disturbed this happy situation; armies were raised, a battle was fought, and then they were disbanded. There was no question (except in some outlying areas in the 1460s) of permanent garrisons waging continuous war.

England's wealth was overwhelmingly rural. The only large town was London, with between thirty and fifty thousand inhabitants. It was 'the flower of cities all' to the Scotsman Dunbar, and probably as large as any city in Europe outside Italy, except for Paris (said to be three times the size of London). Other towns were much smaller; York, Bristol and Norwich had up to ten thousand people each, and perhaps a dozen more were on the five thousand mark. England's most important industry, cloth-making, was largely rural. It had developed relatively late, in the thirteenth and fourteenth centuries. Partly because of the need for water to drive fulling mills, partly because labour was cheaper in the countryside, it had developed outside the towns, in Wilt-shire and Somerset, in Gloucestershire and East Anglia, in Devon and the West Riding of Yorkshire. In the great industrial areas of Europe, in the Netherlands and Italy, the towns were generally larger, and were disturbed periodically by bitter class struggles between the smaller craftsmen and the rich merchants who tended to monopolize town government. Although London had had its troubles at the end of the fourteenth century, and there were occasional outbursts in other towns, the smaller scale of English town life damped down violent urban class conflict.

Historians have disagreed rather violently in their analysis of the general health of English industry. For some, who see the land-lord sector (which included church and king) as the principal customers for industrial products, the decline in landlord incomes, which we will be examining, involved a decline in industrial pro-duction. For other historians this was amply compensated by the rise of a more prosperous peasantry, able to take up any slack in demand on the part of their lords.* The figures are difficult to interpret, and at the moment there seems little alternative to cowardly agnosticism on the point. What is clear, however, is the transformation of the foreign market. In 1300 exports had been overwhelmingly of raw wool: England had been a 'colonial' economy supplying the industrial centres of Europe with raw material. By 1450 exports consisted largely of manufactured cloth, to the great benefit of English employment.

The state of commerce is rather more bleak if we narrow our

* Contrast M. M. Postan, *The Medieval Economy and Society* (Pelican, 1975), and A. R. Bridbury, *Economic Growth: England in the Later Middle Ages* (1962).

perspectives to the years around 1450. The loss of English control over large parts of France, political difficulties with the Netherlands, piracy in the Channel and bad relations with the Hanse (a league of German towns which aimed to monopolize Baltic trade), all contributed to a deep commercial crisis in the years 1440–70. As we shall see this was important for politics. The alienation of London by the apparent incompetence of Henry VI's foreign policy was a major factor in his downfall.

It is difficult to generalize about those Englishmen, the great majority, 'whose occupation stands in grubbing about the earth, as in ploughing and dunging and sowing and harrowing . . .'. Different geographical conditions produced different forms of social organization, and farming regions were interspersed through the country in luxuriant profusion. The most obvious distinction is between the highland areas – variously defined, but perhaps best taken as the area west and north of a line from Weymouth to Teesside – and the rest of the country. The highland areas were largely given over to raising animals, though enough grain was grown for subsistence, generally barley and oats. Their organization was very different from the familiar picture of the 'medieval village'. Settlement was in scattered hamlets, not nucleated villages; what arable land there was had been enclosed for time out of mind; there was often plenty of unenclosed 'waste' for pasture, so that there was no need to impose a limit ('stint') to the number of animals each man could keep. Manorial organization was therefore weak since there was little need for communal organization of the work; the inhabitants had a freer, if at times harder, life than those of the lowland arable areas.

But the lowland zone, too, had large areas devoted to raising animals rather than crops. And in these pastoral districts, as in the highlands, cultivation was individual, fields anciently enclosed. The forests provided opportunities for newcomers to snatch a living, and enabled cows and sheep to graze without restriction, and pigs to root for themselves. The actual amount of land held was therefore less important than in more purely arable areas and men could afford to divide it among their sons instead of restricting it to the eldest. This ability, within limits, to provide a living for all the family was less important in the fifteenth century, a period of low and stagnant population, than it was to be a century later, when the population was expanding fairly fast; then the population of woodland and pastoral regions was swollen, not only by their own natural increase, but by immigration of landless younger sons from the less fortunate arable areas. This abundance of labour, and the fact that looking after animals left a good deal more spare time than ploughing the land, meant that pastoral areas, if they were not too remote, became centres of rural industry. The expanding cloth industry was to be found very largely in pastoral areas; not because the wool was available (that was quite cheap to transport), but because labour was.

The arable areas were radically different in social organization. It is here that we find the allegedly 'typical' village with its three large open fields split into strips and subject to a common agricultural routine. These areas tended to have large 'nucleated' villages, strong manorial organization, inheritance by primogeniture – in short to be a more highly organized and less individualistic society. Even so, the textbook example might not be found in its pure form. In some places the strips had been exchanged between villagers to build up more convenient and compact blocks of land; and those blocks were sometimes hedged off to make little fields whose owners could go their own way, freed from the constraints of communal agriculture Diversity was the keynote to agricultural organization; diversity not only in the organization of the economy, but also in the organization of society and, so far as one can tell, in the outlook of the men concerned.

In these circumstances it is difficult to generalize about standards of living. Vital statistics – how many children were born, how long they might expect to live, what age men and women got married – cannot be quoted with any degree of certainty. Registers of baptisms, marriages and burials were not kept before 1538. Ingenious calculations have been made, based on the inquisitions taken after the death of landholders; these generally mention the age of the heir, and it is then sometimes possible to find the inquisition recording *his* death and so calculate his age at the time. This procedure has its drawbacks – notably, that it only applies to the better-off – but does produce interesting results. The span of life – the maximum age to which a man might live if he was lucky – was not very different from that of today. The number of men claiming to be octogenarians, ready to testify in law cases about land ownership, is often impressive, even if some of the claims to feats of memory are suspect. But, of course, a far greater proportion of the population failed to attain the maximum age than in modern conditions. The average expectation of life at birth was hardly likely to be much above thirty-five years, compared to about seventy or so today. Up to two out of ten babies probably died before their first birthday, one more would die before the age of ten, and the chance of dying in young manhood or middle age was of course much greater than today, so that very few lasted to the end of the course.

Given the deficiencies of medical science, inadequate heating, all too adequate ventilation, and diets which were likely to be deficient or ill-balanced, it is remarkable that anybody ever survived to old age. The truth is, of course, that the less healthy died off quickly, and survivors would tend to be reasonably tough. Natural selection worked with a vengeance. Disease too was kept in check by the fact that so few people lived in the towns; until very recently towns have always produced higher mortality figures than the country (sharing two rooms with the farm animals, as many peasants did, was evidently less unhealthy than crowding together in the squalor of badly-drained towns). Towns traditionally depended on rural immigration to keep their numbers steady.

Another vital matter (in the literal sense) about which we know little is food; though historians are beginning to pay attention to the physical and, even more speculatively, the psychological effect of different diets. We naturally know far more about how servants in great households or soldiers and sailors were fed than we do about the great mass of the population. The great and their dependants seem to have fed on a gargantuan scale; and conspicuous waste was a feature here. (Though it is fair to say that the waste was supposed to go to feed the poor.) A feast to enthrone the personally abstemious William Warham as Archbishop of Canterbury cost £500, at a time when a worker got rather less than 6d. a day wages. But even in normal circumstances a great household would provide its servants with a gallon of ale a day, vast quantities of meat, a certain amount of cheese and fish, and more than ample bread to add to the already considerable carbohydrate content of their ale. Vegetables and fruit, on the other hand, were provided only in small amounts by modern standards, possibly because that was what the poor ate if they could not get anything else. Obesity and waste must have been widespread.

The great majority of men lived more modestly. Two Dorset priests, for instance, provided rather under a gallon of ale a day for themselves and one servant; but still spent a good deal on meat, and were a long way off from abject poverty. The English tended to boast about the 'great plenty' of ale and meat in their country, and above all the good white bread. The French peasantry, by contrast, were said to 'drink water, eat apples with bread right brown, made of rye; they eat no flesh [except occasionally] a little lard, or the entrails and heads of the beasts slain for the nobles and merchants'. But in fact rye bread was common enough in England; and, in the highland areas, oats were the common cereal.

Against Langland's vivid description of the workmen who, with harvest just in and food cheap, 'must have fresh meat or fish, fried or baked and *chaud* or *plus chaud* at that', we must set his poignant picture of the poor in their hovels, over-burdened with children, and rack-rented by landlords. 'For whatever they save by spinning they spend on rent or on milk and oatmeal to make gruel to fill the bellies of their children who clamour for food . . . While the Friars feast on roast venison, they have bread and thin ale, with perhaps a scrap of cold meat or stale fish . . .' And these, after all, were the healthy; for the 'old men with white hair . . . the women with child who cannot work, nor the blind and bedridden whose limbs are broken, nor the lepers', there was little material hope –

> For love of their low hearts, our Lord hath them granted
> Their penance and their purgatory, here on this earth.*

* Langland's *Piers Plowman* is late fourteenth century; but there is no reason to think that conditions were much changed by 1450. I have used the modern prose translation by J. F. Goodridge (Penguin Classics, 1959), except where, as above, the verse is easily modernizable.

The upper classes lived in a good deal of magnificence but, by modern standards, desperately uncomfortably, in huge draughty buildings. The life of a peer and his family was lived in public view, amidst a great mass of under-employed household servants; although to the indignation of the moralists there was an increasing tendency for the lord's family to retire to private chambers rather than eat in state among the whole household in the hall, except on special occasions. There was, in fact, a distinct development in the fifteenth century towards a more domestic style of life, and away from the concept of a castle as a military fortification, in spite of the period's reputation for disorder. Henry VI's treasurer Lord Cromwell built at Tattershall a brick 'castle' which is in fact a large domestic building, and the private quarters of the castle built by William Herbert, Earl of Pembroke, at Raglan in the 1460s have great oriel windows facing the courtyard, though the castle is well defended against the outside world. Below this level, there was an increasing degree of comfort in the houses of rich merchants and the gentry, with the increasing use of glass windows, wainscoted panelling and hangings, though all these things only spread from the wealthy to the moderately affluent in the next century. Glass windows seem to have been a novelty to wealthy Leicester merchants in the late fifteenth century, and were treated as movable furnishings rather than fixtures, to be taken away on giving up a tenancy, bequeathed in wills and so on; in the early sixteenth century the Earl of Northumberland, no less, would still take his glass casements with him when moving from one of his houses to another.

Most people, however, lived in one- or two-roomed houses, generally constructed of fairly flimsy materials; chalk or plaster walls, 'wattle-and-daub' and so on. People sometimes had their own building separate from the livestock. But more often than not those who were lucky enough to own domestic animals had them under the same roof as the family; one end of the house was a byre, the other one or two rooms for living in. Both were entered by the same passage. Windows would be covered by thin horn, or greased linen or paper, floors even of clergymen's houses would be of beaten mud. Chimneys and fireplaces were rare, and smoke escaped through louvres in the roof. 'Full sooty was her bower and eke her hall', says Chaucer of the widow in the *Nuns Priest Tale*, who seems, on that basis, rather well off. Very few houses apparently had more than one floor; the substantial stone or timber-framed houses we tend to think of as typically 'medieval' were in fact built by yeomen and better off husbandmen in the late sixteenth century. Furnishings were minimal, and houses damp, draughty and insanitary; no wonder that surviving skeletons show a high incidence of rheumatic disease.*

An economy of this sort was dangerously dependent on the weather; too much rain in summer, too little in the spring, could cause widespread distress. About one year in four saw food in short supply, about one year in six at danger level, when, to quote *Piers Plowman* again, 'Famine shall judge the world, and Davy the ditcher shall die of hunger – unless God in his mercy grant us all a truce.'

Bad harvests tended to come in batches since there was a temptation to spare less seed for next year's crop so that that too was a thin one unless there was exceptionally favourable weather. Those who normally ate meat and white bread might find themselves reduced to rye bread and cheese. The poor had no alternative but to eat less food; and while actual deaths from starvation seem rare, there seems to be correlation between bad harvests and epidemics which suggests the key role of malnutrition. A few large-scale agricultural producers might benefit from bad harvests; for them the rise in prices more than compensated for the reduced quantity they had for sale. But the small peasant might be reduced to buying grain to feed himself at famine prices; if, that is, he could afford to pay for it. Demand for goods would fall off as men devoted more of their income to food; and there was likely to be unemployment among cloth-workers and so on. The poor found themselves relying on loans from complaisant inn-keepers, corn-dealers and rich peasants – at, of course, a price, a price which all the fulminations of church and state against usury (lending money at interest) was unable to prevent.

Harvest failures were not the only natural disasters. Animal diseases could be equally fatal, and the death of a sheep might

* M. W. Beresford and J. G. Hurst (eds), *Deserted Medieval Villages* (Lutterworth Press, 1971) p. 135.

knock the whole of a family's income off course. The sickness or death of the man of the house were ever-present possibilities, with results too frightening to consider. None of this, of course, was peculiar to the fifteenth century, but was (and is) the everyday reality in most economies. If anything, the fifteenth century, for all its reputation for excessive melancholy and apocalyptic visions, was rather less badly affected than most others by natural disaster of this sort.

This was because of the generally low level of the population. Where in the first half of the fourteenth century, and again in the sixteenth, a large population was pressing on inadequate natural resources, the fifteenth century as a whole represents a long holiday from the Malthusian nightmare of over-population. It has been called both 'the golden age of bacteria' and 'the golden age of labour', and the two are connected. Estimates for total population vary enormously; that for 1400, for instance, is variously quoted as two or three million. But historians are generally agreed that the population was a good deal lower than it had been in 1300. The decline in numbers may have begun then, when pressure on resources was desperately great. Many men died in the notorious famine of 1315–17, a famine still remembered three hundred years afterwards. But the main drop came later. Whether it was due to the Black Death of 1348–9 or to other plagues later in the century is not clear. But from 1377 onwards there are unmistakable signs of depopulation, as wages rose and the price of grain sank.

Even if we were certain about the cause of this dramatic change, we would still have to explain why the level of population remained low for at least a hundred years after that. We might have expected a fairly quick recovery to the old level; greater prosperity, it might be thought, would mean earlier marriages, more children and longer life. But this did not happen. Renewed visitations of the plague may have increased infant mortality, or for reasons which are not clear, a more prosperous people may nonetheless have avoided greater fertility. Not until 1470, perhaps later, was there another upward trend; and by 1520 the pleasant fifteenth-century world of cheap food and high wages had vanished.

One calculation of a builder's labourer's earnings in terms of the goods he could afford to buy shows him better off in 1450 than at any time before the influx of cheap foreign food in Queen Victoria's reign.* The labourer's wages had doubled (from 2d. to 4d. a day) since the Black Death, and food prices had remained about the same. Moralists denounced the damage this new demand for labour had caused to ideas of social hierarchy. 'Now a wretched knave . . . must have a fresh doublet of five shillings or more the price, and above, a costly gown with bags hanging to his knee.' Denunciation of the affluent worker is familiar enough today; generally with as little justification. Prosperity is of course relative, and it was only by pitifully low standards that the fifteenth-century worker could be said to be prosperous.

The effect of the Black Death and the subsequent low-level of population on the rural classes is no less dramatic but very much more complicated. The essential results were stagnant prices for agricultural products, and especially grain due to the slack demand; less demand for land, and therefore lower rents; and higher wages for agricultural workers. Quite how these factors balance out in any particular case depends of course upon the individual's circumstances; and especially on the size and nature of his holding, what crops he could produce, and so on.

There is obviously the world of difference here between the large peasant, with perhaps fifty acres or so, and the smallholder with five acres or less. The former produced primarily for the market, and employed wage-labourers; to that extent he was manifestly worse off through paying higher wages and from lower grain prices. The smallholder, on the other hand, who would have to buy food to supplement what he could grow for himself, and would probably work as a labourer on somebody else's holding, would obviously be in the opposite situation. More difficult would be the case of the middling peasant, with perhaps fifteen to twenty acres; largely self-subsistent, relying on family labour, he would be affected much less by long-term price and wage movements.

Where all peasants stood to gain was in the reduction of rent because of decreased demand for land. This is difficult to quan-

* See below, appendix p. 334.

tify; but, for instance, rents on Duchy of Lancaster estates declined by about a third between 1400 and 1470. The large peasant too, profited from the increased tendency of large landowners to lease out their demesne lands rather than cultivating them themselves; so that there was, in fact, a good deal more land available for peasants. The average size of peasant holdings, at all levels, increased between 1300 and 1450; and the number of substantial, well-off peasants probably grew as well. These were the men who were coming to be known as the 'yeomen', and praised as the 'pith and substance of the country', 'the peculiar glory of England'. The yeoman, without pretensions to gentility, could 'get his living merrily' with his house stacked full of bacon flitches, eggs, butter and cheese. This sort of solid comfort applied only to the lucky few. But a situation in which rents were reduced obviously benefited everybody; except the unfortunate landlords.

Another general benefit was the withering away of serfdom. Once again, this was largely the result of the shortage of demand for land, of conditions in which tenants could sometimes threaten 'to leave the lands vacant, to the final destruction of the aforesaid manors'. The legal status of serfdom was distinct from the obligation to perform labour services; nevertheless, in practice they were connected. In the short term the Black Death had produced a reimposition of labour services which had often been commuted for money-payments earlier; this was in a landlord's interest when wages were rising. This line could not be held, however, as landlords began to compete among themselves for tenants, and the decline of labour services saw the decline of serfdom. The general economic situation had achieved one of the main demands of the peasant rebels of 1381, that there should be 'no serfdom nor villeinage but that all men should be free'. By 1450 serfdom was reduced to an occasional, though irritating oddity; though the last known example is as late as 1635.

Those likely to suffer from the general developments were the great landowners. The greatest was the king, who owned about 5 per cent of the land. Another 20 per cent was held by the peerage (about fifty men) and some 180 other gentlemen with incomes of over £100 a year or more. 20 per cent more at least, was in the hands of the church; the property of individual monasteries, of bishops, of cathedral chapters and so on. In all these, the land-owners were hit by the rising costs of labour. Attempts to deal with this problem by legislation to keep down wages, and increasing labour services had failed; from the late fourteenth century landowners were giving up the direct exploitation of their estates as large-scale agricultural enterprises, and instead leasing them out in small lots. The pace of change varied; but for instance, all the estates of Canterbury cathedral were leased by 1411, and most of those of Westminster Abbey by 1420. Generally the income was appreciably less than that which direct exploitation had produced in the landlords' hey-day a century earlier. Even worse, in many cases rents continued to fall at successive re-lettings.

There were, of course, exceptions; estates well situated to take advantage of new developments, like Tavistock Abbey, in Devon, which benefited from the prosperity of the local tin and cloth industries. Sheep-farming was a useful alternative in the late fourteenth century; prices kept up well, and of course labour costs were much less important than for grain production. But this did not last; in the first half of the fifteenth century troubles in the export market almost halved the price of wool. Individual peers were not necessarily worse off than their predecessors; many of the greatest nobles of the fifteenth century had managed to accumulate into their hands, by marriage and inheritance, the estates of several great families. Nevertheless, the general trend of landlord income was downwards; though quite how far is difficult to say.

Below the great landlords was a class of perhaps three thousand 'gentlemen'. These too lived largely on the income from land; land, indeed, was a necessary qualification for gentility at this time. Here too we might expect (as with the yeoman) that the general situation would have depressed incomes; but here too the great amount of land being made available by the large estates was probably more than ample compensation. Certainly the class of 'gentlemen' in the mid-fifteenth century was considerably larger than it had been a century before.

Essentially the class was an amalgam of two groups; the descendents of the knightly class of the thirteenth and fourteenth centuries (when there had been a continual shortage of knights, vital both for military service and for the running of local government): and the new men, lawyers or merchants who had bought land as a seal of their respectability, or prosperous peasants who had accumulated enough land to change their style of life. Gentlemen were formally distinguished by the right to coats-of-arms; at one time the prerogative of knights alone, but now extended more widely. The essential quality was 'virtue' an amorphous concept which involved a style of life unsullied by manual labour, cultivated manners, and the readiness to take the lead in civil affairs. Ownership of land was a prerequisite, but it was not enough; a substantial yeoman might be richer than a poor gentleman. Ideally, gentility depended on inheritance; but failing that it could be acquired by the right sort of education. In practice this meant that the father made the family fortune, and the son reaped the benefit in social status. The system therefore allowed for a certain degree of social mobility, while guarding against the alleged boorishness of the self-made.

Essentially, though, this was a strongly hierarchical society in which wealth was distributed with extreme inequality (the income of the Duke of York was over a thousand times that of a labourer), in which relations between men of different classes were marked by formal ceremony and extreme deference, at least ostensibly, on the part of the inferior; by arrogance and at times insensitivity by the superior. (Sir Robert Umfraville, who would never 'rebuke nor chide' his servant 'but softly say to him in privity all his default' was considered extraordinarily virtuous.) Moreover, it was a society in which exploitation was more blatant and direct than in modern industrial conditions; paying rent, or surrendering one's produce in tithe left little to the imagination, especially when the result was immediately apparent in conspicuous consumption. Quite what proportion of a peasant's crop went to support landlord and church is not easily calculated. Very roughly, a substantial thirty-acre holding might yield about 90 bushels of wheat and 110 bushels of barley a year. About a quarter of the crop would be needed as seed for next year. The rest would be worth:

wheat — 65 bushels at 8*d*. = £2 3*s*. 4*d*.
barley — 80 bushels at 4½*d*. = £1 10*s*. 0*d*.

£3 13*s*. 4*d*.

Rent would account for about 12*s*. 6*d*. of this (at 5*d*. an acre) and tithe about 10*s*. 0*d*. The remaining £2 10*s*. 0*d*. worth of grain would be available for personal consumption and sale; and that would have to cover clothing, necessities, winter feed for plough oxen (likely to be a major item), the replacement of farm implements and so on. Of course, things were worse in a bad harvest; there would then be little left over once the family was fed, there would be a temptation to economize on seed-corn, with dangerous consequences for the following year, rent might run into arrears and so on.*

In 1381 peasant grievances had erupted in numerous revolts. Most memorably the men of Kent and Essex had marched on London, had killed, among others, the Archbishop of Canterbury, and had extorted from the fourteen-year-old boy king Richard II a (quickly repudiated) promise to end serfdom. In general, though, peasant revolts were rare. Even 1381 had only disturbed the game of power politics within the ruling class for a very short period; the main revolt was repressed in a little over a month. Cade's rebellion of 1450, which also captured London, was, as we shall see, not a revolt of peasants alone but of a cross-section of Kentish society, concerned mainly with grievances about bad government. It was not until 1497 that London was again menaced by an unambiguously peasant revolt; and the Cornish rebels who were then defeated at a pitched battle at Blackheath were protesting about taxation, not landlord oppression.

Whatever resentment there may have been about the social order, it was difficult to mobilize it into any sort of coherent movement on its own. Even the 1381 revolt was sparked off by

* Recalculated at fifteenth-century prices from P. Bowden's seventeenth-century calculations in Joan Thirsk (ed.), *Agrarian History of England and Wales, 1500–1640* (Cambridge, 1967) p. 653. Bowden's own figures are much more sophisticated, taking account of concepts like interest and capital depreciation.

demands for taxation, although it escalated quickly into a more general protest. Political uncertainty could lead to the expression of grievances which normally had no outlet; as when, during the Cade revolt a hundred peasants 'covered with long beards and painted on their faces with black charcoal, announcing themselves servants of the Queen of the Fairies', plundered the Duke of Buckingham's deer-park. From time to time peasants smashed fences, assaulted estate officials, or refused to pay rents and dues. Very occasionally, industrial workers went on strike; the Coventry journeymen-weavers in 1424, for instance, managed to get some increase in pay and recognition for their own gild. The peculiar circumstances of the fifteenth-century economy, the shortage of labour, the threat of vacant tenancies combined to make landlords and employers rather more tender than usual to lower-class pressure.

But we must not exaggerate the effectiveness of social protest. 'Social protest', indeed, may be the wrong expression. Almost always, except in the heady days of 1381, the grievances of peasants or wage-earners were particular, specific grievances; very rarely were they generalized into a criticism of the social order as such. Men could envisage a 'land of Cockaigne', a dream world of ease and plenty for all. They were continually reminded too, of the Last Judgement, when God would in his own good time exalt the humble and meek and send the rich man empty away; and this language could sometimes express a more immediate threat.

> Another year it may befall
> The least that is within this hall
> To be more master than we all;
> Christ may send now such a year.

In general though the very popularity of the millennial visions of the Last Judgement is in a sense an admission of hopelessness; thoughts of vengeance were safely channelled into a dim future. In fifteenth-century Germany millennial dreams of this sort spilled over into real life. The Last Judgement was upon us, or the emperor Frederick II would shortly return to make all things whole again, and peasant action now would forcibly help the process on. But there was little of this in fifteenth-century England. The threat of peasant revolt does not seem to have featured very high among the preoccupations of the ruling class.

Of course, acquiescence, if at times sullen grumbling acquiescence, has been much more common throughout human history than revolt. We have to make an imaginative leap to appreciate a society which did not have modern means of mass communication, the modern appetite for information and the habit of a critical, questioning approach to social problems.

The contrast is best exemplified by the attitude of the church. Hierarchy was God's will. That life was hard was the inescapable result of Adam's fall from grace. It was man's duty to 'see to what state God has called him and dwell therein by travail according to his degree'. So, 'thou that art a labourer or craftman, do thou truely. If thou art a servant or a bondman, be subject and low ... If thou art a knight or a lord, defend the poor man and needy from hands that will harm them.' Denunciation of the rich was common. Preachers would depict the poor as saying, 'They afflicted us with hunger and labours, that they might live delicately upon our labours and goods. We have laboured and lived so hard a life that scarce for half a year had we a good sufficiency ... O, just God, mighty judge, the game was not fairly divided between them and us.' But the moral was not that the social system was wrong; rather that the wealthy had failed in their duty, had extorted more than they ought, and would be duly punished for it. (It is fair to add that rather more radical conclusions were sometimes drawn by congregations, or even occasionally, as in 1381, by preachers.) The great social sin was covetousness, the aspiration for more than one's degree warranted. Even in *Piers Plowman*, that bitter denunciation of corruption in high places, there is the stern warning:

> Look thou grouch not on God though he thee give little
> Be paid with thy portion, poorer or richer.

and the poet is as scathing about the work-shy false beggar or the labourer who demands too high wages as about the dissolute noble or the swindling churchman.

So men were conditioned to seek out the particular injustice which had caused them distress, to ascribe it to the particular sin of the individual, rather than to look for a social explanation. An appeal to the oppressor's conscience was the right procedure; failing that, to higher authority. Rebellious peasants tended to believe that the king, the fount of justice, would be on their side if only he knew the truth. There was precious little ground for this belief; but the alternative would be blank despair.

The very structure of society made an articulate programme of social protest difficult if not impossible. The small scale of industrial or agricultural enterprises, the localized nature of the economy, meant that master and man, lord and tenant would be as likely to be united in their opposition to the trades of a rival town, or to the inhabitants of the next village claiming more than their fair share of the intervening rough grazing land, as at loggerheads with each other about wages or rents.

When a landlord increases rents or an employer depresses wages, the historian might be able to discern a general trend, but this is not obvious to the contemporary, who is much more likely to think of himself as the victim of a particular act of injustice. A village might rise against its lord, but it is unlikely that all lords would be engaged in similar acts of oppression at once, so that a large-scale cohesive movement was impossible. This explains the general importance of taxation as a trigger for revolt (as in 1381); taxation produces a generalized grievance, able to unite men from several parishes and manors, even from several social groups in a concerted protest. Interestingly enough, it is when the oppressors can be seen to be organized, to be acting as a group, that something like class-consciousness is likely to be generated; journeymen gilds form in the towns in opposition to the masters' control of the craft gilds, or (in 1381) wage-earners resent the attempt by landlords to keep wages below their market level by invoking the 1351 Statute of Labourers.

Another obstacle to possible revolutionary action was the degree of vested interest in the existing system by the leaders of village society. It was the substantial peasant, the substantial craftsman who normally acted as church wardens and constables, or formed the jury of the manorial court. Even more important were those who formed the hinge between village society and the outside

33

world; the estate official and the priest. These were natural leaders of protest and revolt; they were also the targets of popular resentment. The ambivalence reflects the ambivalence of their role, in interpreting the village to the outside world of the gentle classes; and in enforcing the demands of authority on the village. An active government propagandist of the next century picked on the weak point of these better-off peasants. 'How can you keep your own if you keep no order. Your wife and children, how can they be defended from other men's violence, if you will in other things break all order; and by what means will you be obeyed, of yours as servants, if you will not obey the king as subjects?'*

Normally these naturally conservative men were able to keep control of protest movements, to keep them on the 'reformist' rather than the revolutionary tack; when, as sometimes happened, they were thrust aside, the movement rapidly fell apart in disorder.

To these general considerations must be added others specific to the fifteenth century. Landlords had thrown in the sponge. They were not trying to counter economic difficulty by reimposing serfdom and holding down wage rates as they had been before 1381. Leasing the demesnes was an admission of defeat. For most of the century taxation could not trigger off popular revolt. Between 1381 and 1489 the normal method of direct taxation, the 'fifteenth and tenth' did not affect the poorer half of the community. Lower-class protest was largely political, directed against the abuses of government (which, in their local manifestations as the actions of corrupt officials, were of immense importance to ordinary people). Popular rebellion was sometimes stimulated by scheming noblemen for their own ends; a useful means of testing the strength of the government while avoiding, with luck, putting themselves at risk. The demand that the king should be advised by 'men of his true blood' (like 'the high and mighty prince the duke of York') rather than by a collection of self-seeking upstart commoners was always popular. Men like York and the 'Kingmaker' Earl of Warwick consistently looked to popular support as part of the political game; and the hopes they held out for change at the top probably helped to emasculate any slight tendency towards more 'class-conscious' movements.

* Sir John Cheke, *The Hurt of Sedition*. (1549: Scolar Press ed, 1971).

This was a perfectly reasonable policy on the part of the people. Reformers held out some hopes of more efficient and less corrupt government, and this would be a definite advantage to the people at large. It was, in any case, safer to involve as many elements of constituted authority as possible in rebellion; and peasant rebels tended to try to enroll their social superiors as leaders, if necessary by force. But there was more to this than rational calculation. Significantly, there was a tendency for dead leaders of noble opposition, from the days of Simon de Monfort in the thirteenth century onwards, to be popularly revered as saints. The behaviour of some three thousand Cornishmen in 1497 seems equally removed from mundane reality when, just after a popular rebellion had been smashed, they were prepared to turn out in arms to back claims of the Flemish imposter, Perkin Warbeck to be king of England. (Rather like Russian peasants of the seventeenth century, who were always liable to revolt in support of a false tsar.) All this betrays an element of despair, of the belief that the social system was too solidly established to be changed except by the intervention of some remote, almost magical agency; King Richard in 1381, or King Jesus at the Second Coming, the millennium. This was a society which knew itself to be fundamentally unjust; but which knew too that for practical purposes it was unchangeable.

BELIEFS AND ATTITUDES

This was an essentially oral culture, in a way which has been less true since the widespread use of printing (though, even so, more true than library-bound historians often imply). In that sense a formal list of great cultural achievements is misleading: it begs the question of diffusion. Chaucer wrote the *Canterbury Tales* at the end of the fourteenth century, but they were much better known in the sixteenth, thanks to the printing press, than in their own day. Much more significant, from the point of view of popular psychology, are works like the Robin Hood ballads; though their interpretation is full of difficulties, not least because we have for the most part to rely on later printed versions.

In terms of achievement in 'high culture', indeed, fifteenth-century England cannot rank very high, at least in comparison with other countries at the time (not only, and obviously Italy, but France, Germany and the Netherlands). Its literary culture was unremarkable, especially in comparison with the great days of Chaucer and Langland; and the only lengthy work (as compared to the occasional short lyric poem) which can be recommended to anybody except a scholar, is Sir Thomas Malory's crystalline English version of the Arthurian legend. Rather surprisingly, one field in which fifteenth-century England did excel was music, where in the person of John Dunstable, court musician to Henry v's brother, the Duke of Bedford, it had a musician of genius. The Flemish theorist Tinctoris, wrote in 1477 that Dunstable had produced the only music worth listening to in the last forty years and was the 'origin and fount' of a new art. But it is significant that not very much is known about Dunstable and that it was in France and the Netherlands that his techniques were developed.

Individual noblemen and ecclesiastics were also responsible for patronizing what little there was in England of the 'new learning'; the attempt on the Italian model, to study the classical authors on their own terms, as representatives of a different and, by implication, superior culture to that of contemporary Europe. (By contrast, traditional culture tended to assimilate the past to the present, sometimes ludicrously; in the Wakefield pageant the shepherds attending the birth of Jesus make the sign of the cross.) The mark of this new school was its insistence on the use of a Latin modelled on that of Cicero, as opposed to the more rough-and-ready, but serviceable Latin in current use; and, if possible, on the learning of Greek. Another of Henry v's brothers Humphrey, Duke of Gloucester, was involved in this, attracting Italian scholars to England in the 1430s, and building up a library part of which he left to Oxford University. The first Englishman to study Greek seriously was Robert Flemmyng, who learnt it in Italy in the 1440s. George Neville, Archbishop of York (and brother of Warwick the 'Kingmaker') fostered Greek studies in the 1460s, and a few enthusiasts were to be found at Oxford and elsewhere. But all this was very much a minority interest, even among the educated. It was not until the next century that the 'new learning' became firmly established in England and transformed the educational system.

Higher education in the fifteenth century was primarily vocational, designed to equip men for careers in the church or the law. The concept of a general education for gentlemen stopped short in most cases at the level of accomplishment of Chaucer's squire.

> Well could he sit on horse and fair ride
> He could songs make and well endite
> Joust and eek dance and well portray and write.

When Archbishop Rotherham of York founded Rotherham school in 1482 he had no concept of a literary education for laymen; those 'who did not wish to atain to the height and dignity of the priesthood' were to study writing and accounts. The universities were intended for the clergy and their 'arts' course was intended at least, in theory, only as an introduction to the 'higher' degrees of law and theology.

The law taught at Oxford and Cambridge was the Roman 'civil law', the foundation of ecclesiastical law. For the ordinary law of the land as expounded in the royal courts the student had to frequent the Inns of Court in London where he was taught by experienced practitioners. The law they taught was arid and technical. Nevertheless, the inns did provide a centre of higher education for laymen, and the legal profession was often the foundation of a successful career. John Wenlock became a royal councillor and a peer after serving as a member of the king's household and Speaker of the House of Commons.

But although education was primarily vocational there were exceptions. Sir John Fortescue talks of 'knights and barons' sending their sons to the inns, though they had no intention of practising the law. Young William Paston, a country gentleman's son, went to the new school at Eton in the 1470s, and a future Duke of Norfolk attended Thetford Grammar School. The statutes of Magdalen College Oxford (founded in 1448) made special provision for the sons of noblemen to be admitted as fee-paying students, and many individual noblemen showed a keen interest in intellectual matters. The education of noble children may have been less perfunctory than is often implied. But all this was a matter of individual initiative; there was as yet no general convention that sons of gentlemen should undergo an elaborate literary education.

The simple ability to read English, however, was much more common than is sometimes imagined. Forty per cent of witnesses appearing in a London court were literate. Of twenty witnesses to Sir John Fastolf's will nine could sign their names (and these included two husbandmen – oddly, one of those who made a mark was a gentleman). Nevertheless, there were two great obstacles to the spread of a large-scale intellectual culture. One was the conviction that abstract ideas were best expressed in Latin. The other, more important, was the prohibitive expense of manuscript books.

Culture, then, was primarily oral in spite of fairly widespread literacy. This was true even of the universities where teaching consisted of the exposition of a text by a master to a collection of note-taking students. (The persistence of this practice in modern universities in spite of the printing press and duplicating machine is a striking demonstration of academic inertia.) The rarity of books increased the students' reverence for them as 'authorities' to be consulted and cited, rather than as fallible guides to be critically compared with each other. This led to credulity. On the other hand scholastic philosophy practised in the universities through oral disputation fostered a severely critical approach. In practice these apparently contradictory tendencies co-existed peacefully; the logical steps in an argument were subject to rigorous criticism, while the facts on which the argument were based were rarely challenged. Outside the university credulity ran riot; men were too conscious of the limitations of their own experience to dismiss a tale too easily. Elephants, after all, were no more likely to exist than dragons.

An aspect of this sort of mentality, the tendency to gape at wonders, was an apparently universal fascination with outward show, with ceremonial. A German visitor to England was taken, as a great treat, to watch the queen dine in state. The whole process took three hours, the queen dining alone, her mother and the king's sister standing or kneeling below; all in silence. The visitor was duly impressed by the great splendour of the arrangements. Putting on tournaments, which were 'great gladness to all the common people', was the way to impress Londoners. Henry VI, newly restored to government after five years in prison made a bad impression because 'he was shown in a long blue gown of velvet as though he had no more to change with'. Londoners did not treat aristocratic ceremonial with bourgeois disdain, but preferred to beat the nobility at their own game. The lord mayor (a significant title) was 'within London next to the king in all matters', and once when a peer, the Earl of Worcester was given precedence at a banquet, the civic dignitaries walked out and at short notice served an equally magnificent feast of their own.

Chivalric ceremonial was at its height in the fifteenth century. Most of it, indeed, was of relatively recent origin. The use of coats-of-arms had spread widely in the thirteenth century; and only in the fourteenth were the elaborate procedures of the heralds and the courts of chivalry evolved to regulate the cere-monial side of knightly life. The Order of the Garter dates only from 1348; and its European rivals, the Burgundian order of the Golden Fleece, and the French order of St Michael, were both of fifteenth-century origin, though following earlier French models.

In Italy the concept that good taste involved restraint was begin-ning to make headway, but elsewhere in Europe men were still impressed by magnificence and show; and therefore, the most characteristic art form was architecture and its associate sculp-ture, which allowed most scope for extravagance. In England this was the great age of 'perpendicular Gothic'; a peculiarly English style which had evolved in Gloucester Abbey (now the cathedral) in the early fourteenth century, and had since spread throughout the country. The stress was firmly on grandeur; taller towers, wider and high walls, above all the creation of a great area of light by the use of huge windows, what Aeneas Sylvius called, 'glass walls held together by very slender columns'. The style was not confined to cathedrals and abbey-churches; many parish churches have their 'perpendicular' extensions, an additional aisle here, a chantry chapel there, while in some cases, notably in areas prospering from the cloth trade, like Northleach in Gloucester-shire or Lavenham in Suffolk, whole churches were torn down and rebuilt in the new style.

In one sense all this building was an expression of community pride; in another of individual self-assertion. (Thomas Spring, the rich clothier, stamped his newly acquired coat-of-arms all over Lavenham church tower, perhaps to emphasize that he had risen into the circle of one of the most blue-blooded of English aristocrats, the Earl of Oxford, who had also contributed lavishly to the rebuilding.) But it was also part of an insurance policy, of a need to stand well with the church to minimize the punishments of purgatory. Many of the most striking works of fifteenth-century art are in fact chantry chapels, where masses were to be said in perpetuity for the soul of the founder; and among the more gruesome examples are the juxtaposition of a prelate or nobleman in all his worldly pomp, with a realistically sculptured cadaver in which the mice gnaw at the great man's decaying flesh.

We have in fact made little reference to the church in this chapter, in spite of its immense importance as part of the social framework, and in determining men's outlook. We shall be looking later at challenges to its authority, and at dissatisfaction with its failures. But we should pause for the moment at the phenomenon of the chantry, since it epitomizes one of the most acute and difficult problems in the understanding of any age. On the one hand, when the historian investigates the manoeuvres of politicians, the dealings of businessmen or the machinations of churchmen for preferment, he seems to be in a familiar and comprehensible world. Men, it would seem, pursue, through different institutions, in different ways, very much the same sort of ends throughout the centuries. Against this we may set what might be called the 'Huizinga' view of history, after the Dutch historian who wrote the most brilliant of books on the fifteenth century (known in English by its misleading and mistranslated title *The Waning of the Middle Ages*).* There the accent is on a mental world radically different to our own, where we must make a conscious effort to understand the extravagant symbolism, the formal ceremoniousness of courts, the 'almost religious significance' of etiquette, the cult of chivalry; and, overshadowing all, the omnipresent fear of death, the obsession with the macabre, which

* English translation, 1924; many subsequent editions. The Dutch title means 'Autumn of the Middle Ages'.

'arose from deep psychological strata of fear'. 'The extreme excit-
ability of the medieval soul', thought Huizinga, was a factor which
historians who confine themselves to official documents are liable
to miss, but which, nevertheless, 'made frequent and violent
irruptions into practical politics'.

Huizinga is primarily concerned with the need to distance
ourselves from the society we have been studying. This tendency
has been carried further by those historians who have taken an
interest in anthropological studies of the much more primitive
societies of Africa or New Guinea. This is not because fifteenth-
century Europe was very like these societies; it was after all very
much more complex in its methods of political and economic
organization, not to mention its radical dissimilarity in terms
of, for instance, literacy. (The tendency to lump together all
'pre-industrial' societies as essentially similar is one of the sillier
modern fads.) But the anthropological approach provides a useful
form of shock treatment, a reminder that societies which may
superficially resemble our own may differ dramatically in their
basic assumptions.

Two fundamental problems arise here. The first is implicit in
the quotations from Huizinga. Just how far were the politicians
we are dealing with concerned with comprehensible 'secular'
aims; acquiring and keeping power, milking church and state of
wealth for themselves and their families and so on? How far, on
the other hand, were notions of divine kingship, or the concept of
honour or the cult of chivalry real factors in their lives? One is
tempted, examining the sordid day-to-day story of politics, to
think 'not much'; but even when cynical politicians manipulate
supranatural symbols like the coronation for their own ends,
the implication must be that the manipulators themselves thought
this sort of propaganda had some effect. Even among the dynastic
changes of the late fifteenth century, loyalty to an established and
crowned king was a real factor in politics, not only among the
people at large, but even within the politically sophisticated
ruling class. (There was a striking case in 1460 – see p. 76.) Even
when reading that hard-headed judge, Chief Justice Fortescue, we
find abstract concepts like the king's 'honour' or his 'magnificence' treated almost as concrete, tangible realities; take, for

instance, his admission that in some cases of good service 'it besate [befits] the king's magnificence to make their rewards ever-lasting'. Quite where to strike the balance between the idealist and the realist view of history, between the notion that men with radically different beliefs led radically different lives, and the more comfortable notion that beliefs are merely superficial, that *au fond* men have had much the same aspirations and ambitions throughout the ages, is something that must be left for indi-vidual judgement. The student of history will find that the harder he strives for understanding the less confident will he be of the answer.

The second difficulty is that in many of these vital areas of understanding not much serious work has yet been done; and in some cases one may doubt if enough of the right sort of evidence survives to provide a basis. Hardly anything has been said in this chapter, for instance, about the position of women or children. The study of childhood is doubly desirable, not only in its own right (children formed about half of the population) but also because of the vital importance for the adult personality, even for such 'political' matters as views on authority and so on, of a man's treatment in infancy; the role of parents or nurses, the strictness or permissiveness of training and so on. A few things can be deduced by common sense. The lives of nobles, for in-stance, were almost entirely lacking in family intimacy. They lived to a large extent in public, surrounded by attendants. Hus-band and wife were often apart, keeping separate households in different parts of the country. Children were sent out to wet nurses at birth, were reared almost entirely by servants, and despatched at a tender age to learn 'courtesy' in another lord's household. In the circumstances the willingness of parents to use their children as pawns in the political game (for instance by marriage), the tendency to sacrifice the happiness of individuals to the good of the long-term interests of the family, become com-prehensible. The rigorous repression of feelings of affection and of tenderness formed the sort of society of which Machiavelli wrote, in which a man was more easily prepared to forgive the death of his father than the loss of his lands.

The general question of the biological approach to history, of the relationship between a man's physical environment and his beliefs, attitudes and instincts is vast and intriguing. It would be fascinating for instance, to know more about the effects of fifteenth-century diet. To take a simple example, it would seem likely that the large-scale consumption of ale by all classes and all age groups helped to make for a society in which the instinctive resort to violence was much more pronounced than it is today. Or again, if we knew whether fifteenth-century Englishmen practised contraception on a wide scale, the methods used, why and how practices changed over generations, we might begin to understand the crucial problems of population stagnation and growth. Questions of this sort are being widely asked by historians; very often the questions go beyond what the available evidence will bear, and the answers are banal or evasive. Increasing ingenuity in the interpretation of often unlikely evidence (for example, the attempt to work out changes in climate from a study of tree rings) may yet produce a more solidly based understanding of the fifteenth century.

Chapter Two

AN ANATOMY OF POLITICS

England was a reasonably coherent national unit. Unlike France, no foreign prince had attempted to substantiate claims to the English throne; no subject of the English king, except occasionally in Ireland, was able to pursue an independent foreign policy like that of the French king's vassals, the Dukes of Burgundy and Brittany. No foreign potentate, with the marginal exception of the pope, claimed any sort of jurisdiction in the realm.

Of course, things were not quite so clear cut. There were complications abroad. Even after their troops had been expelled from Gascony in 1453, English kings kept up their claim to be the rightful kings of France; a claim not dropped in theory until George III's reign, and an important factor in practical politics, at least up to 1544. Calais remained English, a useful base for dominating the Narrow Seas and an outlet for English wool. The claim to suzerainty over Scotland lay dormant. More important, the English kings were 'Lords of Ireland'. In practice this meant responsibility for a small group of English settlers, equipped with their own parliament and law courts, living either in the area immediately around Dublin or in other, scattered towns; and the exercise of a rather tenuous overlordship over a large intermediate area, ruled by 'Anglo-Norman' great lords, though largely Gaelic in population. About half of Ireland was entirely Gaelic, its inhabitants known to the settlers as 'wild Irish' or 'wild men of the woods'. A government report of 1515 called them 'the king's Irish enemies', under some sixty chieftains each of whom 'maketh war and peace for himself and holdeth by the sword and hath imperial jurisdiction within his room'.

More immediate were the barriers to the full exercise of royal authority within England itself. There were various judicial liberties, scattered through the country, especially in the north; areas in which royal authority was, to a greater or lesser extent, exercised by some private individual. The county palatine of Durham under its prince-bishop had its own legal system and was not represented in parliament. Neither was Wales, which was divided between the principality, ruled directly by the crown, though on different principles to its rule in England, and about one hundred and forty marcher lordships, which possessed their own extensive judicial liberties. Both parts of Wales had their own legal system. Since the rebellion of Owain Glyn Dŵr at the beginning of the century, Welshmen had suffered various civil disadvantages; they were forbidden to hold land in England, to intermarry with the English or to hold office under the crown. (This did not prevent one ambitious Welshman, Owen Tudor, holding court office and marrying the widow of King Henry v.) Another barrier to royal jurisdiction was the power of the church. Certain offences were dealt with by church courts, under their own legal system. Clergy (a very wide-ranging category) were exempt from capital punishment. Particular churches possessed varying rights of protecting criminals fleeing from justice. But even more serious than these institutional barriers to efficient government was a less tangible problem; the difficulty of getting the king's officers, at any level, to perform their duty when bribed or threatened by powerful men, or when the law was inconvenient to themselves or their friends.

In spite of these qualifications, the over-riding impression is of unity. England was about as large a country as could be governed effectively as a single unit. Urgent news could get from the West Country to London in three or four days, from the Scottish border in five or six. It was practical for Cornwall or Cumberland to receive the king's judges on assize and to send members to Parliament. The English Parliament was an institution which had won, through the constitutional battles of the fourteenth century, the sole right to grant taxes and to consent to legislation. In France, by contrast, the States-General of the entire kingdom met only rarely, and consent could equally be got from provincial or regional assemblies. The established nature of the English Parliament was obviously of great advantage to the king, in terms of efficiency; and it is as well to remember that the normal relationship of king and Parliament was one of partnership in the promotion of good government, not of rivalry for power. But obviously conflict was always possible and in those circumstances the English Parliament would be a more powerful institution than any representative body in France.

More generally, the point needs to be made that however much disorder there was in fifteenth-century England, there was no challenge to the concept of a unified realm. The 'Wars of the Roses' were concerned with who should be king, not with the division of the realm. No attempt was made to establish autonomous principalities, though existing 'liberties' were jealously guarded. A Venetian ambassador reported in 1497 that the Doge doubtless imagined that the great lords of England 'dispersed justice in their own countries' but in reality they were only 'rich gentlemen in possession of a great quantity of land'. Although disorder was the main problem of English government, it should not be exaggerated; Professor Lander points out that few towns thought it worth while keeping their walls in good repair.*

Government was the king's. In certain contexts, men habitually thought of the realm as his private property, and talked about fines in the law courts as the 'king's profits of justice'. About a fifth of the crown's revenue came from the royal lands, exploited as an investment exactly like those of any other great lord. This personalized view was especially apparent in all questions of foreign policy; in the king's claims to France, for instance. Even a century later, in 1543, John Dudley, a political realist if ever there was one, thought that it would be wrong to attack Scotland after the death of King James V because it would be to 'invade upon a dead body or upon a widow'. But although the kingdom was in some sense the king's private property, it was also a sacred trust. The king was accountable to God, and even to his subjects. Richard II in 1399 was accused of tyranny and deposed; more specifically he had said 'with harsh and determined looks' that 'the laws were in his own mouth' and that 'he alone could

* J. R. Lander, *The Wars of the Roses* (Secker & Warburg, 1965) p. 21.

change or establish the laws of his realm'; similarly, that the lives and goods of his subjects 'are his at his pleasure'. But these accusations did not imply that Parliament should normally control the power of the king. Attempts to make the king formally answerable for his actions were very much a last resort.

Normally the interest of the subject lay in strong effective royal government and Parliament was rather more concerned about weak government than about the dangers of too much royal power. Parliament had already acquired its familiar form. Theoretically, the king could summon, or not summon, whoever he liked to what was, in fact, though not yet in name, the House of Lords. In practice, once a man had been summoned he and his heirs had a prescriptive right to a summons in future; so that the king could in effect create new peerages, but not terminate an existing one. (Occasionally a peer was not summoned to a particular Parliament, sometimes for political reasons; but this did not result in permanent exclusion.) In 1447, 43 lay peers were summoned to Parliament, outnumbered by the 21 bishops and 30 abbots who also had the right to attend. The Commons consisted of 74 representatives of counties, and 222 of boroughs. The county representatives were, since 1429, elected by freeholders with lands worth 40 shillings a year, to prevent the 'manslaughter, riots, batteries and divisions' which were likely if 'folk of small means or not worth' participated. The urban franchise varied a good deal from town to town, though there was an increasing tendency for the electorate to be restricted to a small 'inside' group of the richest and best-established citizens. In fact, most of the smaller boroughs were represented in Parliament by gentlemen rather than by their own burgesses; so that by 1478 gentlemen MPs outnumbered townsmen two to one. The Commons represented a coalition of interests, the landed and the commercial, which in representative institutions elsewhere in Europe were generally separated. Whatever the deficiencies of election, it represented real communities. Given the general tendency to think in terms of corporate bodies rather than, in modern style, individual rights, the notion that 'everyman' was 'privy and party to the Parliament' and therefore bound by its decisions was feasible.

Formally Parliament was a court of law, indeed the supreme court. Theorists tended to maintain that it did not so much make law as declare what the existing law was, just like other courts; for law was not something made by men, but was natural rather, written in the hearts of men and discoverable by reason. Particular laws were the application of natural law to particular cases. But whatever might be said by jurists in their more philosophical moments, in practice statute law was superior to any individual interpretation of the law of nature, or even to the traditions and precedents of the common law. The judges themselves declared in 1453 that 'this high court of Parliament ... is so high and mighty in its nature, that it may make law, and that which is law it may make no law'. Statutes though less revolutionary in their implications than those of the next century, when Parliament found itself concerned with fundamental problems of theology, covered a large range of important topics from authorizing the burning of heretics to regulating the number of attorneys allowed to practise in East Anglia. A large part of the statute book is in fact concerned with the regulation of economic life. Long statutes deal with the marketing of wool abroad, the proper making of cloth and so on. These statutes were frequently repeated and were difficult to enforce. They do, nevertheless, give the lie to the impression that statutes were unimportant in the fifteenth century.

Taxation was a main cause of Parliamentary strength. The customs revenue accounted for about three-quarters of the 'certain' royal revenue in 1433. While these were voted for limited periods only (two, three or five years at a time) they were renewed, apparently without question, so as to provide a continuous source of income for the crown. In 1453 a strongly partisan Parliament voted the customs to Henry VI for life, Edward IV got a similar grant after only four years on the throne in 1465, and thereafter customs were automatically voted for life in the first Parliament of each new reign. A necessary supplement to the customs revenue was the vote of direct Parliamentary taxation. Over the years 1428–54 this brought an average of £18,000 a year, about half the net value of the king's 'certain' revenue (essentially customs and land). But it was politically much more significant than the customs, since Parliaments frequently refused to vote direct taxes, or voted less than the government had asked for. They were a potential bargaining counter in the way that customs revenues were not.

Parliament met only intermittently; between 1439 and 1461 there were twenty-seven sessions, which generally lasted about six weeks each. Policy was the king's, and naturally he took advice from a council and delegated routine affairs to it. In normal circumstances he could summon whoever he liked (though political expediency would suggest the inclusion of the more powerful nobles); and accept or reject their advice. Occasionally, a cry was raised by disgruntled subjects for a 'nominated' council responsible to Parliament, such as had been imposed on Henry IV from 1406–11; and when the king was incapable (during Henry VI's minority, or during his illness in 1453–4) the council might be nominated in Parliament. Any reasonably competent king would wish to pursue his own policy, and could normally do so. The 'Yorkist' opposition to Henry VI demanded a more 'responsible' government, but when Edward of York became king in 1461 such notions were hastily dropped. A nominated council was a response to emergency, not a prescription for normal government.

So far we have been dealing with the formal structure of government. We need now to turn from the constitutional dimension to the political to see, as well as we can, how government actually worked.

Land was the foundation of wealth, social status and therefore political power. The aim of the ambitious merchant or lawyer was to buy land in the country and to establish a landed family. The distribution of landownership therefore provides some guide to political power and is illustrated in Appendix A (page 63). These figures are very rough but do provide some idea of the orders of magnitude involved.

Next to the crown the hereditary peerage, with at least ten per cent of the landed wealth of the country was clearly the predominant political influence (the church's twenty per cent is less impressive than it looks; the Church was not a monolithic institution, and it did not take a united stand on the political issues of the day). The combined share of the various 'gentry' classes (including knights and esquires) comes to over thirty per cent of the national total, over three times that of the peers; but of course it would be wrong to argue that they were three times as influential, since, obviously, one man with £1,000 is a good deal more powerful in practice than ten men with £100 each. The political initiative, then, lay with the peers.

The peers enjoyed a certain cohesion, a class-consciousness implicit in the concept of themselves as an 'order' with the right to be summoned to Parliament. But there were enormous differences among them. Many of the peers were assessed in 1436 at about £300 per annum landed income; the poorest seems to have been Lord Clinton with £60. On the other hand, Richard, Duke of York was assessed at £2,500; if allowance is made for his Welsh lands and for under-assessment, his total net income was at least £3,500 and may have been as high as £5,800. The case of York shows the way in which estates could be amalgamated through female descent and marriage; though his paternal inheritance was considerable (he was the grandson of one of the many sons of Edward III), most of his land came from the great Mortimer estate in the Welsh marches, which came to him through his mother.*

Another leading figure in the politics of the 1450s was Richard Neville, Earl of Salisbury, assessed at £1,238 in 1436, but probably worth over £3,000 a year. He was a younger son, who managed, nevertheless, to inherit a fairly considerable estate in Yorkshire; but he owed his earldom and most of his income to his marriage to Alice, heiress to Thomas Montagu, Earl of Salisbury. Richard Neville's son, also Richard Neville, became through marriage Earl of Warwick and one of the wealthiest men in England while his father was still alive. Whatever may have been true of the mass of landowners, the leading figures in the Wars of the Roses were hardly impoverished.

Marriage was, therefore, a business venture. Child marriages were arranged quite cold-bloodedly. One noble lady contracted for her son to marry 'the eldest daughter to be born within the next

* See Charles Ross, *Edward IV* (Eyre Methuen, 1975) p. 5, and references cited there.

five or six years to Lord Hastings. Great fortunes could be made out of exploiting the laws of inheritance, which were extremely complicated and made more so by marriage settlements, dowers for widows and so on. The high rate of mortality led to frequent marriage, leading in turn to endless disputes between half-brothers or between step-fathers and step-sons. Litigation then, was an almost inescapable fate for the landowner; litigation which was often directed against his own relatives. Law was a major outlet for entrepreneurial talents. To vary the metaphor, a campaign was often waged by a general staff, the lord's council composed largely of lawyers, with legal documents as ammunition. John Paston 'set more store by his writing and evidence than he did by any moveable goods'. But the law was very slow. It was better to enjoy the fruits of possession while a case ground its way through the courts. There was a considerable incentive to use force to settle these interminable disputes; and because of this the peace of the country was disturbed by innumerable noble (and gentry) family feuds.

Another source of feud was the struggle for pre-eminence in an area between two great men. A few nobles were interested in power at the centre. But for most of them it was their standing in their own area, their 'country', which mattered. This depended mainly on ownership of land, but could be reinforced by royal office. It was worthwhile for the Earl of Northumberland to become a warden of the marches or to angle for the bishopric of Carlisle for a relation. The Duke of Norfolk, armed with a royal commission of enquiry, could proclaim that 'next the king our sovereign lord and by his grace and licence we will have the principal rule and governance throughout all this shire of which we bear our name'.

Alliances naturally sprang up between those involved in struggles for land or power at all levels of society, from the court downwards, and something like fortuitous party groupings emerged. 'Get you lordship and friendship because on that depends all the law and the prophets.' Men looked for powerful patrons, whose prestige would help to sway the decision of law courts and lob profitable offices or leases in their direction. The rise and fall of factions at court naturally affected the balance of power at a local level. The composition of parties was largely fortuitous, based on the principle that my enemy's enemy is my friend. For instance, the West Country was disrupted throughout the 1450s by the feud between Thomas Courtenay, Earl of Devon, and Lord Bonville. On a national level, Courtenay was allied to the Duke of York, and Bonville to the opposing 'court' party. In 1455 Bonville managed to switch allegiance to York's victorious party; by reaction the Courtenays became members of the Lancastrian 'court' party, and remained Lancastrian sympathizers when York's son eventually acquired the throne. The Neville Earls of Salisbury and Warwick were allied with York because both families were enemies of the Beauforts; the Percy family, enemies of the Nevilles, were equally naturally 'Lancastrian' and remained so until the York–Neville alliance was disrupted.

None of the leaders in fifteenth-century politics questioned the basic assumptions of their society, and particularly the predominance of their own class. Divisions were partly about policy in particular circumstances; partly about feuds and struggles for office. Conditions could change very rapidly and the most bitter feuds could be healed in time. The Duke of York's supporters hounded the Duke of Suffolk to his death in 1450. Ten years later Suffolk's heir married York's daughter. The political game was waged, therefore, according to an unwritten law which tended to preserve the family, whatever might happen to the individual. Of the 'attainders' (confiscation by act of Parliament of the title and property of a traitor), carried out against peers between 1453 and 1509, eighty-four per cent were ultimately reversed; and while many of these reversals were due to swings of the political pendulum, many were due to the feeling that it was right to let a family recover, eventually, its own property.* Contrary to the general impression, the great peerage families did not disappear during the Wars of the Roses. When families did die out it was because of a failure of male heirs; a phenomenon common enough at this time (a quarter of peerage families died out every twenty-

* J. R. Lander, 'Attainder and Forfeiture', in *Historical Studies of the English Parliament*, ed. E. B. Fryde and E. Miller (Cambridge, 2 vols., 1970) vol. 2. Now reprinted in Lander, *Crown and Nobility, 1450–1509* (Edward Arnold, 1976).

five years, largely from natural causes) and not especially pronounced at the end of the fifteenth century. Obviously death in battle or at the hands of the executioner increases the chance of this happening; but the only unequivocal extinction of an ancient family through political misadventure was due to the disappearance of Lord Lovel, Richard III's associate, in 1487.*

A great man's following was held together by what its adherents hoped to gain. Some of them had a formal contract to him, an indenture which bound them to serve, generally for life, in return for an annuity and his 'good lordship'. Many of these retainers were knights and squires (sometimes even peers) who could turn out their own following, and provided as it were, a cadre of officers for the great man's army. The magnate's own tenants were also an important element in his following.

The former system, of indenture and retainer has come to be known as 'bastard feudalism'; 'bastard' because a cash payment replaced the grant of land in return for service which was characteristic of feudalism proper. 'Bastard', too, thought Charles Plummer, who invented the term, because it was a cause of violence, of the corruption of the law (through bands of armed retainers terrorizing juries), of private war between the lords, ultimately of civil war; 'by a sort of ignoble caricature of the feudal system the whole structure of society from the apex to the base was knit together in a hierarchy of corruption'.† To this the only answer is that the supposed virtues of 'real' feudalism were not very apparent in, say, the England of King Stephen. Nor was 'bastard feudalism' new to the fifteenth century. Indentures for life have been traced back to the thirteenth century and were common in the fourteenth. Both feudalism and 'bastard feudalism' refer to societies in which the central authority is weak, in which political power is diffused among a number of great lords. Both can produce corruption, petty tyranny and anarchy; in both

* K. B. McFarlane, 'The Wars of the Roses' (*Proceedings of the British Academy*, vol. 50, 1964); and his *The Nobility of Later Medieval England* (Oxford 1973) pp. 142–76. Of seven other examples three were revived in a collateral line under the Tudors; the other families were new or undistinguished.

† Charles Plummer, introduction to Sir John Fortescue, *The Governance of England* (Oxford, 1885) p. 25.

cases these tendencies can be held in check by an efficient central government.

The case against 'bastard feudalism' is based on its supposed instability. When, it is argued, allegiance was determined by grants of land, men were less volatile. In 'bastard feudalism' they often contracted with several lords, and switched at strategic moments. 'Lordship lasted only as long as it was found to be *good* lordship or until it was ousted by a better.'* But volatility of this sort decreased rather than increased the stability of the country as a whole. It meant that politics was a game of temporary coalitions, that lords had to consider the interests of their clients, that they had to attract a following by posing as defenders of the common good: above all, that an able king could manipulate the shifting allegiances for his own advantage. A system in which great men continually confronted each other with *blocs* of supporters on whom they could rely absolutely was more likely to produce long-drawn-out feuds than one in which a man's following deserted him when he was down.

Of course, retainers were a major problem. The Percy earls of Northumberland spent a third to a half of their gross revenue on fees; not all of them for soldiers, but for lawyers, chaplains, even cooks whose service the earls hoped to enjoy for life. Lord Hastings, Edward IV's chamberlain retained at least eighty-eight gentlemen and two peers. They were expected to serve 'with so many able persons as every of them might make, to be furnished and arrayed at the cost and charges of the said lord'. They were also useful in other ways; by serving as members of Parliament, as justices of the peace and so on, they helped to increase Lord Hastings' influence. But their principal function was military; and they constituted a formidable fighting force.†

Parliament worried about retaining, but legislation was slow, generally ineffective and was directed against abuses rather than the system itself; the wearing of a lord's livery by bands of armed

---

* K. B. McFarlane, 'Parliament and Bastard Feudalism', *Trans. Roy. Hist. Soc.*, 4th ser., vol. 26, 1944, p. 70.

† J. M. W. Bean, *The Estates of the Percy Family, 1416–1537* (Oxford, 1958) pp. 85–98; W. H. Dunham, Jr., *Lord Hastings' Indentured Retainers, 1461–83* (Connecticut, 1955).

ruffians and 'maintenance' or violent interference with the due process of law. A statute of 1468 (not the most propitious moment) restricted retaining to household servants and for 'lawful' purposes; but these constituted rather wide loopholes.

The military power of the peers posed a dilemma for the king. It was a potential danger. But it was also the source of troops for foreign war or defence against the Scots. Moreover retaining was only a special form, an accentuation, of something much more widespread: the general obligation of loyalty to a lord. Even Henry VIII's armies were normally provided by landowners contributing a specific number of 'friends, favourers, servants and tenants'. Archbishop Cranmer told the western rebels in 1549 that they were naïve in thinking that they could reduce the power of the gentry by reducing the number of their servants 'since all tenants and farmers who know their duties' will be ready to 'die and live' with their lords.

Suppressing retaining would abolish certain 'artificial' relationships between lords and men, over and beyond the sphere of a lord's 'natural' influence. But that 'natural' influence was a far more important thing; a great man's strength depended partly on his social position, on the general respect for lordship, partly on the adherence, willing or otherwise, of tenants and other economic dependants. It was these, not indentured retainers, who formed the bulk of most riotous bands, and the relationship was an enduring one. In 1642 we find the gentry of Cheshire still swearing to a truce on behalf of 'their friends, tenants, servants and all others in whom they have interest'.

Lordship dominated society. Nevertheless, the interesting problem in fifteenth-century politics is to gauge how complete this domination was. Were politics only a noble game, as it is sometimes implied? Or had some account to be taken of the interests, aspirations and prejudices of the non-noble classes?

Although routine meetings of the king's council were attended only by professional administrators – some of them laymen, generally lawyers, of gentry origin, some clerics, the greater of them made bishops for their pains in royal service – meetings at which more important decisions were taken usually included some of the great lords. Chief Justice Fortescue wondered 'what lower man was there sitting in that council, that durst say anything against the opinion of any of the great lords'. This, however, was referring to the reign of the peculiarly ineffective Henry VI. Strong leadership by the king could prevent noble domination of the council, could see that royal government was conducted in accord with the national interest, as the king and his administrators saw it, rather than according it with the sectional interests of the magnates.

The qualification here is 'as the king and his administrators saw it . . .'. If they were to take account of wider interests, those interests had to make their weight felt. Parliament provides some sort of gauge of their ability to do so.

Formally, of course, the Commons had considerable influence. They controlled taxation; and their assent had long been required for legislation (though this was only formally recognized from 1429). The question is how far the Commons actually represented the interest of their constituents? How far were they merely the puppets of the great lords who jobbed them into Parliament for their own ends?

The influence of the magnates in the Commons was certainly considerable. The Earl of Westmorland ordered the authorities of Grimsby to 'appoint two of my council to be burgesses' (MPs), graciously allowing the town to communicate with him and them if it had any Parliamentary business. The Duke of York had at least four servants in the Parliament of 1450, and probably more; one of them, Sir William Oldhall, York's chamberlain, became Speaker. At least seven retainers of Lord Hastings sat in the Commons in 1478. Nevertheless, if we look closely at a particular region – East Anglia where, thanks to the Paston Letters, we are unusually well informed on local politics – we find that matters are not as clear cut as they may seem at first.

East Anglian politics naturally reflected the rival interests of the three great magnate families; the Mowbrays, Dukes of Norfolk; the de la Poles, Dukes of Suffolk; and the de Veres, Earls of Oxford. Their local standing at any one time reflected the state of national politics. The de la Pole interest collapsed when the Duke was exiled and murdered in 1450. The Mowbrays were political allies of the Duke of York, and their influence was naturally high during periods of Yorkist ascendancy. The de Veres were loyal Lancastrians and paramount therefore during Henry vi's brief restoration in 1470–1. But throughout the period, there was another interest to be considered, that of the country gentry. The Duchess of Norfolk wrote somewhat peremptorily to John Paston in 1455 that it was 'thought right necessary for divers causes that my lord have at this time in the Parliament such persons as belong unto him and be of his menial servants'. But in spite of her tone, this was a request, not a command; and Paston demurred at the ducal nomination of John Howard as member for Norfolk because 'it is an evil precedent for the shire that a strange man should be chosen . . . for if the gentlemen of the shire shall suffer such inconveniences in good faith the shire shall not be called of such worship as it hath been'. As it happened Howard was returned but in 1461 Paston was more successful; being elected against Howard, even though the Yorkist party had just managed to get its candidate, Edward iv, installed as king. In 1470 Paston was organizing his friends to 'hold as one body' at the shire meeting so as to impress on the Earl of Oxford 'that some strength resteth' in the gentlemen of the shire. The result was an acceptable compromise.

We know far less about the rest of the country than we know about East Anglia. Nevertheless, the general picture seems to be that particular noble families rarely had a monopoly of power in any one locality; that the rivalry of great families gave the gentry below them some room for manoeuvre: and that this meant that some attention had to be paid to gentry interests and prejudices. As for the boroughs, although the smaller ones had become pocket seats for gentlemen, towns like Coventry, Norwich and Bristol and especially London, were obviously important in Parliament and their influence can be seen in much of the economic legislation. If we try to get below the level of gentry and the richer merchants who dominated the towns the concept of 'political influence' becomes fairly tenuous. Most forty-shilling freeholders were not gentlemen, and some towns preserved a relatively wide franchise, but actual election contests were rare (rival interests preferred to avoid them by patching up a compromise); and even when they took place, it would be unrealistic to expect more than a very marginal influence on the part of the electorates. One exception here was the direct influence that Londoners could exert on Parliament sitting at Westminster. When Lancastrian governments wanted especially tractable Parliaments, they took care to hold them in the provinces; at Reading, at Coventry, at Bury St Edmunds.

The ultimate decisions in politics were too often taken, not in the council chamber or in Parliament, but on the battlefield; and here it might be thought that there could be no challenge to noble dominance. The great nobles were naturally the men best able to raise troops. Nevertheless, precisely because parties were evenly balanced, precisely because no noble could be confident that his followers would stand by him through thick and thin, political ability, the ability to cajole, to neutralize an opponent's forces, was at least as important even in civil war as more purely military talents. The realist French politician and historian Commynes thought that the English normally spared the common soldiers after a battle in the civil wars 'because everyone wants to please them as they are the strongest'.

The essential problem was to get men to turn out; and men's attitudes at all levels were affected by calculation of what they might gain by victory and how much they dared offend their lords. The flexibility of 'bastard feudalism' mattered here. Some retainers were contracted to more than one lord, and they had to make a hasty calculation of the chances; miscalculation could be disastrous. Sir William Skipworth, who refused to obey the Duke of York in 1455, lost various offices on York's estate and an annuity worth £40 as a result. (Service of a great magnate could be highly profitable; Sir William Oldhall whom we have already mentioned as York's chamberlain, allegedly spent over £4,500 on building operations.) Emotion as well as calculation entered into play. In 1471 the Earl of Northumberland had abandoned his traditional Lancastrian loyalties and now supported Edward IV's second bid for the throne. He could not, however, turn out his following for Edward. The most he could do was to stay neutral, since 'many gentleman and others would not . . . so fully and extremely have determined themselves in the king's right' as the Earl was prepared to do. Their memories of

Yorkist slaughter of their kindred at the battle of Towton ten years before remained too vivid.

Political power depended, then, rather more than one might expect, on 'public relations'; to a certain extent on convincing a number of men that one's cause was right and, perhaps more important, that it was likely to win. Political songs were composed and subversive bills distributed in cities.

Throughout the 1450s the Duke of York's party made skilful use of propaganda in its campaigns to have the Duke recognized as the king's leading councillor (not until 1460 did York claim that he, not Henry VI, was actually the rightful king); and with considerable success. By 1459 the Lancastrian government was complaining that 'the people in many places was deceived and blinded by the subtle and covert malice' of the other side. Of course, it was not just a question of manipulating public opinion; the dismal failure of the government's policies provided plenty of ammunition for its enemies. Nevertheless, it is true that, as far as popular opinion in the politically important south-east was concerned, and especially in London, York and his allies had the initiative; and this was to be a political factor of considerable importance from Cade's rebellion of 1450 through to the proclamation of Edward IV as king in 1461. 'We commons have brought King Edward to his prosperity ... and if he will not [be] ruled after us as ... we will have him, as able we were to make him king, as able we be to depose him'.* This was a naïve interpretation; but not entirely an unjustified one.

'Public opinion' could work both ways; not only magnates looking for support among the people but lesser men hoping to influence magnates to support them. Political connection was a two-way process. Take the situation in East Anglia at the end of 1450. The Duke of Suffolk had been murdered, and York controlled the government. This was an awkward situation for Suffolk's henchmen, Thomas Tuddenham and John Heydon, who had tyrannized over the counties of Norfolk and Suffolk for several years. They rushed to make their peace with the new power; and were reported to have offered Oldhall, York's right-

* Quoted in R. L. Storey, *The End of the House of Lancaster* (Barrie & Jenkins, 1966) p. 197.

hand-man, £1,000. This dismayed their enemies in the shire, who had counted on York to redress their grievances. Counter-action was essential; and William Wayte wrote to John Paston urging a plan of campaign. York was due to go on a tour of East Anglia and every opportunity should be seized to show him how unpopular Heydon and Tuddenham were. Popular demonstrations should be laid on. The men of Swaffham should meet York and give him a bill of complaints and 'cry out on them and that all the women of the said town be there also, and cry out on them also, and call them extortioners, and pray my lord that he will do sharp execution upon them'. The mayor and aldermen of Norwich should be 'moved' to arrange similar demonstrations. For unless 'my lord hear some foul tales of them [Heydon and Tuddenham], and some hideous noise and cry, by my faith they are like to come to grace'. Popular demonstrations, then, could be stimulated by the urban upper class and by the neighbouring gentry; though even so, we should not assume that manipulation would have been possible if there had not been real popular resentment at the way the county had been governed. But more important is the point that even York had to choose his allies with an eye to popular acceptability; that he could be deterred from making his peace with Heydon and Tuddenham by being shown that they were a political liability. Even in the fifteenth century, politics was more than a matter of great men passing orders down the social system.

Government depended ultimately on acceptance by its subjects. 'Acceptance' is the word to stress here. There was no question of popular sovereignty; of the people's wishes (however defined) determining the course of events. Acceptance of authority depended partly on a government's conforming to some very generalized maxims; most notably, those embodied in the coronation oath, to keep the peace to clergy and people, to do justice in mercy and in truth, and to maintain the laws 'which the community of the realm shall have chosen'. It also depended on a government's effectiveness in enforcing its will, in keeping order, avoiding military defeat, and so on. Government survived essentially by creating an illusion of its own power. Kings had no standing army, and financial resources which were barely adequate even in quiet times. Faced with rebellion a government's best tactic was to persuade its subjects that it was impregnable, that the rebels were bound to be defeated and that it was therefore the interest as well as the duty of all subjects to rally to the crown. Conversely failure to keep order could be fatal to a government's credibility; and this may be why noblemen are sometimes found surreptitiously stirring up popular rebellion. If it failed, no harm was done; but if it succeeded, it showed that the government could be toppled.

In all this elaborate game the government had the advantage. It existed. In normal conditions it could out-do even the most over-mighty subject in the display of wealth, in elaborate buildings, pompous processions, tournaments or lavish distribution of alms. Government, too, was the greatest source of patronage, not only from its own resources, but also from the church, whose higher offices were normally at the disposal of the king. It even had supranatural sanction which, we must deduce, if only because contemporaries took such pains about it, had some effect. Since 1399 kings had been crowned with oil which was said to have been delivered by the Virgin Mary to St Thomas Becket; a clear attempt to emulate the kings of France, who were anointed with an oil especially brought by an angel for the baptism of Clovis in 496. And, for three hundred and fifty years at least, the king had been credited with a miraculous power, that of healing the 'king's evil' (scrofula) by the laying on of hands; a practice which continued until the reign of Queen Anne. On a more mundane level the crown was the guarantor of social stability; and could therefore normally count on the support of its more influential subjects.

Violence was common enough in everyday affairs; family quarrels among the nobility and gentry, disputes about property or grazing rights were all too often settled by fights between armed mobs. But this was a far cry from civil war; and rebellion against the crown was not undertaken lightly. In spite of the reputation of fifteenth-century magnates for irresponsibility, their long-term interest lay in the maintenance of a stable working political system; and while short-term advantage might sometimes tempt some of them to try their luck in rebellion, the solid core of the peerage were instinctively conservative supporters of established government. In any case, a direct challenge to the crown was dangerous; the odds were heavily against successful rebellion and the penalties (execution, and the confiscation of one's family property) daunting.

Nevertheless, sheer incompetence or exceptional bad luck could lay a government open to successful rebellion. Defeat in a major war was hard for a king's honour; and corrupt government which was too obviously conducted in the interests of a small group could lead to riots, disorder and ultimately rebellion. A successful usurper took time to establish credibility, and had meanwhile an embarrassing backlog of political debts to those who had helped him to the crown. A usurper needed eventually to widen his support to include the former opponents; and in doing so he risked trouble from disappointed supporters. Except in these two cases, however, the presumption of victory in cases of confrontation lay almost always with the crown.

Historians contrasting the political disorder of the late fifteenth century with the apparent stability of the early Tudor period have traditionally preferred to concentrate on institutional change; the foundation of new courts, the improvement in methods of collecting royal revenues and so on. Institutional change of this sort is, however, more a symptom than a cause of monarchial authority. A certain amount of disorder was endemic in fifteenth-century society; and government could never hope to get complete control of its representatives throughout the country. The inability of government to enforce its will in the provinces was, however, also a major problem of Elizabethan and early Stuart times; and noble-inspired affrays were to persist well into the second half of the sixteenth century. The social framework of Lancastrian England did not make government unworkable, did not make the Wars of the Roses inevitable. For that we must look for more particular circumstances, to the weakness of the king personally rather than the crown as an institution. In that context the Yorkist and Tudor 'recovery' becomes much more comprehensible than it does in traditional accounts.

Appendix A to Chapter Two

THE DISTRIBUTION OF LANDOWNERSHIP IN 1436

This is based primarily on H. L. Gray 'Incomes from Land in England in 1436' (*Eng. Hist. Rev.*, XLIX, 1934) modified by certain assumptions made by J. P. Cooper, 'The Social Distribution of Land and Men in England, 1436–1700 (*Econ. Hist. Rev.*, 2nd ser., vol. 20, 1967).

Category	Numbers included	Total landed income	Average landed income	Percentage of total national landed income	Social Description
		£	£		
Crown		20,000	20,000	5	
Church		75–100,000	75–100,000	20	
Lay peers	51	40,000	768	10	
Incomes of £100+	183	38,000	208	10	'Greater knights'
Incomes £40–99	750	45,000	60	12	'Lesser knights'
£20–39	1,200	28,811	24	7	'Esquires'
£10–19	1,600	19,200	12	5 ⎫	Other gentlemen and
£5–9	3,400	19,200	5·65	5 ⎭	greater yeomen
Under £5		100,000		26	Lesser yeomen and husbandmen

It should be noted that:
  (a) The 1436 figures are extremely defective: most figures are extrapolated from the evidence for sixteen counties.
  (b) Peers were often under-assessed; and lands in Wales and

the Marches, in which many of the greater peers had substantial interests, are not included. (*See* C. D. Ross and T. B. Pugh, *Bulletin of the Institute of Hist. Research*, vol. 26, 1953.)

(c) The total for landowners under £5 is based on the subtraction of the other headings from a very rough guess of the total cultivated acreage.

(d) The 'social description' in the last column is inexact. Many had incomes above their social status; e.g. many yeomen, merchants or lawyers had estates appropriate for 'gentlemen'.

Chapter Three

BREAKDOWN OF A REGIME

Two major problems faced the English government in 1450. The war with France, which had won so much glory for Henry V, had collapsed into ignominious defeat. At home, government was in the hands of a corrupt faction which (so it was believed) had murdered its main opponent three years before, and was now engaged in milking the royal finances on an unprecedented scale, interfering with the due process of law, and terrorizing the countryside. In a functioning monarchy, the principal cause of bad government is likely to be in the personality of the king; in this case Henry VI, king in theory since 1422 (when he was just eight months old), and in practice since attaining his majority in 1437.

Henry's confessor, John Blacman, wrote a fascinating account of a king 'more given to God and to devout prayer than to handling worldly or temporal things or practising vain sports and pursuits'. He was conspicuous in an age especially given to flamboyant courtly ceremonial for despising all fashion and wearing 'round-toed shoes and boots like a peasant's'. He was concerned about the moral tone of his court and given to prying 'through hidden windows of his chamber' at the entry of women to the palace. He rebuked lords who swore, and refused to transact business on Sundays and festivals. He was also generous to the poor, and, more damagingly, to his friends.

Blacman was preparing a case for Henry's canonization, and what he considered appropriate there may be only a caricature of the real Henry. But clearly Henry's qualities were not those of a king. It was not so much a question of Henry's uninvolvement in government business; the trouble was that he did interfere, generally wrong-headedly. Chief Justice Fortescue, a loyal subject of Henry's who preferred to go into exile rather than recognize a usurper, had no illusions about the king's inadequacies. The burden of his *Governance of England* was the need for a powerful council to protect the king from himself, especially where grants of land or money were concerned.

The house of Lancaster had held the throne since Henry's grandfather had led a successful rebellion against the tyranny of Richard II in 1399, and, on Richard's forced abdication, had become king as Henry IV, passing over the prior claim of Edmund Mortimer, Earl of March. Mortimer, however, was only seven years old at the time and his claim was not seriously asserted. Henry IV's reign was to be dogged by trouble; not from rival claims to the throne, but from rebellion in the north and in Wales, and from attempts to make the king's council formally responsible to Parliament. But all this changed in the reign of his son Henry V. Henry's brilliant victories in France, his conquest of Normandy, and eventually his recognition by the French king Charles VI as his heir in the Treaty of Troyes in 1420, all helped to appease discontent at home. But Henry died just thirty-five years old, in 1422. Charles VI died two months later. As, literally, a babe in arms, Henry VI had become king of England and France.

Henry's minority passed off surprisingly peacefully. There was no serious challenge to his right to the English throne; and the struggles for influence in the council which governed England until 1437 did not erupt into violence. The council governed England reasonably well, and at first things did not go too badly in France, where Henry's uncle, the Duke of Bedford, was able to maintain the English position as it had been in 1422. The tide turned with the successful relief of Orleans by the French (whether or not inspired by Joan of Arc) in 1429. In 1435 Philip Duke of Burgundy (who was in fact ruler of the prosperous Netherlands, as well as of the duchy of Burgundy in the east of France and premier peer of France) made his peace with the French king; and a year later the English were driven out of Paris. After that the war was a matter of the gradual expulsion of the English from their remaining territories, interspersed with long periods of truce. By August 1450 Normandy had been lost, leaving the English with only Calais and Gascony. Gascony had been ruled by the English kings continuously for some three hundred years, and was closely bound to the English economy by the Bordeaux–London wine trade; but even Gascony was lost three years later.

The odds were probably always against the English crown keeping its conquests in France. Once before, in Edward III's reign the English had acquired control of a substantial part of France: once before, their position had crumbled ignominiously. Nevertheless, Henry VI's personality was a factor in the collapse. He made little attempt to ingratiate himself with his French subjects and never led his own armies; a fatal weakness in an age in which national feeling was conceived very much in terms of loyalty to the king's person. His rival in France, Charles VII was not an impressive personality, at least until victory began to increase his self-confidence. It is not impossible that the French people as a whole would have eventually accepted the Treaty of Troyes, if only the representative of the house of Lancaster had had rather more charismatic qualities, and had been prepared to conduct himself as king of France.

English attitudes to the war were ambivalent. War-weariness was apparent in Parliament; where Henry V had managed to squeeze about £53,000 a year in direct taxation, this fell to a mere £3,000 a year from 1422–8 and then averaged about £25,000 to 1454. Now that Henry VI was king of France his French territories could be made to pay for their own defence; but of course war expenses always exceeded income. It is doubtful if England gained as a whole from the war, though obviously individuals did who acquired land in France or captured valuable prisoners whom they could then ransom. But while there may not have been much enthusiasm for war, defeat was unpalatable, indeed dangerous for the honour and credibility of the crown; and therefore for good government in the country.

Henry's government, not unnaturally, shied away from the classic dilemma; to try to retrieve the territory lost, at the cost of a good deal of money and the risk of greater humiliation, or to accept a compromise peace which would involve an admission of defeat. By attempting (unsuccessfully) to make peace by stealth it got the worst of both worlds.

The whole business was, in fact, inextricably intertwined with politics at home. An attempt in 1440 to use the release of the Duke of Orleans (a prisoner in England since the battle of Agincourt, twenty-five years before) to initiate peace talks had been vociferously opposed by the king's uncle, Humphrey, Duke of Gloucester, who had invoked the memory of his victorious brother Henry V. There was another chance in 1445, when Henry married a French princess, Margaret of Anjou, apparently with Humphrey's approval. But the marriage negotiations involved a promise by Henry to cede the province of Maine to the French king, as a guarantee of his good faith about hopes of a permanent peace. Humphrey was certain to oppose this, in his view, degrading surrender, and he was edged out of the king's confidence. Rumours that he was plotting rebellion led to his arrest in 1447, and shortly afterwards he died in prison; it was immediately assumed that his enemies at court had murdered him. Maine was duly ceded to the French in 1448. The Duke of Suffolk, Henry's leading adviser, was generally held responsible for the marriage and for the surrender of Maine; how true the allegation was is impossible to tell.

The war, and Parliament's unwillingness to vote adequate funds, was the main reason for the crown's financial difficulties. Direct taxation, as we saw, was less than in Henry V's reign, and the rate of custom voted by Parliament to Henry VI was lower than to his predecessors. (This aggravated an already bad situation, since cloth, the staple export of the fifteenth century, paid taxes at a lower rate than raw wool, the main export of the fourteenth century; but here again more amenable Parliaments would have been prepared to compensate for this.) The annual deficit was some £20,000 a year, and the total debt in 1450, £372,000; chicken feed to later generations, used to measuring the national debt in billions, but serious in an age which had not mastered the art of creating credit mechanisms to service long-term loans at low interest. The cries of unpaid creditors (including the Duke of York, owed £38,000 for his service in France) added to the general state of crisis.

It is much easier to personalize a grievance than to consider the long-term causes. Popular anger came to centre on corruption at court. It had a point; Henry was irresponsibly generous and the years 1437–50 had seen 'an unprecedented dispersal of crown lands outside the royal family'.* 'You have made the king poor, / That beggeth from door to door', sang, somewhat unrhythmically, the court's opponents; while the king's foundations at Eton and King's College Cambridge were dismissed by Parliament as 'over chargeful and noyous' [harmful]. Henry had also been extraordinarily lavish with new titles, following the unhappy precedent of Richard II; Suffolk himself was made a duke in 1448, although this dignity was normally reserved for the king's relatives. Government seemed to be a monopoly of a single faction; and its leader, the Duke of Suffolk, was the scapegoat for military disaster and national humiliation.

The politics of the 1450s are rather confused; it is easy to get lost in a welter of names and dates. But it is necessary to follow what happened in order to understand the very specific circumstances which produced the civil war in 1459–61 and the replacement of the Lancastrian Henry VI by the Yorkist Edward IV; the way one thinks of this affects the way one approaches the subsequent problems of Yorkist and Tudor monarchy. What is involved is essentially a struggle for control of the government (not, until 1460, for the throne itself) between the Duke of York and his allies on the one hand, and on the other the court party of the king's friends, headed initially by Suffolk, then by Edmund Beaufort, Duke of Somerset and finally by the queen, Margaret of Anjou. The great mass, even of peers and administrators preferred to avoid committing themselves to one side or the other if they possibly could; only 45 of a possible 105 peers (clerical and lay) attended a vital Parliament in 1454, and there was a suspicious tendency for lords to hang back from battles until they saw how things were likely to turn out. This degree of non-commitment was not just prudent calculation. There was a genuine feeling for the proprieties of good government, a belief that faction was dangerous, and that the service of the crown must come first. The balance of political power was swayed by the temporary

* B. P. Wolffe, 'The Personal Rule of Henry VI', in S. B. Chrimes, C. D. Ross and R. A. Griffiths (eds.), *Fifteenth Century England* (Manchester, 1972).

adhesion of the uncommitted to one side or the other, generally as a result of the excesses of their opponents.

There were three main phases of 'Yorkist' attack. The first is the period 1449–51 when a popular outcry against Suffolk's malad-ministration paved the way for York to force his way into the government. The second involved the period 1453–6, for a good deal of which the king was ill and York was 'Protector'of the realm. The last were the years 1459–61 when an attempt by the court faction to pay off old scores against York produced a rapid escalation into civil war situation resulting in the death of York and the acquisition of the throne by his son Edward, Earl of March. In between these years of crisis, that is, 1451–3 and 1456–9, government reverted to the 'court' party.

The lead in this drama was taken by Richard, Duke of York. We have already seen something of his wealth (see above, p. 50). More dangerous was his birth. He was descended twice over from Edward III (see genealogical table, p. 355). If women could inherit the throne or even transmit a claim to it, York had a better right to be king than Henry VI, since on that basis his great-grandmother, Philippa, daughter of Edward III's second son, had a claim prior to that of descendants of John of Gaunt, Edward III's third son and Henry VI's great-grandfather. There had in fact been a plot in 1415 to make Edmund Mortimer, Earl of March, York's uncle, king on this basis. Edmund, however, had given the plot away, and Richard, Earl of Cambridge, York's father, had been executed for his part in it. But York himself did nothing to assert his right. His claim to pre-eminence in the realm in 1450 was based on the fact that he was, on impeccably 'Lancastrian' principles, heir to the throne as long as Henry himself had no son; for York was descended in the male line from Edmund, Duke of York, John of Gaunt's younger brother.

York's feud was not with the king but with the 'court party' in general, and more specifically with Edmund Beaufort, Earl (later Duke) of Somerset. York's military ventures in France in the 1440s had been hampered, he believed, by lack of support at home, culminating in his dismissal from the command in Normandy and replacement by Somerset in 1446. York had been sent instead to Ireland, then, as later, a useful dumping ground for ambitious politicians; and because of his fortunate removal from the French war was able to pose as the champion of good government and national honour, the successor of Humphrey of Gloucester, against the corruption of the court and the humiliation of English arms. A further complication was that the Beaufort family represented a threat to York's hopes of eventually succeeding to the crown as heir to Henry VI. Like Henry the Beauforts were descended from John of Gaunt, but in their case by his mistress, Catherine Swynford. Gaunt had eventually married Catherine, and the bastard Beaufort children were retrospectively legitimized. Henry IV, in confirming this expressly excluded any Beaufort claim to the throne. But what Henry IV had done Henry VI might undo, dashing York's hopes of his own or his son's eventually acquiring the crown.

The Neville family was also important in the politics of the 1450s; more specifically Richard Neville, Earl of Salisbury, and his son, also Richard, Earl of Warwick. We have already seen how both these men had done well for themselves by marriage, to which they owed their titles. Like York, they were enemies of the Beaufort family; Warwick and Edmund Beaufort, Earl of Somerset, both had claims to the inheritance of the great Beauchamp estates in Wales. It was this which produced in 1453 the York–Neville alliance which dominated English politics for the next fifteen years.

The story opens against a background of the French conquest of Normandy; a large-scale assault began in 1449 and by August 1450 the last English garrisons had surrendered. The Commons had been vociferously attacking government corruption; and a Parliament had to be dissolved in July 1449 when it demanded an 'Act of Resumption'; that is a revocation of grants of lands and annuities made by the crown since Henry VI's accession. In January 1450 Bishop Moleyns of Chichester, a political bishop and a close associate of Suffolk, was murdered by mutinous soldiers at Portsmouth. Suffolk himself was impeached of high treason and only saved by royal intervention; even so, Henry accepted a less drastic charge of 'misprision of treason' and banished him for five years. On 1 May the ship carrying him into exile in France was attacked by a royal ship, the *Nicholas of the Tower* next day Suffolk was beheaded by the sailors and his body thrown up on Dover beach. This was followed by another political bishop, Ayscough of Salisbury, being dragged by a mob from a church where he was celebrating mass, and beheaded.

Even worse than this, in May a full-scale rebellion broke out in Kent under the leadership of a certain Jack Cade. The rebels complained about the extortion of Lord Saye, the treasurer and his associates; the corruption of local government (the sheriff of Kent was Saye's son-in-law, William Crowmer); the pressures exerted by great men at Parliamentary elections; and the low birth of the king's councillors. To remedy this the king should reinstate the Dukes of York, Exeter and Norfolk to the council. In general courtiers were accused of impoverishing the king, and so involving subjects in paying too many taxes; and the rebels raised the ugly possibility that disaster in Normandy was due to treason.

The Cade rebels were not a simple gang of peasants. A knight, 18 squires and 74 gentlemen were involved, many of whom later sat in Parliament or served as sheriffs. Bad government obviously affected the country at large; and Kent of course was especially sensitive to military defeat because of the attacks by French privateers and because of the effect on trade. But it may be that Kentish discontent had been worked on by an agent of the Duke of York. Certainly the belief that they had powerful allies among great nobles must have been an incentive to the rebels; and Cade (whose origin is unknown) won support by claiming to be related to York.

Henry first tried appeasement, ordering Saye to be arrested. Then, deserted by his troops he fled to the greater safety of Kenilworth, opening the way for the rebels to enter London, where they got hold of Saye and executed him. They eventually agreed to disperse on condition of a free pardon and the establishment of a commission to investigate abuses. Cade realized that dispersal meant defeat and tried to keep his army together, but failed. He was captured, and died on his way to London. Nevertheless, a point had been made and the government's unpopularity and inability to defend the capital strikingly shown.

It was this which opened the way for York. Arriving without

permission from Ireland with four thousand troops, he complained that justice was not duly administered (echoing the Kentish complaints). He demanded access to the king and the summoning of a Parliament. He took trouble with the elections and when the Parliament met in November, he got his chamberlain elected Speaker. The lords attended with their retainers who, with the Londoners, besieged Westminster Hall demanding 'justice upon the false traitors'; that is on Somerset and his friends. The Commons successfully demanded a more effective act of resumption, since a previous act, passed earlier that year, had lost a good deal of its force through exemptions inserted by the king. A committee was established to check future royal grants. A list of those who had 'misbehaved' was drawn up, with the demand that they be banished from the court. The list included Somerset, the Duke of Suffolk's widow, and many of those who had been denounced by Cade. The king refused and defiantly appointed Somerset to the key military position of captain of Calais. Eventually, York's allies overplayed their hand when his client Thomas Yong, MP for Bristol, petitioned for recognition of York as heir to the throne. This was an anti-Beaufort, not an anti-Lancastrian move; but even so it was clearly unwelcome to the king and in May 1451 Parliament was dissolved.

The court party had weathered the storm and could now set about re-establishing itself; even though military disasters continued as, in 1451, Gascony, the last surviving bloc of English territory in France, followed Normandy into French hands.

A second attempt by York to force his way into the government collapsed ignominiously in 1452; he had hoped to rally the Kentishmen at Dartford but they failed to appear, perhaps because of what they thought to be York's double-dealing over the Cade rebellion (he had taken his part in the subsequent repression). A new effort was made in the French war; an army was sent to Gascony and managed to recapture Bordeaux. A new Parliament was called in 1453 at Reading, away from the influence of the London mobs, and no fewer than 17 per cent of the Commons were royal servants (compared with only 6 per cent in 1450). Determined management must have been involved in this; but there may have been a swing of opinion, perhaps because of

York's actions raising the possibility of civil war. The loyal Commons proceeded to vote direct taxation, granted the customs to the king for life and attainted Oldhall of treason.

The general situation was still gloomy. The recovery of Bordeaux was a flash in the pan and by October 1453 the French were once more in control of Gascony. There was general disorder in the country; in Yorkshire the Percy–Neville feud allegedly involved contending armies of five thousand men. But these general problems were overtaken in August 1453 by an immediate and unexpected event – the king's mental breakdown. So far Henry, while manifestly incapable of exerting any sort of leadership, had been sane. He was now reduced to total stupor, unable to take any interest even in his new-born son, the long-awaited hope of the dynasty; 'once only he looked on the prince, and cast down his eyes again.' A delegation of lords came to investigate the king's condition and got even less response. The question was of the regency. The court party, frightened of York, the obvious claimant, argued that the queen should be regent, but this evidently offended the propriety of the lords. York was still next heir to the throne after the new-born prince, and was acknowledged as protector by Parliament.

York's regime as protector was efficient and less partisan than his opponents had feared. Unfortunately, at the beginning of 1455 the king recovered his sanity. The court party was evidently planning its revenge on York and the Nevilles (Warwick and his father the Earl of Salisbury); and York decided to get in first. The result was the battle of St Albans; Somerset was killed and Henry recaptured. Parliament, recalled in November 1455, made York protector once again. But the second Parliament was short lived; by February 1456 the king had recovered his sanity once more (if in fact he ever lost it the second time) and York was out of office.

There were now three years of uneasy peace before the third and last period of crisis. There was no repetition in 1456 of the mistakes made by the court party the year before; York's supporters were eased very gradually out of office and there was no threat of a vendetta against the Yorkist lords. York remained lieutenant of Ireland and Warwick was now captain of Calais,

'Christendom's finest captaincy' according to the French writer Commynes, and a useful base for possible intervention in England. Warwick won the favours of the London trading community by using his own substantial fleet (he had about ten ships, at a time when the royal navy was down to one) against French privateers. It was his naval exploits that sparked off trouble again. In London at the end of 1458 to answer charges of attacking neutral German ships, he was set on by the royal guard after a brawl between his servants and the king's. He claimed that there had been a deliberate plot to murder him, and retired to Calais to defy the government.

Perhaps because of this the Duke of Buckingham, who had so far kept himself aloof from either side, threw in his hand with the court party. His support may have persuaded the queen that she could now finish off York and Warwick; and indeed in October 1459 the court party won a crushing victory at Ludford Bridge, near Ludlow. This was followed by the calling of a Parliament to meet at Coventry, in which York, his son Edward, Earl of March, and the two Neville earls, Salisbury and Warwick, were attainted. But there was no way of getting hold of them. York was safely in Ireland, his position as lieutenant confirmed by the Irish Parliament; and Warwick, Salisbury and the young Edward were in Calais; whence they waged a war of nerves against the government, raiding Sandwich, controlling shipping through the Straits, and mounting a powerful propaganda campaign alleging that they were being deliberately victimized by evil influences around the king.

In June 1460 the three earls landed at Sandwich with an army from the Calais garrison, and were joined by a 'multitude' of Kentishmen and the Archbishop of Canterbury, Thomas Bourchier, a man who had previously played a mediating role and had been at the Coventry Parliament. After some hesitation the London authorities opened their gates. The earls got only limited support from the lay peers, but won a battle against the royal forces at Northampton on 10 July; largely, it would appear, because Lord Grey of Ruthin changed sides during the battle, a forerunner of many similar desertions in the next twenty-five years. The king was captured and taken to London.

The three earls had sworn on the sacrament before the bishops that they intended no harm to the king or to his prerogatives; they had only wished to present their case to the king personally, having been prevented from doing so by evil advisers. York, however, decided to capitalize on his allies' victory. He hurried over from Ireland to Westminster where Parliament had been called; strode through Westminster Hall; and laid his hand on the empty throne. Instead of the expected acclamation from the assembled peers, there was an ominous silence; even Warwick was furious when he heard what his ally had done, interestingly enough because he knew that 'the people of London' were 'ill content' about York's claim. When York produced his genealogical evidence, there was an understandable reluctance by peers or judges to commit themselves on so high a matter. The peers objected that they had recently sworn an oath of loyalty to King Henry and his son Prince Edward at Coventry, that York himself had sworn allegiance, and that the Lancastrian title had been recognized by 'great and notable Acts of Parliament' since 1399. York replied that inheritance was God's law and over-rode any other consideration. The peers had little choice against a victorious army. York's claim was upheld in theory, and a compromise worked out in practice. Henry was to retain the throne for his life, but then it was to pass to York and his heirs, cutting out Henry's son, Prince Edward. Meanwhile York was to be Prince of Wales and Protector of the Realm and richly endowed from crown lands.

York did not enjoy this status for long. Queen Margaret and the prince were still at large and there could be no peace till they were defeated. In December 1460 York marched north to deal with them; and was defeated at Wakefield, apparently because of his impetuosity in not waiting for reinforcements. York's head, and his ally's, the elder Richard Neville, Earl of Salisbury, were exhibited in the city of York, and Margaret marched south, defeating Warwick at St Albans. For the second time in a year however, the reaction of the Londoners was decisive. Their fears of barbarous northerners had been stoked by Yorkist propaganda. They knew, too, that Edward of March was still at large, indeed that he had recently brought off a spectacular victory on his own territory at Mortimer's Cross in Herefordshire. A party of Londoners forcibly prevented the civic authorities opening the gates to Margaret's army. Margaret made the fatal mistake of retreating north again taking the unfortunate King Henry, now recaptured by his own supporters, with her. The way was open and Edward of March made for London.

There was little point now in preserving the previous year's compromise; if Edward won he might as well take the throne, if he lost he was doomed. Deposition of a king was a solemn affair, and had been handled in 1327 and 1399 by the usurper calling a Parliament or pseudo-Parliament to legitimize his position. Edward was plainly in no position to do this; and a show of popular opinion had therefore to be arranged in London. His claim to the throne was set out to an assembly of the 'people' (many of them his own soldiers), and Edward was duly acclaimed. A 'great council' corroborated the claim; less impressive than it might appear, since it consisted of the Archbishop of Canterbury, two other bishops, the Duke of Norfolk, the Earl of Warwick, Lord FitzWalter and two knights from York's Welsh estates. So fortified, Edward was ceremonially recognized as king at Westminster, and set out to deal with Margaret. He caught her at Towton near York and crushed her army in a hard-won battle fought in a freak snow-storm on 29 March 1461. Edward was now effectively king; and 'Lancastrian' resistance was reduced to guerrilla warfare from garrisons in the north and in Wales.

The narrative has inevitably become rather breathless and the reader confused by the multiplicity of battles and the rapid changes of fortune. Nevertheless, some general factors stand out.

One point is how small the 'Yorkist' party among the peerage was throughout. Of the fifty or so lay peers only two supported York at Dartford in 1452. The adhesion of the Nevilles in 1453 was useful and wider support was won in 1459–60; but even so, only three bishops and three lay peers took part in the council which made Edward king in 1461.* York could excite a good deal of support for his claim to be protector in 1454 or for the notion that he and his friends had been unfairly condemned in 1460;

* J. R. Lander, *Conflict and Stability in Fifteenth Century England* (Hutchinson, 1969) pp. 83–4, 89–90.

but not for a claim to run the government in normal times or to be king.

In these circumstances public opinion in some senses mattered; whether this was seen in the Parliamentary attack and popular rioting against Suffolk and Cade's rebellion in opening the way to York in 1450; York's failure to repeat this manoeuvre in 1452; or the support or at least acquiescence of Kent and London in the invasion of 1460 and in London's opposition to Queen Margaret in 1461. There was clearly a tradition of popular hostility to the Lancastrian court, or rather to the court party, represented by the Beaufort family and the Duke of Suffolk, and later by Queen Margaret. This tradition had been represented at one time by Duke Humphrey of Gloucester and York was in a sense his political heir. Popular support was reinforced by Warwick's privateering exploits at Calais which appealed to the xenophobic elements in London, and helped protect London merchants from French attacks. Warwick indeed probably had a greater popular following than York. 'If aught come to my lord Warwick but good, fare well ye, fare well I, and all our friends . . . for this land were utterly undone,' thought John Brackley, a Norwich Franciscan friar, well known as a preacher, and a friend of the Paston family, in 1460. Warwick's belief that the new king owed his throne to him was clearly justified. To talk of the Yorkist lords appealing to a popular reforming tradition does not necessarily mean that they were themselves sincere reformers; the Duke of Norfolk, who supported York on, broadly speaking, an anti-Suffolk platform in 1450, terrorized East Anglia in his own interest in much the same way as Suffolk had done; while York's steward in the Isle of Wight was accused of living 'like a lord with as rich wines as could be imagined' out of the proceeds of oppression. But the fact remains that popular opinion was worth courting. In a period when parties were so volatile, when so much depended on the course of events in a battle or the deliverance of a town, it would be foolish to neglect any source of support.

One qualification needs to be inserted here. 'Popular opinion' in this context means opinion in London and the south-east counties. Queen Margaret plainly found that her main support lay in the midlands (Coventry, the venue of the 1459 Parliament) or the north. She was busy recruiting troops in Lancashire and Cheshire in 1459 and obviously regarded Yorkshire as her stronghold in 1460-1. It is too easy to assume that the opinion of the capital was that of the country at large, and we shall come across this point again, especially when dealing with the Reformation. Later in the fifteenth century, Wales or the north tended to provide the route of entry and a good deal of support for pretenders, including the successful bid for the throne by Henry Tudor in 1485. But in the period we have been dealing with, at least, it was the attitude of the south-east that mattered. Only twice, in 1460 and in 1469, was a successful invasion mounted through Kent. Significantly the rebel on both occasions was the Earl of Warwick; and in both cases the invasion was made possible by rebel control of Calais.

London could not have held out against Queen Margaret in 1461 if Edward had not already won the battle of Mortimer's Cross; and even as it was, if Margaret had pressed on, London would probably have fallen and the proclamation of Edward IV would have been impossible. What determined the outcome of battles is very difficult to decide, because of the unreliability of the chroniclers or letter-writers who usually provide the only evidence; their highly coloured accounts are generally based on rumour or on one particular informant. Modern reconstructions of battles, although often extremely ingenious are based even more than history generally is, on conjecture, on what an eminent practitioner calls 'inherent military probability'.* Because of this historians tend to be reluctant to face up to the importance of chance events which may have determined the outcome of a battle; a good deal plainly depended on the desertion of one side by a prominent leader like Lord Grey of Ruthin at Northampton; a good deal, too, on successful generalship such as Queen Margaret's turning of Warwick's flank at the second battle of St Albans (1461) or Warwick's attack through the gardens when the road was blocked at the first battle there in 1455. Relatively minor events like this, especially with untrained and undisciplined scratch armies can quickly produce panic, the collapse of a

* A. H. Burne, *Battlefields of England* (Methuen, 1950) and *More Battlefields of England* (Methuen, 1952).

whole line, and defeat. These factors are difficult, perhaps impossible to reconstruct; but that is no reason for implying that they are unimportant in the general development of the political struggle.

Some historians would reply here that the result of an individual battle may be unpredictable, but whole campaigns are determined by more fundamental factors. Whatever the truth of this in general it is plainly not true for the Wars of the Roses; precisely because we do not have in this case a clash of two clearly defined sides. I have stressed the importance of some degree of general 'Yorkist' sympathy; but this was clearly subordinate to the general mood of caution, the need not to find oneself on the losing side. Once defeated, it becomes very much more difficult for a rebel to raise an army a second time; had, for instance, York been defeated at St Albans in 1455, he and his family might well have ceased to trouble English politics. Given Henry VI's weaknesses, this would have been unlikely to produce internal peace and stability; but whatever the final outcome, it is unlikely that it would have borne much resemblance to what actually *did* happen.

It is impossible, then, to single out a particular factor as *the* significant cause of the Wars of the Roses, or of their outcome. Events inter-relate, inter-react, so that what might seem insignificant in itself takes on overwhelming importance in appropriate circumstances, and in turn sets up other reactions. Historians might begin to look for their metaphors among the physicists' theories of fusion-fission. The war with France obviously posed a host of problems but need not in itself have produced a breakdown of government. Henry's personal character was obviously important and his total incompetence as a ruler was compounded by his mental breakdown; but the events of 1460, the profound shock at the notion of his deposition, show what reserves of loyalty the crown as such possessed, and how these could have been mobilized by even the slightest display of leadership on the king's part. Once a war situation had materialized events could be utterly transformed by chance factors; and in this situation the unpopularity of the government (or equally, the personal grouse of an important peer) might swing the issue. In general the country was prepared to respect an effective king if only because of a general fear of disorder. Of course, once order had broken down, it would be so much more difficult to re-establish. But there was, in the country at large, a deep desire for political stability; and this provided a foundation on which a reasonably skilful ruler might hope to build a more settled polity.

Chapter Four

RECOVERY: EDWARD IV
TO HENRY VII

EDWARD IV

Although Lancastrian forces had been smashed at Towton in
1461 Queen Margaret, with King Henry in tow, carried on the
war in the far north. With Scottish support (for which she handed
over Berwick) she maintained three castles in Northumberland
until 1464. From Alnwick castle the unhappy Henry VI 'reigned'
over England. When these castles were finally captured Henry
disappeared. Eventually a year later, he was betrayed while
staying at Sir Richard Tempest's house, Waddington Hall, on
the Yorkshire–Lancashire border, and brought to permanent
captivity in the Tower of London. Queen Margaret and her son,
Prince Edward, maintained a miniature court in her native France.
A Lancastrian force held out at Harlech, in north Wales, until
1468; otherwise any danger to Edward IV's throne from the
previous dynasty seemed over.

Edward's difficulties came from his allies. The victory of 1461
had been as much a Neville victory as a Yorkist one. Edward
himself was not quite nineteen years old; and although he was
already an experienced and successful soldier, it was likely that
he could be overshadowed by his thirty-three-year-old cousin,
the Earl of Warwick. Commynes thought that Warwick 'could
almost be called the king's father as a result of the services and
education he had given him'. His brother, George Neville, was
chancellor. Another brother, John, crushed the Lancastrian forces
in the north in 1464, and for reward was given the earldom
of Northumberland, vacant since the attainder of the Percy
earl as a Lancastrian in 1461; he also received a large part of
the Percy estates. For the moment it made sense to build up

Neville power; but the potential dangers in the long run were obvious.

English politics were complicated by the international situation. This was dominated by the rivalry of the Duke of Burgundy, now in effect an independent ruler of a state centred on the Netherlands, and the King of France. Both needed the English alliance. The Netherlands were England's great trading partner, the market for English cloth; and it was the Burgundian alliance which had enabled England to dominate France in the minority of Henry VI. But France was the more powerful; and the influence of Margaret of Anjou was dangerous. The best tactics for the moment were to encourage approaches from both sides, and the fact that the king was not married was a useful card in this diplomatic game.

These arrangements were upset when Edward made a sudden secret marriage in May 1464. The bride was Elizabeth Woodville, a young widow. When the marriage was eventually made public, the following September, it scandalized many of the nobility, among them the king's mother. In fact Elizabeth's background was a good deal more distinguished than is sometimes implied (see biographical index, p. 354). Her mother was a member of one of the great European royal families, and an appropriate wife to the Duke of Bedford, Henry V's brother and Regent of France. But her second husband, Richard Woodville, Elizabeth's father, had been a mere knight (widows were able to please themselves, and often married beneath them) and was believed to owe his subsequent peerage as Lord Ryvers only to his high connections. In 1459, when a prisoner at Calais, his future son-in-law, Edward of March, had taunted him as a 'knave's son'. Elizabeth herself had married a knight, Sir John Grey, who was killed fighting on the Lancastrian side in 1461. It was bad enough that the king should marry a subject; what was worse was the plethora of unmarried relatives – brothers, sisters, even sons – that Elizabeth brought with her into the royal orbit. They would have to be found suitable marriages, that is, marriages among the high nobility; and this sudden massive intrusion upset the marriage market. All this may seem petty in modern conditions; to contemporaries it raised questions of honour and of property which were the stuff of politics.

More immediately the secret marriage rankled with Warwick; not least because he had been trying to negotiate a marriage between Edward and a French princess. Some historians have seen the Woodville marriage as a political move, a declaration of independence on Edward's part from Neville tutelage; the subsequent marriages of the queen's relatives into the nobility feature as a definite attempt to build up a counter-weight to Neville influence in the country. But it is more likely that the marriage was an impetuous love-match; and the later marriages its inevitable consequence. For the moment Warwick put a good face on it; especially as Edward, by having George Neville promoted Archbishop of York, seemed to be taking pains to appease him.

The marriage market was soon in full swing. The queen's brother John, aged twenty, married the dowager Duchess of Norfolk; she was eighty according to gossip, and a mere sixty-five or so in fact. The queen's son Thomas married an heiress (to the Holland family, Dukes of Exeter) who was already promised to Warwick's nephew. The queen's sisters were married to noblemen, in one case at least (see below, p. 92) to the bridegroom's intense displeasure. One result was that Warwick had difficulty in finding suitable husbands for his two daughters, who were co-heiresses to his own enormous estates (he had no sons); especially as the king was set against a marriage between them and his own two brothers. 'The Ryvers [run] so high that it is impossible to get through them' quipped Edward's court fool.

The rift between Edward and the Nevilles got worse in 1467. George Neville was dismissed as chancellor. Edward's sister Margaret was betrothed to Charles, Duke of Burgundy, foiling the chance of the French alliance for which Warwick was still working. Edward's machinations at Rome prevented Warwick's daughter Isabel getting the necessary dispensation to marry her second cousin, the Duke of Clarence, Edward's brother. But Warwick held his hand; and as late as April 1469 he was sufficiently trusted to be given command of a fleet.

The final break came against a background of riots and rebellions in the north under the leadership of men calling themselves

'Robin of Holderness' and 'Robin of Redesdale'. In one sense these were popular riots, involving a number of grievances which included purely local affairs. 'Robin of Holderness' had nothing to do with the Nevilles; he demanded the restoration of their rivals, the Percy family, to the earldom of Northumberland, which was at that time held by Warwick's brother John; and John Neville put down the rising. 'Robin of Redesdale', however, was Sir John Conyers, a Neville connection by marriage and in the light of later events, his rebellion was probably encouraged by Warwick to discredit Edward's government.

In July 1469 a papal dispensation had at last been obtained for the Clarence–Isabel Neville marriage, and the ceremony was performed by Archbishop Neville at Calais. The two Neville brothers and Clarence then issued a manifesto in the usual form against the king's 'evil councillors' who had alienated Edward from the lords of his blood, levied too great taxes and subverted justice. They landed, as in 1460, in Kent, and marched to London where they seem to have been well received; Warwick's traditional popularity may have helped here, and there seems to have been some resentment at the terms of the Burgundian treaty which was thought to have sacrificed too many of England's commercial interests. Edward in any case was in the Midlands preparing to face 'Robin of Redesdale'. In the event the decisive battle involved neither Warwick nor Edward. It was fought at Edgecote, near Banbury, between the Earl of Pembroke (William Herbert, in the 1450s York's agent in South Wales) and 'Robin of Redesdale'. With Pembroke's defeat, Edward evidently decided that he had no alternative but to surrender. He was taken as a prisoner to the Neville castle at Middleham in Yorkshire; and many of his prominent supporters, including the Earl of Pembroke, Earl Ryvers, (the queen's father) and John Woodville (her brother) were executed.

Government with the king in prison was impossible. A Parliament was called to meet at York, but had to be cancelled because of the 'great troubles'; it was impossible to raise an army to deal with more rioting in the north and the people refused to obey 'royal' proclamations. Edward had to be released; and once back in London worked assiduously to re-establish his position.

Power was gradually slipping out of Warwick's and Clarence's hands.

Once again, in 1470, crisis was precipitated by local rebellions. Sir Robert Welles, a peer's son, who called himself 'the great captain of the commons of Lincolnshire', raised the commons who were led to think that Edward was coming to punish them for riots and feuds in which they had been involved the previous year. Welles in his confession accused Warwick and Clarence of instigating the revolt. (According to one account the commons had been badly drilled. They shouted 'King Henry, King Henry' instead of 'Warwick' and 'Clarence'.) Edward crushed the rising easily and another which was preparing in Yorkshire (again involving 'Robin of Redesdale') collapsed. Warwick and Clarence fled to France, where King Louis XI could be relied on to back anything to weaken Edward and the Anglo–Burgundian alliance.

The obvious way was an alliance between Warwick and his old enemy, Margaret of Anjou. Louis accomplished this, though with a good deal of difficulty. A French fleet then landed Warwick and Clarence in Devon in September 1470; they issued a manifesto declaring Henry VI 'very true undoubted king of England and [ironically in the circumstances] of France', and went on to make the usual allegation about bad government. A number of Lancastrian peers joined them; but the decisive moment came when Warwick's brother John Neville, hitherto loyal to Edward, defected to their side.

To explain this, we need to go back a stage. As we saw, John Neville had been given the Percy earldom of Northumberland and a large part of the Percy estates. By 1470, however, Edward, needing all the help he could get, decided to restore Henry Percy to the earldom. To compensate John Neville, Edward gave him the higher title of Marquis of Montagu and also arranged for a marriage between Neville's son George (created Duke of Bedford for the occasion) and his own daughter Elizabeth. These concessions failed to mollify John Neville who complained that he had not been given enough land to support his new dignity, only a 'magpie's nest'.

Edward fled when John Neville tried to seize him and managed to escape to the Netherlands, the territory of his embarrassed ally and brother-in-law, Duke Charles of Burgundy. A somewhat bemused Henry VI was hauled out of the Tower, where he had spent the last five years, in moderate but unprincely comfort (some £3 a week had been allocated for his maintenance) and proclaimed the rightful king. Government was carried on by the Nevilles. But Henry's 'readeption' was short lived, a matter of some five months from October 1470. Diplomatic activity was intense. Warwick's victory had shattered the Anglo-Burgundian alliance but Duke Charles had to go cautiously as long as there was hope that Warwick might not go so far as to join France in an attack on Burgundy. By February 1471, however, the garrisons at Calais were being got ready for war, and the Duke decided to provide money and ships for Edward.

In March 1471, therefore, Edward landed with a small army at Ravenspur in the mouth of the Humber; a spot which has now disappeared into the sea, but which had then some significance as the starting point of Henry IV's bid for the throne in 1399. The army seems to have been partly composed of exiled Englishmen, partly of Flemings and other foreigners and even the chroniclers put its numbers at less than two thousand. There was not much enthusiasm for Edward in Yorkshire; Hull refused to open its gates and Edward was only allowed to enter York without his army, swearing first that he had come to claim his rights as Duke of York only, not as king. But the main forces in the area were commanded by Henry Percy, Earl of Northumberland, who had no cause to like the new Neville regime; and although (see p. 82) his troops would not fight for Edward he at least kept them in check while Edward slipped by. Once in the midlands Edward picked up large reinforcements, largely through the exertions of Lord Hastings (a client of Edward's who had given him his peerage and built up his power in the 1460s). Finally Clarence decided that he had more to hope from his brother than from a Lancastrian regime, and changed sides again. With these reinforcements Edward made for London, where he was let in, according to one chronicler, by a plot on the part of the recorder and aldermen – the London merchant class dreaded the thought of a war against Burgundy. He captured the hapless Henry VI once more, and prepared to face the Neville brothers at Barnet. The result was a resounding victory; Warwick and Montagu were killed and their bodies exhibited at St Paul's, perhaps to prevent any nostalgia among Londoners for their dead heroes.

On the day of the battle of Barnet, Margaret of Anjou and her son Prince Edward had landed at Weymouth. Marching west Edward caught them in Gloucestershire on their way to pick up support in the old Lancastrian strongholds of north Wales and Lancashire. At Tewkesbury Edward pulled off his second great victory in three weeks; a large number of Lancastrian notables were killed including Prince Edward, and Queen Margaret was taken prisoner.

King Henry according to the official account, died of 'pure displeasure and melancholy' on hearing the news from Tewkesbury. Contemporaries were convinced he was murdered and the evidence of Henry's skeleton suggests that they were right. Tudor historians blamed Edward's youngest brother, Richard, Duke of Gloucester, the incarnation of all evil; but there is no evidence for this. Henry had aroused no respect as a king but a good deal of sympathy as a person, especially since his captivity in 1465. Before long he was being popularly venerated as a saint and his relics were believed to be working miracles.

There are two main problems in the complicated events of 1469–71. First, why was Edward so easily beaten in 1469 and 1470? Secondly, why did he manage to re-establish himself in 1471? The first is the more difficult. Edward was in a peculiarly difficult position as a usurper, as the representative of a small clique of peers and Londoners in 1461. When Edward III and Henry IV had been put on the throne by *coup d'état* in 1327 and 1399 their predecessors were quickly murdered and constituted only posthumous dangers to the new kings. (Though Henry IV was plagued by rumours that Richard II was still alive.) Henry VI, on the other hand, was at large till 1465, and alive until 1471. Edward, too, had at first been so much the tool of a faction that he had been wildly extravagant in distributing confiscated estates to his allies in the first years; and perhaps clumsy in his handling of a delicate situation when, from 1464 he lurched into the opposite tactic of building up a counter-weight group and reconciling ex-opponents. There was little evidence that he was positively unpopular, although a Lancastrian chronicler mentions popular disillusion with Yorkist promises of reform; the people hoped for the 'prosperity' and 'peace' 'but it came not; but one battle after another and much trouble and great loss of goods among the common people'. The trouble appears to have been that Edward had not managed to convince the subjects that he was an effective king in his own right; and this was reinforced by divisions in the royal family and by Warwick's extraordinary position in the state. Few nobles, other than those he had built up himself (generally ex-clients of his father, like William Herbert, Earl of Pembroke or Lord Hastings) were prepared to rally to Edward in times of crisis; and so he was left deserted, after Edgecote, and again in 1470.

Edward's return shows no more evidence of positive support; a good deal was owed to military skill and rather more to luck. Burgundian support was essential; the role of the Earl of Northumberland decisive. Barnet was fought in a fog, and Edward apparently owed his victory to a group of Warwick's men attacking their own side by mistake and causing general panic. Tewkesbury, on the other hand, was due to Edward's determination and speed in getting his army to Gloucester to challenge Margaret, rather reminiscent of his dash to London in 1461.

The restored regime of Henry VI had achieved even less credibility than Edward had acquired in the 1460s. It would have been better if Queen Margaret had returned to England immediately in 1470 rather than waiting another five months in France. She was obviously suspicious of Warwick and reasonably so; but the result was to prevent a united front between old Lancastrians and Warwick's followers. Warwick himself seems to have lost a good deal of his old support in London. The French alliance would obviously play havoc with the cloth trade, and as Commynes saw, the London merchant community preferred Edward in 1471; though there is some evidence that Warwick still had a party in London. (According to his opponents, men who 'would have been right glad of a common robbery'.) More generally, Warwick's banging of the old reformist drum, the cries of corruption in government and over-taxation, must have rung pretty hollow in 1469–71; his motives were now too clearly opportunistic and self-seeking. Finally, a Warwick–Margaret regime can have offered little prospect of peace; the two principals were bound to be at loggerheads as soon as they had disposed of their mutual enemy.

In fact there seems to have been an absence of general conviction, of positive support, for either side in the crisis of 1469–71. In the circumstances, everything depended on successful seizing of the initiative, and on individual decisions, like those of Northumberland and Clarence. After 1471, however, Edward was in a much stronger position: the rival dynasty had been eliminated and the victories at Barnet and Tewkesbury had been impressive. More firmly established, Edward could now take the initiative in foreign affairs. The major events of the next twelve years were the invasion of France in 1475 and the war against Scotland in 1481–3.

The only significant political event at home in fact was the execution of Clarence in 1478; and that seems to have been as much a settling of old scores as a real immediate danger to the throne. Clarence's conduct since helping to restore Edward in 1471 had done little to dispel the impression of shifty double-dealing in his early years. He had tried to prevent his brother Richard of Gloucester marrying his sister-in-law, Anne Neville, since this would reduce his chance of getting the lion's share of Warwick's estates. In 1476, when Isabel Neville died, Clarence had two of her servants arrested and hanged on a charge of poisoning her, with great despatch and little regard for the king's justice. He was also involved with sorcerers who prophesied that he would inherit the throne. Perhaps the most dangerous circumstance was the attempt by his sister, Margaret, to have him marry her step-daughter Mary, heiress to Burgundy. In 1478 Clarence was attainted (that is effectively declared guilty of treason by act of parliament) and executed.

Clarence's execution was less important than Edward's work in rebuilding the royal finances, and doing something to restore respect for the administration of justice. The new dynasty seemed secure. Edward was not yet forty years old; he had two sons; and his youngest brother, Richard, had proved himself conspicuously loyal through all the twists and turns of the reign. The only rival claim was a far-fetched one; by Henry Tudor, Earl of Richmond, a young man of dubious ancestry little known in England and living in precarious exile in Brittany. Once again, however, the nation's peace was to be shattered by a chance event; the sudden death of Edward in April 1483.

EDWARD V–RICHARD III

With Edward's death the throne passed to a child, his twelve-year-old son, now Edward v. Richard of Gloucester's usurpation and the fate of the young king and his brother are among the *causes célèbres* of English history. To Tudor historians Richard seemed a monster of wickedness, who had brought about the execution of Clarence to improve his own chances to the throne. He had not only betrayed his trust to his nephew Edward v, but had him and his younger brother murdered in the Tower of London. This view was most persuasively put by Sir Thomas More in 1513, and was immortalized by Shakespeare. It was obviously a useful line to a regime which preached obedience to the powers that be, while owing its origin to a successful rebellion. If Richard could be represented as a man of quite exceptional wickedness, a tyrant of monstrous proportions, the paradox might be resolved. In reaction, some historians (and still more amateur enthusiasts) have seen Richard as a paragon of chivalry whose loyal service to his brother in the political crisis of the reign, and whose splendid achievements as a soldier against the Scots, now culminated in the unpleasant duty of taking over, first the regency, and then the throne in the interest of the country. No sort of proof is possible in these cases; all we can do is to hazard plausible guesses about motives. We cannot ignore them, since what contemporaries thought about Richard's actions played some part in determining political attitudes and the outcome of political events. But we do need to put them in context.

First, the killing of innocent members of the royal family was not unusual. Edward IV must be held responsible for the death of Henry VI; Henry VII for the execution on a flimsy charge of the young Earl of Warwick. Time and success divert attention; in a few years, if Richard had lived, the fate of the princes would no longer have mattered. Secondly, we need to consider other factors which made Richard's usurpation possible, and which helped to determine the events of the next two years. The personal drama is inescapable; but it is not the whole story.

Although Edward IV's last years had seemed so peaceful, they had concealed a good deal of simmering resentment. Edward had little compunction in advancing the claims of his own family. He had, for instance, married his younger son, Richard of York to Lady Anne, the heiress of the great inheritance of the Mowbray Dukes of Norfolk. This was not an unreasonable move in the game of landed power politics even though Richard was only four years old at the time and Anne five. But when the Lady Anne inconveniently died in 1481, Edward kept the inheritance in the hands of young Richard, passing a special act of parliament to that effect in 1483, to the displeasure of the next heirs, Lords Howard and Berkeley. Similarly, William Herbert, son of the William Herbert who had been killed in Edward's cause in 1469, was made to exchange his Welsh lands and the title of Earl of Pembroke for the Earldom of Huntingdon and a much smaller estate in the west of England. The beneficiaries were Edward's sons, Edward Prince of Wales and Richard of York. Nor had the old breach between the queen's family and the rest of the court been healed with time; indeed, it seems to have got worse. Richard of Gloucester was notoriously hostile to the queen and her relations. The Duke of Buckingham seems never to have reconciled himself to his marriage in 1466, when he was a royal ward, to the queen's sister; Edward had also frustrated his political ambitions by building up the queen's son, Thomas Grey, Marquis of Dorset, as the leading power in the south-west. Lord Hastings, the lord chamberlain, one of Edward's staunchest supporters, was also a bitter enemy of Dorset; they had apparently quarrelled some years before over a mistress. The queen and her family seem to have been unusually tactless and unpopular. Acts by Edward, like the execution of Clarence, were automatically ascribed to her influence. Resentment about the past and fears for the future fused in 1483 at the prospect that the boy king might be the tool of his mother's family.

Edward had realized the danger of faction after his death and had tried to share power between the two sides. Richard of

Gloucester may have been named protector in Edward's will but he also gave his brother-in-law, Lord Ryvers, charge of the young prince at Ludlow, with extensive powers to raise troops. The Woodville faction was remarkably well entrenched; another brother, Edward, controlled the fleet, and the queen's son, the Marquis of Dorset, had charge of the Tower of London.

Ryvers seemed to expect no immediate danger when Edward IV died on 9 April 1483. On 24 April he set out with the young king from Ludlow to London. On the way, however, they were met by the Dukes of Buckingham and Gloucester. Ryvers and Sir Richard Grey, another of the queen's sons, were arrested without much difficulty, and sent off to prison in Yorkshire, where in June they were executed. Dorset and the queen attempted to arrange resistance in London, but to no avail. Reported the Italian Dominic Mancini, 'Some said openly that it was more just and profitable that the youthful sovereign should be with his paternal uncle.' Dorset abandoned the Tower and with the queen, her younger son, Richard of York, and her daughters, sought sanctuary at Westminster Abbey. Gloucester paraded cart-loads of arms as proof of a Woodville conspiracy, had his title as protector confirmed by the council and arrangements were made for the coronation of Edward V.

So far Gloucester may have acted in self-defence; the need to get at the Woodvilles before they got at him. By June, however, he had his eye on the throne. Lord Hastings, until then Gloucester's ally, was suddenly accused of treason and killed in the ensuing scuffle; Archbishop Rotherham of York and Bishop Morton of Ely were arrested at the same time. Hastings may have heard of a plot to depose the king; or he may have been annoyed at being less influential in the new regime than he had hoped to be.* On 24 June Buckingham explained to the Londoners why Richard should be king: Edward IV's children were all, he claimed, illegitimate, since Edward, before marrying Elizabeth Woodville,

---

* The tortuous way in which motive has to be deduced from events can be seen from an article by Alison Hanham, 'Richard III, Lord Hastings and the Historians' (*Eng. Hist. Rev.*, vol. 87, 1972). If, as she argues, Hastings was killed on 20 June, the first explanation is more likely; if, as according to traditional accounts, 13 June, the second. (*See* B. P. Wolffe, *ibid.* vol. 89, 1974.) 13 June is almost certainly correct.

had been 'pre-contracted' to Lady Eleanor Butler, and this barred any subsequent marriage. Clarence's children were barred by their father's attainder. Gloucester was therefore the rightful king. Parties of Londoners, duly encouraged by armed troops, shouted their approval and an assembly of Lords and Commons begged Richard to take the throne.

A deputation of peers had meanwhile persuaded the queen to let her younger son Richard join his brother in the Tower; if she refused they threatened to break sanctuary. What happened then is largely guesswork. The boys disappeared from public view in the summer of 1483. Skeletons found in the Tower in 1674 point to their being killed during 1483; but these may not be the right skeletons, and even if they are the evidence is not conclusive.

Rumours of their death circulated rapidly in London; they were picked up by the Italian Dominic Mancini before he left London on 6 July and they formed the basis of an accusation by the French chancellor in January 1484.* Rumour of this sort could obviously be dangerous, though fifteenth-century men were used to political murder. But the rumours played some part in assembling support for the Duke of Buckingham when he rebelled against Richard in October 1483.

In any case, 1483 was a peculiarly difficult year. The harvest of 1481 had been bad, that of 1482 was atrocious and wheat reached an average for the year of ten shillings a quarter – the first break into double figures for a century, except for one peculiarly disastrous year, 1438–9, when it had been fourteen shillings. The new harvest brought in in August 1483 was rather better (an average price of seven shillings) but this was still well above the normal price, and accumulated dissatisfaction may have persisted. The Buckingham rebellion was an odd combination of disparate movements. Lady Margaret Beaufort was busy plotting for her son, Henry Tudor, in exile in Brittany, to be king. The Woodvilles were planning revenge; and if the princes were really dead,

---

* One popular argument can be discounted; that since the boys had been proclaimed bastards, there was no point in killing them. The realities of fifteenth-century politics illuminate the naïveté of this thesis. Nor does the belief that they were kept alive, close prisoners, to be eventually murdered by Henry VII seem at all convincing.

these two interests could be combined by a marriage between Henry Tudor and the eldest daughter of Edward IV, Elizabeth. What impelled Buckingham himself is hard to say. He had, after all, made Richard king, and had done well for himself as a result; royal offices, grants of land, judicial commissions, had made him practically viceroy in Wales and south-west England. Possibly he resented not getting even more; perhaps he was genuinely shocked at the death of the princes; perhaps he was an unscrupulous intriguer plotting his own devious way to the throne.

The plot was fixed for 18 October; Buckingham was to mobilize an army in Wales, various members of the Woodville family and their connections and some old Lancastrian families were to raise the southern and south-western counties. Unluckily for the plotters, the Kentish rebels rose a week early, on 10 October. The Duke of Norfolk thought they were coming to rob London, an accusation traditionally made against Kentish rebels since 1450 if not 1381, but possibly indicating that economic distress may have been a factor in the rising. This premature move gave Norfolk and Richard time to get their forces ready. Buckingham was unable to raise his own territory in south Wales; his own retainers, Sir Thomas Vaughan and his family, harried his troops and captured Brecon, other gentlemen preferred to lie low and pouring rain discouraged the commons. Henry Tudor set sail from Brittany with fifteen ships, but bad weather dispersed all except two, and his reception at Poole discouraged him from landing. Henry's stepfather, Lord Stanley might have been expected to join the rebels; he had after all been one of those arrested with Hastings earlier in the year. But possibly because the time was not yet ripe he remained loyal and was able to protect his wife from the worst consequences of her machinations. Buckingham and a few others were executed. The rebellion had been a fiasco, but it did have one important consequence: the Woodville–Tudor alliance. Many of Henry Tudor's closest allies two years later – men like Sir Richard Guildford, Sir Thomas Cheyney, William Brandon – had been Woodville dependants and leaders in the revolt. On Christmas day in 1483 Henry Tudor, back in Brittany, solemnly contracted himself to marry the Lady Elizabeth.

Buckingham's fall resulted in large-scale confiscation of lands to the crown. Richard, naturally enough, set about rewarding his supporters. Three in particular have become immortalized in a seditious rhyme, 'The Cat, the Rat and Lovell our dog'; that is, William Catesby, who had betrayed Hastings, Sir Richard Ratcliffe and an old friend of Richard's, Lord Lovell. Many of the beneficiaries were northerners, Richard's allies from his long years of border service under Edward. They represent to some extent the intrusion of a new party into England and a disturbance of the pattern of landholding which inevitably created temporary difficulties for Richard among the more established landowners. But it is easy to exaggerate this point, and there is no reason to think that Richard's 'new men' any more than those of his predecessors would not in time have been comfortably assimilated into the established order.

Henry Tudor's position seemed hopeless after the fiasco of 1483. Queen Elizabeth gave up her hopes of a Woodville–Tudor alliance in March 1484, when she left the Westminster sanctuary and allowed her daughter Elizabeth to live at Richard's court. (A curious action if she believed that Richard had murdered her sons or even if he was keeping them close prisoner; but it is very dangerous to draw conclusions from the reactions of noble ladies, who seem to have been motivated far more by politics than by family affection. She may in any case have been giving in to *force majeure*.) Some people thought that Richard intended to marry his niece; and ugly rumours had to be denied when in March 1485 Richard's queen, Anne Neville (daughter of the 'Kingmaker') died. Henry Tudor's claim to the throne was extremely weak; it came through his mother, but if a woman could transmit a claim to the throne the Yorkist case was better than the Lancastrian one. Even if Richard himself was dismissed as a 'tyrant' there were plenty of young Yorkist princes who had far better claims than the Tudors.

Henry's second attempt came at last in August 1485. He landed at Milford Haven in Pembrokeshire with two thousand men provided by the French government (who also provided the money). With him were his uncle Jasper Tudor, who had upheld the Lancastrian cause in Wales in the sixties, the Earl of Oxford, another staunch Lancastrian and John Morton, Bishop of Ely – Morton had been arrested when Hastings was killed in 1483 and as Buckingham's prisoner may have been the *eminence grise* of the Buckingham revolt. Henry obviously hoped for support in Wales and was seen by some Welsh bards as the expected descendant of the British king Cadwallader, who was destined to restore their freedom to the Welsh people; but hopeful bards had also seen Edward IV as the same light. More important were the attitudes of a few key men who, it seems reasonable to suspect, had been fixed in advance; among them Rhys ap Thomas, the most powerful man in south Wales, whose defection surprised Richard, and Henry's stepfather Lord Stanley and his brother Sir William who controlled vast lands in Cheshire and north Wales. Lord Stanley had to be cautious; he was a natural suspect and he could not come out openly for Henry since Richard held his son Lord Strange as a hostage for good behaviour. But the collusion of Rhys and the Stanleys meant that Henry could march through central Wales to Shrewsbury, unmolested.

The decisive battle took place at Bosworth in Leicestershire on 22 August 1485. The outcome was certainly not predetermined, any more than previous decisive battles had been. It is true that Richard had only ten peers with him and that only two of them were of the first rank: John Howard, Duke of Norfolk and William Berkeley, Earl of Nottingham. Both of them had been granted their titles by Richard and confirmed in their joint inheritance of the Mowbray estates which Edward IV had conferred on his younger son (above, p. 92). But even so, Richard's army was bigger than his enemy's; almost two to one by one reckoning.* His defeat was due to treachery; the Earl of Northumberland hovered with his troops away from the battle and the Stanleys threw off the mask and joined Henry. The decisiveness of the battle was due to an extraordinary chance: Richard's being killed, the first time an English king had been killed in battle since Richard I in 1199. If he had lived and escaped capture he could have fled abroad to the court of his sister, Margaret of Burgundy; and given the trouble that Yorkist pretenders were to give Henry VII, a real Yorkist king might well have reconquered the country as Edward

* P. M. Kendall, *Richard III* (Allen & Unwin, 1955) p. 361.

IV had done in 1471. But with Richard dead, there was nobody for the moment to stand in Henry's way. Appropriately it was Sir William Stanley who placed the crown on his head.

What seems to characterize 1485, like 1469–71, is a general reluctance to get involved; a caution, perhaps a lack of enthusiasm for any cause on the part of even influential subjects. The result was that events could be thrown entirely out of balance by the chance outcome of a battle, the decision of one or two key figures and so on. All this seems to be at odds with the attempt to depict fifteenth-century England as a complex political society in which political decisions were not merely the whim of a few great lords, and in which a wider public opinion carried a certain amount of weight. That was certainly the case through most, if not all, of the 1450s. The difference is that between an established regime, however corrupt, inefficient or even disastrous, Henry VI's for instance; and regimes like that of Edward IV before 1471 or Richard III's, which had not yet achieved general credibility, and which still carried the marks of their origin as the creation of faction. Above all, these latter regimes did not enjoy the presumption of stability and continuity, and were liable therefore to collapse after a single defeat in battle.

The difference is reflected in the decline of Parliament as a politically significant body (as opposed to its constitutional importance which of course continued unchanged). In 1450 nobody had been prepared to challenge Henry VI's right to rule. Dissatisfaction took the form of attempting to hedge in the king's powers in certain respects, by making the government more responsive to the nation in Parliament; and so Suffolk was removed by impeachment, and Parliamentary treasurers were appointed to oversee the spending of taxation. When, however, with Henry's breakdown, politics became a matter of who should exercise the supreme power; and when, with the 1455 battle of St Albans, a slide into armed conflict began, Parliament was inevitably devalued. Politics had become more personalized; dissatisfaction with a king, at a time of conflicting dynastic claims, would increase support for a rival claimant, rather than suggesting the need to limit the king's powers; and in any case the final court of appeal had become the battlefield. After 1455 successive Parliaments reflected the dominant military power; strongly 'Yorkist' after the first battle of St Albans in 1455, vindictively 'Lancastrian' in 1459, prepared to work with Edward IV after 1461 and to proclaim him a usurper during the re-adeption.

How far the refusal of retainers or tenants to follow their lords continued to be a politically significant factor is much more difficult to tell. We have seen examples of this; the hostility of Northumberland's followers to Edward IV in 1471 for instance, or Buckingham's failure to raise his Welsh tenantry in 1483. But there were specific reasons in the first case; and the second was probably due to Buckingham's harsh record as a landlord. The more general brake on raising troops was probably fear of the consequences of royal retribution; and this brings us back to the point that the apparent fluidity of the sixties and of the years 1483-5 (or indeed 1483-7) was the result of the peculiar circumstances of those years, and did not apply, for instance, to the period after Edward IV had successfully established himself. In 1478 Edward IV could arrest Clarence without, apparently, any fear of his following. Ten years before it would have seemed impossible. Had Richard won at Bosworth it would have made his regime as impregnable as Edward's before him.

HENRY VII

As it happened, Henry VII founded a dynasty which presided over one of the most momentous centuries in English history. There is a tendency, therefore, for 1485 to acquire a spurious importance, as if it marked a decisive change in English political history. In one sense it did. Henry VII was the last claimant to fight his way to the English throne (his granddaughter Mary's accession in 1553 and that of William III's invasion in 1688 are not quite in the same category). But that would have been a rash prediction in 1485. There were several candidates for the throne with claims at least as good as Henry's; and although Henry did much to foreclose Yorkist opposition by marrying Edward IV's daughter Elizabeth, there was still some danger from other Yorkist princes. Fortunately only one of them was old enough to be an immediate danger; John de la Pole, Earl of Lincoln, son of

Richard III's sister Elizabeth, whom Richard had considered as his heir. He had fought at Bosworth, but submitted and was given a place on Henry's council.

The Yorkist tree had many flourishing branches. Lincoln himself had three younger brothers. Two of the Duke of Clarence's children were still alive. Their claims to the throne had been passed over in 1483 because of their father's attainder; but attainder had been no bar to Henry VII's becoming king, and would not prevent a subsequent claim on their behalf. Fortunately for Henry, the boy Edward, Earl of Warwick was only ten years old, and had been imprisoned by Richard III. Henry kept him a prisoner, and married off the other child, Margaret, to Sir Richard Pole, one of his most trusted supporters. (Her royal blood eventually helped to bring her to the block, as Countess of Salisbury, in 1541.)

Elizabeth of York, Henry's queen, had four sisters, three of whom married nobles in Henry's reign (the other, conveniently, became a nun). As it happened, only one of these produced a child who reached manhood, Henry Marquis of Exeter, (eventually executed in 1538). Finally there were potential Beaufort claimants (*see* genealogy, p. 355). Fortunately Lady Margaret Beaufort, in spite of four marriages, had only one child, Henry himself. But a Beaufort claim could also be mounted by Edward Stafford, to whom, in gratitude for his father's rebellion in 1483, Henry had restored the dukedom of Buckingham. He was descended twice over from Edward III, by the Beaufort route from John of Gaunt, and also from Thomas of Woodstock, Edward's youngest son. Fortunately he was only seven years old; but he posed a real threat for the future, a threat which cost him his life in 1521.

The idea that the Wars of the Roses had got rid of great men with possible claims to the throne, is totally untrue. But Henry did at least have a breathing space in that Lincoln was the only plausible claimant for the moment. Even so, if real claimants were not available they could be invented, especially at the court of the dowager Duchess of Burgundy, Edward IV's sister Margaret. Presumably her intention was to set up a stool-pigeon who could be used to overthrow Henry VII after which a genuine Yorkist would be installed.

The first of these pretenders was Lambert Simnel, son of an Oxford tradesman, who appeared in Dublin in 1487 and was accepted by the Lord Deputy of Ireland, the Earl of Kildare, as being the young Earl of Warwick. The ramifications of the Simnel conspiracy were wide. Margaret of Burgundy sent two thousand highly trained German troops. Queen Elizabeth Woodville, Henry's mother-in-law and her son the Marquis of Dorset were involved. Most seriously of all the Earl of Lincoln joined Simnel. A Yorkist army crossed to Lancashire, moved on to York and was only defeated at a bloody battle at East Stoke near Newark.

From 1491 another impersonator was active, one Perkin Warbeck, a Fleming who claimed to be Richard of York, the younger of the princes in the Tower. Warbeck's success was considerable. Like Simnel he was supported by Margaret of Burgundy. Charles VIII of France supported him as long as it was convenient; so did the Holy Roman Emperor, Maximilian. James IV of Scotland gave Warbeck a state reception and married him to Lady Catherine Gordon. Sir William Stanley, Henry's ally at Bosworth and now his chamberlain was executed in 1495 for, allegedly, plotting with Warbeck. An attempted landing at Deal in 1495 came to nothing; so did an invasion from Scotland in 1496. But in 1497 just after the Cornish peasant revolt (*see below*, p. 102), Warbeck landed in Cornwall and gathered a fairly substantial army, and held it together to Taunton, where he abandoned it and fled to sanctuary at Beaulieu. Two years later after yet another plot, Warbeck and the real Earl of Warwick were executed.

Simnel and Warbeck often figure as rather comic characters in the *1066 and All That* school of history. In fact their careers signified both of possibility of a pretender raising support and the foreign rulers being prepared to help them. Henry himself, after all, owed his throne to French support and English treachery. He was in no position to despise that sort of threat and his official panegyrist, Bernard André, described Stoke as the 'second triumph of Henry VII'; it could easily have been a second Bosworth, with Henry in the role of Richard III. The disposal of Warbeck and Warwick did not end the run of potential rivals. Lincoln had been killed at the battle of Stoke; but in 1503 his younger brother, Edmund, Earl of Suffolk, was being entertained at the imperial court, and spent the next four years at various German courts as the 'White Rose' before being betrayed to Henry by Philip of Burgundy in 1506. Yet another brother, Richard, was a useful card for the French king as late as 1525.

Henry's military weakness was shown in 1497. In May riots broke out in Cornwall about taxation. The rioters soon coalesced into an army led by Michael Joseph, a blacksmith, and Thomas Flamank, a lawyer. Marching on London, they acquired respectable leadership *en route* in the person of Lord Audley. The degree of spontaneity and of prompting in this sort of affair is always difficult to judge. Whatever the background it seems odd that no peer was able to block their march – or even to try to do so – before they got to London. Perhaps they were lying low to see how things turned out.

The rebels encountered a substantial army for the first time at Blackheath, on the outskirts of London; and not surprisingly they were defeated. The leaders were executed; the rest faced massive fines. About three thousand of these then rallied to Warbeck and were defeated. Officials were at work collecting fines in the south-west as late as 1506.

After 1497 Henry was faced with no more armed challenges. But the Tudor dynasty was not unquestioned; all too much still depended on the hazards of life and death, and the presence of adequate but not too many heirs. About 1504 the officers of Calais garrison were discussing the succession after the death of Henry's elder son, Prince Arthur, and while the future Henry VIII was about twelve years old. 'Some of them spoke of my lord of Buckingham . . . [others] . . . of Edmund de la Pole, but none of them . . . of my lord prince.'

GOVERNMENT

The king's relations with his nobility were of first importance. He had to avoid being dependent on one particular group and leave himself room for manoeuvre, for playing off parties against each other. If he did not, rather like Henry VI in the 1440s, he risked welding the various feuds and enmities of aristocratic society into a dangerously united opposition. But while he had to take care not to be dominated by them, a strong nobility remained essential for the peace and security of the country. This was obvious in the case of defence. But it was also true of internal security, of the prevention of disorder. The nobility were, or should have been, a firm island amidst the flood waters of the common people, according to the chancellor in 1483. A great nobleman might provoke local disorder and rebellion, sometimes as a deliberate political ploy. But equally a nobleman doing his duty would often damp down disorder, mediate between the aggrieved commoners and the central government and, if it came to the point of riot, organize the forces of order. Significantly, the Cornish rebellion in 1497 broke out in an area where there was no dominant magnate. The presence of a great man simplified things for the crown: if he failed to prevent disorder, the king knew whom to blame. The perspicacious Francis Bacon, indeed, thought that Henry VII had been too strict with the nobility and that 'this made for his absoluteness, but not for his safety' for though his nobles 'were loyal and obedient, yet [they] did not co-operate with him but let every man go his own way'.

Success in kingship consisted, therefore, not in suppressing the nobility even if that had been possible, but in using them for the king's own purpose. Reliable information was important here. Edward IV and Henry VII both had capable ministers, but worked hard at the business of kingship to keep a check on what was going on. Edward, according to the Croyland chronicler, could remember the name and estates of everybody in the country down to 'the rank of private gentleman' and by appointing trusted servants to local office, had all suspicious incidents reported to him immediately. Henry VII's well-known habit of signing his treasurer's accounts may not have been merely a check on financial efficiency; it had the additional advantage of keeping the king up to date on problems of wardship, debts, the succession of lands and so on. An intimate knowledge of local power structures was invaluable.

Within these limits there was a difference of emphasis between the policies of the two kings. Edward essentially established his position by playing the game of noble power politics in his own interest. Henry on the other hand, was able to go further in putting the crown above the battle, repressing all rival groups impartially, and using a nicely judged lack of generosity in dealing with his supporters.

The difference can be seen in attitudes to new peerages, in which Edward was more open handed than Henry. Edward created nine new earls or above; Henry VII only one, his step-father, Lord Stanley, who became Earl of Derby. (In addition his uncle Jasper Tudor was promoted within the higher grades of the peerage from Earl of Pembroke to Duke of Bedford.) Edward created two viscounts and thirteen barons; Henry no more than five barons and most of these could be regarded as recognition of ancient claims rather than actual new peerages.* Through not creating new peerages to replace those which became extinct during his reign (mostly through natural causes) Henry allowed the number of peers to drop from about 57 to 44. There are special circumstances which blur this apparently clear-cut con-trast. Eight of Edward's nine higher peerages were created in the sixties (the exception was to make his stepson Marquis of Dorset in 1475), and ten of the lesser peerages. There was an obvious need to reward his allies, establish a vested interest in the new regime (largely out of the lands of attainted Lancastrians) and, later, build up a countervailing power to the Nevilles. Henry on the other hand could win support by restoring to their old titles and estates the Lancastrians or deviant Yorkists attainted by Edward and Richard. Nevertheless, more than this might have been expected of a new king. It is remarkable that neither Sir William Stanley nor Rhys ap Thomas, to whom Henry owed so much in 1485, became peers.

---

* These calculations are difficult and rather arbitrary. I have omitted mem-bers of the royal family and certain oddities (eg, George Neville, who became Duke of Bedford in expectation of marrying Edward's daughter and was sub-sequently deprived, or Louis de Bruges, a Burgundian who became Earl of Wiltshire under Edward IV but played no part in English affairs.); also restorations after attainders. See T. B. Pugh, 'The Magnates, Knights and Gentry' in *Fifteenth Century England*, eds. S. B. Chrimes, T. B. Pugh and R. A. Griffiths (Manchester, 1972); also J. E. Powell and K. Wallis, *House of Lords in the Middle Ages* (Weidenfeld & Nicolson, 1968), and S. B. Chrimes, *Henry VII* (1972).

Two conspicuous examples of Edward's policy are provided by William Herbert and William Hastings. Herbert had been steward of both York and Neville estates in south Wales in the 1450s. In 1461 he became chief justice and chamberlain of south Wales, and accumulated land and offices; and in 1468 became Earl of Pembroke. Next year he was killed fighting for Edward at Edgecote. Hastings was a servant of Edward's when he was Earl of March. He became a baron in 1461, was given extensive lands and offices in the east and north midlands (Leicester, Nottingham, Derby), and kept, as we have seen, a peculiarly distinguished set of retainers. From 1471 he was also captain-general of Calais; a vital strategic position as Warwick had shown in the fifties and sixties. He was also the king's chamberlain; and more important, his close friend and companion. Edward's trust paid off; Hastings provided Edward with his first substantial support in his bid for the throne in 1471, and, as we have seen, it looks as if it was his loyalty to Edward's son which caused his death in 1483.

But loyalty of this sort was hard to find. Edward preferred to trust his relatives; and the various Woodvilles were useful in this connection, since they owed their social standing almost entirely to their connection with Edward and his children. He was also generous to his brother, George, Duke of Clarence, with disastrous results; and to Richard of Gloucester. Richard was built up as the great representative of royal power in the north, on the basis of royal grant and of his Neville inheritance (through his wife, the daughter of the Kingmaker). In 1483, after a great victory over the Scots, and just before Edward's death, Richard *and his heirs* were given extraordinary powers in the north-west; the perpetual right to be warden of the West March, one of the most valuable, prestigious and powerful offices in the hands of the crown; all crown lands and judicial prerogatives in Cumberland, including the right to nominate the sheriff; and possession of any lands he might win from the Scots. This amounted to the creation of a permanent, quite independent county palatine which could have become a huge menace to the crown in the long run. Even granted Richard's loyalty to Edward, it seems unlikely that his descendants would remain undeviatingly loyal to Edward's children or grandchildren. In effect Edward was creating in England something like the division between the royal house and the house of Burgundy which had shattered political unity in France. It was a heavy price for the build-up of an effective military force against Scotland.

In his last years, Edward began to concentrate lands and offices on his children. William Herbert's son was made to surrender a large part of his Welsh lands and the earldom of Pembroke in 1479, for the benefit of the Prince of Wales: Herbert became Earl of Huntingdon instead and was given some rather meagre lands in the West Country in exchange. Edward's younger son Richard was, as we have seen, married to the Mowbray heiress, and would have become a great force in East Anglia. All these moves had obvious political advantages; new lands for the Prince of Wales meant, as long as the prince was a child, greater powers for the king himself, and this was used to improve the government of Wales. The policy of enriching the royal family at the expense of the peerage had been followed with some success by no less a king than Edward I. Nevertheless, it did alienate a number of influential and aggrieved lords; and, as important, was essentially a storing up of trouble for the future by the creation of a number of royal over-mighty subjects. Political calculation obviously inspired a good deal of Edward IV's actions; but there was rather too much concentration on short-term advantage in his policy, and possibly, too, a certain amount of reckless impetuosity.

Henry VII was much more cautious; he was also a good deal luckier. His only close male relative was his uncle Jasper Tudor, who, as Earl of Pembroke and Duke of Bedford, was set to do William Herbert's old job of running south Wales; fortunately Jasper was conspicuously loyal (his nephew was after all, his only claim to political importance) and he had no legitimate children. Here again, political stability probably benefited by the death of Henry VII's elder son, Prince Arthur. The man we think of as Henry VIII would probably have been a thorn in his brother's side as a mere Duke of York. The problem of the younger son was insoluble, since he had to be given a dignified position which could constitute an independent source of power. Nevertheless, it seems unlikely that Henry would have provided for younger members of his family quite as bountifully as Edward had done.

Henry's caution can be seen from his northern policy. In 1489 the Earl of Northumberland was murdered while putting down a tax riot in the North Riding. Henry sent to replace him Thomas Howard, Earl of Surrey, son of the Duke of Norfolk who had been promoted by Richard III and killed at Bosworth Surrey, too, had fought at Bosworth, and had spent the time since in the Tower. He was now granted some of his lands, and his former title; though his father's dukedom was kept from him until, in 1513, he redeemed it by smashing the Scots and killing their king at the battle of Flodden. His appointment in 1489 as lieutenant-general of the north was in some sense a risk; if he was too weak to be an over-mighty subject he might be too weak to keep out the Scots. Fortunately it was a risk worth taking, since the Scots were deeply involved in civil war after deposing and killing their king, James III, in 1488, and there was not much chance of an immediate attack.

Surrey is the classic example of Henry's cat-and-mouse policy with the nobles. Henry was, in fact, rather more generous than Edward in reversing attainders; sixteen peers were attainted in Edward's reign, of whom only four were pardoned during his life; the corresponding figures for Henry VII are nine and five. But Henry granted back only a part of the forfeited lands at one time, so keeping the family at his mercy if it wanted the rest of them back; and did so at a price which made them financially indebted to the crown. On top of this, from about 1502 onwards, Henry systematized a policy which the Yorkists had adopted sporadically. He demanded from a large number of his subjects 'bonds' or 'recognizances', by which they would forfeit to the king a named sum of money, if they offended in a certain way. This often related to carrying out a particular duty or paying a fine, but was sometimes much more widely a matter of keeping the peace or not deviating from their allegiance. On top of this in the later part of the reign, huge fines were sometimes levied on noblemen. Lord Abergavenny was fined £70,000 in 1507 for unlawful retaining; the Earl of Northumberland £10,000 for nominally 'ravishing' a royal ward. Of course, these monstrous fines were soon commuted into smaller sums, payable in instalments (£500 a year in Abergavenny's case, possibly about half his annual income), and backed up by recognizances of over £8,000. In these various ways Henry could keep a tight financial hold on his peerage; some four-fifths of peerage families fell into his clutches in one way or the other during his reign, a large proportion of them at the very end.*

Henry's vindictiveness towards the nobility was partly a matter of opportunity (a statute under which Abergavenny could have been prosecuted for retaining had existed since 1468, but Henry was hardly in a position to enforce it before the end of his reign), partly a matter of temperament. But however harshly he treated them, there is no justification for the view that he in any way was a 'middle-class' monarch; indeed, as we shall see, his treatment of London was as harsh or harsher than his treatment of the nobles. Of course, Henry's most trusted advisers were nonnoble; men like Sir Reginald Bray, Richard Empson and Edmund Dudley, all of gentry origin, who had made a career for themselves as lawyers involved in estate management. Much the same applies to William Catesby under Richard III, or to men like Sir William Herbert, Sir William Hastings and Sir John Wenlock under Edward IV (though these last were all ennobled). Men like this had long played an important role in the king's administration and in the council; York's propaganda had complained about them in the 1450s and they were to be found in Richard II's reign, if not earlier. Their numbers may have been increasing, but at the expense of the clerical civil servants, not of the nobility. It was part of the general process of the emergence of a more educated laity. Of course there was a difference between the council of Edward IV and Henry VII, and the more 'aristocratic' councils imposed by York in the 1450s or in Henry VI's minority. But these latter were essentially an opposition device, a remedy for exceptional circumstances. In normal conditions the proportions of different social groups who were members of the council remained

---

* For the calculations, see the works of J. R. Lander, especially his *Attainder and Forfeiture 1453–1509* and *Bonds, Coercion and Fear: Henry VII and the Peerage*, published respectively in 1961 and 1971, and reprinted in *Crown and Nobility, 1450–1509* (Edward Arnold, 1976).

fairly constant throughout the fifteenth century. Of course, counting heads does not indicate political influence; and it does seem that Henry VII relied more than most of his predecessors on non-nobles for political advice. Nevertheless, this was more a personal preference, a question of his own inherent distrust of powerful men, rather than any formed policy to force the nobility out of central politics. He had no compunction in appointing the Earl of Surrey, once his loyalty was proved, to the important post of lord treasurer.

Neither Edward IV or Henry VII established, as is sometimes alleged, special courts to deal with nobles. It is still sometimes thought that a 'Court of Star Chamber' was established by Act of Parliament in 1487. There was certainly an act of that year, which established a special tribunal to deal with those who browbeat juries and generally perverted the course of justice through the use of armed force. But the tribunal was *not* the Court of Star Chamber. It seems to have been an *ad hoc* body, of which little is known, and which had ceased to function by 1509. 'Star Chamber', on the other hand was nothing more than the king's council sitting on judicial business; its powers derived from the royal prerogative and long tradition, and needed no special foundation. It was only later, in the 1530s with an increased definition of various aspects of council business and the creation of a more specific 'privy council' to handle political affairs, that the council sitting in Star Chamber on judicial business came to be thought of as a specialized court. Although a large number of cases of 'riot' were heard by the council in Henry's reign, these were not cases of 'over-mighty subjects' being prosecuted by the crown. Cases were brought by subjects against each other, and rarely involved peers. As we have seen, towards the end of Henry's reign, peers were harshly treated. But they were either fined in the common law courts (as in Abergavenny's case) or put under recognizance for good behaviour by the council; they were not dealt with by any sort of special court. Henry, according to Polydore Vergil, 'vigorously punished violence, manslaughter and every other kind of wickedness'. But if he did so it was by traditional means (except in so far as he systematized the recognizance system); by having the determination and, by the end of the reign, political strength to proceed harshly, rather than by institutional innovation.

There was nothing revolutionary either about the use of justices of the peace. Justices had been exercising practically unlimited criminal jurisdiction since the fourteenth century; they could handle at quarter sessions, with a jury but without necessarily the attendance of any of the king's judges, all capital cases except treason. They administered a wide variety of economic legislation – most notably the Statute of Labourers (1351, revised 1388) on wages, but also multifarious acts about apprenticeship, standards of cloth-making and so on. There was nothing specifically Tudor either about such cases or about the use of the justices to administer them. Certainly their competence was extended by Edward IV and Henry VII. In 1461 the criminal jurisdiction of the sheriff was transferred to them; in 1495 they were allowed to try certain non-capital offences without a jury. (This was repealed in 1509.) But there was no revolutionary break with precedent. The justices were in a sense representative of the gentry class; and very slowly, very gradually, over the sixteenth century as a whole, the political balance swung somewhat away from the nobility, and towards the gentry, and away from feud and towards litigation. But that was the result of peace and slow social evolution; also of painstaking care by a succession of talented statesmen; it was not the result of any formal transfer of power by a particular monarch.

Something was done to increase royal power in Wales and the north. The Marcher lordships of Wales were a nest of privileges in which nobles exercised all the judicial rights of the king; to a lesser extent the same was true of the north, but there the major problem was distance from London, on the one hand, and the need for a strong nobility to keep out the Scots. In both cases Yorkists and Tudors attempted to establish regional councils to make the royal will more effective. A council was created in 1471 to supervise the estates of the Prince of Wales, Edward's new-born son, on lines analogous to the estate councils of great noblemen. From 1473, it was given powers to oversee the administration of justice in the principality, the border counties, and, in so far as it could, the Marcher lordships, and may have had some success in an area which had been pretty well neglected by the central authority in the previous twenty years. But it disappeared in 1483, when the prince became (briefly) king; something like it was revived for Buckingham later that year (as the greatest of the Marcher lords himself, Buckingham would have been in the powerful position of poacher turned gamekeeper); and, after Buckingham's fall, was not heard of again until 1493, when it was re-established as Prince Arthur's council. It remained in existence when Arthur died in 1502 – a significant indication of a change from a personal council to a national institution – but it does not seem to have been very active.

The northern council is more hazy. It originated as Richard of Gloucester's council while he was governing the north for his brother, and was commissioned to deal with breaches of the peace, if possible, or if not to report them to the king. It still functioned when Richard was king, but then lapsed. It seems to have been revised under Thomas Savage, who became Archbishop of York in 1501. It may have continued under the aegis of Henry's mother, Lady Margaret Beaufort. On her death in 1509 the northern council, unlike the Welsh one, apparently lapsed.

The councils were primarily attempts to maximize royal power in the areas by concentrating existing royal rights – rights of jurisdiction, of landownership, of appointment to offices and so on – and entrusting them to a body of men with a specialized knowledge of the area and its pattern of local political power.

The Welsh council was one weapon – though an important one – in the local political game. Its power was considerable, because the crown itself had swallowed up a number of the more powerful lordships; the Duchy of Lancaster in 1399, the Mortimer inheritance (earldom of March) when Edward became king in 1461, the Herbert lands in 1479. Had this gradual concentration of lordships continued, Edward might eventually have been strong enough to remodel the government of Wales; but the political upheavals of the next few years prevented that. Richard III granted the most extraordinary powers, in both Wales and the west, to Buckingham, and Henry VII relied at first on his uncle Jasper Tudor until the re-establishment of the prince's council in

1493. The council had no jurisdiction in the Marcher lordships, other than those in the Crown's possession, and no direct attack was made upon them. Henry proceeded by his favourite device of recognizance, binding the lords to see that their legal system functioned efficiently; and especially, that fugitive criminals were not granted refuge. Jasper Tudor himself, no less, was subject to such a bond; and towards the end of the reign there was an attempt to apply the system generally; not, as we shall see, with very striking success.

An extreme example of the outlying area in which the royal authority was weak was provided by Ireland. No English king had any effective power in the half of the country inhabited by the 'wild Irish'. The real question was the extent of power exercised over the Anglo-Irish lords or even the English settlers. The English had been on the defensive since the early fourteenth century. The last English king to attempt to re-establish royal authority there was Richard II. (He was, in fact, the last English king to visit Ireland before James II and William III fought each other there in 1689.) The English Pale had shrunk to about fifty miles around Dublin, while the Anglo-Irish lordships were becoming increasingly Irish in law, social institutions and culture. The colonists, in despair, begged Henry VI to get the pope to authorize a 'crusade against the said Irish enemies'. York had had some success against the Irish in 1449–50, and, by winning the gratitude of the settlers, had been able to use his lieutenancy in Ireland as an independent base to which he could retreat when things turned against him in England. It was through York's inspiration that the Irish Parliament (representing the settlers) declared in 1460 that Ireland was only bound by laws passed in Ireland; the intention was to protect Yorkists from Margaret of Anjou's government.

Edward IV was therefore faced with a situation of *de facto* independence on the part of the settlers, engineered by his father. Not until 1467 did he attempt to assert royal authority by sending over John Tiptoft, Earl of Worcester, as Lord Deputy of Ireland. Worcester managed to have Thomas Fitz-Gerald, Earl of Desmond, one of the great Anglo-Irish lords (and his predecessor as lord deputy) executed in 1468; but it soon became obvious that strong rule by an Englishman was only possible if the crown would subsidize the Irish government. Edward balked at this, Worcester was recalled, and the government of Ireland was entrusted to the greatest of the Anglo-Irish lords, Gerald Fitz-Gerald, Earl of Kildare. Attempts by Edward to replace him by Englishmen were frustrated by the colonists (Kildare protected them more efficiently against the Irish) and from 1478 Kildare's son, Thomas Fitz-Gerald, the eighth earl, ruled Ireland.

Thomas was reasonably successful in conciliating both the native Irish and the settlers. But he was not amenable to control from England, and demonstrated this in 1487 when he had Lambert Simnel crowned as 'King Edward VI' in Dublin. In spite of this Henry was not able to replace him until 1492, when the welcome given to Warbeck by another Fitz-Gerald, the Earl of Desmond, gave him a chance. Sir Edward Poynings was sent to Ireland with a small army. The Irish Parliament was induced to agree that in future it should not be called without the authorization of the English king who would first be informed what business was to be transacted. In spite of this apparent triumph, however, Henry could not do without Kildare's support, and in 1496 he was brought back as lord deputy, and governed Ireland until 1513. 'He is meet to rule all Ireland, seeing all Ireland cannot rule him,' Henry is supposed to have said. Essentially, Henry had recovered the pre-1460 position. He had reasserted English authority over the settlers, and he had prevented the Anglo-Irish lords from conducting an essentially independent foreign policy. But nothing had been done – or could be done – to make the royal will effective *within* the Anglo-Irish lordships, let alone among the 'mere Irish'.

Ireland is, of course, exceptional. Nevertheless, its story is, in its way, an exaggerated version of the two kings' relations with the English nobility. They could not crush their nobles, they could not do without them; but they could apply sanctions in an attempt to repress disorder and discourage rebellion. Both kings were successful in avoiding rebellion during the second half of their reign, although obviously the situation could not be guaranteed for their successors. It is usually assumed that harsh measures against nobles were both justified (because nobles are inherently assumed to be rebellious, and given to oppression of the people at large), and politic. The former is debatable; the latter is only true given the right circumstances. Henry VII's actions in his last years – vindictive fines, the widespread use of recognizances, the dangling of a permanent sword of Damocles in the shape of financial sanctions above the heads of the nobles – are uncomfortably reminiscent of the reign of King John. Of course, society and politics had changed enormously in three hundred years, and any simple comparison would be naïve. Nevertheless, it does seem true that John's repression provoked rebellion because he was in a position of weakness; most notably because he had been humiliatingly defeated in foreign war. Henry had managed to avoid this situation, and was in a position of strength because of his victories against rebels at home. But whether he could have gone on much longer with the harsh policy inaugurated in 1502 had he lived (he was only fifty-two when he died in 1509) is not at all certain. As it was, the young Henry VIII had to make large concessions to his affronted subjects, aristocrats and commoners, and throw two of his father's principal agents, Edmund Dudley and Richard Empson, to the wolves in earnest of good intentions.

If rebellion was averted, the general problem of disorder was much wider. Edward IV personally accompanied his judges on progress from time to time, to try and reinforce the sullied majesty of the law by his own presence. Henry VII acquired a reputation for 'cherishing justice'; though even that is doubtful. Recent research suggests that not much vigour was shown in prosecuting cases, except in those in which political implications or rich pickings were involved.* The propensity to violence was so widespread, so deep seated, among all classes, that it was not until the end of the sixteenth century that more civilized habits began to prevail even among the nobility and gentry. As late as 1578, twenty-five retainers of Lord Rich could set on Edward Windham in broad daylight in Fleet Street, and away from London armed feuds indistinguishable from those of the 1450s were common even later.† Politics remained the art of the possible;

---

* S. B. Chrimes, *Henry VII* (Eyre Methuen), chap. 10.

† Lawrence Stone, *The Crisis of the Aristocracy 1558–1641* (Oxford, 1965) chap. 5.

no waving of a magic wand, no creation of institutions, no personal attention to government, could transform the habits of a nation overnight.

This is, of course, to try to judge by too high a standard. It would not be necessary if Edward and Henry (both together, or either one or the other) had not so often been credited with founding an authoritarian 'new monarchy', different in style and aims from their predecessors. Within a realistic framework of what was possible, however, they were successful and efficient kings. And this is mirrored in the parliamentary history of their reigns; or rather, in the lack of a parliamentary opposition like that of 1449–50. Partly this was because, as we have seen, the impetus of an informed, critical parliamentary tradition had been lost in military conflict. But partly too it was because Edward and Henry gave their Parliaments very little to complain about. (Henry's last Parliament met in 1504, before his repressive measures had begun to bite.) By strengthening royal finance through better administration the two kings were effectively carrying out the 'parliamentary' programme of 1450. In these circumstances men were glad that Parliaments, and therefore taxes, were infrequent.

One test of efficiency was finance. And in this respect Edward and Henry both did well. Edward has been described as 'the first English King since Henry II (1154–89) to die solvent'.* Henry improved on this, leaving a positive surplus, though less than is sometimes thought. (Quite how much is difficult to say – only £9,100 in cash, and a considerable amount in plate and jewels, bought partly at least as an investment. Total spending on plate and jewels in the reign was about £140,000.†) The impression of Henry's wealth was carefully fostered at the time to impress ambassadors and deter rebels. As early as 1497, when he was certainly not wealthy, the Milanese ambassador could talk of his 'immense treasure'. The Spanish ambassador the following year was a bit more perspicacious. Henry, he said, 'likes to be thought very rich' but in fact was 'less rich than is generally said'.

There had certainly been a considerable improvement in the

---

* J. R. Lander, *Conflict and Stability* (Hutchinson, 1969), p. 111.
† R. L. Storey, *Henry VII*, p. 114; B. P. Wolffe, *The Royal Demesne in English History* (Allen & Unwin, 1971) chap. 7.

crown's income; most notably, in the income from crown lands. For the first time these made up a really substantial part of the crown revenue, roughly equal to the yield of the customs. Net value rose from about £8,000 a year in 1433 to about £40,000 by 1504. This was partly due to improved management. In 1433 crown lands were administered by the exchequer, through an immensely complicated system designed to prevent fraud of the simplest sort; that is, to make sure that the accounting officer actually paid in the money that he owed the crown. But there was little or no incentive to improve the revenue by more efficient management, in the sense of renewing leases to try and raise rents, cutting out unnecessary payments and so on. Edward therefore adapted for the crown's use the much less formal accounting system used on noble estates. He appointed receivers and special auditors to manage particular groups of estates, and these were to account to the king's chamber, a department of the royal household, and not the exchequer. The chamber became in effect a rival treasury which was soon handling almost all the landed revenue. Henry VII did not appreciate this new system at first, but within a few years he had become an enthusiast, personally supervising the whole system in minute detail, and on occasion writing accounts in his own hand.

Historians have made a great deal of fuss about this new 'chamber system'. The sad truth is that it is impossible to tell just what effect it had on revenues. Some estates have dramatically improved rent rolls under the new system, others seem hardly affected. Administrative efficiency in fact was probably less important than the sheer increase in crown possessions; partly through the 'resumption' policy of 1450, partly through the workings of attainder and forfeiture. The spectacular figure of £40,000 a year landed income in 1504 was due at least in part to the small number of relatives Henry had to provide for. Nevertheless, whatever the reason, the improved income from crown lands was important; this was the only time in English history (except, briefly, after the Norman Conquest) when they made a really substantial contribution to royal finance.*

* See B. P. Wolffe, *The Royal Demesne in English History* (Allen & Unwin, 1971), or more briefly, his *The Crown Lands 1461–1536* (Allen & Unwin, 1970).

The other main prop of royal income was the customs. Net yields rose rather slowly, from £31,000 a year in the late 1450s to about £40,000 in the last years of Henry VII. Improved administration may have played some part; but the increase is more likely due to increased trade. Both Edward IV and Henry VII devoted attention to the possible profits to be derived from the 'feudal' forms by which land was held; and especially the rights of the crown to the wardship of minors who inherited lands held 'in chief' of the crown. Edward's interest seems mainly to have been political; the chance of arranging marriages and so on. Henry VII, in his last years, concentrated on the financial proceeds; wardships could be sold, and the profits increased from £343 in 1491 to over £6,000 in 1507. Even so, neither king did more than nibble at a problem which effectively deprived them of considerable revenues; the creation of 'uses' or trusts which, rather like modern devices to avoid death duties, effectively prevented lands being subject to wardship.

There were other more questionable financial expedients. Forced loans to the government had been common for a long time, justified by the argument that it was a subject's duty to help the king in times of need. Under Edward these escalated from loans to gifts, known as benevolences, levied in 1474 and 1480-2. Richard III's Parliament in 1484 declared them illegal, but they were levied again in 1491. In addition, a good deal of Henry's activity in enforcing the law had at least the incidental advantage of increasing the crown's income from fines; and there were complaints that men were being prosecuted for mere technical offences under statutes which had been disregarded for some time past.

Both kings, then, were active in maximizing income, but control of expenditure was equally important. The main factor here was the avoidance of large-scale war in France, whether by accident or design. Less important, but still substantial, was the saving of expenditure at court. This was not achieved (contrary to the popular impression of Henry VII, at least) by skimping on ceremonial; investment in court show paid useful dividends in terms of public relations, in creating the impression of the king's wealth, his majesty and so on. Edward deliberately modelled his court on that of his brother-in-law, the Duke of Burgundy, the most magnificent court in Europe, at least north of the Alps. The Croyland Chronicler wrote proudly that Edward's court 'fully befits a most mighty kingdom, full of riches and with people of almost all nations'. Henry, too, impressed ambassadors by his costly dress, and promoted tournaments, and court festivities on a large scale. All these, however, seem to have been achieved for less cost than the court of Henry VI and, apparently, to more effect. Neither Edward IV nor Henry VII skimped on building, the most tangible expression of a man's wealth. Edward began to build St George's Chapel at Windsor. Henry continued it; continued, too, Henry VI's magnificent King's College at Cambridge (the famous chapel is more Tudor than Lancastrian), and built the 'Henry VII chapel' at Westminster Abbey; a chantry chapel on an overwhelming scale, a conspicuous (and well sited) symbol of both royal piety and royal resources.

Edward promised his Parliament in 1467 to 'live upon mine own', only troubling them for taxes 'in great and urgent causes'. About £120,000 was raised in 1472–5, but this was for the French war. After that there was no more direct taxation till 1483. Henry VII stepped the rate up smartly in his first twelve years to average about £22,000 a year. This was rather less than half the rate of taxation under Henry V, and about equal to the direct taxation of 1428–54; but peacetime conditions made it the more intolerable, and one result was the Cornish rising of 1497. Perhaps because of the rising, there was an abrupt change in the second half of the reign; 1504 saw the only vote of direct taxation, and there was increased pressure on other financial resources.

Henry was becoming increasingly self-confident in his final years, daring to attack vested interests on a big scale, catching the nobility out on legal technicalities, binding them tight with unrealistic recognizances. He extended the scope of his victims beyond the nobility. He was at odds with powerful groups in the City of London, and especially the Merchant Adventurers; and their complaints of his grasping extortions found their way into the *Great Chronicle of London* written about 1512, and from there into the mainstream of historical writing.

Henry and his ministers were violently attacked in the first year of his son's reign. Henry's will established a committee to investigate wrongs done by himself to individuals which might harm his immortal soul. The injured were loud in their complaints. Lord Abergavenny, no less, was one of the commissioners to investigate abuses. Of course, dying kings tend to have qualms about actions that may have been necessary for reasons of state, and new kings like to make a bid for popularity. But it is clear from the list drawn up by Edmund Dudley, after he had been condemned to death in 1509, that Henry personally was responsible for a good many individual cases of injustice; of men 'hardly entreated and much sorer than their causes required', Lord Abergavenny's 'sore end' was achieved without 'any proof that was against him to my knowledge', while 'one Windial, a poor man in Devonshire, lay long in prison and paid £100 upon a very small cause.'*

In general, restoration of the crown's finances was more a symptom than a cause of the crown's general political recovery. Henry VII could afford to be high handed because he faced no immediate challenge; as long as he lived (like Edward IV after 1471) he was safe, and he was lucky to hand on to a son who had (just) reached manhood. Political stability, too, depended on the absence of a threat from abroad; and it is to foreign affairs that we must now turn.

FOREIGN AFFAIRS

Foreign affairs were intimately connected with events in England. The rift between Edward and Warwick in the 1460s stemmed from disagreement about a French or Burgundian alliance. Burgundian aid restored Edward in 1471; the various pretenders to Henry VII's throne were supported from the court of Burgundy by Edward IV's sister the Duchess Margaret. Henry VII's intricate foreign policy was partly, at least, dictated by fear of rivals being harboured in foreign courts and launched

* The list was discovered by C. J. Harrison and printed in *Eng. Hist. Rev.*, vol. 87, 1972.

upon England, as he himself had been from the French court in 1485.

Although Edward and Henry kept their options open as far as they could, France was the main enemy. They kept alive their claim to be King of France, and their more jingoist subjects called upon them to repeat the glorious achievements of Edward III and Henry V. William Caxton published Arthurian romances and works of history specially to stir up Edward to martial exploits. The wily Louis XI, King of France since 1461, was principally concerned with the Dukes of Burgundy and Brittany, nominally his vassals but *de facto* independent princes. Any French attempt to deal with them, however, was opposed to English interests. Acquisition of the long Breton coastline would give France a precious strategic and tactical advantage in the Channel, especially as the prevailing winds are south-westerly. Attempts to push back the frontier with the Burgundian Netherlands (which ran within eighty miles of Paris) also threatened English control of Calais and the Straits of Dover, and, ultimately, the Netherlands cloth market on which English trade depended.

As we have seen, Edward's alliance with Burgundy had been a main cause (or perhaps result) of the breach with Warwick; and had paid off for him in 1471. Once re-established as King of England, Edward set about turning the alliance into a more positive channel. An attack on France from all fronts was planned; by Edward, the dukes of Burgundy and Brittany, even by an Italian army provided by the pope, the King of Naples and the Duke of Urbino. In 1475 Edward mounted his great invasion, involving some eleven thousand men, the largest English army sent to France in the fifteenth century.* The intention was serious: to vindicate his claim to the French throne; but the result was a fiasco. The Italian project, as might have been expected, came to nothing. More important was the fact that Duke Charles of Burgundy was more interested in the politics of the Rhineland, and was in fact engaged in besieging a town called Neuss, near Cologne. Edward, therefore, was forced to make the best of a bad job; after marching his army into France he concluded a treaty at

* *See* J. R. Lander, *Crown and Nobility, 1450–1509* (Edward Arnold, 1976), cap. 9.

Picquigny in which he agreed to call off the invasion in return for a down payment of £12,000 and an annual one of £4,000.

Picquigny was a truce, not a formal peace. Edward had kept his claims to the French throne; and had he lived longer he might well have tried again to assert them. (The notion that he was too wily to involve himself in foreign war and that the 1475 expedition was just a device to get money is without foundation.) After Picquigny, however, things went badly. Duke Charles was killed in battle (by the Swiss) in 1477. His heir was an unmarried girl of twenty, the Duchess Mary. Louis took the opportunity to conquer the Duchy of Burgundy itself; more important, the French had ripped away the protective band of Burgundian territory in which Calais had been ensconced and now controlled the Channel coast as far north as Boulogne.

Mary's position was saved by her marriage to the Archduke Maximilian, heir to the Holy Roman Emperor and to the Habsburg territory in Austria. Edward flirted with the idea of dismembering the Burgundian Netherlands in alliance with France, and then with another invasion of France in alliance with Burgundy; in the end he did neither and turned his attention to Scotland. There the enmity between King James III and his nobles encouraged the notion that a puppet regime could be established under James's brother, the Duke of Albany. These hopes collapsed; but an expensive war fought in 1481–2, largely by Richard of Gloucester, at least recovered Berwick (which Margaret of Anjou had ceded to Scotland in 1461, in return for Scottish support for the fugitive Henry VI). Berwick was vital for the defence of the borders; and still more as a symbol of the balance of power between the two kingdoms.

Richard III was in no position to do very much in foreign affairs, except to defend his throne. His diplomacy denied Henry Tudor his base in Brittany after the attempted invasion in 1483; but Henry took himself instead to France, where the government welcomed him on the principle of sheltering one's enemy's rival. So it was that French troops landed with Henry in Milford Haven. Once he was king, however, the logic of events outweighed whatever gratitude Henry may have felt. The immediate problem was Brittany itself, and French attempts to control it after the death of its duke, Francis II, in 1488. As in Burgundy eleven years before, the heir was a girl, Anne; and the French promptly claimed that she should marry their young king, Charles VIII. Henry sent an army to shore up the anti-French party. But resistance crumbled. Anne married Charles. The whole southern coastline of the English Channel, from Brest to Boulogne was now in French hands.

In 1492 it was Henry's turn to plan a major invasion of France. The fact that his army was not ready until the end of October, right at the close of the campaigning season, might suggest that he was never serious in his intentions; but it might just be due to the usual administrative muddle. In the event, like Edward before him, he allowed himself to be bought off, at the Treaty of Etaples. This was to the mutual advantage of Henry and the young French king, Charles VIII. Charles wished to win military glory in Italy, and was glad to be rid of fears for his northern border; Henry, naturally, found it convenient to encourage these romantic dreams. It was in fact the Italian mirage and the international complications that followed from it which removed any temptation the French may have had to extort revenge from England for the Hundred Years War; more immediately it spared Henry VII the awkward decision of what to do if the French had concentrated on the less glamorous but more lucrative conquest of Flanders. As it happened Charles actually abandoned, in 1493, some of the gains made in 1477.

Even so, Henry had to pursue an active diplomatic policy in case a new anti-French alliance should one day be necessary. The natural alliance with Burgundy was with some difficulty preserved. The difficulties rose primarily from the activities of Edward IV's sister Margaret, now Dowager Duchess of Burgundy and her readiness to support Yorkist pretenders, true or false. Henry retaliated with economic sanctions; Burgundian support of Perkin Warbeck was countered by a trade embargo in 1493–4. In 1496 a comprehensive treaty was concluded, the *Intercursus Magnus*, which attempted to facilitate trade by ironing out jurisdictional conflicts about commercial affairs: both sides, moreover, promised not to support each other's rebels. This did not prevent fresh commercial and political disputes. From 1497–9, the Eng-

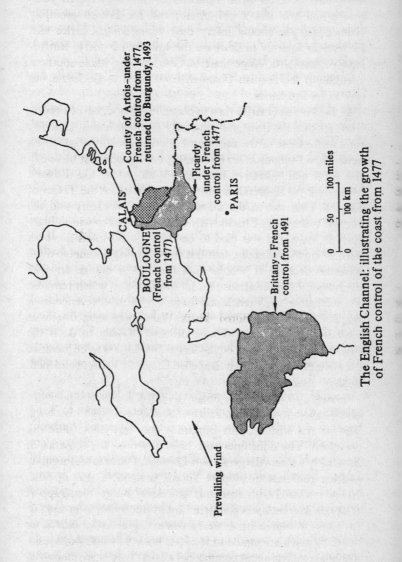

County of Artois—under French control from 1477, returned to Burgundy, 1493

Picardy under French control from 1477

CALAIS

PARIS

BOULOGNE (French control from 1477)

Brittany – French control from 1491

Prevailing wind

The English Channel: illustrating the growth of French control of the coast from 1477

100 miles
50 100 km
0

lish Merchant Adventurers transferred their mart from Antwerp to Calais because of commercial disputes. In 1506 similar sanctions were used when Philip, Duke of Burgundy, Margaret's grandson (she died in 1503), flirted with the support of yet another Yorkist pretender, Edmund de la Pole, Earl of Suffolk.

Burgundy was a possible but unreliable ally. Fortunately for Henry, the emergence of a new Spanish monarchy, with the marriage of Ferdinand, King of Aragon, to Isabella, Queen of Castile, made possible another counter-weight to France, and a natural ally. The alliance was not to be concluded without endless haggling. A marriage between a Spanish princess and an English prince was first mooted in 1488; eventually in 1501 Catherine of Aragon arrived to marry Prince Arthur. Both of them were fifteen years old. Unfortunately Arthur died next year, and the whole process of negotiation began again, this time for a marriage between Catherine and Arthur's younger brother Henry. Both sides blew hot and cold in turn as it suited them; and a further complication was the need for a papal dispensation to let Catherine marry her brother-in-law. This provided a splendid chance for Pope Julius II to delay proceedings and extract a political *quid pro quo*. The marriage did not in fact take place till 1509, when the young bridegroom had already become King Henry VIII. Nobody could have foreseen that these squalid but essentially mundane affairs would give rise to one of the great turning points in English history.

Another royal marriage with unexpected long-term consequences was that of Henry VII's daughter Margaret to King James IV of Scotland. James had for a time supported Warbeck; and, as a headstrong young king with a passion for military glory (which could only be satisfied in England), was always a potential danger. French concentration on Italy, however, was leaving Scotland dangerously isolated. Negotiations started in 1499, and the marriage was celebrated in 1503. The immediate consequence was quite satisfactory. James maintained peace for the rest of Henry VII's reign, though in 1513 he could not be prevented from invading his brother-in-law's country (with fatal consequence for himself and for Scotland) while Henry VIII was campaigning in France. The unlooked for long-term result was, of course, the union of the crowns through the succession of Margaret's great-grandson to the English throne in 1603.

Henry's last years were full of fevered diplomatic activity. The death of Isabella of Castile in 1504 produced enmity between Henry's allies. Philip of Burgundy claimed the throne of Castile in the right of his wife, Isabella's daughter; his father-in-law Ferdinand of Aragon tried to stop him. Meanwhile in the maelstrom of Italian politics alliances were formed, re-formed and dissolved with unprecedented speed. Henry had to work hard to retain his own alliances; and in spite of his activity found himself isolated in 1509 when by an extraordinary turn of events, the leading continental powers united in a grand coalition against Venice. Such a league could not last long, and represented no long-term threat to England. But Henry died before the alliance split, with England still uncomfortably isolated.

Henry had worked hard at diplomacy, and achieved solid results; protection against rivals, a reasonable trading agreement with the Netherlands, and an (irregularly paid) pension from France. Above all he had avoided involving England in a major war; and, in Bacon's words, 'though his reputation was great at home yet it was greater abroad'. He was helped by the general suspicion of France among all her neighbours, and the attractions of an English alliance; and also (through the marriage of Maximilian and Mary of Burgundy) by the involvement of the Germanic states in western European affairs; by contrast during the early fifteenth century the political game had centred almost entirely on the triangle of England, France and Burgundy. But the major factor was an uncovenanted bonus: the attraction which Italy had for Charles VIII and later kings of France. Had they devoted themselves to extending French power in the Netherlands, or to an all-out attack on England, Henry's life would have been more difficult and his finances less healthy.

As it was, English kings were spared large military expenditure. No attempt was made to create a professional army or even to improve the efficiency of the militia system. The growth of French power in the Channel did involve a development of the royal navy. When Edward IV came to the throne the crown possessed just one ship, the *Grace Dieu*, bought from John Taverner of Hull. Naval force depended on ships hired from private owners like Warwick and Sir John Howard. Edward was building up the royal navy in the seventies and owned about fifteen ships by 1481. The number fell away under Henry VII, so that there were only five by 1509. Two of these, admittedly, the *Sovereign* of 1487–8 and the *Regent* of 1490, were much more heavily gunned than their predecessors, more specifically warships rather than adapted merchant ships. Henry also contributed the first permanent establishment for the royal navy, the dry dock at Portsmouth. Nevertheless, especially in view of the threat from the French acquisition of Brittany, his achievement was not impressive. Henry, like his predecessors, had to rely mainly on hiring merchant ships, just as for his armies he had to rely on what noblemen and gentlemen would raise.

Edward IV and Henry VII had, between them, provided a large measure of peace at home, and kept England safe without involving the country in major war (except in Scotland in 1481–2). As I have stressed, good fortune entered into this to a large extent; the good fortune that the upheavals of 1470–1 and 1483–5 were so short lived (it could easily have been different if the battles of Barnet, Tewkesbury and Bosworth had been less decisive), and that there was no problem about the succession in 1509. Good fortune, as well as skill, preserved England secure from invasion. It is tempting to exaggerate the achievement of the two kings, especially by exaggerating the propensity for civil war of fifteenth-century noblemen and taking the events of the 1450s as the norm rather than the outcome of very exceptional circumstances.

The monarchy, after all, possessed considerable assets; in the fact that there was a government machine, an established bureaucracy which could keep going, albeit at reduced efficiency even during civil war and dynastic change; in ingrained habits of obedience and reverence; and in a commonsense dislike of the dangers to life and property which civil war inevitably posed. Henry VI's reign had drawn heavily on these assets; but they were not yet exhausted.

Within this context, then, Edward IV and Henry VII's achievement was to play the game of politics with skill. Their reigns differed, both because of different circumstances and of different personalities; Edward extrovert, personable, approachable, in some respects impulsive, a man of moods, rather like his grandson Henry VIII; Henry VII, more withdrawn, tight-lipped, non-commital, suspicious. Both, however, took pains about their business; both worked hard, first to secure their throne against rivals, and secondly, to build up the resources of the crown. Both acquired a good deal more self-confidence in the second half of their reigns; Edward from 1471, Henry from about 1500. Both then proceeded to create potentially dangerous situations: Edward by treating his nobility unfairly in building up the power of his family; Henry in going beyond the conventional decencies in his treatment of many of his subjects, especially the more prominent among them.

Neither was able to revolutionize society and neither tried. The councils in Wales and the north were more a part of the general game of power politics in those parts rather than far-reaching institutional innovations. There was no fundamental change in methods of administering justice. Nothing was done, or perhaps nothing yet could be done about the judicial privileges of many of the nobles, notably in the Welsh Marches and in the north. Little was achieved in the general suppression of riot and disorder. Not much more could be done in Ireland than to prevent a drift towards complete defiance of the English crown. Nothing was done to modernize recruitment for the army, and surprisingly little, given the foreign policy situation to improve the Navy. Cautious conservatism, the adaptation of existing institutions, was, in contrast to what followed, the hallmark of these two reigns. Historians tend to prefer institutional change. In this case it was probably impossible; and perhaps not even desirable.

ECONOMIC AND SOCIAL DEVELOPMENTS

A real, if fragile return to political order had taken place by 1509, though involving no fundamental change in the nature of politics. The years since 1450 had also seen important changes in more fundamental matters; the first signs of an end of that peculiar situation of a shortage of people and an abundance of land which had characterized the early fifteenth century; a considerable expansion in foreign trade; and, perhaps most important of all in the long run, the introduction of the printing press. All these developments really bore fruit in the sixteenth century; England changed far more dramatically in the half century after 1500 than in that before it. Nevertheless, the mid-point is a useful place to take stock.

Before 1450 the question was whether population was stagnant, or in continued decline. From about 1470, at least, there is no question of decline; instead, it seems likely that the population had already begun to rise, though not yet to such an extent as to force up food prices and agricultural rents faster than wages, as was to happen later. The interpretation of prices is extremely difficult, and no more direct evidence of population trends is available. But it looks as if a steady and continued upsurge of population only began in the 1510s; only then does a growing population begin to put pressure on scarce resources, leading to that disastrous decline in the standard of living of the poorer half of the population which was to characterize most of the century.

One major problem of the sixteenth century which did become acute as early as the 1480s, however, was the creation of rural distress through landlords amalgamating peasant holdings into larger units, and also converting arable land into pasture. The lord chancellor in a speech prepared for Parliament in 1483 mentioned the dangers of 'enclosures and emparking . . . drawing away of tenants and letting down of tenantries'. An act was passed in 1490 against the depopulation of the Isle of Wight, citing the obvious military dangers, and a more general one the same year against 'pulling down and wilful waste of houses and towns . . . and laying to pasture lands which customarily have been used in tilth'.

This was probably the result of a rise in wool prices since the 1450s, due partly at least to the recovery of trade, which encouraged landlords to convert to pasture. It probably aroused particular concern because the years 1481–4 saw very high *short-term* grain prices, due to freak bad harvests, which suggested to statesmen that conversion had gone too far, and that the country would soon be unable to feed itself.* In fact the concern was short lived; both wool and grain prices fell in the 1490s, and little was done to enforce the 1489 act. The years 1500–4 saw abysmal harvests and high grain prices; but wool prices were low. Not until grain and wool began to rise together, from about 1512, was general concern shown. Parliament was legislating about conversion in 1515, and in 1516 More's *Utopia* was published; 'the sheep that were wont to be so tame' were now become 'so great devourers and so wild that they eat up ... the very men themselves'. In 1517 a commission was established to investigate breaches of the law since 1488, and a large number of prosecutions followed. These early developments have attracted a good deal less attention among historians than have the similar events of the 1540s, although the rate of change was probably greater in the earlier period. This is partly because the 1540s produced more contemporary comment (in turn, the result of the growth of the printing press, and the social conscience of many early Protestant writers), partly because, by then these problems were superimposed upon a situation of continuously rising grain prices and of currency disorder which were fortunately absent in the early years of Henry VIII.

A good deal of this new pasture land was devoted to sheep; and part at least of its products went towards the boom in cloth exports. These had continued depressed in the 1450s and 1460s; between thirty and forty thousand cloths a year, compared with nearly sixty thousand in the 1440s. Recovery began in the second half of Edward IV's reign; and in 1481–2 they first topped the sixty thousand mark; they then fluctuated at around this level, to begin another surge in about 1500, and to reach ninety-three thousand in 1507–8. At its fastest, in the middle years of Henry's reign, this represented a growth of about 2·4 per cent a year, as fast an expansion as that of the much better-known 1540s.†

* Peter Bowden in J. Thirsk (ed.), *Agrarian History of England and Wales, 1500–1640* (Cambridge, 1967) pp. 637, 841; T. H. Lloyd, '*The Movement of Wool Prices in Medieval England* (*Econ. Hist. Rev.*, Supplement No. 6, 1973).

† Figures in E. M. Carus-Wilson and O. Coleman, *England's Export Trade 1275–1547* (Oxford, 1963). Their findings are conveniently summarized in a diagram in Carus-Wilson, *Medieval Merchant Adventurers* (2nd ed.,

There are obvious political factors in this development; especially better foreign relations. The privateering war with France and bad relations with Burgundy had disrupted trade in the 1450s; the re-invigoration of the Burgundian alliance, the treaty with the Hanse in 1474, were all favourable to trade. So, probably, was Henry VII's diplomacy, especially with the Netherlands treaty of 1496. This is not to say that either Edward or Henry were 'middle-class kings' who had turned their backs on the irrelevant trappings of feudal militarism and had realized that their country's destiny lay on the high seas. Their real interest was more immediate; to foster shipping for defence purposes, and to increase the yield of the customs. Next to this perhaps, might be set the need to secure the loyalty of the towns, especially London. When Henry VII felt secure enough, at the end of his reign, he was perfectly willing to treat London capitalists as harshly as he treated the nobles.

One by-product of English commercial activity ought to be mentioned here, though its immediate importance was small. About the end of Edward IV's reign Bristol merchants began fitting out ships to explore the Atlantic, in search of the mythical island they called 'Brazil'; they may in fact have reached Newfoundland, possibly even before Columbus reached the West Indies in 1492, but they did not publicize their activities, presumably to reap the benefit undisturbed from whatever they might discover.* In 1496 a Genoese sailor, John Cabot, who had probably heard something of these voyages from Bristol, approached Henry for official backing for a voyage across the Atlantic to China. (The bits of land already discovered being assumed to be either the extremities of Asia, or odd islands which could be got round.) Henry had turned down a similar suggestion from another Genoese, Columbus, some years before. This time he decided to chance his arm; it was, after all, a cheap piece of speculative investment which might provide enormous divi-

---

1967) pp. xxii–iii. J. D. Gould, *The Great Debasement* (Oxford, 1970) pp. 118–33.

* See D. B. Quinn, *England and the Discovery of America, 1480–1620* (1974), part 1. There had been considerable trade with Iceland in the mid-fifteenth century.

dends. Unfortunately on his first voyage in 1497, Cabot only reached Newfoundland. He was given a pension of £20 a year for his pains, and set out once again on a voyage from which he never returned. There were other attempts to reach Asia by the western route, including some by Cabot's son, Sebastian; especially as the discovery of Hudson's Bay gave hopes that a way had at last been found round those inconvenient desolate lands which stood between England and the riches of China. But the immediate result was nothing more than the unglamorous exploration of Newfoundland fisheries by Bristol seamen. With Henry VII's death interest in exploration lapsed. Whatever grandiloquent ideas his son may have had of English power, the concept of world empire was not among them.

Commercial prosperity probably contributed to the boom in church building and church decoration at this period. For the most part this was firmly traditional; though Henry VII's tomb at Westminster, by the Italian Pietro Torrigiano, represents a striking breakthrough to the classically based realism which flourished in Italy. Henry's court, in fact, was a centre of Italianate classical influences. An Italian was employed as the king's Latin secretary, so that diplomatic correspondence might not be soiled with post-Ciceronian barbarisms. Another Italian, Polydore Vergil (in England as papal tax collector) wrote the first history of England to show much sophistication in its handling of sources. The royal children apparently learnt Greek and moved Erasmus to conventional plaudits.

Classical education was gaining ground in the country at large. The earliest English humanist schoolmaster is normally reckoned to be John Ankwyll, the first master of Magdalen College School at Oxford, which was founded in 1480. The first specifically humanist foundation on a large scale was John Colet's St Paul's School in London in 1509. The concept that servants of the state should have had a literary education was gaining ground. Edmund Dudley, Henry VII's fallen minister, was to complain in 1510 that 'the noblemen and gentlemen of England be the worst brought up for the most part of any realm of Christendom, and therefore the children of poor men . . . are promoted to . . . the authority that the children of noble blood should have', a sentiment which, with decreasing justification, was to be a platitude for the next fifty years. There was considerable foundation of colleges at the universities; most notably, by Henry's mother, Lady Margaret Beaufort, who founded St John's at Cambridge, substantially refounded Christ's, and endowed chairs in divinity at both universities. Her interests were primarily in rather traditional theology; there was no university equivalent to St Paul's School, of a college specifically founded on humanist principles, until Bishop Fox (Henry's old minister) founded Corpus Christi College in Oxford in 1517. But long before that in 1496 or 1497 Colet had been applying humanist principles of criticism in his exposition of St Paul's Epistles at Oxford. What had been primarily a diversion for literary men, little more than a stylistic affectation, had become a means of advance in theological and philosophical thought.

Even more important than these intellectual developments was a small-scale business recently established in Westminster by William Caxton. The use of the printing press in Europe is usually taken to date from Johann Gutenberg's use of movable type in about 1450. Similar experiments were being made elsewhere; and the press may be seen as a response to the increasing literacy of fifteenth-century Europe. But printing was slow to spread to England. Caxton was the master of the English Merchant Adventurers at Bruges in the 1460s. He went in for translating works from French as a hobby, with the encouragement of Duchess Margaret, Edward IV's sister. He had imprudently promised copies of his translation of the Trojan histories to several people, and blanched at the scribal labour involved. He therefore learnt printing at his own expense, and produced the *Recuyell of the Historyes of Troye* as the first English printed book, at Bruges in 1475. This is according to his own account; we may also guess that as a shrewd businessman with literary tastes he realized that printing could be profitable and pleasant (like all early printers, Caxton also played what would now be the separate role of publisher). In 1476 he began his press at Westminster (rather than London – court patronage by men like Earl Ryvers was important). His example was soon followed, at Oxford in 1478, at St Albans in 1479 and in London in 1480. By 1500 some

360 books are known to have been printed in England, and, of course, foreign printed books, including editions of the classics, which English printers neglected, were also becoming available

Even these small beginnings made books far more widely available than they had been earlier. In the long run print was to make possible the large private library, running, by the end of the sixteenth century, into several thousand books; even relatively modest gentlemen could, if they liked, get hold without too much trouble of libraries of about five hundred books, the sort of total which, in pre-print days, had only been available to wealthy enthusiasts like Duke Humphrey or Bishop Grey of Durham. Not that everything which was published suddenly became available overnight. Bookshops were rare, and their stocks extremely limited. Most of it was firmly traditional. Caxton's own taste, for instance, was for tales of adventure which reflected the ethos of chivalry. He also had great success with the *Golden Legend*, a vast accumulation of wonder stories of the saints. A good deal of early printing was strictly utilitarian; church-service books, books of legal practice and so on. Nevertheless, when all these qualifications are made, it had become possible to buy works by Erasmus and Luther at Oxford at about 4*d.* or 6*d.* a copy in 1520. At about a day's wages for a craftsman, this was hardly cheap, but at least it brought books into the purview of the merely comfortably off rather than of the wealthy only, with far-reaching consequences for that religious faith so eloquently symbolized by Henry VII's great building at Westminster.

Chapter Five

RELIGIOUS LIFE ON THE EVE OF THE REFORMATION

We have so far neglected one very important part of life: the spiritual. In our secular age it seems natural enough to concentrate on man's painful attempts to feed and clothe himself, and to organize society to minimize violence. Economics and politics are the fundamental issues; all else is top-dressing. This order of priorities would not have been intelligible in the fifteenth century, or, indeed, three centuries later. Men may frequently have been lax in their religious duties, may sometimes have scoffed at the church's doctrines or regarded the pretensions of priests with scepticism. Nevertheless, they were locked into a system of belief in the supranatural by the brute facts of life; a hazardous, unpredictable world could only be understood in terms of the operation of possibly arbitrary spiritual forces. Far from superstition being imposed upon people by an unscrupulous clergy, it was the people themselves who tended to push religion into what we might consider the realms of magic, and to interpret religious phenomena in a grossly materialistic way. So much so, in fact, that when with the Reformation a form of religion was introduced which was less easily adapted to a superstitious interpretation, one result was, apparently, an increase in 'unofficial' magic; in sorcery, witchcraft, divination, astrology and so on.*

How far was this thirst for the spiritual in fact met by the Catholic Church? How far, even before the Reformation, was that monolithic institution beginning to crack, its own spiritual life so lukewarm, its wealth and worldly pretensions so blatant as to undermine its credibility as a divine institution? These are diffi-

* See Keith Thomas, *Religion and the Decline of Magic* (Weidenfeld & Nicolson, 1971, Penguin 1973).

cult questions, and a confident answer would be a mark of shallow judgement. The difficulty is not so much the commitment of historians to Protestantism or Catholicism, although for centuries theological blindness befuddled the issue. That obstacle has disappeared now that most historians have ceased to be Christians, and Christians themselves have taken to treating each other more charitably. More important is the question of hindsight, the historian's knowledge of the Reformation, and his tendency, therefore, to see the fifteenth century in terms of the background to the Reformation. This is inevitable since the Reformation has to be explained. But of course contemporaries knew nothing of what was coming. To most of them the existing structure of the church was unquestioned and apparently immutable. If they attacked a corrupt clergyman, grumbled about a tithe assessment or questioned a sermon, they were not necessarily expressing premature Protestantism or implacable anti-clericalism. The problem is not to show whether or not there was dissatisfaction with the church; but whether it had reached a critical level. And this is a delicate matter of judgement.

The church's troubles derived in large part from its dual role; representing God upon earth, on the one hand, and an earthly potentate on the other. It owned about a quarter of England, its leading officials were great men of the realm, its parochial structure was financed by a compulsory levy of tithe, and a good deal of its business was conducted according to strict forms of law rather than in a spirit of spontaneous charity. The resulting contradictions are vividly illustrated in the case of excommunication. Theoretically this was a dire spiritual penalty, involving refusal of the sacraments to the offender, and, unless he repented, almost certain damnation. In practice it was so often imposed for relatively trivial offences (disobeying church courts over tithe or will disputes, for instance), that many offenders treated it so lightly as not to bother to have it rescinded when they could easily do so. So, too, the friction which necessarily entered into the relations of landlord and tenant, of tax collector and tax payer, generated tensions which could be usefully exploited by the church's opponents.

The church was its own major critic. The pulpit poured out denunciations of clerical indolence and ignorance, lasciviousness and self-seeking. It was no anti-clerical layman, but John Myrc, the early fifteenth-century author of a handbook for parish priests, who wrote that 'in modern times far more priests have gained promotion by adulation and simony than by uprightness of conduct and learning'. The vivid paintings of the Last Judgement in parish churches showed priests and prelates prominent among the damned dragged screaming off to Hell's mouth.

The church was an international institution, with jurisdiction distinct from that of the secular authority; all questions involving marriage, legitimacy and the probate of wills, for instance, were matters for the church courts. So, too, the principle of 'benefit of clergy' for which Archbishop Becket had died, that clerks were not to be subjected to penalties by a secular court, was still in force; convicted 'clerks' (who might be for practical terms laymen who had acquired 'minor orders' or even merely the tonsure which denoted, in theory, an intention of taking up the clerical life) were handed over to their bishop, to be imprisoned in the episcopal prison until sufficient fellow clerics would swear to their belief in their innocence; not hanged like common offenders. The ecclesiastical courts administered canon law, an international system in which, in spite of some national variations, ultimate appeal lay to the pope. Finally, and perhaps most important, doctrine was international, though with local variations. The English, for instance, had a particular devotion to the Immaculate Conception of the Virgin, a belief which did not become an official doctrine of the Catholic church until the nineteenth century.

An international church could co-exist with even the most powerful national monarchy, but certain strains were inevitable. (For support for both parts of this statement, consider the France of Louis XIV.) During the eleventh and twelfth centuries the papacy had made a determined effort to establish itself, not merely as the spiritual leader, but in some sense as the political leader of Europe. Its efforts had been resisted by English kings (and by others) with considerable, but not total, success. Papal influence reached a peak in the thirteenth and fourteenth centuries. Two of Edward I's three archbishops of Canterbury were papal nominees, although he had pressed the claims of his own candidates. Papal influence in the more lucrative non-episcopal benefices (canonries, and the better-endowed parish livings and so on) was considerable. Of the 68 members of the cathedral chapter of Lincoln in 1334, 25 had been appointed by the papacy, and 23 by the king.* The residence of the popes at Avignon, while England was at war with France during the fourteenth century, and the subsequent papal schism of 1378–1415, naturally led to an assault on papal privileges in England. The various Statutes of Provisors (passed between 1351 and 1389) were designed to limit papal appointments to English benefices. The Statute of Praemunire (1393), appeared to forbid any exercise of ecclesiastical jurisdiction or appeal to Rome which had not been sanctioned by English law

Had Praemunire been consistently applied the English Reformation would have occurred a hundred and fifty years earlier than it did; but its application was spasmodic, a useful weapon for the king in marginal disputes about jurisdiction, rather than an affirmation of English independence of the See of Rome. In fact relations between king and pope were regulated by a sensible system of compromise. With only occasional exceptions cathedral chapters elected the king's nominee to bishoprics, and the pope confirmed the choice. Henry VII began the practice of appointing Italians to certain English bishoprics; most notoriously, to Worcester, which had four non-resident Italian bishops in succession between 1497 and 1535. But this was an indication of royal strength, not weakness. The Italians were appointed as a reward for looking after English interests at Rome. In fact the crown's control of the church had grown enormously since the fourteenth century. By 1444 not one of the Lincoln chapter had been appointed by the pope.† Papal involvement in the routine business of the English church had been reduced to granting dispensations (eg, licences to hold two 'incompatible' benefices) and the receipt of money. The bulk of this comprised a portion of the first year's revenue of the more lucrative benefices. These 'annates' and services' were worth, in the early sixteenth century, about £5,000 a year.‡

* R. W. Southern, *Western Society and the Church in the Middle Ages* (Penguin, 1970) p. 164.

† *Ibid.*, p. 467.

‡ J. J. Scarisbrick, 'Clerical Taxation in England, 1485–1547' (*Journal of Ecclesiastical History*, 11, 1960).

It would be wrong to think of the pre-Reformation papacy too much in terms derived from modern Roman Catholic practice. The doctrinal position of the papacy was a good deal less clearly defined before the Reformation than after it. During the fifteenth century there were several competing views of papal power. The Great Schism had strengthened the view that general councils were superior to the papacy, especially when it appeared that the deposition of obdurate rival popes was the only way to end the schism. The role of the papacy was undefined; definition was only in fact accomplished at the Council of Trent (1545–63) and the modern doctrine of papal infallibility only proclaimed very much later, in 1870. Of course conciliar views were anathema to fifteenth-century popes, and were vigorously condemned. The proposition that the pope was the successor of St Peter and vicar of Christ was used as a test of orthodoxy in heresy trials. But papal supremacy was not one of the more fundamental tenets of the faith of a fifteenth-century Catholic in the way that it would be for a post-Reformation one. Even Sir Thomas More who, in 1535, was to die for refusing to acknowledge the royal supremacy in ecclesiastical affairs, had earlier regarded papal primacy as of human rather than divine institution.

To most men their bishop must have been almost as remote as the pope. The bishops lived in pomp as great lords, attended Parliament, and enjoyed incomes to match. The richest of them, the Bishop of Winchester, had about £3,800 a year, roughly equivalent to the income of the Percy earls of Northumberland. Many poor curates, manfully doing the duties of absentee rectors or vicars, got under £5 a year. The more important bishoprics were usually rewards for loyal service in the royal administration. The lord chancellorship was normally held by a bishop until 1529, the keeper of the privy seal was almost always a clerk, and usually a bishop. There was little time left over from politics for diocesan matters.

In fact only a minority of bishops were involved at any one time in central government, though these tended to occupy the best sees. But even non-political bishops were primarily administrators and judges rather than spiritual leaders. Paradoxically this resulted from the lack of financial centralization. The parish priest derived his income from tithes and dues paid by his parishioners, and was appointed to his benefice (a revealing word, which stresses the profits rather than the duties of the post) not by the bishop, but by whoever owned the right of presentation; a monastery, a cathedral chapter, or, most frequently, a layman, who might be the king or the local lord of the manor. Monasteries, cathedral chapters and so on were all independent property-owning corporations. The bishop, therefore, did not control the career structure of his clergy. Most of them owed little to his favour, and expected little from it; if they were ambitious they could look to other patrons. To the clergy, the bishop was not so much a leader as an external figure who had certain jurisdictional rights only. Any dealings of bishops and clergy (beyond moral suasion) had to be conducted in legalistic fashion; and often not very effectively at that.

Indeed, because of a host of competing jurisdictions (several churches, for instance, claimed independence of episcopal visitation through papal grants) the more energetic the bishop, the more likely he was to be involved in complicated legal disputes. Not surprisingly a training in canon law was a better guarantee of ecclesiastical advancement than training in theology, while pastoral gifts counted not at all (few, if any, bishops had active parochial experience). Many dioceses were in any case much too large for any personal attention by the bishop; the see of Lincoln stretched from the Thames to the Humber, and Lichfield from Stratford-on-Avon to Preston. When in 1428 Archbishop Kempe proceeded on the first visitation of Richmond archdeaconry for a hundred and fifty years the dismayed clergy bought him off. Even the bishop's disciplinary officers, the archdeacons, were frequently absentees. The church's disciplinary machine was extremely cumbersome and often inefficient, and clerical abuses could persist unchecked for years.

The best-known abuses were those of the monasteries. Visitors commissioned by the crown to report on their condition seized with joy on the evidence of corruption; principally drunkenness and sexual indulgence of various sorts. These charges are sometimes found in less biased sources; for instance, our knowledge of the behaviour of the monks of Thame, in Oxfordshire in 1526, comes from correspondence between the diocesan bishop and the Abbot of Waverley, who had been sent to investigate the complaints. The Abbot of Thame was accused of scandalous relations with a boy, running the estates in the interests of his favourites, letting buildings decay, keeping too many servants and too good a table. He also let women into the monastery, and failed to prevent his monks (many of whom showed total ignorance of the monastic rule) enjoying themselves in the town.

This sort of scandal is entertaining, but not typical. The monasteries as a whole were not dens of iniquity. The trouble was rather that the scandals and defects which might be expected in any institution were not counter-balanced by many very striking examples of spiritual exertion. The high ideals of a movement are soon dissipated. It becomes established, set in its routine. Its leaders are selected for their statesmanship rather than for their heroic virtues. They begin to ask 'What is practical?' rather than 'What is right?' In the case of the monks, their great age of expansion in the eleventh and twelfth centuries had been too successful. There were too many monasteries, and they were too rich. An increasing number of monks was involved in administration, especially estate-management; and frequent absence disturbed that even, regular tenor of life which is the Benedictine ideal. The head of the house, the abbot or prior, had long since ceased to live with his monks, and kept state in a separate establishment, with his own servants, his own meals, more like a great lord than a mere monk. The life of the ordinary monk had got easier over the centuries with 'the gradual relaxation of the prescriptions of the Rule in the matter of fasting and abstinence, a relaxation not in itself directly evil but indicative of a weakness of faith and spiritual purpose, and, most corrosive of all, the introduction of private ownership and privilege and exemption in numberless occasions of daily life'.*

The slow unwinding of the contribution of the religious orders to the church could only be countered by a major upheaval within the existing orders, or by the creation of new ones. This had not happened since the early thirteenth century, when the new orders

---

* David Knowles, *The Religious Orders in England* (Cambridge, 1959) vol. 3, p. 463.

of friars had arrived in England, more outgoing in their vocation than the monks, dedicated less to the life of worship, prayer and meditation in cloistered seclusion, more to preaching and ministering to the world, especially the urban poor. As with the monks, the original idealism of the friars was largely spent long before the fifteenth century. The dedication of the Franciscans to a life of absolute poverty had passed away. (Indeed, those who clung to St Francis's own ideals found themselves condemned as heretics.) But compared to the monks, they were still poor and depended on donations, which they worked hard to get; an ironic perversion of the original ideal of freeing themselves from the shackles of property. Chaucer drew a neat distinction between the monk, 'a lord full fat' with his well-made boots and sleek horse, and the friar, always ready to give an easy penance in return for a 'good pittance'. The monastic temptation was idleness, cushioned by wealth. The friar, by contrast, had to be shrewd, sharp, on the make. His life necessarily involved competition with the parish clergy, an influential group in a good position to get their own back by spreading tales of the friars' iniquities.

In this gloomy situation there were some exceptions; the Franciscan 'Observants', who sought to return to the spirit of St Francis, flourished with royal patronage from 1481; the Bridgettines of Syon, established at Syon, near Richmond, by Henry V in 1415, and sufficiently new and exclusive to maintain a high standard of monastic life; and the Carthusians, an austere order which had kept its purity by resisting the temptation to expand numbers. Significantly these three were the only monastic groups to put up much resistance to the imposition of the royal supremacy on the church in the 1530s. The religious orders, were hardly a spiritual inspiration, except to a small minority.

More important was the parish. It is difficult to talk of a 'typical' parish. There were fundamental differences between the ways that priests were paid which could affect the whole structure of the parish. In some cases the parish priest was a rector, who was entitled to the tithes of the parishioners. In others, the 'rector' might be an institution, generally a monastery, and the parish was served by a vicar, entitled only to a part (and the lesser part) of the tithe. Rector or vicar might be non-resident; holding another benefice, working in the royal or episcopal administration, studying at the university. In these cases his duty would be performed by a badly paid, often ignorant, curate. Non-residence did not mean, as is often imagined, complete spiritual neglect. The sacraments were always available. But the ability of the curate to instruct the people was often abysmal, and there was a startling contrast between what parishioners paid, in tithe, and what was actually spent on their spiritual ministration in the form of stipend.

This haphazard system produced enormous disparities of income. The Earl of Northumberland's uncle got £73 a year as rector of Spofforth in Yorkshire; the average West Riding rector had £20 a year, the average vicar £9. Curates were often paid under £5. There were, in fact, far too many clergy; about twenty thousand of them, or one for every 125 people (the modern ratio, including clergy of all denominations is 1:1,300).* There was a real clerical proletariat, even a 'reserve army of unemployed' from which parishes could sometimes take on extra priests for peak periods like Easter. Sometimes priests behaved in the way that this Marxist analogy would suggest. In 1531 fourteen curates and chaplains attacked the bishop of London's palace, and went on to assault the bishop himself and his officers at St Paul's.

Priests were not formally trained. There was admittedly an examination of competence; but it tested little except ability to read Latin, and was frequently evaded. Of 311 Gloucestershire clergymen examined by their bishop in 1551, 10 could not repeat the Lord's Prayer, 39 could not find it in the Bible and 34 did not know its author.† Admittedly this may be untypical; and the test may be unfair, set as it was by a new-broom, reforming Protestant bishop. But it does show that the clergy were inadequately equipped to refute heretics, whether Lollard or Protestant, from the Scriptures.

* R. B. Smith, *Land & Politics in the England of Henry VIII: the West Riding of Yorkshire 1530–46* (Oxford, 1970) p. 93; Peter Heath, *The English Parish Clergy on the Eve of the Reformation* (London, 1969) pp. 22–3; A. R. Myers, *English Historical Documents, 1327–1485* (Eyre & Spottiswoode, 1969) p. 615.

† F. D. Price in *Transactions of the Bristol and Gloucestershire Archaeological Society* (1938) vol. 60, p. 101.

All this may suggest that dissatisfaction with the church round about 1500 is easily explained; the simple answer is corruption, a decline of standards. But it is difficult to be sure that there was in fact a decline; and an alternative explanation may be that higher standards were now being demanded by an increasingly educated and spiritually-aware minority of laymen, and that greater vigilance was bringing imperfections to light. Popular dissatisfaction may result from rising expectations, rather than from an absolute decline in standards.

The rise of lay piety is best appreciated by comparing the situation around 1500 with the eleventh and twelfth centuries, the great age of monasticism. Then the laity had been almost entirely rural, uneducated and unquestioning. The vocation of the greatest saints had been to the monastic life, the cultivation of the corporate worship of God in institutions cut off from the world, rather than to the cure of souls, the pastoral care of the people. Change was already apparent by the thirteenth century; the growth of towns produced a more questioning, a more critical laity, demanding some degree of personal involvement in the affairs of the church. There was an increase in devotional activities in the parish church, morning and evening prayers, the expectation (not always fulfilled) of an occasional sermon. The popularity of the friars was partly based on their ability to preach. Religious associations of all sorts multiplied; guilds enrolling members of a particular craft, fraternities devoted to a particular saint and so on. The parish church itself became the focus of corporate pride. The upkeep of the nave was the parish's responsibility, exercised through elected church wardens. The great rebuilding of parish churches in the fifteenth century was carried out largely by lay initiative. The popularity of service books and manuals of private devotion among the early products of the printing press epitomizes the demand among certain of the laity for a sophisticated understanding of their religion, and a meaningful involvement in it.

Of course, a passionate interest in religion would be confined to a minority of laymen. Most would probably view the more awesome teachings of the church with some scepticism, at least as far as they themselves were concerned; a commonsense belief that everything would be all right in the end was widespread, to judge, at least, by the number of sermons preached against this comfortable doctrine. (Sudden death was a popular theme with preachers.) We do not in fact know how many attended weekly mass, as they were bound to do, and how many fulfilled their obligation of annual communion. But certainly many of them who did attend spent their time chatting irreverently during the service, or stayed outside the church until the elevation of the host A manual for pious laymen, published in 1530, assumed that anybody saying prayers in his bedroom would be mocked by his fellows ('O Jesu bone, oh good lord Jesus, what hear I now') while he did so.

There were, too, very different sorts of lay piety. Much the commoner was the exuberant cult of particular devotions, of saints, of images, of pilgrimages; a cult which could very easily degenerate into mechanistic superstition. On the other hand, lay piety might take the form of the cultivation of the inner spiritual life, the attempt at a direct communion with God, through concentration on the person of Jesus. Both movements sprang from the same theological need; the reconciliation of God as the righteous judge with the individual's hope of personal salvation. The first approach involved appeasing God by a multiplicity of good works or of liturgical acts; or an indirect approach, through the intercession of the much more human (and, by implication, more merciful) Virgin and saints. The second stressed the Jesus of the Gospels, the suffering man full of compassion for his fellows, the ethical teaching of the Sermon of the Mount; Jesus the friend 'who speaks inwardly to the soul', rather than the mighty judge. From this viewpoint the practices of their fellows would appear useless, offensive, even downright blasphemous. The growth of lay participation had saddled the church with a potentially explosive contradiction.

The grosser superstitions were officially discouraged. But in practice they were often encouraged by clergy who had themselves an unsophisticated view of the spiritual life, or had a vested interest in pushing the fame of their particular shrine or image. This applied right through the church up to the popes themselves whose finances were swelled by the crowds attending

Rome in 'jubilee' years. The cult of the saints filled an obvious psychological need and their services ranged from the supra-natural to the purely mundane or even vindictive. Derfel Gadarn, whose image was venerated at Llandderfel in north Wales, was said to rescue souls from purgatory; he also cured diseases of men and beasts or, if offended, might even cause them. The massive *Golden Legend*, the most comprehensive collection of stories of the saints, was one of Caxton's great publishing successes; it ran through seven printed editions between 1483 and 1527, and its contents provided the staple of many parish sermons.

The cult of the saints was most strikingly shown by the popu-larity of pilgrimages. Crowds flocked to the miraculous statue of the Virgin at Walsingham. Henry VII sent his standard to Wal-singham after the defeat of Lambert Simnel; Catherine of Ara-gon went there to give thanks for the great victory over the Scots in 1513. Motives for pilgrimages were often mixed, as they had been for Chaucer's pilgrims. Wolsey visited Walsingham in 1517 to fulfil a vow, 'and also to take air and exercise which may correct the weakness of his stomach'. Erasmus went there to scoff, but bore witness to its continued popularity: 'the most frequented place throughout all England, nor can you easily find in that island a man who ventures to reckon on prosperity unless he yearly salutes [the Virgin] with some small offering according to his ability'.

The objection of the more 'spiritually-minded' to these practices was that they encouraged a mechanical, calculating attitude. 'They calculate the time to be spent in Purgatory down to the year, month, day and hour as if it were a container that could be measured according to a mathematical formula', wrote Erasmus. Good works, equally quantified, could be entered on the other side of the balance sheet. Officially the church rejected calculations of this sort. In practice, by putting a 'price-tag' on particular devotions, it encouraged them, especially in relation to penance. Earthly penance might consist in saying so many prayers or going on a particular pilgrimage. An 'indulgence' (often in practice a money matter) might remit either an earthly penance or a purgatorial one. So, too, there was a general assumption that a multiplicity of masses would reduce the soul's time in purgatory.

And the pains of purgatory were depicted, even by such urbane writers as Sir Thomas More, as hardly less than those of hell itself. 'If ye pity any man in pain, never knew ye pain comparable to ours; whose fire so far passeth in heat all the fires that ever burned upon earth, as the hottest of all those passeth a feigned fire painted on a wall.'

Provision of masses for the dead was therefore a major concern. About a quarter of all charitable bequests in the 1520s was for prayers for the dead. A great army of chantry priests, clergy with no benefice or cure of souls, existed to cater for the demand. Learned bishops as well as anxious laymen tried desperately to reduce their chances of purgatory; Bishop Skeffington of Bangor arranged two thousand masses for himself. There seems in fact to have been a difference of opinion about the best tactics; whether, like Henry VII or Cardinal Beaufort ('10,000 masses to be said for my soul as soon as possible after my decease') to take heaven by storm, or whether a series of masses said regularly over a long period of time was preferable. The church had fallen foul of Jesus's injunction against using 'vain repetitions as the heathen do', and of this the more spiritual, introspective, gospel-reading Christians, whether clerical or lay, were all too aware.

One major attack had already been launched on the institutional church in England; that of John Wycliffe in the 1370s and 1380s. Wycliffe, an Oxford academic, had attacked several orthodox doctrines, but most notably that on the eucharist; where the church taught that the body of Christ was present in some real, objective sense in the consecrated host, Wycliffe held that it was only so spiritually. This difference reflected a fundamentally different way of thinking about religion. The orthodox belief was that the church was a divine institution, offering through its sacraments and teaching a sure means by which all men could be saved. To Wycliffe, on the other hand, the church consisted of all those who had been predestined by God to salvation; no human action could alter this, and the institutional church was largely irrelevant. The papal primacy was a trap (after all, the pope need not be among the predestined), and the practices of clerical celibacy, of monasticism and so on, were all pointless.

Wycliffe had developed his radical critique within the framework of orthodox academic debate. But his doctrine had an appeal to laymen, especially in its denial of the importance of the sacraments and therefore of the clergy. Somewhat inconsistently, much of what Wycliffe had taken away from the church, he gave back again to the lay state; it was the duty of the civil power to reform the church, and (the better to reduce it to evangelical poverty) to confiscate its property. The traditions of the church were of no value. The Scriptures were the repository of all truth, and clergy had no especial claim to interpret them. Scripture reading by the laity should be encouraged, and to this end the Bible was translated into English. For a time Wycliffe got some powerful lay support; most notably that of John of Gaunt, Duke of Lancaster, who saw in him a useful ally against clerical pretensions and papal claims. Gaunt, however, dropped him when his progress to heresy made him an embarrassing ally politically, and Wycliffe's following in Oxford was rigorously repressed by the ecclesiastical authorities with the connivance of the state. The popularity of one aspect, at least, of Wycliffe's teaching can be seen in the demand by the Commons in the 1410 Parliament for the confiscation of church lands. A botched rising in 1414, however, sealed the fate of Lollardy (as Wycliffe's doctrine was now called) among the respectable classes, and it was driven underground.

By the end of the fifteenth century Lollardy was largely a movement of certain artisans and tradesmen; rigorous, independent-minded, prepared to run great risks for their beliefs (at least seventy-four were put to death between 1414 and 1520*), but neither politically nor intellectually influential. Its most notable result in England had been to hinder attempts at reform of the church by making bishops extremely sensitive to anything that might smell of heresy; the panic caused by Lollard translation of the Scriptures may explain why England, alone among major Catholic countries, had no officially approved vernacular translation. Lollardy contributed to anti-clericalism among the laity; and Lollard groups provided a means by which newly introduced Protestantism could establish a hold among the people at large rather than merely among intellectuals alive to new trends in

* Figures calculated by Margaret Aston (*History*, vol. 53, 1968, pp. 87-8) from J. A. F. Thomson, *The Later Lollards 1414-1520* (Oxford 1965).

Germany. Since its doctrines were more radical than anything that the 'official' church in England taught, even after the Reformation, the most notable legacy of Lollardy may well have been the popular Puritanism of the Elizabethan period. But once the chance had been lost at the beginning of the fifteenth century, it seems clear that Lollardy could not in itself have brought about a thorough-going change in the English church.

More insidious than outright heresy, however, was the existence of a critical attitude within the church, stressing the simplicities of the Gospel, as opposed to the infinite elaboration of current practice, Jesus's commendation of a contrite heart, rather than the multiplication of works of penance, poverty rather than possession, spirit rather than law. Oddly enough, in spite of a tradition of English mystical works in the fourteenth century, fifteenth-century England produced no outstanding book of popular devotion, while the best known of continental works of this sort, Thomas à Kempis's *Imitation of Christ* circulated mainly among a small group of Carthusian monks.* The lay spirit was, however, vividly illustrated in Langland's *Piers Plowman* at the end of the fourteenth century. Langland combined savage satire of the churchmen of his day from parish priest to pope (though lawyers are also a major target) with a vision of Christ's passion and the redemption of mankind. *Piers Plowman* remained popular throughout the fifteenth century; and in the Tudor period 'Piers' was conscripted into the Protestant ranks as a popular figure of social and religious satire.

To describe these developments simply as a manifestation of 'lay piety' is in a sense misleading. The English mystical writers were clerics, à Kempis was an Augustinian Canon; even Langland was in minor orders. Nor was the concentration on the simplicities of the Gospel in any way heretical. Langland's message was a commonplace in medieval sermons; so were his attacks on corrupt clergy. Nevertheless, it was 'lay' in the sense that the cultivation of the individual's soul, the concentration on the central Christian mysteries, tended to by-pass the corporate life of the church, and to suggest that a

* R. Lovatt, 'The Imitation of Christ in Late Mediaeval England' (*Trans. Roy. Hist. Soc.*, 5th ser., vol. 18, 1968).

good deal of its liturgical life, a good many of the doctrines it encouraged, and certainly the whole legalistic and bureaucratic framework within which it was run, was unnecessary and even actively harmful. It provided the individual with a criterion by which to judge the church as an institution; and in this sense represented the *possibility* of lay revolt against clerical domination.

Printing enormously increased the potential impact of these developments. The Protestant propagandist John Foxe rightly hailed the printing press as an ally. 'Hereby tongues are known, knowledge groweth, judgement increaseth, books are dispersed, the scripture is seen, times compared, truth discerned, falsehood detected ... Through printing the world beginneth now to have eyes to see and hearts to judge.'* Of course, he was writing later in the century. As we have seen, the initial impact of the press was limited. But, although the majority of early printed books were orthodox works of piety, printing did make it easier to circulate subversive works such as those of Luther. The availability of books made possible a critical comparison of texts and an attempt to search out the original meaning of the author, which was as important in Biblical studies as in classical ones.

This fusion of the tradition of lay piety with the potentially corroding effects of modern scholarship aided by the press may be seen in the movement known to historians as 'Erasmianism'; not because there was a conscious school of followers of Erasmus, in the sense that there were Lutherans and Calvinists; but because Erasmus typifies a number of widespread assumptions among an educated elite.

Erasmus himself was a Dutchman, an Augustinian canon sent by his order to Paris to study theology; the result was a hatred of the monastic life, at least as it was commonly practised, a contempt for the scholastic philosophy of the universities, and a love of classical literature. In a series of popular works Erasmus mounted a scathing attack on the ecclesiastical establishment of the day; contrasting its hypocrisies, evasions and distorted sense of priorities with the stark simplicities of the Gospels. His was an essentially optimistic, reductionist view of Christianity. Tradi-

* Quoted Heath, *The English Parish Clergy*, p. 193.

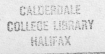

tional Christian thought emphasized original sin, man's degradation, and redemption through Christ's sacrifice. Erasmus's assumption was rather of human dignity, of man's potential for good. 'It is fitting first that we come to recognize the inclinations of the mind, and that we realize that none of them is so violent that it cannot be restrained by reason or redirected towards virtue.' Scripture pointed the way to the good life; and that way was the fulfilment, not the negation, of the best of the ancient authors.

This humanist, ethical interpretation of Christianity sapped the importance of the sacraments, and therefore of the church which was, ultimately, a sacrament-dispensing institution. One of Erasmus's English friends, Richard Whyteforde, a monk of Sion (in most respects an orthodox Catholic) believed that if laymen could not attend both mass and sermon on Sundays, they would do better to miss mass. The Scriptures, Erasmus wrote, should be freely available to all so that 'all women might read the Gospel and the Epistles of Paul . . . the countryman might sing them at his plough, the weaver chant them at his loom, the traveller beguile with them the weariness of the journey'. Their meaning should not be distorted by quibbling and logic-chopping. Hence Erasmus's hostility to academic philosophers. 'You will more easily escape from a labyrinth than from the snares of the Realists, Nominalists, Thomists, Albertists, Occamists and Scotists.' St Paul, by contrast 'divided and defined with very little logical skill', but taught instead the virtues of charity.

Erasmus was a familiar figure in English intellectual circles, paying several visits between 1499 and 1519, including a three-year stay at Cambridge working on his edition of the New Testament. Among his English friends was John Colet, who, in a revolutionary series of lectures on St Paul at Oxford, had broken with the tradition of looking for layers of allegorical meaning in Scripture, and had concentrated instead on a straightforward exposition of the meaning. Colet later, as Dean of St Paul's, delivered in 1512 a violent attack on the condition of the clergy; he also founded St Paul's School (see above, p. 131), dedicated to the Erasmian concept of 'faith and letters', and placed it, significantly, under the control of a city company rather than of the cathedral chapter. Another close friend was Sir Thomas More, author of *Utopia* and future lord chancellor. (The Latin title of Erasmus's *Praise of Folly*, *Moriae Encomium*, is a pun on his name.) *Utopia* is essentially a paean to an orderly, educated society, despising luxury and display and organised on lines of primitive communism; if that was the teaching of natural reason, how much more, by implication, should Christians, their reason reinforced by their master's teaching, aim at the same sort of satisfying simplicity.

The examples of Colet and More illustrate how misleading it is to think of 'Erasmianism' as a monolithic doctrine. When Colet preached against the sins of the clergy, it was not because he wished for lay control of the church, but rather to improve clerical standards so as to preserve the clerical state. If More despised hypocritical, arrogant or unlearned monks, he nevertheless spent four years in the London Charterhouse wondering whether to become a Carthusian, published a refutation of Luther which involved a detailed defence of Catholic doctrines, and preferred to lose his life rather than acknowledge Henry VIII as head of the English church. Erasmianism was not a definite movement, but rather a set of intellectual values; a tendency to question, a belief that the waters were clearest at the spring, that intellectual elaboration distorted rather than illuminated. It did not in itself imply heresy. Indeed, Erasmus's optimistic humanism was poles apart from the central Protestant doctrine that man, because of his utter depravity, could be saved only by faith in Christ, and that faith was a free gift from God, unrelated to the merits of the individual; Erasmus saw this clearly, and engaged in violent controversy with Luther on the subject.

Nevertheless, the appeal of Erasmianism was obvious; on the one hand to the laymen, seeking for a more personal, inner-directed interpretation of religion; and also to younger clerics, brought up on the new, more direct approach to classical literature, impatient of what they saw as the arid complexities of traditional theology, perhaps more generally inclined to a rather glib dismissal of accepted ideas. Although the humanist approach was anathema to Protestantism, it none the less helped to prepare the way for the acceptance of Luther's ideas among an influential circle of intellectuals. This was partly through the stress on the return to the sources, which fitted very well the Protestant emphasis on the individual's interpretation of Scripture as the sole standard of belief. In part, the Erasmian contribution was more indirect; by emphasizing the crimes and follies of the church, by stressing the need for free criticism, by its scornful attitude to current superstitions, by its hostility to a sacramental view of religion, it helped to discredit the existing orthodoxy; and in doing so opened the way for a new, equally un-humanist doctrine. In spite of Erasmus himself the paths of many sixteenth-century intellectuals lay through humanism to Protestantism.

Martin Luther first openly challenged Catholic orthodoxy with his 95 *Theses* published at Wittenberg in Saxony in October 1517. Of course, many of his views had been held by others before him, including the central doctrine of justification by faith. His ideas were not yet fully developed and indeed, with rather more sympathetic understanding, might still have been incorporated into a Catholic framework. Nevertheless, the *Theses* represent the first coherent 'Protestant' alternative to Catholicism. His works were circulating in England by 1520; a year later they were being publicly burnt, while the king himself was preparing a refutation. Groups of Protestant intellectuals were meeting at the White Horse Tavern at Cambridge; and from there they spread to Oxford, imported, ironically enough, by Cambridge men brought over to staff Cardinal Wolsey's new college.

The first major achievement of English Protestantism was William Tyndale's translation of the New Testament published at Cologne in 1526. A native Protestant tradition had been founded, largely as yet among intellectuals and a few merchants and seamen with German connections; but, through contact with Lollard groups, and, still more, through the diffusion of printed English scriptures with their explosive denunciation of hypocrisy and formalism in religion, bound to build up a considerable following in England as it was doing everywhere in western Europe.

Alongside this degree of spiritual dissatisfaction, there existed a more straightforward resentment of clerical wealth and privilege. There was nothing new about this; such feelings were inherent in the powerful situation in which the church found itself.

'Anti-clericalism' of this kind was not in itself heretical (the hostility to wealthy clergy combined with a rather simplistic doctrinal orthodoxy was characteristic of the early Robin Hood ballads) but was obviously a useful weapon in the hands of opponents of the church. Issues flared up from time to time, and the particular one round about 1500 was concerned with benefit of clergy, the privilege by which clerics escaped the more extreme penalties of the secular law.

Matters came to a head in the Hunne affair. Richard Hunne was a Londoner who, in 1511, refused to pay a 'mortuary' fee to his rector on the death of his baby son. The rector sued him in a church court; and Hunne retaliated by suing the rector in a secular court for 'praemunire'. He was then arrested for heresy, on the bishop's orders; and was later discovered hanged in the 'Lollard's Tower' at St Paul's, which was used as an ecclesiastical prison. Three ecclesiastical officials were then accused of murder, but the church prevented their being brought to trial, and proceeded to burn Hunne's body as a heretic.

The result of this conflict of jurisdiction was an attack on 'benefit of clergy' in the 1515 Parliament. A friar, Dr Henry Standish, defended Parliament's right to legislate on this issue, to the fury of his fellow clerics; Standish was near to being tried for heresy himself. In the end, through the king's intervention, a compromise was patched up. Parliament withdrew its bill to restrict benefit of clergy, and did nothing to regulate mortuary fees; but, by implication, its right to deal with this sort of issue had been vindicated.

The Hunne case shows how a relatively minor matter could generate a major constitutional crisis. It also shows the deep hostility between Londoners and their bishop. The Londoners believed that Hunne was being vindictively prosecuted as a heretic purely for exercising his rights in the secular courts; the bishop believed that a London jury was bound to be 'so maliciously set in favour of heresy, that they will ... condemn any clerk, though he is as innocent as Abel'. The House of Commons obviously felt strongly about clerical jurisdiction; and this anti-clerical feeling would obviously be a useful weapon if the king chose to use it. But traditionally it had been royal policy to use

Parliamentary resentment to strengthen the king's hand when bargaining with the pope, not to press matters to schism.

The church faced formidable difficulties by the early sixteenth century. The growth of an educated lay piety, the great impetus given it by the printing press, the general scepticism about many of the devotional practices which the church encouraged or at least tolerated, the widespread resentment of church wealth, church privileges, church power; all this provided material which could be shaped into a revolutionary movement. Luther's protest was to weld these somewhat disparate trends into a rival system – partly by providing a theologically and psychologically satisfying justification for an alternative, partly by forcing Catholicism into a defensive posture in which many previously tolerated opinions, such as those of Erasmus, became anathema. There is little doubt that, through most of Europe for the thirty years or so from about 1525, Lutheranism and its various derivatives were far more intellectually and emotionally satisfying to the religiously committed than Catholicism. Catholicism was not yet able to measure up to the competition; to the enthusiast its disadvantages were too apparent, the opportunities it offered for zeal were too few. In short, it was too much associated with the established abuses of the status quo.

All the same, none of this made the Reformation in England inevitable. Conservatism, too, has its strength which it is easy for a historian, intent on isolating the elements of change, to ignore; the strength of familiarity, of solidity, of the distrust of novelty and its dangerous consequences, social as well as religious. It is very easy to overstate a case, and we need some cautionary counter-examples. Against all the evidence of parochial anti-clericalism involved in disputes about tithe, for instance, we must also set the occasions when peasants turned out in rebellion led by their parish priests. Sometimes, as we shall see, these revolts were in defence of church interests. But the clergy are often found leading riots about taxation, enclosure, rack-renting and so on. They were, after all, part of the village community, in a position of natural leadership; they often came from the same social origins as their parishioners; they were involved, as cultivators, as well as receivers of tithe, in the economic life of the village, and while this produced tensions, it also produced solidarities and shared interests.

Protestantism was to triumph in England, initially at least, because it was given a lead from above by the king; and that lead came, not because the general problems of church–state relations were irreconcilable (they had been settled often enough before, and were to be again, in Catholic Europe), but because of the peculiar and, in the circumstances, insoluble difficulty of Henry VIII's matrimonial status; a matter which could not have been foreseen. Without that lead, it is impossible to know what would have happened in sixteenth–century England. Almost certainly there would have been a powerful Protestant party; very probably powerful enough to exploit particular political situations and bring about civil war. But there is no guarantee that a Protestant rebellion would have succeeded; any more than it succeeded in France, which had at least as impressive a record as England of anti–clericalism, strain between king and pope, and successful assertion of royal rights against papal pretensions. In that sense the developments we have been describing did not make the Reformation inevitable. But we should also look at this the other way round; these developments made Henry VIII's break with Rome possible. One could, indeed, put the case more strongly; it was the dedication to Protestantism of a small but influential minority working on the discontents of their fellows which transformed what might otherwise have been a minor jurisdictional affray into a thorough–going change, not merely in the beliefs of the English people, but ultimately in their way of life.

Chapter Six

HENRY VIII

WOLSEY'S MINISTRY

Henry VIII's reign was to be one of the most momentous in English history. But there was no hint of this during its first twenty years – over half the reign. These were years of domestic peace and tranquillity, which promised a steady development under a respected and able king who was the undoubted master of the country. Used all his life to the deference due to a royal prince, heir to the throne since the age of ten, king at seventeen, Henry seemed totally self-confident, a man who could afford to be carefree and trusting, where his father had had to be prudent and suspicious.

Henry's court experienced one of those occasional periods of sunlit dignified classical ease to which later more crisis-hardened generations look back nostalgically. With no urgent domestic problems, with an inheritance which, if less munificent than is sometimes thought, was, thanks to his father, at least free from debt, Henry could afford the luxury of concentrating on the princely pastimes of diplomacy and war; war which was for the most part conveniently fought abroad. In any case routine business (and more than that) could be left in the competent hands of the ever-willing Thomas Wolsey. Henry's days were filled with hunting and jousting, music and dancing, poetry and intelligent talk, interspersed with agreeable flirtation; for all of which the king had considerable talent. He was also an accomplished musician, both performer and composer, and a passable amateur theologian.

Of course, the even tenor of court life was sometimes disturbed. Wolsey's high-handedness led to muttering discontent, among the influential as well as among the people at large. Difficulties increased during the twenties; Parliament was sticky about taxation, the people jibbed at paying an un-parliamentary 'amicable grant', and foreign policy began to go disastrously wrong. From 1527 the problem of Henry's marriage and the succession came to dominate politics against a background of bad harvests which pushed grain prices to record levels. But, when all such qualifications are made, there had been no such period of internal tranquillity and confidence in the monarchy since the reign of Edward III in the mid-fourteenth century. The experience may have done a good deal to buttress Henry's position to that apparent impregnability with which he faced the storms of his later years.

Henry's reign began with a bid for popularity which produced the execution of his father's old ministers, Empson and Dudley, on trumped-up treason charges; two of the worst cases, in fact, in a reign which was to see a good many others of the same sort. Nobles, London merchants and others were released from the financial bonds in which Henry VII had entangled them. The young king's thoughts turned to 'virtue, glory and immortality' on the battlefield, which would knit together the upper ranks of society in a common and, it might be hoped, profitable adventure.

New dockyards in the Thames hummed with activity as some eighteen new royal ships were launched between 1510 and 1515, including the mighty *Henry Grace à Dieu*, or 'Great Harry'; eleven others were bought abroad. To put this in perspective, we must remember that Henry had only inherited five ships from his father. Europe was scoured for naval stores, for body armour, for new-fangled handguns, for gunpowder for great cannon, like the 'Twelve Apostles' ordered from Hans Poppenruyter at Malines; and a set of Italian merchants at court grew fat on the proceeds.

The great coalition against Venice from which England had been excluded at the end of Henry VII's reign soon cracked. By 1512 Henry was able to ally himself with Spain and the papacy against France, and promptly despatched an army to invade France from the Spanish border and reconquer the old English possession of Gascony. The result was a disaster which ended in the mutiny of the starving troops, and their unauthorized and ignominious return home. Next year, however, Henry did rather better, personally leading an army of thirty thousand men along the northern border of France, winning, with the help of the Emperor Maximilian, the Battle of the Spurs, and capturing the town of Tournai; all a less impressive achievement than it seemed, since the main French army was away in Italy, but enough for the moment to feed Henry's dreams of military glory and redeem previous failure. Even Niccolo Machiavelli, far away in Florence, was impressed, and concluded that the English must have kept in remarkably good training in the years of peace. Tournai remained in English hands, at enormous expense (Henry went as far as to build a wholly new citadel) until 1519; a striking monument to royal vainglory.

The king's achievement was, however, upstaged by his lord treasurer, Thomas Howard, Earl of Surrey. While Henry was in France his brother-in-law, James IV of Scotland, had decided to fulfil his treaty obligation to Scotland's old ally by invading England. The English, however, were prepared. The Scots were soundly beaten; and James himself was killed in the battle at Flodden, just inside the border in Northumberland. Henry's exultant queen sent him the news. 'You see I can keep my promise to send a king's coat. I thought to send himself to you, but our Englishmen's heart would not suffer it.' The victory was important, because James's heir, James V, was only one year old, and the regency went to his mother, Henry's sister Margaret. The immediate danger from Scotland had been removed. In the circumstances Henry could hardly refuse to give Howard back his father's old dukedom of Norfolk, which had been withheld since the Howards, father and son, had backed the wrong side at Bosworth.

Henry's success sealed the fortune of the rising star among his councillors, Thomas Wolsey. Wolsey, son of an Ipswich butcher, and ex-bursar of Magdalen College, Oxford, had entered the royal service in 1507. By 1513 he was one of the leading councillors and organized the supply services for the French expedition; and it was through his unglamorous service in organizing travelling mills and ovens that Henry was able to cut a dash in the European battlefield. For the next sixteen years English government *was* Wolsey, or so it seemed. A Venetian ambassador noted that by

1519 he no longer said, 'His majesty shall do so and so' but, 'I shall do so and so'. Appearances were deceptive. The final decision was always the king's, and Henry was always liable to listen to others. Wolsey could never quite be sure of his position. Nevertheless, day-to-day running of affairs seems to have been left to him; and the events of his ministry clearly bear the stamp of his personality.

Wolsey's contemporaries admitted his ability, but agreed too in stressing his 'pride covetousness and ambition'. His admiring gentleman-usher George Cavendish described his daily procession to Westminster Hall 'all in red in the habit of a cardinal ... the best he could get for money'. The Great Seal of England was carried before him, then his cardinal's hat 'by a nobleman or some worthy gentleman right solemnly, bareheaded'. 'Two great crosses of silver', carried by the 'tallest and comeliest priests that he could get within all this realm', two other silver 'pillers' and a 'great mace of silver gilt' also preceded him. His enemies compared this splendour with his lowly origins, his 'greasy genealogy' as the poet John Skelton so elegantly put it.

He accumulated power, wealth and honour on an unprecedented scale. He dominated the machinery of government. As lord chancellor from 1515, he headed the judicial system. From 1514 he was Archbishop of York; and held his archbishopric in plurality with another major bishopric (Bath and Wells, Durham and Winchester successively), a combination unprecedented for over four hundred years. As papal legate *a latere*, from 1518, he was the pope's special representative, exercising almost dictatorial powers over the church, and outranking the elderly Archbishop of Canterbury, William Warham. He enjoyed several ecclesiastical revenues, including those of the abbot of St. Albans. All told, he was reckoned to have an income of £35,000 a year, about six times as much as the richest peer, and a similar sum to what Henry VII had from the crown lands; while the estimate is probably exaggerated it is not wildly out.* He became a cardinal in 1515, and made much of his rank as a prince of the church. When his hat arrived from Rome the citizens of London (still snarling from the Hunne case) were turned out to do it

* A. F. Pollard, *Wolsey* (Longman, 1929) pp. 320–5.

honour, and its reception was compared to the 'coronation of a mighty prince'.

Wolsey had an enormous appetite for work, and the confidence to shoulder a huge burden of responsibilities. He was a conscientious servant of the king, and even, in a mechanistic way, of God. Cavendish remarked that many would be surprised to know that he normally heard two masses a day, and that he 'never went to bed with any part of his divine service unsaid, yea not so much as one collect'. He defended his pomp as necessary to create respect for authority; his silver 'pillers and pollers', he told one critic, were better used 'to maintain the commonwealth by them as I do' than melted down and given away 'to five or six beggars'. Nevertheless, even in an age always eager to be impressed by ceremony and show, Wolsey overdid things, and what was fitting for a king was slightly ludicrous in his case. Foreign monarchs flattered Wolsey grossly as a diplomatic ploy, and we may suspect that Wolsey's self-glorification was not unwelcome to Henry himself. The more the cardinal made himself ridiculous with crosses and pillers and mules decorated with crimson velvet, the more noblemen, prelates and civic dignitaries gagged at his arrogance, the easier it was for the king to shrug off responsibility for awkward decisions and to pose as the indulgent father of his people. There is an amused and rather calculating condescension about Henry's attitude to 'his' cardinal.

Much of Wolsey's attention was devoted to foreign affairs; and English foreign policy in his time has been endlessly debated. There are two main questions involved; the respective roles of the king and of Wolsey; and the aims of foreign policy, whether there was a genuine desire for peace, or whether the quest for military glory was dominant. Neither question admits of a clear-cut answer; and both involve a detailed study of events which would be out of place in a book of this sort; especially since alliances were so fluid, and princes so busily engaged in double-dealing (at the least), that the story is a complicated one. The following outline can only be a crude simplification.

After the successes of 1513, English policy seems to have been pacific. Peace was made with France in 1514, and Henry's younger sister Mary married the French king Louis XII. Louis died almost immediately, worn out, the bawdy suggested, by the demands of his young wife. But, in spite of the militaristic propensities of the new king, Francis I, peace was precariously preserved, and in 1518 both Henry and Wolsey basked in the glory of a grand European treaty signed in London.

Hopes of universal peace were shattered, however, when the Emperor Maximilian died; his grandson Charles, who had recently become King of Spain, was elected as his successor. Charles therefore ruled the Netherlands, Spain, Austria, Naples and as well as exercising, as emperor, some power at least over Germany as a whole. This posed, or seemed to pose, a threat to France. Moreover, the three monarchs of western Europe, Henry, Francis and Charles, were all young men, jealous of each other, and touchy about their military reputations. War was all too likely; and England could hardly help but choose to ally with one or the other.

In spite of the extravagant pomp of the meeting between Henry and Francis in 1520 (the 'Field of the Cloth of Gold') the choice was for alliance with Charles V. Charles represented the traditional Anglo-Burgundian, anti-French alliance. Henry still called himself King of France, and still had hopes of emulating Henry V. The Netherlands, in any case, were the major market for the cloth industry. Other advantages have been suggested; the possibility that Charles would help Wolsey to the papal throne, or that he would marry Henry's daughter Mary (his only living legitimate child). But although the marriage was agreed in a treaty of 1521, it never seemed likely, since Mary was only five and Charles twenty-one, while recent research has tended to discount the notion that scheming to become pope was one of Wolsey's main preoccupations. The explanation of the imperial alliance is probably a good deal simpler; that it was the natural one which England might be expected to pursue unless there was strong reason not to.

The treaty was followed by two military expeditions to France That of 1522 did little except burn villages, in the vain hope that the French would be provoked to fight. The 1523 expedition was more ambitious; the English invasion was to be part of a coordinated attack, which was to include a thrust towards Paris by imperial troops from the Netherlands and another invasion from the Spanish border. But no advance decision was taken about the objective of the English force; whether to attack Paris, or merely to besiege and capture Boulogne. Henry himself argued very cogently for Boulogne; but then allowed himself to be converted by Wolsey to the more ambitious scheme. The result was disastrous. Although military and financial sources had been squeezed hard to prepare an impressive army, the planning was bad. There were not enough guns to besiege Boulogne. There were not enough carts to provision a dash for Paris. Everything was left too late; the army was not ready until September, though the campaigning season normally ended in November. Henry gave orders that the army was to stay in being through the winter, but the soldiers slunk off home, since, 'It was no worse being hanged in England than dying of cold in France.' Wolsey became the target for general abuse. The contrast to his achievement in 1513 was painful.

After this the English, disgruntled at the lack of imperial cooperation, did little to forward the war, and began secret negotiations for peace. In 1525, however, Francis I was spectacularly defeated by imperial troops at Pavia, in Italy. Francis himself was captured, and France seemed available for the asking. Henry proposed an immediate attack; Henry would become King of France, Princess Mary would marry Charles, and their heir would one day rule an empire extending from Ireland to Hungary and Spain to Frisia, with the whole of America thrown in as a bonus. But rebuffed by Charles, and too short of money to raise an army, the English had little alternative but to make peace. In 1526 Henry went further by supporting the League of Cognac, which was meant to re-establish French power of Italy and prevent imperial hegemony over that vital peninsula.

In all this there is little evidence of an English policy of 'balance of power'. Throughout the 1520s Charles V was, arguably at least, the stronger power which on a 'balance of power' basis England should have opposed. Instead England supported Charles, in the hope of an imperial victory. Henry's first instinct in 1525 was not to defend distressed France, but to share out the spoils. Annoyance at Charles, the growing problem of the English succession, and the consequent need to prise the papacy free from imperial domination, are the best explanation of the pro-French policy of Wolsey's last years.

England would probably have done better by keeping aloof from continental adventures. But Henry's temperament, if nothing else, ruled this out. His whole personality, his passion for tournaments and chivalric literature, his rivalry with Charles and Francis made this unpalatable. Unglamorous involvement in the sordid politics of Scotland, as Thomas Cromwell suggested, was hardly an adequate substitute; even if in the event continental adventures turned out to be unglamorous too. In these circumstances it seems idle to wonder what Wolsey's own feelings were; he was hardly in a position to indulge them. Henry may have allowed himself to be persuaded, even in major issues of military strategy, as in 1523. But in the general direction of foreign affairs, which men tended to see in terms of the personal relations of individual monarchs, the king's prejudices were decisive.

Wolsey was more his own master in ecclesiastical affairs; and here the story is one of missed opportunities. No churchman had been in a better position to reform the English church since Lanfranc became Archbishop of Canterbury in the wake of the Norman Conquest. As legate, Wolsey's power was immense. It was as if the pope himself had come to England; he outranked any English prelate and over-rode their jurisdiction. Even religious houses which were 'exempt' from episcopal jurisdiction were subject to Wolsey. The ancient game of stymying a reforming bishop by appeal to the pope was of no effect. It was no use, either, trying to play off secular and ecclesiastical jurisdictions against each other when one man was head of both.

Wolsey talked a good deal of reform, and did nothing, except suppress some small monasteries to endow his new colleges at Ipswich and Oxford. There was a scheme to finance thirteen new bishoprics out of monastic revenues, so improving episcopal oversight by creating less unwieldy dioceses, but it came to nothing. The net result of Wolsey's activities was to decrease episcopal control; by occupying two bishoprics himself, by encouraging the appointment of non-resident foreigners, and by keeping bishoprics vacant for long intervals while he enjoyed the revenues.

Episcopal jurisdiction, temporarily in abeyance during the leg-ate's presence, could only be carried on on payment of a fee to Wolsey. Cases were transferred to legatine courts, including pro-bates of wills, for which extortionate rates were charged. The clergy was taxed heavily for secular purposes, even more heavily than laymen.

It is often asserted that Wolsey's jurisdiction disillusioned English churchmen with Rome, and made them readier to accept Henry VIII's claim to ecclesiastical supremacy. This may well be true. It might also have suggested to the more far-sighted the dangers of too close a concentration of ecclesiastical and secular power.

Much of Wolsey's hardest work was done in the king's courts. He was no institutional reformer. He drove the existing machinery hard in order to stress authority, and rode rough-shod over vested interests. As lord chancellor he presided over the court of chancery, a court concerned with civil jurisdiction — property, contract and so on. Chancery was administered by a system of 'equity', as opposed to the complex rules of the common law. In the course of the century 'equity' developed into a system as hide-bound as the common law itself; chancery was a target of seventeenth-century reformers precisely because of its slowness and subservience to precedent. But in Wolsey's time it still re-tained something of its original flexibility, as a useful means of doing right where the technical procedures of the common law had produced injustice. As a churchman rather than a lawyer, Wolsey pushed the claims of equity hard; to the disgust of the common lawyers, who believed that to invoke the subjective laws of conscience was to open the way to arbitrary judgements.

The judicial activities of the king's council, sitting in Star Chamber were exercised energetically. Riots were prosecuted, and the judicial system supervised; cases of perjury, contempt of court, and of juries which had brought in blatantly false verdicts were all dealt with. Edward Hall, no admirer of the cardinal, commended his prosecution of lords and knights for riots and maintenance so that 'the poor men lived quietly'. Indeed, he adds that when 'the poor people perceived that he punished the rich, they complained without number, and brought many an honest man to trouble and vexation'. Skelton accused Wolsey of humiliating the nobility for 'every light quarrel'. There was certainly a vast increase in Star Chamber cases; though the general expansion of litigation meant that the common-law courts did not suffer from this.

Wolsey also encouraged the poor man's traditional right to appeal direct to the council; and pressure of work led to special arrangements for poor men's cases which later developed into a formal court, the 'Court of Requests'. Ad hoc councils to deal with the Welsh Marches and the north (the latter had lapsed at Henry's accession) were re-invigorated in 1525. In all this Wolsey merely followed the precedent of Edward IV and Henry VII. He was doing what any strong ruler might be expected to do. But his energy and drive involved a vast increase in the business of chancery and the various conciliar courts; this seems undeniable from the volume of the surviving records. So great was the flood of business that, by 1528, Wolsey had in a sense to admit defeat and order that minor matters brought to the council should be referred to the assize judges.

One aspect of the enforcement of the law was the appointment of commissioners in 1517—18 to report on rural depopulation, the amalgamation of holdings, and conversion of arable land to pasture. Some prosecutions followed; there were more in 1526; and there are signs that another campaign was to be launched in 1529. As so often, Wolsey's activity here consists of spasmodic bursts of energy rather than a consistently pursued policy.

Not surprisingly, Wolsey was disliked by the nobility. This was not primarily a question of his low social origins. The church was a recognized ladder for the advancement of talented offspring of the lower classes, and (presumably because a notionally celibate clergy could not found dynasties) this does not appear to have aroused resentment in itself. What really hurt was Wolsey's flaunting of his own power, and the fact that he seemed to monopolize it. To all appearances the council had ceased to be a body in which policy was thrashed out, and had become, apparently, a collection of the cardinal's yes-men. Wolsey had cheated the nobles of the victory which they had apparently won in 1509. This was most spectacularly demonstrated in the trial and execution of the Duke of Buckingham in 1521.

The circumstances surrounding this *cause célèbre* are obscure. Buckingham was the son of that Duke of Buckingham who, in 1483, had attempted a general rebellion against Richard III. He was the richest peer in England, reputedly worth about £5,000 a year. He was in the process of building what, in the event, turned out to be the last privately owned fortified castle in England, at Thornbury in Gloucestershire. He was descended, twice over, from Edward III. He was obviously a potential danger to the dynasty, not so much while Henry was alive but in the increasingly likely event of his death without a male heir; Buckingham might well appear a more likely guarantor of peace than the young Princess Mary. He laid himself open to attack by consulting an astrologer who predicted that he would be king one day. He also derided Henry and Wolsey in his own household. 'It would do well enough if the nobleman durst break their minds together, but some of them mistrusteth, . . . and that marreth all; so that there is no remedy for us but to suffer till that a convenient time may come.'

On top of this he had taken an armed force with him to collect rents in Wales, in spite of being refused permission by the king. This was interpreted as preparation for rebellion; though the truth seems to be that Buckingham treated his tenants so badly that this was the only way to get in his rents. That made it unlikely that he could raise a successful rebellion; and there is in fact no evidence that Buckingham ever thought of doing so. Nevertheless, the result was a treason trial, presided over by the Duke of Norfolk, a verdict of guilty, and execution.

This sort of treatment kept the nobility quiet. They might grumble; but there was nothing positive they could do as long as the king supported the cardinal. Wolsey seems to have been prepared to ride rough-shod over traditional local power structures. In the north where, as Archbishop of York and (from 1523 to 1528) Bishop of Durham, he controlled an immense amount of patronage, he seems to have used it to instal his own men, largely clerical lawyers, in key positions. A half of the West Riding commission of the peace had no roots in the area; a contingent of eight influential local knights who had been on the commission in 1513 had been elbowed out by 1525. That year a special northern council was revived, as a council to 'advise' Henry's bastard son, the Duke of Richmond (then six years old), on his duties as lieutenant of the north; none of its members were peers, two-thirds of them were lawyers, and its president was the Dean of York.* In 1529 Lord Darcy, a Yorkshire peer, accused Wolsey of packing the northern council with his personal servants, 'spiritual men not meet to govern us'.

This contempt for the northern nobility was only possible because, from 1523, the threat from Scotland was neutralized by the successful maintenance of an anglophile party of Scottish lords. It was also helped by the acquiescence of Henry Percy, the fifth Earl of Northumberland, when he was kept out of the offices traditionally held by his family, the wardenships of the east and middle marches. His son, the sixth earl, also Henry Percy, who succeeded in 1527, was less cautious. He evidently stirred up one of his clients, Sir William Lisle, to create such disorder on the borders that the northern council recommended that 'the power of some nobleman continually lying in Northumberland' was needed to put a stop to it, and Northumberland was made warden of the east and middle marches. Wolsey had the last word in this trial of strength. Lisle knelt in the mud at Alnwick, and Northumberland pleaded for his life, only to be angrily rebuffed by the cardinal. The earl had to have his own client hanged; a fatal blow to his honour in the highly personalized society of the borders.†

There is some evidence that Wolsey was thinking of supervising outlying areas by some sort of conciliar system. In 1525, the same year as the Duke of Richmond's council, the council for the Welsh marches was re-organized. It was nominally under the Princess Mary, who was still a child, but like Prince Arthur and the future Edward v before her, had been sent to keep court at Ludlow; and the execution of Buckingham meant that there was a power vacuum to be filled. In Ireland the old Earl of Kildare had been succeeded by his son as lord deputy when he died in 1513. But in

* R. B. Smith, *Land and Politics in the England of Henry VIII; the West Riding of Yorkshire, 1530–46* (Oxford, 1970) pp. 153–5.

† *See* M. E. James, *A Tudor Magnate and the Tudor State* (University of York, Borthwick Papers, No. 30, 1966).

1520 Thomas Howard, Earl of Surrey (and heir to the Duke of Norfolk) was sent over as lord lieutenant, with the incidental advantage of getting him out of the way during the attack against his father-in-law, Buckingham. Surrey was soon complaining of inadequate funds; he would need six thousand men and a massive castle-building programme to bring order to Ireland, and Henry preferred to use his resources for French wars. The Anglo-Irish lords resumed their sway, though now there was an attempt to play them off against each other rather than to entrust everything to Kildare. Just possibly Wolsey was contemplating a further advance in 1529, probably some variation in the conciliar pattern, headed by the new Archbishop of Dublin, John Alen, who had been one of his ecclesiastical agents in England.* But the most important reason for the contrast to the 1530s was probably the lack of any sense of urgency; religious change was to produce a dangerous situation in which it became much more vital to restrict the political power of the nobility.

In all this there was a lack of perseverance. There were sporadic stabs at reform, but nothing like the thorough-going institutional changes of the 1530s; the revived northern and Welsh councils seem to have had little impact. This may be in part because Wolsey had too many irons in the fire. It may also be due to the lack of whole-hearted support by Henry. While the king sometimes thought of the greater nobles as potential threats to the dynasty, they were also his friends, and personal ties could counter Wolsey's policy at key points. The young Henry Courtenay, Earl of Devon, was a close friend of the king, and this is probably the reason why, in 1523, he was given important royal offices in the West Country (Steward of the Duchy of Cornwall, Warden of the Stannaries) which boosted the immense power he already had as the principal landowner of the area; and all this in spite of the fact that he was a grandson of Edward iv and potentially at least as great a danger as Buckingham had been. (In 1525 he was promoted Marquis of Exeter, and was eventually executed, in 1538, for allegedly plotting for the throne.)

Wolsey talked a good deal of reform and reorganization in the state and in the church, to little effect. Nothing came, for in-

* D. B. Quinn, 'Henry VIII and Ireland' (*Irish Historical Studies*, 12, 1961).

stance, of a thorough-going scheme of 1525, the Eltham Ordinances, to reform the royal household in the interests of efficiency and economy. But he made full use of whatever powers he had, as the king's or the pope's representative; and his natural inclination was to browbeat rather than conciliate.

This is nicely illustrated by his dealings with Parliaments. The 1515 Parliament was dismissed because of its anti-clerical agitation after the Hunne affair. The next Parliament, in 1523, was faced with a demand for a tax of four shillings in the pound. It refused, because, so it was maintained, the sum was impossible, especially as it came on top of a massive forced loan in 1522; instead the Commons offered half as much. Wolsey blustered; his suggestion that the general prosperity of the country showed that the tax could easily be paid, was interpreted by members 'as though he disdained that any man should fare well, or be well clothed, but himself'. It was left to the astute More as Speaker to retrieve the situation and arrange a compromise.

The news of Pavia in 1525 produced a sudden need for more money if the king was to take the opportunity of claiming his own in France. Commissioners were to demand an 'amicable grant' to the king, equivalent to a sixth of their goods in the case of the well off. The clergy (Wolsey came down especially hard on his own order) were to pay the equivalent of a third of their possessions. Open rebellion broke out among the cloth-workers of East Anglia and Kent, and Londoners, in spite of Wolsey's threats, refused to pay. Henry himself saved the situation by declaring that he had no knowledge of the rate Wolsey was demanding (either a downright lie, or a flagrant confession of royal irresponsibility) and allowing contributions to be voluntary.

Wolsey's general insensitivity is striking here; but so is the need of money produced by Henry's foreign policy. About £258,000 was produced in direct taxation in the first twelve years of Henry VII's reign, and this had produced the Cornish rising.* Between 1513 and 1527 something like £413,000 was raised in direct taxation, even without the amicable grant; in addition

* This paragraph relies on an unfortunately unpublished Cambridge Ph.D thesis by R. S. Schofield, 'Parliamentary Lay Taxation, 1485–1547' (1963).

£250,000 was raised and not repaid in the forced loan of 1522-3. (Back to the levels of taxation of Henry v's time, whose policies Henry VIII was trying to emulate.) Moreover, a good part of this was raised by a new method of taxation, the subsidy, which involved a direct assessment of each man's income and possessions. Henry VII had had considerable success with a tax of this sort in 1497 and 1504 (though of course the 1497 levy had provoked the Cornish revolt). But the pattern for the future was in fact set by the tax of 1513. The subsidy was to become a regular method of Parliamentary taxation; and, as the century went on, and assessments were mechanically repeated, it became notoriously and comfortably unrealistic. But in Wolsey's time the system was new, and reasonably accurate, and therefore bit hard. Even so, Wolsey was not satisfied; and in 1522, under the guise of an enquiry into military capacity, he set in train a detailed survey of the financial resources of the country.*

Wolsey's taxation was also resented because it penetrated exceptionally far down the social scale. In 1513 even those with less than £1 wages a year were supposed to pay 4d. There was no repetition of this attempt to tax the destitute; £1 a year in wages or goods worth £2 was the minimum which rendered men liable to tax in the 1520s, and on this basis something like a third to a half of the adult population of the big towns was exempt.† Even so, a greater proportion of the population had to pay taxes in the 1520s than at any later time in the sixteenth century, except possibly for the years 1544-47; and this probably accounts in large part for Wolsey's unpopularity with the people in general.

Taxation was likely to mobilize a larger and more diverse group of protesters than, say, the estate policies of a particular landlord; and the taxation policies of Henry and Wolsey had produced a situation which was common in Europe, but rare in England. Discontented aristocrats and discontented commons might easily have formed a common front. Londoners, who had suffered rigorous repression of the race riots of 1517 (directed against foreign merchants accused of battening on the wives and

* J. J. Goring, 'The General Proscription of 1522' (*Eng. Hist. Rev.*, vol. 86, 1971).

† W. G. Hoskins, *Provincial England* (Macmillan, 1963) p. 83.

livings of citizens) had to be prevented from visiting Buckingham's grave in 1521, 'reputing him to be a saint and holy man and saying he was innocent'. The 1525 revolt did not in fact bring about a noble–commons alliance. The Dukes of Norfolk and Suffolk and the Earl of Essex did their duty as the king expected, moderating the fury of the rebels and urging the government to make concessions. But the incident illustrates the dangers which Wolsey ran by attacking all vested interests simultaneously. He was unpopular on a scale unknown since the murder of Suffolk in 1450, largely because of his forceful but tactless domestic policy, and his popularity was hardly helped by the vagaries of the weather (wheat which had averaged about 6s. 6d. a quarter in 1526–7, rose to over 13s. in 1527–8, and was still at over 10s. in 1528–9).* Growing opposition might eventually have forced Henry to drop him in any case. But in the event it was not his domestic policy which brought Wolsey down, but a problem involving his two great fields of expertise, ecclesiastical law and foreign policy. The problem was, of course, that of annulling Henry's marriage to the queen, Catherine of Aragon.

The marriage had taken place in 1509, after wearisome years of negotation (see above, p. 124). Among the difficulties had been the need for a special dispensation, because Catherine was the widow of Henry's brother Arthur. But this had been duly granted by Pope Julius II. For the first ten years of the marriage Catherine was frequently pregnant; but, by extraordinary bad luck, even by sixteenth-century standards, only one child survived babyhood, and that was a girl, Princess Mary. After 1518 Catherine had no more pregnancies.

Whether a woman could claim to be queen in her own right was doubtful. On the precedent of Lady Margaret Beaufort, Henry VII's mother, she could only transmit a claim. But whether or not the young Princess Mary could become queen, it was as well to marry her off as soon as possible; her husband might help her establish her right or, better still, she might produce a son who could eventually become king. Efforts were in fact made,

* W. G. Hoskins, 'Harvest Fluctuations and English Economic History, 1480–1619' (in *Essays in Agrarian History*, ed. W. E. Minchinton (Newton Abbot, 1968) vol. 1).

as we have seen, to marry her to her cousin, Charles v. But Henry showed little enthusiasm for this sort of solution; and no attempt was made to find an acceptable husband for Mary after the imperial marriage had fallen through, even though a marriage to the young James v of Scotland, Henry's nephew, and nearest legitimate male relative, would have had obvious advantages. Instead Henry preferred the expedient of preparing his bastard son, Henry FitzRoy, to be his heir; in 1525 he was created Duke of Richmond, made lord lieutenant of Ireland and of the north, and given precedence over Mary. But this in turn was dangerous. Better than either of these dubious alternatives was another marriage for Henry himself with the chance of a legitimate son at last.

Dynastic and legal considerations were complicated by human passion. By 1526 Henry was desperately in love with Anne, the nineteen-year-old daughter of one of his ministers, Sir Thomas Boleyn. Although Henry had had affairs before (among others, with Anne's elder sister Mary), this was clearly different. Possibly, as tradition asserts, Anne refused to be his mistress; more likely, Henry had come to realize that he needed a new marriage, and that any anticipation of marriage could have dangerous consequences for the future succession. (Impatience finally overcame this high-minded resolve in 1532.) His conscientious scruples about the marriage to Catherine could be given free rein. Henry's conscience was an adaptable instrument; he managed, for the moment, to stifle the awkward fact that, since he had had sexual relations with Anne's sister, his marriage to her would be as canonically invalid as his marriage to Catherine.*

The complicated proceedings by which Henry hoped to have the marriage to Catherine annulled began officially in 1527. At this stage Henry was not denying papal power. His contention was merely that Pope Julius had had no power to dispense when there was a direct scriptural prohibition. This point was accepted at

* Henry knew about this point; indeed, ironically, he sought a papal dispensation to let him marry Anne, at the very time that he was arguing that the papal dispensation for the marriage to Catherine was invalid. The difference is that marriage to a brother's widow was prohibited by Scripture; but to a mistress's sister only by canon law. Henry held that a pope could dispense in the latter case, but not in the former. (See J. J. Scarisbrick, Henry VIII (Eyre Methuen, 1968) pp. 160–1.)

Rome; what was not clear was whether there was any such scriptural prohibition against a man marrying his brother's widow. Henry cited the words of the Mosaic book Leviticus; 'If a man shall take his brother's wife it is an impurity; he hath uncovered his brother's nakedness; they shall be childless.' In opposition to this stood the command of another Mosaic book, Deuteronomy, that it was a man's duty to marry his brother's widow if she were childless. If that were so, the prohibition in Leviticus could not be a prohibition against marriage. Marrying a brother's widow was indeed prohibited to Christians, but only by the church's law, not by Scriptural command; and in that case Pope Julius had the right to dispense the prohibition. Asking Clement VII to deny this right was asking him to deny a fundamental papal prerogative.*

Given the legal expertise available at Rome, a way could probably have been found to grant Henry's request without damage to papal prerogative, but for the complications of Italian politics. Since the battle of Pavia in 1525, Italy had been dominated by the Emperor Charles V. To papal eyes Charles was much more dangerous than Henry. There was no guarantee that he might not change his mind about the stand he had taken against Martin Luther in 1521; if he had done, he would have gained a good deal of popularity among his German subjects; and booty for himself. He was also in a position to take over the papal states, and even abolish the papacy itself. Charles was strongly opposed to the dissolution of Catherine's marriage; not only because she was his aunt (he frequently sacrificed family feeling to reasons of state), but because it symbolized the repudiation of the Anglo-Burgundian alliance. Henry's cause at Rome depended on the French being able to redress the balance of power in Italy, and so restoring some freedom of manoeuvre to the Pope. Henry went as far as to declare war on the emperor in 1528. But the practical effect of this was nullified by East Anglian cloth-workers; they protested so vociferously at the threat to their export market that, after some blustering by Wolsey, a local truce was concluded exempting the Netherlands from the war. An attack on any other part of Charles's dominions was out of the question.

* This is a very rough sketch of a complicated issue; see Scarisbrick, *Henry VIII* (Eyre Methuen), chap. 7.

The case began in England in May 1527, conducted by Wolsey as legate. The intention was probably to rush it through quietly and quickly. But on 6 May Charles's armies took and sacked Rome; Clement became the emperor's prisoner, and hopes of his acquiescence in Wolsey's proceedings were at an end. Wolsey went to France to concoct a scheme by which he would become papal vicar (and in effect, acting pope) as long as Clement was imprisoned. But this came to nothing because not enough cardinals were prepared to swallow the scheme.

Clement was playing for time, presumably in case of a French victory. Eventually Wolsey and Cardinal Campeggio ('protector' of English interests at Rome and absentee Bishop of Salisbury) were granted a commission to hear the case in England. The court sat at last on 31 May 1529 and proceeded to hear a good deal of scandalous evidence about whether or not Catherine's marriage to Arthur had been consummated. But on 31 July, before a decision had been reached, Campeggio declared an adjournment; and the effect of this was to give Clement time to revoke the case to Rome. Since French forces had just sustained, on 21 June, a final defeat in Italy, this effectively ended the chance of a quick decision for Henry.

It was also the end of Wolsey's political career. He was convicted in the court of King's Bench of exercising a foreign authority in England as papal legate, against the provisions of the statute of *praemunire*. The charge was patently true; and the fact that Henry had condoned Wolsey's action was legally irrelevant. But it was quite obvious that Wolsey's real crime was his failure on the divorce issue. His enemies took the opportunity of producing a list of accusations in the Parliament which met in October 1529. These amounted to a general indictment of royal policy for the last fifteen years. There had been too much papal interference, and this had led to a deplorable lack of respect for the papacy (a nice indication that there was as yet no thought of cutting loose from Rome). Wolsey had oppressed the clergy, misused judicial offices, neglected national defence and conducted foreign affairs without reference to the king. He had even endangered Henry's life by 'blowing upon your most noble Grace with his perilous and infective breath'. In the event nothing was done with the parliamentary charges; and Wolsey, having surrendered a good deal of his property to the king, was sent off to take up residence in his diocese of York; it was the first time he had been there.

He died a year later on his way back to London to answer a charge of treasonable correspondence with the French court. It is difficult to come to a just appreciation of his work. The failures since 1525 tend to overshadow the very considerable achievement of his first twelve years. The French alliance had turned out badly; but before that Wolsey's rule had seen England treated as a major European power, and for a time, at least, a force for peace. He had increased the judicial business of the chancery, the council sitting in Star Chamber, and the embryo court of requests, but had made no institutional innovations, other than the revival of the northern and Welsh councils. He did little to reform the royal revenues, except to revive Henry VII's chamber methods, which were being dismantled in the first years of the reign. (Landed income was down from about £40,000 to £25,000 by 1514–15, but there seem to be no figures for the later period.*) Nor in spite of much trumpeting, did he do anything to reform the church.

Wolsey took too much on himself; and that was probably one result of his notorious arrogance. Acting as judge in chancery and in Star Chamber took up a good deal of Wolsey's day; foreign affairs were always urgent; and there was little time for anything else. (By contrast Henry's next great minister, Thomas Cromwell, although astonishingly busy, carefully avoided becoming lord chancellor, and so did not find his time eaten up by judicial matters.) The military disasters of 1522 and 1523 were largely the result of inadequate planning, mainly due to Wolsey's unwillingness to delegate. But it would be wrong to end on a note of condemnation. Three points need to be made in his defence. First, that although Henry took little interest in the details of government, responsibility for the main lines of policy (above all the concentration on a bellicose and expensive foreign policy in the 1520s), could only be his. Henry liked to shrug off responsibility for important decisions on his efficient but unpopular minister.

* B. P. Wolffe, *The Crown Lands 1461–1536* (Allen & Unwin) p. 84.

It was a convenient arrangement – but that is no reason for historians to indulge Henry as his subjects did. Second, the failure of Wolsey's foreign policy in 1529 was hardly his fault. There was not much that England could have done to prevent Charles v's triumph in Italy, and, in those circumstances, there was little that could be done to secure Henry's divorce except by resorting to radical measures which neither Wolsey nor Henry at that stage were prepared to contemplate. Third, institutional reform is not the only test of a government. Its main business was to keep the peace and dispense justice; and this Wolsey did. The period of the cardinal's rule seems tame compared to the bustling reforms of the next decade; but there is a good deal to be said for mere stability.

THE BEGINNING OF THE REFORMATION

After Wolsey's fall the leading figures at court were Thomas Howard, Duke of Norfolk, England's premier peer, son of the victor of Flodden, and uncle of Anne Boleyn; the hearty, bluff, Charles Brandon, Duke of Suffolk, Henry's brother-in-law (he had married Henry's sister Mary, so briefly Queen of France in 1514); and Anne Boleyn's father, now Earl of Wiltshire. The new chancellor was Sir Thomas More, an associate of Wolsey, but a common lawyer; and, of course, a distinguished author and wit. The choice fell on More because the king wanted a layman, while Norfolk was too jealous to let Suffolk become chancellor. The choice of a layman in this traditionally clerical office shows the anti-clericalism which was prevalent in the wake of the fiasco of the divorce proceedings. (When Campeggio had so fatally adjourned the legatine court Suffolk had burst out, 'by the Mass, now I see that the old said saw is true, that there was never legate nor cardinal that did good in England'.) But More was an odd choice, in that he had refused to support the king's case on the divorce; he may have made non-involvement a condition of accepting office. For all his 'Erasmian' humanism, he was a firm opponent of Protestantism; he had written against Luther and Tyndale and, as chancellor, did all he could to help the bishops hunt down heretics. Whatever the frustration of the divorce proceedings, there was no question yet of doctrinal change; a little show of anti-clericalism, and perhaps the pope would be frightened into compliance. It had happened often enough before.

In the new Parliament the Commons were allowed to rail against ecclesiastical abuses. Acts were passed against the extortion of excessive fees for the probate of wills and to regulate mortuary dues (the old grievance in the Hunne case); another set a limit on clerics holding a plurality of benefices and on their absenteeism. These echoed old parliamentary grievances, exacerbated by the ecclesiastical counter-attack in Wolsey's time.

The king's case dragged wearily on. Henry's agents at Rome, who had previously fumed at papal procrastination, were now trying to prevent a decision, in the belief that Clement was bound to find against the king. Their argument was that the case might have to be settled in England, because Englishmen could not be cited before a foreign jurisdiction. This was not a challenge to the papal headship as such; but if admitted it would have been a serious blow to the array of jurisdictional powers the popes had built up over the last five hundred years. It followed logically enough from the *praemunire* charge against Wolsey; and in December 1530 the whole clergy was charged under *praemunire*, for an ill-defined offence. On one interpretation it consisted of the mere fact of exercising spiritual jurisdiction; and although they were pardoned on payment of £118,000, the point was made that their jurisdictional powers depended on the sufferance of the state. This was followed up, in February 1531, by the demand that the clergy recognize the king as 'protector and only supreme head of the English Church'. Canterbury Convocation eventually agreed, after inserting the saving clause 'as far as the law of Christ allows'.

Early in 1532 – with affairs at Rome still deadlocked – the attack was resumed. The Commons drew up, possibly on the basis of complaints first aired in 1529, a 'Supplication against the Ordinaries' (that is, the bishops or their deputies in ecclesiastical courts). This complained about ecclesiastical jurisdiction in general, and about the unfair and extortionate proceedings of church courts in particular. It is not clear how much this was a genuine Commons measure, or to what extent it was engineered by the king's new minister, Thomas Cromwell.* Canterbury Convocation stood firm on the principle of ecclesiastical jurisdiction, though it was prepared to make some practical concessions. The king, already furious at a charge of heresy levied against one of his favourite preachers, Hugh Latimer, exploded. The clergy, he had discovered, rather late in the day, 'be but half our subjects, yea scarce our subjects'. A rump Convocation, browbeaten by the presence of six peers, gave way. In the 'Submission of the Clergy' it acknowledged that convocation was not to assemble without a royal writ, and that ecclesiastical legislation should be subject to a royal veto. This was too much for More, who promptly resigned as chancellor. Parliament meanwhile was launching its first direct attack on Rome, in a bill to prevent the payment of annates (payments made by bishops to the pope on appointment to their sees). Opposition in the Lords produced a modification: the provisions were not to take effect until the king decided that they should. What had been a rather clumsy anti-papal demonstration had been accidentally transformed into a useful bargaining counter in Henry's negotiations.

The pace quickened. In August 1532 the Archbishop of Canterbury, Warham, died. Although over eighty years old, Warham was no nonentity. He had invoked the memory of his predecessor, Thomas Becket and taken his stand on the liberties of the church. He had eventually acquiesced in the submission of the clergy, but could not be relied on to take the king's side on the divorce issue. His death, therefore, cleared the way; the king would now be able to play Canterbury against Rome. Perhaps heartened by light at the end of a very long tunnel, Henry took Anne Boleyn with him on a visit to Francis I, and had her treated as a queen; he found that neither Francis nor the English nobles were unduly shocked. Evidently about this time the caution and self-restraint which the king had exercised so far gave way, and by the end of the year Anne was pregnant. In January a new archbishop was appointed, Thomas Cranmer, one of Anne's

* For different interpretations *see* G. R. Elton in *Eng. Hist. Rev.*, vol. 66, 1951; J. P. Cooper, *ibid.*, vol. 72, 1957; Michael Kelly, *Trans. Roy. Hist. Soc.*, 5th ser., vol. 15, 1965; M. Bowker, *ibid.*, vol. 21, 1971; S. E. Lehmberg. *The Reformation Parliament* (Cambridge, 1970) pp. 138-40.

protégés. The appropriate bulls were issued at Rome, and Cranmer took the customary oath of obedience to the Holy See. In March 1533 Parliament passed the Act in Restraint of Appeals to Rome. 'Whereas by divers sundry old authentic histories and chronicles it is manifestly declared and expressed that this realm of England is an empire, and so hath been accepted in the world. . .' trumpeted the preamble; and the act went on to affirm that the king was 'furnished by the goodness and suffrance of Almighty God with plenary, whole and entire power . . . to render and yield 'justice' to all his subjects without restraint from 'any foreign princes or potentates'. After this trumpeting, the substance of the act, prohibiting all appeals, came as something of an anti-climax.

So armed, Archbishop Cranmer pronounced Henry's marriage to Catherine null. Henry had already secretly married Anne in January 1533. In June she was crowned as queen; in September the Princess Elizabeth was born. The pope excommunicated Henry, who appealed to a general council of the church. But the break was still not complete. The Act of Supremacy was not passed until the end of 1534; this incorporated and extended what had been done before; affirming that the king was 'supreme head of the Church of England', the source of all ecclesiastical juris-diction, armed with full authority to 'restrain and amend all such errors, heresies, abuses' and so on in his realm. Henry was now credited with the power to control the spiritual life of the church, rather than merely its exercise of certain jurisdictional rights.

What had begun as a complicated but, in principle, soluble matrimonial case had been transformed into a political revolution. The details of this process have produced a massive and inevitably technical controversy. The essential problem is why the whole thing was so long drawn out. Was it, as Professor Elton suggests, that nobody in government had a clear view of how to proceed until the admission of Thomas Cromwell to the inner ring of councillors towards the end of 1531; and that the notion of an assertion of national sovereignty by parliamentary statute was his, and that this cut the Gordian knot, provided a clear way forward which had not been apparent before? Or are we to believe, following Professor Scarisbrick, that the ideas which eventually took form in the Acts for Restraint of Appeals and Supremacy were familiar from an early stage in the controversy? In that case we need to explain why the threats made to the pope were not carried out earlier; and why they were eventually activated in 1533 and 1534.*

The issue is complex; a good deal depends on the interpretation one puts on particular phrases in a long and tortuous game of bluff and counter-bluff. But it seems clear that there was no need for Thomas Cromwell, or anybody else, to put the idea of taking over spiritual jurisdiction into Henry's head. English Protestant controversialists, such as William Tyndale in his *Obedience of a Christian Man* and Simon Fish in his *Supplication of the Beggars* (both 1528) were urging that papal power was a usurpation, that in general the clergy possessed no rights of jurisdiction – their duty was to exhort men to follow the right way, not to compel obedience through the use of church courts and so on – and that political power in England belonged exclusively to the king. (According to a later story, Anne Boleyn gave Henry a copy of Fish's book, and Henry 'kept the book in his bosom for three or four days'.) The notion that Henry was head of the church was implicit in the *praemunire* action of 1530. The assertion that he owed no obedience outside his realm was made at various times during the negotiations. Finally, the decision to proceed by parliamentary statute was almost inevitable. Where else but in Parliament could Henry find sufficient authority for a hazardous move against a well-established ecclesiastical authority? After all he had to be able to assert that the changes were due to the will of the realm, not merely to his personal whim. And the fourteenth-century statutes of provisors and *praemunire* provided a clear precedent for parliamentary action.

In that case, the question remains why Henry waited so long. Professor Scarisbrick suggests that this can be explained by Henry's caution. He was, he argues, increasingly taken with the idea of sovereignty which was advanced in this case; so much so,

* J. J. Scarisbrick, *Henry VIII* (1968); Professor G. R. Elton's views as expressed in *England under the Tudors* (Methuen, 1955) are very much qualified in his *Reform and Reformation* (Edward Arnold, 1977), cap 6; he would now push the new ideas (and Cromwell's influence) back to 1530.

indeed, that whatever the outcome of the divorce proceedings he would have proceeded at a fairly drastic redefinition of papal and royal authority. For the moment, however, this aim was held in check by a more important consideration; there must be no doubt of the legitimacy of any child of the Boleyn marriage, and a favourable papal ruling on the divorce case was highly desirable. Indeed, Henry, and most of his courtiers, seem to have over-estimated the degree of opposition there would be to a unilateral solution, and, in the event, must have been pleasantly surprised when the whole thing turned out to be so easy. Even so, Henry's patience was not inexhaustible. He stepped up the pressure forcibly in 1532; and the death of Warham in August of that year made a more radical solution possible. Henry and Anne at last began to cohabit; drafts of a bill for restraint of appeals were concocted; and Anne's pregnancy eventually made what had now become likely, inevitable.

This seems to be the more convincing explanation. Nevertheless, two points need to be made. The first is that Henry tried as long as possible to keep all options open. He was notoriously inconsistent (and adept at making others scapegoats when he needed to change his policy, as we saw over the amicable grant of 1525), and it is dangerous to assume that he would eventually have put into effect the ideas about royal jurisdiction with which he was playing from 1529; though obviously the further he went along the road to carrying out his threats, the more difficult it would be to retreat. Even if we could establish when the Reformation first became a practical possibility, we are a long way from establishing when it first became likely, let alone inevitable. From that point of view Anne Boleyn's pregnancy, or rather Henry's cohabitation with Anne towards the end of 1532, retains its traditional importance.

Secondly (and Professor Scarisbrick would not deny this), the implementation of the ideas about jurisdiction which were bandied about during the controversy would not necessarily have resulted in the supreme headship in the form which did in fact materialize in the 1530s. They might well have produced a more limited jurisdiction, something like the considerable rights which the kings of France exercised over the 'Gallican' church (or, come to that, the kings of Spain in their dominions), while acknowledging the spiritual leadership of the papacy. The essence of the Henrician Reformation, on the other hand was far more than this, the claim to control doctrinal issues, even defining what should be the true teaching of the church.

Although the last stage was implicit in the Supremacy Act, even that could, if necessary, have been interpreted in a minimizing way concerned with organization and jurisdiction, not with doctrine. The specific tenor of the Henrician headship came from its implementation in the following years; the beginnings of interference with the church's teaching, the attack on the monasteries and so on. This was partly, as we shall see, due to the logic of events; partly because, as it happened, Henry found his most reliable allies in the battle with Rome among men of specifically Protestant tendencies, most notably Thomas Cromwell (who had rapidly become the king's principal minister as the anti-Roman policy got under way), and Archbishop Cranmer. Cromwell, if he did not sow the idea of the supreme headship in Henry's mind, did more than anybody to forge it into an active, aggressive, instrument of the royal will. In general, most of those involved in bringing about the Reformation, including the king himself, had little understanding of the implications of what they were doing.

In sum, then, some form of drastic redefinition of royal and papal power was a possibility from the beginning of the divorce. But the form that the redefinition eventually took, involving schism and secular intervention in matters of church doctrine, was due to specific circumstances, to the way in which events actually worked out; and could very easily have been different. (If, for instance, Catherine had conveniently died in 1532 rather than four years later.) It is easier to determine when change becomes possible than when it becomes inevitable; and it is dangerous to confuse the two.

There was popular sympathy for Catherine during these proceedings. Even Edward Hall, a passionate supporter of Henry, wrote that 'the common people being ignorant of truth' especially the women, impugned the king's motives and 'abhorred and reproved' anybody who put in a word for the divorce. But there was very little open opposition.

Nevertheless, the king could not afford to be sanguine. The possible dangers were illustrated by the case of Elizabeth Barton the 'Nun of Kent'. She was a visionary and prophetess who had had a large popular following around Canterbury since experiencing a miraculous cure, so it was believed, in 1525. She was a well-known figure among the spiritually minded in London and had impressed, among others, Bishop Fisher of Rochester and (with some reservations) Thomas More. She had spoken out against the divorce since the beginning, indeed, had told the king to his face that it was wrong. By 1533 she had progressed to the more dangerous proposition that if the king married Anne Boleyn he would be deposed within a month. She was arrested, and, for three days, an extraordinary meeting of councillors, bishops, noblemen and judges discussed what was to be done. Eventually she was declared guilty of treason by Parliamentary act of attainder and, with four clerical associates was hanged. Bishop Fisher was similarly attainted of 'misprision of treason' (for failing to report her treasonable remarks) and fined £300; a charge against More was dropped, apparently because of opposition in the Lords.

The proceedings had been necessary because the judges ruled that Elizabeth Barton's offence would not amount to treason in the courts. An act of attainder, on the other hand, merely declared guilt, without tiresome legal quibbles. (Attainder had normally been used as a substitute for a trial if the defendant was not available, because he was dead or had fled the country; this was clearly not the case on this occasion.*) This highlighted the point that the treason law needed updating to cope with the new situation; and this was duly done under the Treason Act of December 1534.

The problem was to extend the existing treason law, basically that of 1352, which had defined treason as bringing about or imagining the death of the king (or queen or heir apparent), adhering to his enemies, or levying war against him. It was now treason to speak maliciously against the king's title (which now

* G. R. Elton, *Policy and Police* (Cambridge, 1972) pp. 274–5; J. G. Bellamy *The Law of Treason in England in the Later Middle Ages* (Cambridge, 1970).

of course included the supreme headship), or to declare that the king was a schismatic, heretic, tyrant, infidel or usurper of the crown. Speaking against the king's title had sometimes been interpreted as treasonable in the past, but the new act erected the concept of 'treason by words' into a principle.

In May 1535, under the new act, three Carthusian monks and Richard Reynolds, a monk of Syon were executed. This was followed a month later by the execution of Bishop Fisher, a man of stern unbending orthodoxy who had been the most outspoken champion of Queen Catherine and opponent of the supremacy among the bishops.

In July the trial of Thomas More took place. More defended himself with the skill of a professional lawyer. He had managed to avoid offending under the new law by refusing to declare his position on the supremacy. Eventually he was found guilty on the unsupported testimony of the solicitor-general, Sir Richard Rich, about what More evidently regarded as a private and hypothetical conversation. Once convicted More launched out into a general condemnation of the king's proceedings, denying the competence of Parliament to meddle in spiritual matters. 'For one parliament of yours, and God knows of what kind, I have all the general councils for a thousand years . . . The church through all Christendom is one and undivided, and you have no authority . . . to make an act of parliament against the union of Christendom.'

Although the issue was clear to More, the arguments had so far been too abstract, too jurisdictional to affect the people at large. Perhaps the bishops should have appreciated what was happening. They had, after all, put up quite considerable resistance in the early stages. Tunstall of Durham had protested vigorously against the king's first claim to some form of supremacy in 1531. Stephen Gardiner, Bishop of Winchester, composed the reply of Convocation to the Supplication against the Ordinaries in 1532. Yet all, except Fisher, eventually acquiesced in the new order, and Gardiner, in his *De Vera Obedientia* ('On true obedience') produced the ablest defence of the supremacy from a conservative point of view.

This was partly a reflection of their personality. In general, as we saw, administrative ability, often shown in the royal service, was the best qualification for the episcopacy. Significantly, the bishops tended to have degrees in law, not theology. Realists, they were well aware of the deficiencies of the papacy, and of the shabby way in which Henry had been treated by Clement VII: Gardiner indeed had seen the *Curia* at close quarters during the early stages of the divorce proceedings. As practical statesmen they were alive to the dangers of disputed succession and civil war. By acquiescing in the king's proceedings they might at least prevent schism developing into the worse sin of heresy. In any case, the whole thing might soon blow over, as jurisdictional disputes between king and pope had blown over before. It was not worth sacrificing one's life and more important, the peace of the realm, to a point of principle which might soon be forgotten. It is easy to condemn this in retrospect, because the particular point at issue turned out to be so significant; that was not so apparent to contemporaries, many of whom, like the Warden of New College, Oxford, thought that 'although the king hath now conceived a little malice against the bishop of Rome . . . yet I trust [he] will wear harness to fight against such heretics' as the Warden's nephew.*

It would be wrong, though, to see these events purely in terms of opportunism and miscalculation. We should not forget the extent to which most sixteenth-century thought was deeply corporate. The nation (or indeed, other corporate bodies – a monastery, a cathedral chapter, a guild, or town) was not a mere collection of individuals, but in some sense an organic unity. There was little room for private conscience; or rather private conscience could be 'discharged' and responsibility assumed by higher authority.

Gardiner once put this very strikingly. Faced with a heretic who believed that each man had the right to judge doctrine according to his own interpretation of scripture, Gardiner held that no private man's judgement should stand 'against the determination of the whole realm'. Not that Parliament was infallible. It was the duty of those in authority to urge their view, in council, in convocation, in Parliament, while matters were under discussion.

* Quoted Elton, *Policy and Police* (Cambridge) pp. 352–3.

But 'private persons' should not discuss these matters, and, once Parliament had decided, everybody should stifle their private reservations and obey. When in 1554, partly through Gardiner's own urging, England returned to the papal obedience, it was done through Parliament; more significantly, the realm was *corporately* granted absolution by the papal legate, in Parliament, for the sin of schism.

Of course, not everybody held to this notion of corporate responsibility embodied in the realm. More and Fisher clearly believed in the prior claim of the corporate international church. Protestants held, ultimately, to the view that conscience must be sovereign; and in the long run this was to constitute a far more effective challenge to the supreme headship than the Catholics were able to mount. But even Protestants, when in a position of authority, freely used 'corporate responsibility' arguments against their opponents, whether Catholic or radical Protestant. So Hugh Latimer denied the plea that even though laws were outwardly obeyed, 'my heart in religion is free to think as I will' when it was advanced by Gardiner in the Catholic interest; even though it was a plea that Latimer himself made when he in turn was out of sympathy with the current orthodoxy. Theologians were rarely consistent on this sort of issue, and habitually denied to opponents what they claimed for themselves; but then, they rationalized their inconsistencies by denying the good faith of their opponents.*

If this was the sort of argument which carried weight among the theologians most people could be excused for thinking that religion was too complicated to settle themselves, that national unity was essential, and that doctrine should therefore be determined by those in authority; and that that supreme authority was Parliament. This belief in established authority was the ultimate justification of the supreme headship; that the nation was the highest *effective* corporate body, that notions like Christendom or the universal church were too vague and amorphous, that the papacy was, in the words of the seventeenth-century philosopher Thomas Hobbes (whose thinking has a very 'Tudor' colouring), 'none

* For an excellent discussion of these complicated issues, *see* D. M. Loades, *The Oxford Martyrs* (Batsford, London, 1970).

other than the ghost of the deceased Roman Empire sitting crowned upon the grave thereof'; and therefore, given the un- certainties of private interpretation and the danger of anarchy, doctrinal matters could only be settled within the framework of the state. The modern religious mind may find this notion ana- thema; many sixteenth-century men would retort that religion was too important to be left to the individual.

In England that authority was to be found in Parliament; in this case that remarkable Parliament which had been called at the fall of Wolsey, lasted until 1536, and has become known as the 'Reformation Parliament'. 'God knows of what kind' of Parlia- ment, More had remarked. How far in fact did the Reformation statutes represent the views of the parliamentary classes? Or were the statutes, as More suggests, passed only by intense and unusual government manipulation?

As far as can be seen, there was nothing particularly odd about the composition of the Reformation Parliament. There is no evi- dence of unusual government interference in elections. The great majority of members were 'independent' in the sense that they did not owe their seats to the government.* On certain issues the Commons were prepared to put up a long-drawn-out fight; against, for instance the government proposals on 'uses', a matter which affected property rights (see below, p. 223). As far as religion was concerned, the government obviously had the advantage of the Commons' anti-clericalism; stemming from the pent-up frustrations of 1515 and stimulated by the way the Commons had been treated by Wolsey.

Yet there was a certain amount of opposition to the new religi- ous measures. There was considerable hesitation in the Com- mons about the Annates Act of 1532 and the Act in Restraint of Appeals in 1533; possibly because of the fear that the emperor would retaliate by an embargo on English trade with the Nether- lands. There is evidence of some concerted opposition, involving a group of members, which included Bishop Fisher's brother, which met at the Queen's Head tavern. Opposition was more sub- stantial in the Lords, where bishops and abbots made up 50 out of 107 members. There was some intimidation; Henry at-

* S. E. Lehmberg, *The Reformation Parliament* (Cambridge, 1970).

tended both houses at vital moments to overawe them, and some peers (the Archbishop of York, the Bishop of Durham and Lord Darcy among them) were ordered not to attend. It would be naïve to argue that the Reformation statutes represented the positive will of the nation. But they could not have run directly counter to the views of the governing classes. The papal connection, in spite of the extreme caution with which Henry had approached the matter, was cut away amidst general indifference.

Chapter Seven

HENRY VIII Continued

REFORMATION CONSOLIDATED

So far the results of Henry's divorce had not affected the lives of his subjects or fundamental matters of doctrine. In 1535, however, there began a more definite move towards Protestantism. This was largely due to the balance of power at court. While the Catholic bishops had accepted the supreme headship, and had continued in office, there was a reasonable doubt about their whole-heartedness. For a few years two men, Archbishop Cranmer and Thomas Cromwell, were able to use the situation to undermine Catholic beliefs, in spite of Henry's own conservative theological views.

Both men were over forty when first appointed to important office; rather old, by Tudor standards, to be beginning a top-flight career. Cranmer was the son of a minor Nottinghamshire gentleman. In the course of a placid academic career at Cambridge he had been drawn into the Protestant group which used to meet at the White Horse tavern. He had attracted notice in 1529 by the suggestion that the universities of Europe should be canvassed for their opinion on the divorce. Cromwell, on the other hand, was neither cleric nor graduate, but one of that under-estimated class of lawyers turned men-of-business, and entirely self made. (His father had been brewer, smith and fuller at Putney and had rented a little land.) Cromwell in his youth visited Italy (apparently, and surprisingly, in the French army), dabbled in Netherlands trade, went into the money-lending business, got himself a legal training, and was a member of the 1523 Parliament. He then became man-of-business to Wolsey, found a seat in the Reformation Parliament in spite of Wolsey's fall and set about bringing his talents to the king's notice. By the end of 1530 he was a member of the council, a year later one of the inner ring; and from 1534 he was the principal secretary. He was the leading man in the government, and in 1535, without relinquishing the secretaryship, he became the king's vice-gerent in ecclesiastical affairs; responsible, that is, for exercising the royal supremacy, with a closer, more centralized control over the church than anybody before him except his old master Wolsey.

Both Cromwell and Cranmer were convinced, if cautious, Protestants. Their position was a delicate one. The credibility of the traditional structure of belief might be surreptitiously undermined, but the Catholic doctrine of the mass, which Protestants regarded as blasphemy, remained the official doctrine of the English church as long as Henry lived; so, too, did that Protestant bugbear, the doctrine of purgatory. The citadel of Catholic belief had not been taken; but the outworks were heavily sapped while Cromwell was minister (he fell in 1540), and, in spite of theological reaction in Henry's last years, the foundation had been laid for popular Protestantism.

Cranmer and Cromwell were well suited to handle a situation of this kind. Neither was cast in heroic mould; that Cranmer was eventually burnt for heresy and Cromwell executed for treason are among the ironies of Tudor history. As long as Henry lived Cranmer was prepared to be discreet about his opinions (and about his wife, niece of a prominent reformer, whom he had married in Germany). He was prepared to argue with Henry on peripheral theological matters, and to run a risk in pleading for those condemned to death, but he knuckled down on all matters of importance; perhaps in part because he had a genuine belief in the divinity of kings. Cromwell, too, was prepared to dissemble his opinions; though he too can be seen in retrospect to have had to run considerable risks in sponsoring Protestant men and measures.

Among their achievements was the production and dissemination of an English Bible. Orthodox opinion distrusted the Scriptures, and there had in fact been no official translation into English. Copies of the edition produced by Tyndale in Antwerp in 1526 were liable to be burnt. The climate was more hopeful when

Miles Coverdale produced a whole Bible in 1535, probably at Zurich; Henry was induced to sanction a London printing. In 1538 parish churches were ordered to equip themselves with an English Bible for public reading; and in 1539 an official translation, the 'Great Bible', largely due to Coverdale, was published. Its frontispiece showed Henry handing down the Word of God to Cranmer and Cromwell for general distribution, while Jesus looked on approvingly.

The newly accessible Bible was explosive. The educated heard the familiar truths expounded in a modern, hard-hitting, down-to-earth medium rather than encapsulated and distanced in all the dignity of a learned language. To the people at large the Bible must have burst with something of the impact of film on an impoverished Indian village. Scriptural denunciation of clerical hypocrisy and mechanical observances could only harm the tarnished image of orthodox Catholicism; especially when theologically sensitive words were translated in a 'protestant' way: *sacramentum*, for instance, as mystery, not sacrament. Scriptural denunciation of the rich might also be awkward. Soon Henry was complaining that 'the word of God is disputed, rhymed, sung and jangled in every alehouse' and the 1543 Parliament tried to stop lower-class laymen reading this dangerous work. But it was too late; the English Bible had ensured that Protestantism should be the religion of at least a substantial and dedicated minority of Englishmen, a force to be reckoned with when official policy went into reverse.

Equally significant was the dissolution, in 1536, of a number of monasteries. The long-term result was to give a large number of influential men a material stake in the new order. But the immediate circumstances were more mundane. The king needed more money. Little in the way of taxes had been demanded of the Reformation Parliament, presumably because its cooperation was so essential in other spheres; and the danger of foreign invasion was acute. The church was a tempting source of revenue. Already in 1534 a scheme had been mooted for the confiscation of all episcopal lands, and the great valuation of ecclesiastical benefices of 1535, the *Valor Ecclesiasticus*, had provided a tempting mass of information about clerical wealth. But the bishops and the other secular clergy were spared, and instead agents were despatched on a general visitation of the monasteries. They were to ask the questions traditionally asked by bishops on their 'visits' (or inspections) of monasteries, but their purpose was different; the aim of the bishop's visitation was to uncover faults and reform them, that of the king's visitors to collect useful evidence on the low state of morals and spiritual life of monks, nuns and friars, the better to justify confiscation. The visitors' report was used to get from the new Parliament of 1536 an act for the suppression of the smaller monasteries, those with revenues less than £200 a year. These, it was alleged, used their income only for the 'maintenance of sin'. In the larger houses, on the other hand, 'thanks be to God, religion is right well kept and observed'.

The implication that there was no threat to monasticism as such was clearly intended to deceive the king's subjects: perhaps to deceive Henry himself. (He founded a completely new abbey at Bisham in 1536.) But some of the larger monasteries were declared forfeit in 1537 because their abbots were convicted of treasonable involvement in the rebellion known as the Pilgrimage of Grace; and a campaign of threat and blandishment began, to get the remaining monasteries to dissolve themselves and surrender their estates to the king. The process was complete by April 1540. A conspicuous, wealthy, if spiritually somnolent, branch of the church in England had disappeared.

The religious departed, with relief or resignation. A few were dedicated enough to carry on the religious life in private; four monks of Monks Bretton set up house together and attempted to live by the rule, and so did five nuns of Kirklees. The fate of the ex-religious varied. At one extreme heads of houses, abbots and priors, accustomed to living in considerable state, did well for themselves, with high pensions (£100 a year for the Abbot of Fountains – well into the gentry level of income) and, often, high church office. The majority of monks and nuns got pensions. At £5 a year for monks (some poorer parish livings were worth less than that) this was reasonably generous, and, again, many soon supplemented their pensions by acquiring benefices or becoming chantry priests. (This sudden influx into the parochial world of priests looking for benefices was countered by a sharp drop in ordinations; probably because career prospects became less attractive in conditions of clerical unemployment.) A nun with her £2 pension was in desperate condition and would have to depend on her family for support; especially as Henry's respect for the perpetuity of religious vows meant that she was still forbidden to marry. Fortunately most nuns came from reasonably well-off families.

A substantial number of the religious – at least 1,800 out of a total of 9,000 – got no pensions, and rarely received benefices.* These were the monks and nuns whose houses had been dissolved in 1536, and had refused transfer to another house; they were therefore held to have chosen the secular life voluntarily. It also included the friars who had never enjoyed the same affluence as the monks. Outdoor servants were hardly affected; agriculture continued, whoever owned the estate. But many domestic servants, who often outnumbered the monks themselves, were thrown on to an over-crowded labour market. The distribution of alms at the monastery gate came to an end. This represented only two and a half per cent of monastic revenues and hardly shows the monks indulging in self-denial for the sake of the poor; but from the recipient's point of view, it had been a tangible, even a substantial benefit. The dissolution of the monasteries was not, as has sometimes been thought, a major cause of that increasing poverty which is so depressing a feature of Tudor England; far from it. Nevertheless, in individual cases its effect was considerable. While in the long run state-organized and private poor-relief was to be on a larger scale and more rationally administered than anything the monasteries had done, Maynard Keynes's dictum 'in the long run we will all be dead' has a special application to the sixteenth century.

At the same time as the monasteries were dissolved, the government was conducting an assault on popular superstition; shrines were dismantled, and miraculous images were revealed as frauds. The 'Holy Rood' of Boxley, in Kent, a figure which amazed the multitudes by bowing its head, opening its mouth, and rolling its eyes, was shown to work mechanically. Officially,

* G. W. O. Woodward, *The Dissolution of the Monasteries* (Blandford, 1966) pp. 139–57.

none of this attacked traditional belief, but only its perversion But the destruction of relics and images, and the fact that it produced no apparent divine retribution, must have caused many men to abandon the practice of praying to the saints. Similarly, if institutions like the monasteries which had the duty of praying for the souls of their founders and others were abolished, it was harder to believe in purgatory; unless that is, one was prepared to accept that the king was indifferent to the purgatorial suffering of those souls. The dissolution brought the whole Catholic doctrine of intercessory prayer into question.

More tangibly, it created a vested interest by laymen in the new order. We shall look later at the effect on landownership. Certainly Henry had no intention of distributing monastic lands to the nobility and gentry at large; the aim was to enrich the crown. But even at the beginning some monastic land went to appease the influential or to gratify courtiers. The beneficiaries did not necessarily become Protestants. The Duke of Norfolk doubled his Norfolk estates through the dissolution, but remained a conservative in doctrinal matters. Still, the possession of monastic lands obviously induced a certain wariness of Catholicism; it was visible, for instance, in Parliament in Mary's reign, where the papal legate had to strike a bargain on the land issue before reconciling England to Rome.

Official formularies of faith in the 1530s lagged a good way behind these empirical changes. Such elements of Protestantism as they contained were introduced cautiously, implied rather than stated; it was more a question of not stressing certain Catholic doctrines rather than positively proclaiming Protestant ones.* Of the various formularies, the most Protestant was the 'Ten Articles' of 1536, drawn up by convocation on Cromwell's initiative. This failed to mention four of the traditional seven sacraments, and quoted a good deal, without acknowledgement, from German Lutheran sources. The 'Bishop's Book' of 1537 restored the missing sacraments (matrimony, holy orders, confirmation and extreme unction); but rather grudgingly, as of less dignity than the first three (baptism, penance and the eucharist).

* For rather different views on this, see Dickens, English Reformation, pp. 167–74; and Scarisbrick, Henry VIII, chap. 10.

Finally, in 1539 the Act of Six Articles swung the tiller hard back in the Catholic direction. Denying transubstantiation (that is, the belief that the priest in the mass actually changed the 'substance' of the bread and wine into the body and blood of Christ, though their physical form remained unchanged) was heresy. The act also affirmed the Catholic practice of communion in one kind (that in the eucharistic bread only, without the wine, being taken by the laity); auricular confession; the binding character of monastic vows; clerical celibacy; and private masses. Two Protestant-minded bishops, Hugh Latimer and Nicholas Shaxton resigned the sees to which they had been appointed in 1535, Cranmer sent his unfortunate wife back to Germany, and various heretics were burnt for advocating what the government itself had condoned a year or two earlier.

The 1539 act remained the standard of orthodoxy for the rest of the reign. The movement towards doctrinal reformation had come to a full stop before it had much effect on what was probably the most vital and sensitive area, the life of the parish church. Except for the newly installed chained Bible, service books mutilated by the erasing of all mention of the pope, and occasional homilies against Rome and superstition, parochial life went on much as it always had. 'Catholicism without the pope' probably represented the views of most of Henry's subjects. Nevertheless, the trend was still towards Protestantism. The Conservative party, the party of Bishop Gardiner and the Duke of Norfolk (indeed, of the majority of bishops and almost all the peers) failed to follow up the victory it had won in 1539 by any sustained propaganda campaign to balance the harm already done to the Catholic cause by widespread Bible reading, the mockery of Catholic practices, and the disappearance of the monasteries.

THE REFORMATION AND GOVERNMENT

One obvious and immediate result was a vast increase in royal financial resources. The dissolution roughly doubled the crown's ordinary income (that is, exclusive of special parliamentary grants of taxation) which had been running at about £150,000 a year in 1529. First fruits and tenths (the payment by the clergy of the whole of the first year's income from a benefice, and ten per cent of each year's income afterwards) alone yielded about £40,000 a year; the sort of figure which Henry VII, with great skill and attention to detail, had squeezed out of crown lands.

A new 'Court of Augmentation' was established to deal with the ex-monastic lands. A special treasurer dealt with first fruits. But there was a good deal more administrative reorganization than was necessary to deal with new developments. Cromwell had a penchant for overhauling the machinery of government, and creating new, more formal, institutions. The king's right of wardship (the administration of the lands of minors who held of the crown by knight service) previously handled by an inadequately serviced 'master of the wards' became the responsibility of a special court in 1540. The office of works (responsible for royal buildings) acquired a formal board from 1539; more significantly, the administration of the navy was probably reformed in the same way about the same time, though the changes were not formally recognized until 1546. Most important of all was the reform of the king's council. With its large, unwieldy, and often honorific membership, this had always depended for its efficient working on the existence of an informal inner-ring of councillors; but from about 1534–6 this arrangement was formalized. The inner-ring became the Privy Council, a body with about twenty members only, regular meetings and (from 1540) a clerk and a minute book. It was this definition of the Privy Council which finally separated the political activities of the council from the judicial activities of the council in Star Chamber; in that sense, the 1530s saw the establishment of the Court of Star Chamber as a separate, definite body. Whether all this amounts to a 'revolution in government' (Professor G. R. Elton's phrase*) we must discuss later. But it certainly shows a genius for organization on Cromwell's part, a readiness to grapple with new problems, which makes a refreshing change from the usual habit of muddling along until accumulated chaos makes change inescapable.

The very act of enforcing religious change strengthened royal authority. Richard Layton, one of the monastic visitors, thought that 'there can be no better way to beat the king's authority into

* *The Tudor Revolution in Government* (Cambridge, 1953).

the heads of the rude people of the north than to show them that the king intends reformation and correction of religion'. The various acts, injunctions and official formularies of doctrine drove home again and again the awesome responsibility laid on the king to keep his subjects on the right road. No texts were more familiar to a sixteenth-century congregation than St Paul's 'The powers that be are ordained of God; so that who ever resisteth the power, resisteth the ordinance of God,' and St Peter's 'Submit yourselves unto all manner ordinance of men for the Lord's sake: whether it be unto the king as unto the chief head, or unto rulers.' Government propaganda made Henry 'not only a king to be obeyed, but an idol to be worshipped', thought the French ambassador.

Nevertheless, as Professor Elton has shown, acceptance of the new ecclesiastical order was not automatic.* Cromwell had to work hard at propaganda; providing model sermons for now-preaching clergy, commissioning books to defend the king's proceedings and so on. He also had to investigate disloyal remarks, subversive rumours, fantastic prophecies or minor affrays, even if they were apparently trivial (like the uproarious Coventry stag party which finished the evening by tearing down a royal proclamation and so technically committing treason), since anything of this sort might conceal a major plot or (as happened in October 1536) trigger off a rising.

Disaffection was widespread throughout the country (it was the popularity of her cult that had made the Nun of Kent so important). Nevertheless, the 'extremities of the realm' were obviously the areas of greatest danger; those in which rebellion could be most easily fermented, in which local loyalties were greatest, and in which potentially dissident nobles enjoyed the greatest power. The problems of the north and west of England, of Wales, even of Ireland, highlight both the determination of the government to enforce its will, and also the practical difficulties of doing so.

In Wales, the attainders of Sir William Stanley in 1495 and the Duke of Buckingham in 1521 had done a good deal to remove the

* G. R. Elton, *Policy and Police – the Enforcement of the Reformation in the Age of Thomas Cromwell* (Cambridge, 1972).

dangers of over-mighty subjects. As we have seen, Wolsey had tried to invigorate the Council in the Marches in 1525; but it remained a rather ineffective body under the elderly Bishop Veysey, and its authority hardly extended beyond the English border counties. Wales itself remained a tangle of marcher lordships and lands under direct royal control with distinctive methods of government and law. In 1533 Cromwell reminded himself of the need 'to reform the administration of Wales so that peace may be preserved and justice done'.

There were two parts to the policy. First, the appointment of the vigorous, brutal, rough-and-ready Rowland Lee (who also became Bishop of Coventry) as president of the council in 1534. A Welshman reckoned that 'over 5000 men were hanged in the space of six years' by Lee; an exaggeration, but a testimony to the bishop's reputation. Secondly the parliamentary statutes of 1536 and 1543, known to historians as the Acts of Union, revolutionized Welsh government. Both parts of Wales were united, and law and administration assimilated to the English model. Welsh law was abolished, legal proceedings were to be conducted in English and JPs were introduced; Wales was to send members to Parliament and to be liable to parliamentary taxation. The acts might have been expected to provoke opposition. But the Welsh gentry (the only class capable of activating opposition) regarded them as emancipation from the disabilities suffered by Welshmen since the Glyndwr rebellion, over a hundred years before, a reward for loyalty. Any danger came from the affronted marcher lords who were losing not only status and power but income derived from their judicial privileges. The more important were, however, bought off (the Earl of Worcester got Tintern Abbey as compensation) and, in spite of some fears when the north of England revolted late in 1536, the reforms were carried through peacefully enough.

Wales follows a pattern with which we will become familiar; the abolition of ancient noble 'liberties', integration into the realm, the entrusting of government to a council rather than reliance on the local nobility. But in the event government could not be entirely 'depersonalized', could not be entrusted to men whose only claim to obedience was the king's commission. In the

1540s the powers of the council were supplemented by building up, on the old style, the powers of a reliable great man; in this case, William Herbert, the descendant, by an illegitimate line, of the Yorkist Earls of Pembroke.

In Ireland, Cromwell again reinvigorated what had been a rather half-hearted policy of Wolsey's. Kildare's enemies were encouraged to send complaints to Westminster, and in 1534 Kildare himself was brought to court on a treason charge. In June his son 'Silken Thomas' raised a revolt, at a delicate moment for Henry, just before the passing of the Supremacy Act. But although Thomas tried to use the religious issue, it was premature; and the 'Geraldine revolt' was crushed easily by a small English army and the Butlers, the ancient enemies of the Geraldines among the Anglo-Irish aristocracy.

The fall of the Geraldines made the problem of Irish government urgent; especially in the context of the Reformation. An Irish Parliament passed a supremacy act easily enough; and also agreed to dissolve the monasteries, after some opposition based on the suspicion that the proceeds would be used for English, not Irish purposes ('Irish' in this context means, of course, the English settlers). In 1541 Parliament recognized Henry as King, not merely Lord, of Ireland; the old title was embarrassing because it had been granted to Henry II by the pope, and 'the Irish have a foolish opinion that the Bishop of Rome is King of Ireland'. An attempt was made to win over the native Irish chiefs, hitherto almost entirely ignored by the English government. Some of them attended the 1541 Parliament. Many surrendered their lands (which, according to Gaelic law were not theirs, but their clan's), and received them back on feudal terms from the king, along with the grant of new titles. As grateful subjects they would, it was hoped, spread English law and customs among their followers; and to reinforce this, their sons were brought to England to be educated in English ways.

In the event this policy was a dismal failure. Attempts to impose English norms on a fundamentally different social system produced endless disputes about the succession to land, disputes which had been endemic in Irish society, but now constituted a challenge to English law and therefore to the English crown.

Royal control was fairly nominal over the Irish church. Many of the bishops were less than whole-hearted supporters of the Henrician Reformation, and in any case they had little control over their clergy. Ominously for the future, the orders of friars, though legally dissolved, continued their ministry with little interference. Nevertheless, the 1530s do mark a watershed in Irish history. For two centuries the English had been stuggling to maintain some sort of political suzerainty in Ireland and to resist, none too successfully, the advance of Gaelic society. 1495 was little more than an attempt to stabilize a none too strong position. From 1534, on the other hand, the initiative lay with the English crown; from now on it was Gaelic society which was on the defensive.

Rebellion was crushed in Ireland and avoided in Wales. A large-scale rebellion also took place in the north of England towards the end of 1536; known from the use of religious symbols in its banners and in its slogans as the Pilgrimage of Grace. It is worth examining the Pilgrimage in some detail; first, because it was the greatest manifestation of opposition that Henry ever faced in England: secondly, because it illustrates many of the realities of political power, of the practical limitations of royal power, on the one hand, and of the difficulties of organized opposition on the other. And while the Pilgrimage is often dismissed as a dismal failure, an anachronistic but harmless manifestation of the backward and feudal north, it is arguable that it had important results in first slowing, and ultimately reversing, the trend towards Protestantism which was apparent in 1535-6.

Although Wolsey's reconstructed council in the north had survived his fall, it seems to have had little influence. Aristocratic power at court was paralleled by aristocratic power in the north. But a renewed attack on magnate privilege was launched under Cromwell's aegis. An act of 1536 abolished franchises and liberties for most practical purposes; that is, areas, especially common in the north, in which the king's writ either did not run or was heavily restricted by local privileges. In the same year a spectacular coup was achieved in relation to the great house of Percy when the childless Earl of Northumberland was induced to bequeath his estates to the crown, so disinheriting his brother, Sir Thomas Percy. How this was achieved is not clear; it may be because of the earl's financial troubles, it may be that he was open to blackmail in some form (perhaps because of his one time youthful passion for Anne Boleyn). Nor do we know what the crown hoped to achieve, since Sir Thomas would in any case have inherited the earldom itself, and it would be against Tudor concepts of social order to let an earl be impoverished. Presumably he would have been re-granted some, at least, of the Percy estate, but on conditions which would provide a useful guarantee of good behaviour.

All this could be represented as interference with the established local order by a blundering and tactless government. Cromwell does seem to have been remarkably confident in the early months of 1536, indeed over-confident; 'to make or mar' had always been his motto in a crisis. Church doctrine was being moved towards Protestantism. Vested interests were under attack in all directions; the dissolution of the smaller monasteries; the rooting out of ancient 'liberties'; the apparent attack on the interests of the landowning classes in general represented by the Statute of Uses (*see below*, p. 233) which prevented them leaving their lands by will.

All this came on top of a difficult economic situation; the harvest of 1535 had been bad, and the new one which was got in during the summer of 1536 was not much better. Conditions were ripe for the spread of wild rumours. The king, it was said, was going to rob parish churches of their plate and jewels (in which a lot of community pride was invested), reduce the number of parish churches, levy taxes on baptisms, marriages and burials and on lower-class men who aped their betters by eating white bread.

In retrospect these rumours seem fantastic. In a time of rapid, even revolutionary change, they were credible. The extraordinary things which *were* happening seemed to confirm the truth of the rumours as a whole; as one of the rebels put it 'the people saw so many abbeys pulled down in deed, they believed all the rest to be true'.

The result was a large-scale rebellion by the commons, in Lincolnshire, Yorkshire and the northern counties. There was, as we shall see, a good deal of upper-class prompting, even participation; nevertheless, in form at least, it was a popular rather than a noble rebellion, even to the extent of having a commoner, Robert Aske, as its 'Great Captain'.

It began in Lincolnshire at the beginning of October 1536. Three sets of commissioners were at work simultaneously: one collecting a subsidy, one suppressing the smaller monasteries, and one, sent by the bishop, enforcing the Ten Articles (*see above*, p. 194) and Cromwell's injunctions. These involved a drastic cut in the number of saints' days; in particular patronal festivals were not to be kept as holidays. Worse still, the commission was investigating the morals and general competence of the clergy. Trouble began at Louth on 1 October, and spread very quickly in north Lincolnshire; by 5 October an army was occupying Lincoln, led by a motley mixture of peasants, craftsmen (Nicholas Melton, *alias* 'Captain Cobbler'), parish priests and gentlemen; the latter, who included the sheriff of Lincoln, claimed that they had been forced to take part. A petition was drawn up demanding an end to taxes, except in wartime; a guarantee of the liberties of the church; no more suppression of monasteries; and a purge of heretics in high places, including Cromwell and Latimer. It also demanded the repeal of the Statute of Uses which, not surprisingly, most of those involved had never heard of; this was obviously put in at the instigation of the gentry. The king returned an indignant answer, in which he referred to the rebels as 'the rude commons of one shire, and that one of the most brute and beastly of the whole realm'. An army approached under the Duke of Suffolk, and the rebels dispersed. The whole episode had lasted less than a fortnight.

Much more serious were events further north. News from Lincolnshire produced rebellion across the Humber, in the Beverley area of the East Riding. Soon the whole Riding was involved. About the same time trouble broke out in the wild northern areas; in Cumberland and Westmorland, in Durham and the North Riding and in Craven in the far west of Yorkshire. York itself was taken on 13 October, and six days later the king's castle at Pontefract surrendered, with suspiciously little resistance. In the castle were its constable, Lord Darcy, the Archbishop of York, Edward Lee, and other members of the council in the north; after their capture they sat in the rebel council of leadership. Other great men who were involved included the Earl of Northumberland's brothers, Thomas and Ingram Percy.

The Pilgrimage showed the military weakness of the crown and its dependance on the great nobles. Henry, significantly, did not lead the army sent against the rebels (perhaps to allow himself room for manoeuvre if it were defeated). It was commanded by the Duke of Norfolk, although he had been out of favour since the execution of his niece, Anne Boleyn, earlier that year; a substantial part of the troops were his own tenants. In spite of the Boleyn connection, his inclinations were generally conservative; and he might have been tempted to join the Pilgrims against his enemy, Cromwell. The Pilgrims themselves believed other leading peers (the Earls of Shrewsbury and Derby for instance) to be sympathetic; and although they were wrong, the chance of a great magnate joining the rebellion could not reasonably be ruled out. Had one done so, others might have followed. In the circumstances the royal forces could not risk pitched battle.

Instead the king issued a free pardon and promised to consider the Pilgrims' demands. These were complex. Their programme demanded an end to heretical innovation, the restoration of suppressed monasteries, and the punishment of 'heretic bishops' (led by Cranmer). Opinion was divided on the papal supremacy; a compromise formula involved an essentially 'Gallican' solution of acknowledging the pope's primacy but restricting his jurisdiction in England. Vengeance was demanded on Cromwell, a 'free Parliament' was to be summoned, away from the corrupting influence of Westminster, and Princess Mary should be restored to the succession. The interests of the gentry were represented in a demand to repeal the Statute of Uses, and of the peasantry in those for enforcing the enclosure legislation and the fixing of fair 'entry fines'.

Henry gave a sympathetic but non-committal answer which encouraged the Pilgrims. It was now December, they had been under arms for two months, and their farmwork was neglected; and so they dispersed. But before the king's intentions could be tested, there broke out yet another rising, in the East Riding in January 1537. The commons were on edge. They believed that the gentry would abandon them if they had the chance, and that the king's pardon was worthless. The gentry, too, had had time to consider the implication of the undercurrent of class-hatred which the Pilgrimage had revealed. This crack in regional solidarity opened the way for Norfolk and his troops. The new rebellion was crushed with the aid of the gentry. Local ringleaders were hanged; bigger fish were sent to London for examination, and, eventually, trial. 178 men all told were executed; remarkably few, compared, for instance, to the much smaller 1569 northern rebellion.* But it was an effective deterrent, none the less, and was probably the main reason why the north of England was not involved in the later rebellion of 1549. Henry had survived the greatest challenge he ever faced from his English subjects by keeping a cool head in the crisis and playing for time.

The Pilgrimage was a complex set of events and it is not easy to sort out its causes.† There are two main problems; which of the long list of factors one considers relevant; and how much weight then to give any particular factor in the general picture. One approach is to search out one factor as the indispensable key; the rest then can be dismissed as mere 'occasions' for revolt. The difficulty with this approach is that no single factor will fill the role. The harvest situation was obviously important; it is a reasonable supposition that without high prices, general distress, even near starvation, the revolt might not have happened. But harvest failure is not a *sufficient* explanation; since harvests as bad or worse had occurred in the past and would occur in the future without producing any comparable rebellion. Isolating the various factors from each other is a necessary first stage in any analysis; but only a first stage.

The second stage is to try and see how the various factors interact and fuse to produce a situation which any one of them is unlikely to generate on its own. To take a single example, that

* *See* Elton, *Policy and Police* (Cambridge), p. 389; and *see below*, p. 275.
† For two interpretations which disagree more in emphasis than in substance, *see* Dickens, *English Reformation* (Batsford), pp. 122–8, and C. S. L. Davies, 'The Pilgrimage of Grace Reconsidered' (*Past and Present*, 41, 1968).

of the dissolution of the monasteries, which historians have tended to see as either the main cause of the Pilgrimage or, by reaction, as almost totally irrelevant. Quite obviously the dissolution was not the sole, or even the main cause. Whatever may have been true of the highland areas of the remote north-west, the inhabitants of the East Riding or of Lincolnshire had no more reason to love the monks than had those of similarly rich agricultural areas in the south. But it is no use, therefore, ignoring the monastic factor. The suppression featured in both the Lincolnshire and the main rebel programme, and monks from the suppressed houses were, sometimes forcibly, restored to their old homes. We should rather ask why these unlikely events took place. The answer involves at least two factors. The first is the belief that replacement of the monks by an absentee, the king, would produce economic difficulties, of which one manifestation would be to denude the north of coins, sent south as rent. The second is the extent to which the attack on the monasteries was seen as part of a general attack on local institutions, whether the pattern of landownership, or the traditional ordering of the parish church; and here we come back to the point that so much apparently was being changed at once. In these circumstances defence of the monks took on a symbolic importance which it would otherwise have lacked.

Overlapping these problems of causation are those of the involvement of different social groups. Although most of the gentry and nobility claimed later to have been forced to join, they clearly took the opportunity to insert their own demands about the Statute of Uses. Close investigation reveals a number of suspicious circumstances about the origin of the revolt; for instance Aske, the 'Great Captain' had been in the service of the Percy family, and his account of the spontaneous outbreak of the East Riding revolt hardly rings true. The attitude of the younger Percies to the Pilgrimage is as suspicious as that of York towards the Cade rebellion or Warwick towards the Lincolnshire revolt of 1470; and for similar reasons. Monks and parish clergy were heavily involved in spreading rumours, encouraging the revolt, and drawing up the programmes. The clergy clearly resented the increased taxation which the Reformation had involved for them, the threat that their morals would be investigated, and the blow to their status involved in the recognition of a layman as Head of the Church. This, rather than a positive feeling in favour of the pope seems to be behind the demands about the supremacy.

Nevertheless, both gentry and clergy had to work through the common people, had to manipulate popular prejudice to their own ends; and the way they did so can tell us something about popular attitudes. A conservative revolt could be mobilized in terms of defence of local rights and opposition to religious change; and these motives could hold together, briefly, social groups with differing, even contradictory, aspirations. (Compare the demand for enforcement of the enclosure laws with the participation in the revolt of Lord Darcy, a prime example of an enclosing landlord.) The heart of the matter, the issue on which these two aims fused, may have been the defence of the parish church; the embodiment of the village community, the centre of its pride, the symbol, too, of the belief that there might be more to life than an unending and precarious fight for subsistence.

This may be too romantic a view. Many historians would say that the priests merely manipulated an ignorant peasantry. But even that should dispel the myth that Tudor England was irredeemably anti-clerical, however much at various times and in various circumstances anti-clericalism was a real factor. The ability of monks to turn out their tenants in their own defence must be set alongside the clear signs of anti-landlord, anti-gentry feelings which sometimes broke to the surface; any interpretation of Tudor society must encompass both tenant loyalty and tenant resentment. Nor was the Pilgrimage merely the dying spasm of a backward feudal society. The Yorkshire revolt began in the East Riding, as rich an arable area as any in England, organized in the classic nuclear-village, three-field system; open, via the thriving port of Hull, to the influence of London and of Germany. Much the same applies to north Lincolnshire. Indeed, throughout England there was a mass of conservative opinion, unlikely, by its very nature to burst into open revolt; but ready to be mobilized should the circumstances arise; should there be, for instance, a fight for the succession to the throne. As long as Henry VIII provided effective government, successful rebellion was unlikely; the Pilgrims acknowledged this by preferring to petition the king to change his policies and ministers. But this is not to say that even Henry had nothing to fear. Had, for instance, Norfolk thrown in his lot with the rebels, rather than, as he did, working more subtly at court for much the same ends (the overthrow of Cromwell and the end of religious innovation), the Pilgrimage would have been a very much more serious affair. To ignore the danger of armed opposition is to misunderstand the essential problems of the 1530s. The Pilgrimage was not a peripheral irritant but the crisis of the reign.

Its immediate result was a drastic change in the power structure of the north. The two younger Percies were attainted, and when their brother the Earl of Northumberland died in 1537, there was no challenge to the crown's taking over the estate. The council of the north, which had played an inglorious, even a disloyal role, was reconstructed and took on the form it kept for over a century, dispensing justice and keeping a wary eye on possible disaffection. Even those peers like the Duke of Norfolk and the Earl of Cumberland who had been actively loyal got fewer rewards than they might have hoped for. A definite policy of entrusting power to men of gentry origin was followed, in spite of Norfolk's protest that only 'men of estimation and nobility' could govern the north. To this Henry replied, in his own hand (an unusual exertion), 'We will not be bound of necessity to be served with lords. But we will be served with such men, what degree soever, as we appoint to the same.' As Sir Thomas Wharton, the new warden of the middle march, and beneficiary of the new policy, wrote, 'In the late Lord Dacre's time there was a cry "A Dacre, a Dacre" and afterwards "A Clifford, a Clifford" . . . Now only "A King, a King".'*

* *See* M. E. James, *Change and Continuity in the Tudor North :* (University of York, Borthwick Papers, No. 27, 1965). M. L. Bush, 'The Problem of the Far North' (*Northern History*, 6, 1971) suggests that Henry would have preferred to employ magnates if suitable ones had been available, and was only making a virtue of necessity in his reply to Norfolk. Against this, it could be argued that Henry had difficulty finding suitable magnates only because he demanded far higher standards of loyalty from them than his predecessors had. He preferred a loyal gentleman to a potentially disloyal nobleman, and the fact that he could make this choice is significant.

Even so the old social pattern was not so easily disrupted. Whatever the king might say, his officers would be better obeyed if they had standing in their own community; and Henry recognized this by giving Wharton lands and eventually making him a baron. 'New men' did not remain new for long; Wharton's heir was a notable Catholic and political ally of those Nevilles, Dacres and Percies his father had been promoted to supplant. The crown won a notable victory in the north in the 1530s; but it would need more than that to effect a permanent change in northern society.

Lastly, it is worth considering briefly the situation in the west of England. This evolved from the execution, in December 1538, of Henry Courtenay, the Marquis of Exeter, Henry's one-time friend. Exeter had been closely involved with the Pole family, whose most distinguished member, Reginald, was an exile at Rome, a cardinal and the author of a book against Henry's ecclesiastical proceedings; he had also been employed in trying to stir up Charles V to invade England. Investigation of treasonable correspondence between the cardinal and his family brought to light various indiscretions of Exeter's, including threats against the king's ministers; and to these were added older allegations, investigated originally in 1531, that Exeter's servants speculated openly on the chances of his eventually becoming king.

Exeter's execution made possible a re-allocation of power in the west, much as the Pilgrimage had done in the north. In 1539 a Council of the West was appointed, to administer justice, put down sedition and so on. Its president was a courtier John Russell, a distinguished soldier and diplomat; and to support his new dignity he was given a large estate from the lands of Tavistock Abbey and created a baron. The western council, unlike those of Wales and the north, did not survive the fall of Cromwell in 1540; the task of keeping the peace in the West Country fell rather on Russell personally. It was Russell who took the lead in putting down the western rebellion of 1549. Created Earl of Bedford in 1550, he is the founder of one of the great noble houses of England. A new power had been built on the ruins of the Courtenays; a family which had no claim to the throne, but which, by its long-term patronage of Puritan clergy and members of Parliament, was to constitute a more subtle long-term danger to Henry's successors.

In Wales, and Ireland, in the north and west of England, the 1530s had seen both the opportunity and the will to reduce noble privilege and noble influence; and to introduce, as far as possible, conciliar institutions rather than relying on great men. But the policy had to compromise with the realities of power; not only the need for military strength against Scots or 'wild Irish', but the importance of a great nobleman's role in ensuring peace in 'his' country. The Duke of Norfolk, though frequently out of favour, played the political game so skilfully as not to be caught on a treason charge until 1546; and because of this no 'modernizing' policy was therefore possible in East Anglia, which was as firmly under the duke's influence as Devon had been under that of the Marquis of Exeter. Significantly enough, in the duke's absence in prison nobody seems to have been able to organize the Norfolk gentry to resist the peasant rebellion which broke out in 1549.

But if there were limits to an anti-noble policy in the 1530s, the period after Cromwell's fall saw something of a reaction. Although the Welsh and northern councils continued to function, the institutional approach had to be supplemented increasingly by a policy reminiscent of that of Edward IV in building up reliable supporters of the crown, in this case men like Wharton, Herbert and Russell.

The trend was to be accelerated during the reigns of Edward VI and Mary, when political uncertainty, *coup d'état*, and rebellion, put a premium on a man's ability to raise troops. Edward's reign was also to see a wholesale distribution of lands and titles, so that the 'new men' of the 1530s soon became a 'new nobility', and new nobilities are soon assimilated into the old nobility. It was the long period of internal peace in Elizabeth's reign, after the northern rebellion of 1569, which finally changed the life style of the English nobility and reduced their military proclivities. Nevertheless, the new families of the 1530s, with the possible exception of the Whartons, never quite played the role of 'overmighty subject' in the way that some of their predecessors had done; and the rivalry between the Cromwellian new men and the older nobles was to be a major theme of politics up to 1569. Although the victory was not and could not be complete, the years of Thomas Cromwell's ascendency had shaken radically the traditional structure of power.

FACTION POLITICS, AND WAR, 1536-47

In considering these changes we have lost the narrative thread. We need therefore to retrace our steps to 1536, before the first dissolution of the monasteries and the Pilgrimage of Grace. We are back to Henry VIII's matrimonial problems, and in a context peculiarly ironical, given the sound and fury of the years 1527-33. Catherine of Aragon died in January 1536. A few days later Anne Boleyn, whose only child so far had been a daughter, the Princess Elizabeth, had a miscarriage; and she soon fell victim to a sordid intrigue by an oddly assorted coalition which included Thomas Cromwell. She was accused of adultery with several men and of incest with her brother. Even though the evidence was thin, to say the least, this was held to amount to treason and Anne was executed in May 1536. Thomas Cranmer obligingly found that, like Catherine, she had never in fact been married to the king, because his sexual relations with her sister constituted an affinity between them. The succession problem was now worse than in 1527. Henry had a bastard son (the Duke of Richmond) and two bastard daughters, Mary and Elizabeth. Parliament went to the extraordinary lengths of passing an act allowing the king to leave the crown by will, in default of legitimate issue; but the probable intended beneficiary of the provision, the Duke of Richmond, died a few weeks later.

Fortunately Henry's third attempt at matrimony was more successful. Eleven days after Anne's execution he married Jane Seymour, lady-in-waiting to both her predecessors. In October 1537 Jane died in childbed; but at least the child was saved. Henry had a son at last. Danger was not over; since Henry was forty-six there was a very good chance that the young prince Edward would succeed while he was still a child, involving the country in the uncertainties of a minority government. In any case, he might die; and another marriage and more sons were obvious insurance for Henry. The chance of being Queen of England became a factor in international affairs, in spite of the understandable reluctance of several royal ladies.

In general, foreign policy since 1526 had been pro-French; or at least, anti-Habsburg. The two great European monarchs, Charles V and Francis I were, as it happened, at peace between 1529 and 1536. But they were too suspicious of each other to combine against Henry. After another war in 1536-7, however, Charles and Francis met each other in 1538, and declared that they were ready to cooperate in defence of Catholicism – against the Turks, the German Lutherans and Henry. Henry took the threat seriously; the royal navy was enlarged, an impressive series of fortifications were built along the south coast, and negotiations began for an alliance with the Lutherans.

Henry, however, was not prepared to commit himself whole-heartedly to a 'Cromwellian', Lutheran-orientated policy. The Pilgrimage of Grace had shown the dangers of pressing on with a Protestant policy at home (fortunately the Pilgrimage had co-incided with the latest bout of fighting between Francis and Charles); and the Germans, although hoping to persuade Henry to follow their own example, needed his support too much to quibble over theology. So in 1539 Henry was simultaneously pro-moting the Act of Six Articles, with its fierce insistence on doc-trinal orthodoxy, and negotiating, through Cromwell, a German marriage. The principality of Cleves in the Rhineland seemed to fit the bill exactly; the duke was a Catholic, but he was allied to the Protestant princes. The affair proceeded by proxy, helped by a flattering portrait, which Henry's court painter Holbein made of the duke's sister Anne. The lady arrived in England, in Janu-ary 1540. Henry was acutely disappointed in her looks; but, on hearing the news that Charles V was in Paris being fêted by the French king, did his duty, and the marriage duly took place.

This act of heroic self-sacrifice turned out to be unnecessary. Charles and Francis were drawing apart again, and Cromwell's enemies determined to press home the victory they had already won on the doctrinal front in 1539. The Duke of Norfolk was sent to Paris to explore the possibility of a new French alliance. His ally Stephen Gardiner, the conservative Bishop of Winches-ter, accused Cromwell's protégé Robert Barnes of heresy;

Barnes was an ex-friar turned Lutheran. Norfolk's niece, Catherine Howard was meanwhile groomed to repeat the coup of her cousin Anne Boleyn. The balance wavered. For a moment it looked as if Cromwell had won. He was made Earl of Essex in April 1540, and got his own back on Gardiner by having a conservative bishop, Sampson of Chichester, arrested on suspicion of Roman sympathies. But Henry then had one of his sudden and violent changes of mood. Cromwell himself was arrested on 10 June and charged with treason. The allegations ranged from taking too much business on himself (like Wolsey), to planning to marry the Princess Mary, and, less absurdly, protecting heretics. Parliament passed an act of attainder declaring his guilt (it might have been difficult to prove the case according to due legal process). The Anne of Cleves marriage was annulled (Cromwell testifying from the Tower how Henry had told him, in intimate detail, that it had never been consummated), and Cromwell was executed. Anne retired gratefully to life as a spinster with a comfortable pension of £500 a year.

The king soon repented of Cromwell's execution. In a sense the charge against him was justified. Cromwell *had* protected heretics, he *had* influenced national policy to his own ends. There is no question about his Protestantism and his use of office to further Protestantism. But the charge is distasteful and disingenuous; Henry could only now wax indignant at how Cromwell had manipulated state policy by implying that he himself was either politically innocent, or totally negligent. Once again, as in 1529, Henry was refusing to accept the responsibility which was ultimately his for the direction of policy.

Cromwell has traditionally been presented as a cold, calculating, businesslike, self-effacing, reliable subordinate, prepared to put up with any humiliation to grasp and retain power. (Gossip had it that 'the king beknaveth him twice a week, and sometimes knocks him well about the pate', but that Cromwell would come out 'with as merry a countenance as though he might rule all the roost'.) His reputation has suffered from the political executions which marked his ministry; but the case of the Duke of Buckingham, or the Countess of Salisbury (attainted in 1539 but not executed until 1541), or indeed of Cromwell himself shows that any political executions were not confined to his ministry, and that blame for them must fall at least as much on the king.

The image of the shrivelled bureaucrat is misleading. He was a cultivated if largely self-educated man who could more than keep his end up with a bevy of talented intellectuals; men like Thomas Wyatt the poet, Sir Thomas Elyot the educational theorist or a social and political thinker like Thomas Starkey. Cromwell had none of Wolsey's appetite for show. As a layman instead of arch-bishop and legate, as the king's secretary and lord privy seal rather than lord chancellor, he had less opportunity. Nevertheless, something could have been made of the vice-gerency in spiritual affairs (as vice-gerent Cromwell took precedence over all members of the House of Lords) if pomp had been part of Cromwell's style. Wolsey ostentatiously ran the government on behalf of the king; Cromwell was more concerned to keep up appearances, to give the impression of a subordinate who knows how to mani-pulate his master. There was certainly a meticulous attention to detail; whether drafting statutes, investigating the spread of sedi-tious rumours and keeping his finger on the pulse of the localities or establishing government departments. Memoranda and agenda, preserved at length in the state papers, seem characteristic of his orderly businesslike mind. But there was also a rashness, an im-petuosity, a desire to get things done at all costs, very evident in 1535-6, when, faced with a major Irish rebellion, he was also manoeuvring the English church into a more Protestant stance, attacking noble privileges and destroying the smaller monas-teries. Possibly the Pilgrimage of Grace taught him caution; or possibly it suggested to Henry that Cromwell should be kept on a tighter rein.

Cromwell's fall marked the end of a decade of radical change. Henry's last years were a period of consolidation, dominated by war and court intrigue. Their most striking feature was the solidity which Henry's government had now acquired, its apparent im-munity from opposition. Parliament voted some £670,000 in direct taxes over seven years with no apparent protest; rather less, admittedly than the £800,000 over five years that had been refused to Wolsey in 1523, but a good deal more than the £152,000 eventually voted for the years 1524-7. In addition there were forced loans (1542) and benevolences ('voluntary' gifts to the crown, theoretically illegal) in 1544 and 1546, and yet none of these provoked large-scale protests like that of 1525.

Scotland took up a great deal of attention. Its king, James v, was strongly anti-English, and had re-affirmed the 'auld alliance' by marrying a French princess in 1537, and, when she died, another one in 1538. He had also contrived to wring a good deal of money out of the church (partly by the implied threat of following the English example) and so saw no need to cut loose from Rome. The threat of a Scottish attack if Henry were at war with Francis (or worse still, with both Francis and Charles) was always menacing. Henry decided to try to win over his nephew to the advantages of friendship with England and profitable Reformation. A meeting between the two kings was arranged in 1541 to take place at York. Henry duly set out, the only time he ever travelled so far north. But James failed to arrive; he may have suspected an English plot, he may have been dissuaded by his clerical ministers (who had their own reason for suspicion about the meeting). Henry exploded; and the two countries were again at war.

Operations began in 1542, with a totally bungled invasion by the Duke of Norfolk. Two strokes of luck followed. A Scottish counter-attack was driven into the marsh at Solway Moss, and no less than seven lords and five hundred gentlemen were captured. A fortnight later James died, leaving as his heir his baby daughter Mary, just seven days old. Everything had fallen into Henry's lap. The new regent of Scotland, the Earl of Arran, was ready to cooperate. Cardinal Beaton, symbol of Rome and French alliance, was arrested, the Scottish Parliament sanctioned a translation of the Bible, and negotiations were opened for the baby queen to marry Prince Edward. This was duly settled at the Treaty of Greenwich in July 1543.

But Scottish politics were nicely balanced, and there was a deep distrust of England. Henry hardly reassured the Scots by asserting the old, and long dormant, English claim to suzerainty. By the end of the year the Anglophile party had lost control, the Scottish Parliament had repudiated the treaties, Beaton was back in power, and the French alliance re-established. In May 1544 the Earl of Hertford (Edward Seymour, Henry's brother-in law) was sent to burn Edinburgh and the Lowlands, a task he accomplished with efficient brutality. But this was only a punitive raid which did nothing to bring the marriage any closer. Henry had fumbled his chance; and in any case was now more interested in the more glamorous battlefields of France.

It has been argued that the new French war was not a distraction from Scottish affairs; that if the English added Boulogne to Calais they could cut off French communications with Scotland and the anti-English party in Scotland would then crumble.*

This seems to be a rather roundabout way of proceeding, however, and if Henry was really concerned about French communications with Scotland, a more determined effort on the naval side would have made more sense. As it was, even when Boulogne was in English hands, enough French ships got through to keep up Scottish resistance. It does look rather as if Henry had been inveigled into continental diplomacy largely for self-glorification, a desire, perhaps, to relive in late middle age the triumphs of youth. Accordingly in July 1544 an army of forty-eight thousand men, with a huge supply train (six thousand five hundred horses were needed just to haul the guns and ammunition carts) set out from Calais. This was a larger army than any sent to France during the Hundred Years War; indeed, it was the largest English army to be sent abroad before William III's reign. Even without hangers-on it was equivalent to two-thirds of the population of London and was two or three times as large as a provincial city.

The plan was for Henry to lead his own army (something he had not done since 1513), and for Charles V to invade at the same time from Alsace. The two armies were to converge on Paris and finally wrest the kingdom from Francis I. Probably neither Henry nor Charles ever intended to keep their bargain; it was a question who would double-cross the other first. Henry probably remembered the fiasco of Suffolk's dash for Paris in 1523 and wanted something more solid. He therefore sat down to besiege Boulogne. Charles got halfway to Paris, and then, blaming Henry

* R. B. Wernham, *Before the Armada: The Growth of English Foreign Policy, 1485–1588* (Cape, 1966) chap. 12.

for not supporting him, signed a profitable peace treaty. Boulogne was duly captured; and immediately there was a flurry of work to protect it from French counter-attack.

Few of his council shared Henry's enthusiasm for the war. The young Earl of Surrey, in command of the Boulogne garrison, got a stinging rebuke from his father, the Duke of Norfolk, when he won a skirmish in particularly gallant fashion against the French; six days' work by the council persuading the king to give up the war had gone for nothing. Certainly, while Boulogne remained in English hands, a massive French counter-attack must be expected; possibly an attempt to get compensation in England (the Isle of Wight, for instance) which could then be traded for Boulogne.

The attack came in the summer of 1545, when 55 ships and 25 galleys, with an army of 25,000 men on board, appeared off Portsmouth. 100,000 men stood in arms ready to engage them if they landed, and some 90 ships stood by. Henry arrived to direct operations in person. What might have been the first great inter-fleet gun battle in history (before that fleet engagements were mainly concerned with boarding the enemy ships), failed to come off. Virulent disease broke out in both fleets, and the French returned hastily home. The only spectacle for Henry was an unfortunate one, the capsizing of his own, top-heavy, *Mary Rose*. Fate always cheated the king of the military glory for which he craved. Theoretically he had won a victory; his fleet controlled the Channel, his troops were in Boulogne, and, when peace was made in 1546, the French promised to resume payments of the pension first promised to Edward IV in 1475. The English were to keep Boulogne for eight years, after which the French would buy it back. But it was a hollow victory, and the whole war had been an expensive fiasco; especially as nothing had been done to stop French assistance to the Scots.

The Scottish war had dragged wearily on. The only success for the English was the murder of Cardinal Beaton in 1546 by a group of Scottish conspirators (who included John Knox). But the cardinal's death did nothing to further the hoped-for marriage. The war continued into the next reign; indeed, on an increased scale. Boulogne had to be kept on a war-footing even after the French peace, and was in fact handed back, four years early, after another outburst of war in 1549–50. It was reckoned that it had cost £1·3 million to capture and defend it, and that another million had been spent on the Scottish war. In addition, about a million had been spent on the navy, on garrisons and so on. Some of this expenditure would have been necessary even in peacetime, but the total cost of the war itself probably came to nearly three million pounds. Of this direct taxation raised about £1·2 millions, and loans and benevolences about £300,000.* This left another £1·5 million to be found by other means, probably in fact rather more than this, since the estimates of total cost seem to be on the low side.

One way was to sell off crown lands. This raised about £1·2 million between 1539 and 1554.† This sale, was, of course, mostly of the newly acquired monastic lands; and it is reckoned that, one way or another, about half the monastic lands had been lost by the crown by Henry's death, and another quarter disappeared by 1558.‡ Henry's war was not of course the only reason for this, but it was a major one, and so played a large part in undermining the 1536 plan for a permanent 'augmentation' of the crown's endowment. Another expedient was the debasement of the coinage. 'Debased' new coins were issued which contained less precious metal, gold or silver, than their predecessors. Individuals brought in their old coins to be melted down, to receive a greater value of new coins in return, and although in the long term the process put up prices, the individual would have made a real immediate profit. The government's profit came from charging for the operation; anything up to forty or eighty times the usual fee.§ The mint business boomed, and the profits for the crown

* Calculated from R. S. Schofield, 'Parliamentary Taxation 1485–1547' (Cambridge Ph.D. thesis 1963) table 40; and figures quoted by C. E. Challis, *Econ. Hist. Rev.*, 2nd ser., vol. 20, 1967, p. 454: *see also* F. C. Dietz, *English Government Finance 1485–1558* (Urbana 1921) pp. 164–6.

† L. Stone, *Crisis of the Aristocracy* (Oxford), p. 166.

‡ *See* Joyce Youings, in Thirsk, ed., *Agrarian History, 1500–1640* (Cambridge), pp. 338–9.

§ It is often suggested that the crown merely pocketed the difference between the metallic content of the old and new coins, but this is not true.

were considerable; about £450,000 from 1542-7, and another £750,000 from 1547-51.*

The economic consequences were complex, and we will discuss later what effect the debasements had on inflation. For the moment the important thing is that the debasements were *believed* to cause inflation. The coinage was, in a sense, a symbol of the stability of the state and the circulation of debased, false coins was seen as a confidence trick on the part of the government.

> These testons look red: how like you the same?
> 'Tis a token of grace: they blush for shame.

On top of this, from 1544 onwards, Henry was raising loans in Antwerp at about fourteen per cent. This was not, in fact, a high rate compared to what was usually charged to other kings; the credit of the English crown was better than that of its rivals. Nevertheless, it was dangerous to be so dependent on the subjects of Charles V, and there was some £75,000 owing at Henry's death. The crown was not free from foreign debt until 1574.†

While these expensive and ultimately disastrous wars were being fought, politics at home were largely concerned with court manoeuvres. These seem petty and sordid, but important issues were at stake. The ins and outs of court determined the education of the heir to the throne, and control of policy in the next reign. They determined, therefore, the religious future of England.

The Protestant–Catholic division of Cromwell's last years continued; although, as then, it would be wrong to think of clearly defined parties. Politicians preferred to conceal their private feelings and bow to the prevailing wind. Cranmer remained Archbishop of Canterbury, in spite of the Act of Six Articles. Henry's brother-in-law Edward Seymour, Earl of Hertford, was cautiously inclined to Protestantism, and, because he was Prince Edward's uncle, he was an important figure at court. Of the prominent Catholics, the Duke of Norfolk was now an old man

* Rough calculation from C. E. Challis's meticulous figures in *The Tudor Coinage* (Manchester Univ. Press, 1978).

† R. B. Outhwaite 'The Trials of Foreign Borrowing' (*Econ. Hist. Rev.*, 2nd ser, vol 19, 1966). Earlier editions of this book were at error in suggesting a debt of £750,000 at Henry's death. Although Henry raised about a million pounds all told from 1544-7, most of it was promptly repaid.

(he was born in 1473), but remained influential. So did Stephen Gardiner, still Bishop of Winchester, the most articulate and forceful of the Catholic bishops, and an extremely competent administrator, nicknamed Simon Stockfish for his part in organizing food supplies for the army.

As always, political struggle involved the king's bedchamber Catherine Howard had been put forward by Norfolk in 1540 to supplant Anne of Cleves. She was young, pretty and more than a little naïve. Henry had rediscovered the joys of youth in his fifth marriage. Catherine, however, found her corpulent and middle-aged husband less than attractive. She began to flirt with men of her own age, a dangerous pastime in a court full of enemies waiting to strike her down. Soon Archbishop Cranmer was able to rush to the king with evidence that Catherine had been unchaste before her marriage; and that she had probably committed adultery since, or had at least come near to committing it. An act of attainder was duly passed by Parliament in January 1542, and Catherine, like Ann Boleyn before her, ended her life on the executioner's block.

Norfolk, however, survived his niece's execution. Henry lived as a disillusioned widower for another eight months before marrying, in July 1543, a rather more suitable lady, Catherine Parr, thirty-one years old, and already twice a widow. Catherine was actively interested in religion. Her views were perhaps more Erasmian than 'Protestant', at least ostensibly, in that she was more concerned with undogmatic, scripture-based piety than with controversial matters of doctrine. She went in for daily scripture readings, and set her entourage to translate pious books. Princess Mary, for instance, worked on Erasmus's paraphrase of St John's Gospel. None of this offended against the official religious policy. But Erasmianism has a tendency to corrode Catholic certainty. The Gardiner faction smelt danger and the chance to avenge Catherine Howard. Gardiner told Henry 'how perilous a matter it is to cherish a serpent within his own bosom', and, on the king's orders, a heresy investigation was begun. Catherine got to know of it in time, and came to plead for her life. Never again, she promised, would she overstep wifely duty by instructing the supreme head in theology; she had only done so to distract Henry when he was ill (interesting evidence that theology was a subject for small talk as well as a serious intellectual pursuit, rather like politics in the twentieth century). Henry, satisfied, declared that 'perfect friends we are now again as ever at any time heretofore' and dismissed the accusers with a drubbing.

Henry seems to have been playing an elaborate cat-and-mouse game, designed apparently, to keep the courtiers in a constant state of apprehension and, by encouraging charge and counter-charge, find out what was really going on around him.* He had, after all, suffered twice from powerful and all too competent ministers, and was now anxious to prevent this happening a third time. An attempt was made to topple Cranmer in 1543; once more Henry encouraged the preparation of the prosecution case, then stepped in to protect the victim, after giving his archbishop the chilling information that he knew who was the greatest heretic in Kent. He also protected Gardiner from an attempt to involve him in the treason proceedings which were taken against his nephew (who was also his secretary) for upholding the papal supremacy.

Throughout these years the 'Catholic reaction' of 1539 was officially maintained. The Act of Six Articles remained in the statute book, the 'King's Book' of 1543 (written by a committee of bishops but revised by Henry) was a theological justification of its doctrine, and, in a *cause célèbre* of 1546, a well-connected Lincolnshire lady, Anne Askew, was burnt for denying the Catholic doctrine of the mass. It was afterwards alleged that two of the king's ministers, Wriothesley and Rich, operated the rack themselves in a vain attempt to get her to implicate the queen.

But there were signs of change. It remained a capital offence to deny the existence of purgatory, but an attack was prepared against the chantries, special foundations designed to endow masses for the souls of the dead. An act of 1545 authorized their dissolution and the transfer of their endowments to the king. Henry died, in January 1547, before any of this was put into effect. But he may have been contemplating in his last year a resumption of the march towards Protestantism and the abolition of the mass.

* See Lacey Baldwin Smith, *Henry VIII* (Cape, 1971).

Henry's religious vacillations were less important than the arrangements he was making for government after his death. This was complicated by the fact that, legally, Henry had only one legitimate child, Prince Edward, born in 1537. An act of 1544 inserted Mary and Elizabeth into the succession in spite of their bastardy; and allowed Henry to determine the further succession by will. In the event, Henry's will of December 1546 gave the descendants of his younger sister Mary precedence over those of his older sister Margaret, who had married James IV of Scotland; presumably the intention was to prevent a Scot taking over the throne of England, revenge perhaps for Scottish perfidy over the marriage. But more immediately important was the question of who should govern in Edward's name during his minority.

In December 1546 the equilibrium which Henry had maintained in the council for the last six years was suddenly broken. The Duke of Norfolk and his son, the Earl of Surrey, were arrested on a charge of treason. Surrey, a distinguished poet and a dashing soldier, was an arrogant young man, completely lacking in the prudence and readiness to crawl that had preserved his father through so many crises. He had displayed, privately, a coat-of-arms which underlined his royal descent. His servants, like those of Buckingham and Exeter before him, had gone in for loose talk about the succession. He had been openly contemptuous of the king's ministers (and ruined a prudent scheme of his father's for a marriage alliance with the Seymours); and had suggested to his sister (the widow of Henry's son the Duke of Richmond) that she should try to become the king's mistress, an old Howard ploy.

Surrey was found guilty and beheaded. His father would have followed him to the block; but his extraordinary luck held. Henry died before signing the warrant. Norfolk spent the next reign in the Tower, to emerge for a brief and final triumph when Mary became queen. Bishop Gardiner was excluded from the council which Henry had appointed to rule in his son's name. Without these leaders the remaining 'conservatives' were unlikely to stand up to the Protestant inclination of Seymour. The battle which Archbishop Cranmer had waged, long and surreptitiously, was won.

Whether or not Henry had planned the fall of the Howards long before, is difficult to say. He may have realized that the tactic of having a divided, faction-ridden council, which suited his own purpose well enough, would spell disaster in a minority; that therefore a choice between the Seymour and the Norfolk–Gardiner faction would become inevitable at some stage. Seymour had many advantages; not least the fact that as the future king's *maternal* uncle, his position depended entirely on his relationship to Edward, so that he would not be tempted to act against the king's interest. On this view, the Catholic faction was eventually doomed; and Henry's choice of three Protestant intellectuals (Richard Cox, Sir John Cheke and Sir Anthony Coke) as Edward's tutors was a recognition of this.

Against this, it may be suggested that Henry's policy was not so premeditated; that the Protestantism of Edward's tutors (who all suffered, in varying degrees, for their faith under Mary) was not apparent at the time but was merely the result of the tendency for intellectuals to have advanced religious views. On this view the downfall of the Howards was part of the normal see-saw of Henrician politics; it could have been the turn of the Seymours next. But whatever Henry may have intended, the situation he had created in 1547 resulted in the establishment of an unequivocally protestant regime in his son's reign. It also had the odd result – and a significant one – that only one man among Edward's councillors, the Earl of Arundel, had inherited his title. The rest were either commoners or newly created peers. In any minority, faction is likely to spill over into violence, if (remembering Edward v) nothing worse. Now religion threatened to complicate and intensify the traditional struggles, against a background of acute economic and social problems. When Henry died, on 27 January 1547, the new regime sensibly kept the news a secret while it prepared its dispositions.

RETROSPECT

Henry's reign had been one of the most crucial in English history. So much seems generally agreed, though agreement is less general on the significance of the various changes, or even how to define them. Controversy has its disadvantages. It tends to polarize issues, to force historical truth, which is many sided and rough edged, into the debating chamber artificiality of 'either-or': either the reign saw introduction of the sovereign state into England, or it did not; Henry was either a 'constitutional monarch' or he was a despot. Controversy seems inevitable; for the issues concerned raise stark fundamental questions of political values. No general agreement is likely on these. But controversy is also useful in stimulating research; and research can cut away legend and misconception, and provide as solid a foundation as possible for the value judgements which must be made in the end.

The most obvious change was in religion. Although not much had changed on the parochial level, Catholicism had been put on the defensive. Some indication of this is available from wills Traditionally the testator began by bequeathing his soul to God, the Virgin and the saints. But, as Professor Dickens has shown, by the end of Henry's reign about a third of testators even in Yorkshire and Nottingham, were omitting this 'Catholic' invocation and a few were venturing on a specifically Protestant affirmation of being saved through faith alone.* This is a significant indication of a popular mood; though we should not over-estimate it. Edward VI's reign was to see considerable resistance to the introduction of Protestant liturgies, and in Mary's reign Catholic forms were restored with little trouble. But the initiative was with Protestantism, for the moment at least; and if Catholicism were to survive it would need more than the old unthinking acceptance of the familiar.

Protestants might rejoice at the gains made. But in sober fact their cause had prospered not so much because of its inherent merits, but by an alliance with the forces of secularism; the king's fury at papal procrastination and dissimulation, and at the clergy's daring to assert the superiority of canon law to statute law, the grievances against the clergy of the Reformation Parliament, and so on. All over Europe, the reformers had forged an uneasy alliance with anti-clericals; a marriage of convenience between those who wished to reform the church to make it more

* A. G. Dickens, *The English Reformation* (Batsford, 1964), pp. 191–2. D. M. Palliser, on the other hand, finds the citizens of York itself remarkably conservative in his *Tudor York* (Oxford University Press, 1979), pp. 248–54.

effective, and others who resented ecclesiastical interference with everyday life.

As long as there was a common enemy, the Roman church, the alliance held. As soon as it came to positive action, there were signs of a split. The reformers wished not merely to pull down the monasteries, but to use their resources for positive religious and social purposes. Bishop Latimer asked that Great Malvern priory should continue, 'not in monkery ... God forbid', but 'to maintain teaching, preaching, study with praying and ... hospitality'. There was in fact a plan to make church government more efficient by using ex-monastic revenues to create new, manageable, dioceses. But in the end only six new bishoprics were founded, one of which (Westminster) was quickly suppressed again. Some schools and colleges were founded from monastic proceeds, but, given the opportunities, very few. Instead the revenues went to strengthen the crown and the landowning class. By 1549 Latimer was asserting that 'abbeys were ordained for the comfort of the poor', and that it was wrong to use them as stables for the king's horses. He was soon complaining that laymen would not support good gospel preaching in the way that they used to pay for 'Romish trifles'. His attitude foreshadowed the disappointment of the Elizabethan Puritans at the spectacle of a church inert and supine under lay domination, in which 'but halfly ... hath God been honoured, his church reformed ... his people taught and comforted, his enemies rejected and subdued, and his lawbreakers punished'.

This dichotomy between the spiritual and secular aspects of the Reformation was also noticeable in the realm of theory: on the one hand, God's everlasting truth had been rediscovered after being hidden for centuries, on the other, it was the state which had set forth the truth. Obviously nobody maintained that king or Parliament could alter the supranatural, or disputed More's *reductio ad absurdum*: 'suppose it were enacted that God was not God and that if anyone were to deny this it would be treason ... would you want to say that God was not God according to the statute?' Henry's bishops, while glad (or so they said), to have Parliament proclaiming the supreme headship, justified it in *theological* terms; the king was supreme head because God said so, not because Parliament had made him so. Parliament had done no such thing, but had only belatedly recognized the truth. (The fact that Parliament had done so before the bishops is incidental.) Indeed, the Supremacy Act was carefully couched in declaratory terms. 'Albeit the king's majesty justly and right fully *is and ought to be* the supreme head of the church of England ... yet nevertheless for corroboration and confirmation thereof ...' God's laws were eternal, and it was the state's duty merely to enforce them; 'diligently to foresee and cause, that not only the most holy word and commandments of God should most sincerely be believed and most reverently be observed ... but also that unity and concord in opinion ... may increase and go forward', as the preface to the 'Ten Articles' of 1536 proclaimed.

So much for theory. Unfortunately God's laws were far from self-evident. Parliament was therefore taking upon itself to define what they were, as well as enforcing them. A view of the eucharist condemned as damnable error in the Act of Six Articles was later (1552) asserted by Act of Parliament to be gospel truth. In practice, therefore, Parliament, and the nation which it represented, created for itself an image of omni-competence. Henry's ability to defy the pope, confiscate church property and despoil shrines, without much harm to himself and the kingdom, strengthened the impression of overwhelming state power.

The destruction of the tomb of Thomas Becket was especially significant here. Becket was, after all, well known for having been martyred for opposing King Henry II. His story, repeated and embroidered in countless sermons, and depicted in stained glass, was a powerful reminder of an alternative source of authority to the state; and this was now forcefully denied.

Between them king and Parliament now seemed capable of setting aside some of the basic assumptions of society, and not only in the religious sphere. Take, for instance, the succession acts of 1536 and 1544 which, by allowing the king, in certain circumstances, to leave the crown by will, and (in the second case) inserting Mary and Elizabeth into the succession in spite of their bastardy, constituted an astonishing claim of parliamentary authority as against customary, indeed fundamental, law. Historians have argued at some length about how far the Reformation introduced the 'sovereign state' into England. The arguments are highly technical. But in practical terms there can be little doubt that the way the Reformation was effected in England increased immeasurably both the power and the pretensions of the state.

That Leviathan had also been strengthened in more material respects. Defence against foreign threats had been improved by a huge increase in the royal navy (five fighting ships in 1509, about forty-five in 1547), with all the paraphernalia of permanent dockyards to service it. A chain of fortifications had been built along the south coast, and the garrisons at Calais, Hull and Berwick modernized. (Armament, however, often involves running to stand still; the new fleet served to counter the equivalent increase in the French fleet which the incorporation of Brittany had brought about.) Internally, the ability of the state to enforce its will had increased. For all the qualifications that we have made, the introduction of new and more effective permanent councils in the north and in Wales, and the transformation of Irish policy, had been a striking achievement. So, too, the dissolution of the monasteries, in spite of grants and sale of some of the lands, left the crown far better endowed by 1547 than it had been in the past. (Although Henry VIII, unlike his father, left a large debt, that was due to the demands of war rather than to any deficiency in income.) Henry was able to get away with unusually high demands for taxation in the 1540s. He also, in 1544, broke with precedent by ordering men to serve overseas in virtue of their militia obligation (hitherto confined to home defence). This foreshadowed the Elizabethan method of conscripting men for foreign service so ending the reliance on great landowners raising men from their tenants and dependants.

Much of this, as we have seen, involved a drastic change in government machinery. Did this, as Professor Elton claims, amount to a 'revolution in government' engineered by Thomas Cromwell?* The essence of his case is that 'medieval' government was always essentially personal. The work of such undoubtedly 'bureaucratic' bodies as the exchequer could be supplemented by

* G. R. Elton, *The Tudor Revolution in Government* (Cambridge, 1953).

more informal means, generally by using the king's 'household' offices for government purposes; such as the use of the king's chamber as a treasury by Edward IV and Henry VII. 'Modern' government, on the other hand, is seen as essentially 'bureaucratic' and 'formal'. The change is held to have taken place in the 1530s; and to have determined the general framework of English government for at least two hundred and fifty years.

This over-arching thesis can be criticized on several levels. Did Cromwell consciously plan any such 'bureaucratization'? Professor Elton himself admits that as an administrative reformer he did not, sensibly enough, tie his own hands. He kept, for instance, the receipt of ecclesiastical 'first fruits' on an informal basis; no formal court was established until after his fall. And the same applies to the final 'establishment' of the Privy Council. What emerged from the Cromwellian reforms, at least as far as finance was concerned, was a not very rational system; various courts (the exchequer, augmentations, first fruits, wards, etc.) all handling different sorts of income with no mechanism to bring together the various revenues. A warrant for £2,000 for ship repairs might involve the naval treasurer collecting money from two or three different departments. The problem bothered Cromwell's successors, and under various reform schemes all the revenue courts, except wards and the Duchy of Lancaster (anciently privileged) had been re-absorbed into the exchequer by 1554, though retaining their own accounting systems; from this point of view, Cromwell appears as the last statesman to proliferate new departments on 'medieval' principles, and William Paulet, the Marquis of Winchester, the lord treasurer responsible for unification, was the initiator of bureaucracy. Finally, even if the Cromwellian achievement is accepted, it seems hard to argue that it lasted two hundred and fifty years. The massive change imposed upon government by much closer parliamentary control after 1689, the development of the treasury, and the evolution of a sophisticated system of public credit, can hardly be written off as 'only a shifting of emphasis', as Professor Elton claims.*

But even with all these qualifications, the administrative

* *Tudor Revolution* (Cambridge) p. 424.

achievements of the 1530s are impressive. The period 1540–1640 was one of administrative consolidation, rather than innovation (the Paulet reforms would fit this scheme); one might say, of administrative sclerosis. Bureaucratic routine helped to perpetuate inefficiency (for instance, the Elizabethan failure to adjust the income from crown lands to inflationary conditions) and corruption. Arguably, if a personal initiative like that of Edward IV or Henry VII had been possible, this might have been prevented. It is in this context, rather than the much longer one which Professor Elton claims, that the 'Tudor Revolution' carries conviction. Why this should be so is not clear. Elizabethan and Jacobean administrative history is a largely uncultivated field of study. But it seems a reasonable supposition that sheer weight of business made a personal initiative impractical. Increased government business in the 1530s demanded new methods. That the demand was met, and efficiently so, without any intervening period of chaos, is a striking personal testimony to Thomas Cromwell's administrative genius.

Cromwell's fall was sudden, and his work incomplete. He encouraged a good deal of discussion about the reform of the law, but nothing was achieved. Nor was anything done about local government, except for the northern, Welsh and western councils. (Professor Youings suggests that the Council of the West may have been intended to be the model of a regional conciliar scheme for the country as a whole.*) It may be that a continued Cromwellian regime would have modified the system of amateur justices of the peace which was one of the great obstacles to administrative efficiency and the enforcement of the law.

Even confining ourselves to what was done, rather than what might have been done, the state in the 1530s was considerably stronger than it was to be under Henry's successors. One obvious point here is the financial benefit of the monastic lands. But it was not only a financial advantage. Land involved considerable patronage in the appointment of stewards, the grant of leases and so on, which the crown lost when monastic lands were sold. It lost, too, valuable ecclesiastical patronage. The monasteries had con-

* J. A. Youings, 'The Council of the West' (*Trans. Roy. Hist. Soc.*, 5th ser., vol. 10, 1960).

trolled the right of appointment to about a third of the country's parochial livings. Had these rights remained with the crown, royal control of the church would have been immeasurably stronger in the next century, and the ability of Puritan peers and gentlemen to ensconce their clerical protégés in comfortable livings and snap their fingers at crown and bishop, would have been very much less. The larger the crown's patronage, the less frequently would ambitious clergy have been tempted into unorthodoxy. If the crown had kept control of the benefices, Puritanism might never have become a respectable body of opinion within the church; it might have been driven instead to being merely a politically ineffectual underground movement.

The church provides one vivid illustration of the sort of active, interfering, omnicompetent government to which none of Cromwell's successors could aspire; his interpretation of the supreme headship. As vice-gerent, Cromwell controlled both provinces of the Church of England, as Wolsey had done before him. No other subject, lay or cleric, ever exercised a similar jurisdiction after him, at least in theory. (The jurisdiction of Archbishop of Canterbury was confined to the southern province, although of course, archbishops like Whitgift and Laud who received considerable support from the crown came in practice to run the church as a whole.) As vice-gerent Cromwell possessed his own court (whose existence has only recently come to light) and interfered drastically with the normal jurisdiction of the bishops. Their rights were suspended during the royal visitation of 1535. Thomas Legh and John ap Rice explained why. By taking 'all jurisdiction and power' into his own hands for a time, the king would establish 'a perpetual monument' of his power. If the bishops retorted that their jurisdiction came from God, not the king, 'let them bring forth scripture, but I think them not so impudent as to say so'. This blunt assertion of state power underlines the realities of the Henrician Reformation.

It is within this context, of a crown stronger than at any time before or since, that we must consider its relations with Parliament. Here again, we must take issue with an influential view of Professor Elton's; his statement that 'in the last analysis it was [Cromwell] who founded the modern constitutional monarchy in England, and organized the sovereign national state'.* There is some truth in the statement; but put so baldly it is liable to mislead.

As we have seen, the parliamentary tradition in England was very strong, long before the Reformation Parliament; although the tendency towards parliamentary self-assertion against the crown had declined since the early fifteenth century, Parliament's legislative supremacy was unchallenged. Parliamentary statute was as much the obvious way for Henry VIII to proceed against the papacy as it had been for Edward III and Richard II. In the sense of sharing its legislative functions with Parliament and, perhaps more important, relying on Parliament for extraordinary taxation, the crown had been 'constitutional' for at least two centuries. We may grant that Cromwell had a particular penchant for proceeding by parliamentary statute even when it was not strictly necessary – for instance, in establishing the Court of Augmentations; but that hardly amounts to the foundation of constitutional monarchy.

Secondly, although the term 'constitutional monarchy' can, strictly speaking, be applied to the government of Henry VIII (as of his predecessors), it is misleading; in that it must suggest to a modern reader, not a situation in which the crown needed parliamentary approval for legislation and taxation, but one in which the degree of parliamentary control over the everyday workings of government was considerable; in other words, something like the eighteenth-century situation. Obviously no one would suggest that Cromwell was thinking of anything of this sort. But it is worth making the point that 'constitutional monarchy' in this sense was the result of seventeenth-century developments which were due to royal weakness, precisely in those areas which Cromwell had tried to strengthen; royal finance, for instance. Had the crown retained the revenues acquired through the dissolution

* *England Under the Tudors* (Metheun, 1955: rev. ed., 1974) pp. 128–9. Professor Elton has now modified his views on fifteenth-century parliaments, and acknowledges the evolutionary nature of their development, though still insisting on a significant change with the Reformation. *See* his 'Body of the Whole Realm: Parliament and Representation in Medieval and Tudor England', in *Studies in Tudor and Stuart Politics and Government* (2 vols. Cambridge, 1974), vol. 2.

of the monasteries, it would not have freed itself from the need for parliamentary taxation; but its bargaining position with Parliament would have been very much stronger, and at certain key moments (Charles I's 'personal rule' provides a possible analogy), extra resources might have been decisive.

Nevertheless, the Reformation Parliament does represent an important stage in parliamentary development. If an attack on the church was envisaged, Parliament was the obvious means of proceeding; but the *fact* that this had happened, that Parliament had been used to annihilate a jurisdiction which had been, in a sense, a rival to the whole secular state, obviously resulted in a tremendous increase in its standing. In one sense the Reformation represented a practical affirmation of positive statute law over natural law, the notion that there was an independent law of God which was not only incumbent on a man's conscience, but which he might plead in a court of law against the positive law of the state; the position, essentially, taken by Thomas More. Defence of the royal supremacy involved defence of Parliament as the institution which had activated and in a sense authorized it. So Cromwell personally sponsored a translation of the fourteenth-century Italian theorist, Marsilio of Padua. Marsilio argued that legitimate political power emanated from the people; the translation added the significant gloss that 'people' did not mean 'the rascal multitude' but Parliament.

The practical significance of this lay in the sheer importance of Parliament's business in a period of bewildering and fundamental religious change. When Elizabeth I tried to stop her parliaments discussing religion, MPs were armed with a host of precedents to quote back at her; and the parliamentary history of her father's reign bulked large among them.

Parliament, then, was Henry's indispensable ally, once he had determined to cut loose from Rome; its authority was necessary to buttress his own, and Henry was prepared to acknowledge it. 'We at no time stand so highly in our estate royal as in time of Parliament, wherein we as head and you as members are conjoined and knit together in one body politic . . .' Even so conflict might develop on occasion, and the art of parliamentary management was studied by the crown's ministers, and sometimes rather roughly applied. The crown naturally used its own influence and that of its ministers in elections. On one occasion, at least, Cromwell went further than this. At Canterbury in 1536 the authorities were ordered to quash an election which had already taken place and to elect instead two royal nominees. As we have seen (*above*, p. 187) a good deal of pressure of various sorts was brought to bear on the Reformation Parliament, while blatant intimidation was practised to get the Submission of the Clergy out of Canterbury Convocation. Lord Herbert of Cherbury, Henry's seventeenth-century biographer, wrote that 'when gentle means served not, he came to some degrees of the rough; though the more sparingly in that he knew his people did but too much fear him'. More contemporary evidence is that produced by Cranmer, resisting a demand by the western rebels of 1549 for the reintroduction of the Act of Six Articles. 'If the king's majesty had not come personally into the parliament house those laws had never passed.'

But, when vested interests were involved, Parliament could oppose the royal will, and to good effect. In 1539 a bill was introduced about the validity and enforcement of royal proclamations. What was in the bill is not known. But it excited considerable discussion in both houses, and was so amended, that a new bill was eventually introduced and enacted. This Statute of Proclamation now seems a rather innocuous measure; it is concerned primarily with the better enforcement of proclamations, and to this end gives explicit statutory sanction to rights which the crown already had. Some historians have suggested that the original bill was more sinister than this, and sought to extend the crown's right to issue proclamation to new spheres, so threatening the normal method of legislation by parliamentary statute.* Within twenty years the 1539 Parliament was credited with preventing Henry VIII giving proclamations 'the force of statute'. But against this there seems no evidence, either before or after the statute was passed, of the crown wishing to employ proclamations in a

* Compare J. Hurstfield, 'Was there a Tudor Despotism After All?' (*Trans. Roy. Hist. Soc.*, 5th ser., vol. 17, 1967) with G. R. Elton, 'Henry VIII's Act of Proclamations', *Studies in Tudor and Stuart Politics at Government*, vol. 1.

novel manner. Perhaps the best answer to this riddle is to suggest that the act was badly drafted, seemed to threaten more than was intended, and that vigilant parliamentarians therefore caused trouble. Whatever the truth of all this, the incident certainly demonstrates Parliament's capacity to make the government think again on important issues.

Even more striking is the controversy on 'uses' which dogged the Reformation Parliament for the whole seven years of its life. It stemmed from the ambivalent status of land at this time. In theory nobody 'owned' land in the modern sense; all land was held by tenancy from somebody else, ultimately from the king. In practice land was regarded as a commodity, which could be bought and sold and bequeathed by will. Nevertheless, the king (and indeed, the lords) still possessed their rights of overlordship, and could levy certain dues, which historians háve come to call 'feudal dues'. In particular the lord had the right to wardship of the lands of his immediate tenants if the occupant were a minor; and this could be very profitable.

To avoid the danger of land being subject to royal rights of wardship, there was an increasing tendency to put lands into 'trust' or 'use'; rather like modern devices to avoid death duties. In 1529 the government introduced a bill to plug this loophole by outlawing uses, in return for a restricted royal right to feudal dues. It met with so much opposition in the Commons that it had still not passed in 1533. Henry, exasperated, got a ruling from the judges, that land could not be bequeathed at all. The judges, by upholding the full rigour of the ancient land law, had invalidated all existing uses and caused endless other difficulties in the whole complicated world of landownership. Parliament was faced with a *fait accompli*; and in 1536 passed the Statute of Uses. In return for legalizing existing uses, it acknowledged the crown's right to feudal dues; but land could still not be left by will. The king had achieved total victory.*

The statute was, naturally, extremely unpopular and its repeal figured among the rebel demands in the Pilgrimage of Grace.

* *See* E. W. Ives, 'The Genesis of the Statute of Uses' (*Eng. Hist. Rev.*, vol. 32, 1967); J. M. W. Bean *The Decline of English Feudalism* (Manchester, 1968).

In the event, it was impractical. In 1540 a new statute permitted lands to be bequeathed once more, and compromised on the dues question. From one point of view the story of the Statute of Uses shows the length to which the crown would go to get its own way. But more significant is probably the Commons's ability to resist an unpopular measure; and, in the long term, the impracticality of a statute which had to be forced on them. Parliament was a useful sounding board which the government would be foolish to ignore.

In essence, then, parliament was likely to resist measures it found to be against its interest; but to accept those to which it was indifferent, or even perhaps mildly opposed. Its normal working assumption, after all, was cooperation, not opposition. The pressures exerted by the crown to manage the assembly smelt to Victorian historians of despotism. To late twentieth-century eyes (more accustomed to studying the realities of power, and aware of the immense powers of the executive in modern parliamentary democracy) Tudor attempts to manage Parliament may look no more than the minimum requirement for ordered government. 'Constitutional monarchy' may stand; provided that there is no implication that it was new, or that Parliament was the majoi partner.

'No king was so careful of law as Henry, but he was not so careful of justice', wrote A. F. Pollard.* It is, of course, perfectly possible for laws to be passed by due constitutional process and still to be unjust, even tyrannical; it is also possible for trials to take place without violation of the proper judicial forms, and yet for injustice to be done. Debate here centres on the Treason Act of 1534 (*see above*, p. 183), which, by making possible the conviction of a man for treason on evidence by one witness that he had called the king heretic or schismatic, clearly had enormous scope. It aroused a good deal of contemporary hostility; and was repealed in the first Parliament of the next reign as likely to 'appear to men of exterior realms and many of the king's majesty's subjects very strait, sore, extreme and terrible'. More generally, many treason trials and acts of attainder seem manifestly unjust; More, tricked into denying the royal supremacy, Anne Boleyn,

* *Henry VIII* (Longman, 1905 ed.) p. 435.

victim of a far-fetched accusation, Thomas Cromwell, against whom the political–theological balance had swung at an awkward moment; as well as those more humble men and women who called Anne Boleyn 'that whore' before king and Parliament came round to the same opinion.

Some points need to be made to put this in perspective. Dubious evidence had always been a feature of political trials; the trials of Clarence in 1478, and of Warwick in 1499 provide cases in point. A man could be executed for speech rather than action well before 1534; as well as the cases in which speech had been 'constructed' as treason, wrong opinion about religion had after all been a capital offence under the heresy laws since 1401. Professor Elton has argued that the purpose of the 1534 act was to bring the law up to date, to cope with the existing situation (clearly, calling the king a heretic was a dangerous threat to good order in the 1530s), so that treason trials could take place according to due process of law rather than by resort to acts of attainder, or other dubious expedients. He has also argued that the number of convictions has been exaggerated; that cases were minutely investigated and that those based on frivolous accusation, or the result of careless or drunken talk, were usually dropped.*

But some awkward points remain. If some two-thirds, at least, of those accused of treason were acquitted, pardoned, or had their cases dropped, none the less, anything between 50 and 130 people did in fact lose their lives for 'treasonable words' between 1532 and 1540. (Though it might be worth making the point that these numbers are relatively small compared to that of executions for normal criminal offences like theft; *see below*, p. 302.) Many of the others found themselves arrested, interrogated by justices, even by Cromwell himself, for what, very often, amount to little more than ill-considered remarks. Moreover there is a difference between the occasional 'construction' of words as treason, and their normative treatment as such. That introduces a new situation; a principle is erected, men are duty bound to report idle

---

* G. R. Elton, *Policy and Police* (Cambridge, 1972) *passim*. The point might also be made that justice in criminal trials generally, was rough, and that the standard of proof required even for capital offences like theft was unlikely to have been high.

tittle-tattle; and indeed are themselves guilty of misprision of treason if they do not. When it comes to the point, moreover, we do not know how convictions were obtained; even in the More case which is exceptionally well documented, a good deal remains uncertain. The victims of treason trials customarily made a speech from the scaffold acknowledging that they had been rightly convicted. But Henry himself told Cranmer, 'if they have you once in prison, three or four knaves will be soon procured to witness against you', and Anne Boleyn laughed when the lieutenant of the Tower told her 'the poorest subject the king hath, hath justice'.

A better justification probably lies in *raison d'état*; the argument that England's welfare required the Reformation, that national unity needed to be preserved against the threat of political collapse, and that in politics no lesser moral principle can or should stand against an overwhelming national interest. Contemporaries certainly accepted the point that the preservation of order was vital; and that any means, or almost any means was justified to that end. To quote Pollard again, 'The nation in the sixteenth century deliberately condoned injustice, when injustice made for its peace.'* So Bishop Tunstall of Durham, a man who at various times showed a good deal of personal political courage, could write (to clear himself of suspected sympathy for the Pilgrimage of Grace) of his detestation of all traitors and those 'accused of the same', a nice pre-supposition of guilt. All these were worse than Turks, 'for the Turks, albeit they be infidels, yet they be of the same nature men as we be'. Rebels clearly were not.

Nevertheless, one's doubts remain. First, the suspicion that under Henry the treason law was sometimes used, not so much to preserve the king and kingdom, but as an everyday weapon of politics. Secondly, that this in turn depended as much on the king's whim, as on any consideration of the public good. It is just possible to accept that the divorce from Catherine of Aragon was necessary for the national interest; it is much harder to do so (though in other respects Catherine is the more sympathetic figure) in the case of Anne Boleyn. In this sense Henry's actions

* *Henry VIII*, p. 437.

236

came close to what contemporaries understood by tyranny: 'all things pertaining to the state of [the] realm to hang only upon [the ruler's] will and fantasy'. So Luther bluntly dismissed the English Reformation as 'What Squire Harry wills'.

But whatever the motives of the king (and according to Tudor theory he would have to answer for it before God), it is possible to understand why, in the interests of the community, and not necessarily for cowardly reasons, men were prepared to accept royal authority; even when, as with Cranmer on the Anne Boleyn issue, they were reduced to solemnly contradicting what they had recently solemnly affirmed. Henry was, after all, the only king they had, indispensable to the good of the realm, both in theory and practice. A modern analogy might be those often heroic communists who were prepared to put up with the tyranny of Stalin, and even persuade themselves that Stalin was not a tyrant, for what they saw as the ultimate greater good.

What might have happened had Parliament resisted the king's will on a matter of overwhelming importance (as opposed to the merely important, like the Statute of Uses) or if the judges had pronounced against proceedings in a major state trial, we cannot tell. As it was, their very malleability, the readiness of Parliament to enact a treason law which could have been used, even if it were not, as an instrument of tyranny, the readiness of the courts to find men guilty on sometimes very thin evidence indeed, had the paradoxical result of ensuring that parliamentary and common-law institutions survived and were even strengthened.

Henry's political skill was important in his success. He was a consummate politician, in spite of his habitual laziness about business and his tendency to leave decisions to his ministers; indeed this was an advantage, because he could dissociate himself from an unpopular policy, and, if necessary, ditch the minister. He was able to keep his options open, encourage opponents of present policies with the hope that they might soon be changed; whether by his friendliness to the great aristocrats who were Wolsey's opponents in the twenties, or his careful balancing of court parties after 1536. Henry had considerable personal charm, the result both of his utter confidence in his own royal role, and of his natural abilities. He was adept at the friendly confidence, the reassuring arm round the shoulder, the implied promise that favour would be restored. Wolsey's hopes of being recalled to service were kept alive to the end of 1529 by a series of ambiguous signs of royal favour. Henry also knew how and when to strike, and how to humiliate a man; as when the Earl of Northumberland was forced to be one of the judges of his one-time sweetheart, Anne Boleyn.

The state had to sustain the belief that it was wealthy and invincible; that it was also in some sense a manifestation of the divine on earth, rather than merely a human device to maintain order (or, as Thomas More put it, 'a kind of conspiracy of the rich, who are aiming at their own interests, under the name and title of the commonwealth'). Henry's expenditure on building, (Whitehall and Hampton Court, both taken over from Wolsey, and the brand-new and never-completed palace at Nonsuch in Surrey, with a good many others), on pageants and tournaments, on clothes (his tailors did more than anybody else to create the myth of Henry VIII), even arguably the expenditure on war, were all productive investments, the dividend respect and fear and therefore peace.

The effect of this sort of propaganda was limited by the fact that Henry very rarely ventured out of the home counties. But of course the London area was the most important part of the country politically and, through the reports of those who came to London to attend the courts at Westminster or on business in the city, the image which Henry had created was spread through the country at large. Servants, petty hucksters, drovers and all that army of men who travelled the roads of England reported events and impressions; treason trial records show that news about politics and public personalities, often distorted but never entirely fanciful, had a place in ale-house conversation. To judge by the attitudes of Edward Hall in '*The union of the two noble and illustre famelies York and Lancaster*', spectacle was effective propaganda; although he was MP and a lawyer, Hall was easily, naïvely, impressed by 'the order and setting out of dinner', by royal processions, the performance of allegorical pageants (he was especially taken by any 'marvelous cunning' mechanical contrivance), all of them enthusiastically described at tedious length.

Henry went in for a good deal of this sort of ceremonial in his younger days. The pace slackened in the mid-thirties. Anne Boleyn was given a magnificent entry into London (at which, incidentally, the Londoners showed their marked lack of enthusiasm for the new queen), but nothing was done for her successors. Henry gave up competing at tournaments in 1536, when he was knocked unconscious while tilting at Greenwich. He was now forty-four, and his health was deteriorating fast; what had been impressive strength and virility had now become gross corpulence, and Henry (though probably no more than most other men of his age) was wracked by often painful disease. The ceremonial tradition died, not to be revived on a large scale until the days of that other royal showman Queen Elizabeth; but by then it had done its work in establishing an ineradicable image of the king.

Still, public relations, although important, cannot provide a complete explanation of why Henry was able to challenge the pretences of the clergy, abolish the monasteries and in many respects undermine the privileges of nobility, and get away with it. There were obviously solid advantages to the country in accepting Henry's government. It is usual to argue that responsible opinion in the Tudor period was frightened of a recurrence of the Wars of the Roses, and prepared, therefore, to allow considerable latitude to the crown. These fears undoubtedly existed, and Tudor propaganda exploited them with some success. But the implied contrast with the fifteenth century is unwarrantable. Men tended then, too, to prefer peace to war, and to go to great length to preserve it and to prevent the authority of the crown being trampled underfoot; civil war was the result of government weakness, its failure to fulfil its basic duty of providing security and protection, not of an irresponsible or self-indulgent protest against strong government. Henry VIII's government could, by no stretch of the imagination, be accused of the sort of incompetence which had caused the downfall of Henry VI.

Two other points need to be made here. First, the obvious but crucial one, that Henry faced no immediate dynastic threat, in the way that Edward IV and Richard III had; nobles who were involved in 'dynastic' treason were speculating about the succession, not about replacing Henry. Secondly, that Henry was not faced with the possibility of opposition on ideological grounds; which, in sixteenth-century terms, meant religious grounds. There was little danger from the Protestant side. Although Henry persecuted Protestants, sometimes viciously, he had nevertheless opened the way to a possible Protestant Reformation; the martyr-ologist John Foxe could write that he was 'of his own nature and disposition . . . so inclinable and forward in all things virtu-ous and commendable that the like enterprise of redress of religion hath not lightly been seen in any other prince', though sadly liable to be misled by 'snuffling prelates' like Gardiner. On the other hand Catholics had not yet organized themselves to fight ideological battles. For the moment they were too much imbued with the conservatism, with the general respect for the *status quo* and acceptance of the familiar which formed the strength of their church, to attack an errant secular authority; especially one as theologically ambivalent as Henry VIII.

Of course Henry's government at times offended vested in-terests; and sometimes gave way to protest, as it had in 1525 on the Amicable Grant and in 1528 on war with the Netherlands (*see above*, pp. 169, 173). But the question of how Henry was able to get away with his attacks on the clergy in general, and more especi-ally the monks, and to a lesser extent the old nobility, remains to be answered.

As far as the clergy is concerned, it seems reasonable to argue that there was no reason for general enthusiasm in defence of their interests; partly for long-term reasons concerning the relative position of clergy and laity in the church; more immediately be-cause, although both secular clergy and monks had suffered from Wolsey's regime, they nevertheless fell victim to the reaction against him. Nevertheless, the Pilgrimage of Grace shows that, in certain circumstances, defence of the church could be inte-grated into a more general protest movement, and when this happened the result was explosive and the clerical interest itself by no means negligible. But there was no explosion in the country at large. In part this was due to the advantages which other classes got from the humiliation of the clergy; most notably, of course, the distribution of a part of the monastic lands to influential and potentially dangerous great men, like the Duke of Norfolk. In part it was the result of the collapse of the Pilgrimage itself; and here again, Henry's skill in handling the rebellion in prevaricating until it fell apart is important, as was the subsequent reversal of what had seemed to be a helter-skelter progress to radical reform.

The Pilgrimage had shown the key role of a number of influential peers; any chance of success would depend on the decisions of men like Derby, Shrewsbury and Norfolk. The old nobility had after all, suffered some hard knocks under Henry. As Sir Philip Sidney later put it, Henry had preferred to favour the gentry, in case the nobility 'might be tempted, by still coveting more, to fall (as the Angels did) by effecting equality with their Maker'. Some of the most prominent (Buckingham, Exeter) had been executed, and their lands confiscated. The great Percy inheritance had been threatened before the Pilgrimage, and was of course confiscated after it. Many of the nobles' judicial privileges, especially in Wales and the north, were lost in the wave of modernizing efficiency of the 1530s. Edward VI's regency council seemed to set the seal on the developments of the reign (*see above*, p. 221); the old peerage could, apparently, now be dispensed with as a political class.

What seems to us, looking backwards, part of a formed, definite policy of monarchical aggrandizement at the expense of the nobility was not so clear to contemporaries. Henry's policy was not consistent, even towards noblemen who had dangerously Yorkist descent, as the favours showered on Henry Courtenay in 1523–5 show. At various times – at the beginning of the reign, after the fall of Wolsey, after the fall of Cromwell – it looked as if Henry might adopt a more 'aristocratic' policy and let himself be guided by his 'natural councillors' instead of those whom Surrey spurned as men 'of vile birth' who 'loved no nobility'. In the circumstances, it might seem politic to keep quiet for the moment in the hope of a change in the king's mood; especially when this could be helped on by backstairs and bedchamber intrigue.

In any case, any feeling of caste solidarity that the nobility may have had was qualified by jealousies and rivalries between nobles. A treason charge against one of the great northern magnates, Lord Dacre, in 1534 was brought at the instigation of his enemies the Earls of Cumberland and Northumberland. In the event the charge was rejected by a court of twenty-one peers; but it had served the king's purpose in frightening Dacre, and providing an excuse for replacing him as warden of the west march by the much more malleable Earl of Cumberland. A staple factor in northern politics from 1489 onwards was the desire of the Howards to establish themselves as a great northern family; bringing them into conflict with established families like the Percies and Dacres. One of the strongest cards of any monarch was his power of patronage. He could appoint to offices which brought profit and status; he could cancel old debts; he could make gifts of land, or sell on easy terms. The Reformation put Henry in a uniquely powerful position here. He could endow new peers, like Russell, on a lavish scale from the monastic lands, and hold out tempting bait even to such families as the Howards (*see above*, p. 158) in return for good behaviour.

Transcending all these particular points is the sheer increase in the standing and prestige of the crown under the first two Tudors, due partly to sheer luck (the dynastic factor and especially the avoidance of a minority government at Henry VII's death), partly to able leadership; and epitomized in the absence of major, noble-led dynastic rebellion since 1487. The longer the crown was unchallenged, the more unchallengeable it was likely to be. But this was the result of particular circumstances, as Edward VI's reign was to show. The possibility of noble rebellion could not be ruled out for ever. But for the moment, the absence of noble opposition meant the absence of any effective opposition. The English monarchy stood unchallenged; Holbein's image of the solid, arrogant, even contemptuous, Henry its perfect epitome.

Chapter Eight

THE MID-TUDOR ECONOMY

With Edward VI's reign the flow of political narrative is brusquely interrupted by economic considerations. 1549 saw the only occasion in our period when social tensions played the major part in ruining a great political figure. Edward's reign provides, therefore, a convenient excuse to stand back and examine the slow development of the economy over the previous hundred years.

By far the most important change had been in population trends. As we have seen, population had been static in the middle of the fifteenth century, at a level considerably lower than it had been a century before that. Historians dispute about when exactly it began to rise again. But certainly from the 1520s, if not earlier, the trend is unmistakable. Population was growing faster than agricultural production. The price of food soared ever higher. At the same time, there was increased competition for jobs, so that wages rose much more slowly than food prices. The result was therefore a dramatic drop in real wages, in the goods that wages could buy.

By 1560 a building craftsman could buy with his daily wage only 60 per cent as much food as his predecessor could have bought in 1500; by 1600 it was down to 40 per cent.* Of course these figures are abstract and divorced from everyday reality. Not all expenditure was on food. Wage-earners may not have bought many industrial goods; but they did pay house-rent, and this is a subject about which we know very little. Moreover wage figures

---

* E. H. Phelps Brown and S. V. Hopkins, 'Seven Centuries of the Prices of Consumables, compared with builders' wage-rates' (in E. M. Carus-Wilson, ed., *Essays in Economic History* (1962) vol. 2, pp. 179–96).

are wage *rates* per day; we cannot tell whether in fact the number of days worked per year was, on average, less or more in the sixteenth century than in the fifteenth. Theoretically it should have been more, with the drastic diminution of non-working saints' days at the Henrician Reformation, but this may have been countered by there being more unemployment or under-employment. Lastly money wages were not everything, even for the townsman; many urban workers could keep cattle on the commons, and many riots (for example, at Coventry in the 1480s) resulted from the determination of the poorer citizens to defend these rights. Nevertheless, the trend in the standard of living of the urban worker was unmistakably downwards; from the point of view of the bottom half of the population, the sixteenth century was disastrous.

The pressure of population showed itself rather differently in the countryside. There too money wages were important, whether for farm labourers or for the increasing number of rural industrial workers who produced cloth or other goods in their own cottages. But the balance was much more towards growing one's own food. The rural labourer or artisan would be affected more by the availability of common rights, by decisions to 'stint' (limit) the number of animals to be kept on the common, by the chance of acquiring a smallholding, than he would by a daily wage rate. And here local generalizations are more than usually hazardous. By and large things were better in the pastoral areas, whether forest or highland (*see above*, p. 191). There was still a good deal of waste land available in those regions and so the labourer was able to improve his living by keeping animals and taking wood for fuel. In addition he had more chance for industrial by-employment – spinning wool, knitting stockings, making nails and so on – because looking after animals was less of a full-time job than working an arable holding. In arable areas land was in greater demand. There the trend was towards prohibition of the ancient right to run-up a makeshift cottage on the waste, a further tightening of grazing rights in the interests of the propertied, and, sometimes, the disappearance of commons altogether. In some cases men resorted to straw and cow dung for fuel, and cooked at a communal fire.

There is a paradox here which historians have not yet begun to solve. The natural explanation of rising population would involve postulating a general rise in living standards, which would permit a higher birth rate or greater expectation of life. (And there seems some evidence both for an unusually high degree of fertility and for an unusually high expectation of life in early Tudor England.) Yet we have just been arguing for a decline in income for wage-earners. But the two points are not necessarily incompatible. After all, wage-earners were only a minority of the working population. They were less likely to be married than master-craftsmen or peasants. Even among this minority, a substantial number were only temporary wage-earners, while they waited to take over the family farm or set themselves up in business, and then marry. The master craftsman, the peasant farmer (provided he was securely in possession of his land) were well placed to profit from the opportunities available, not least from the buoyant demand for food. The trend was not towards all-round impoverishment, but rather to a greater polarization between the respectable, possessing, propertied classes on the one hand; and those whose only capital lay in their hands. The increased prosperity of the former may well explain the rise in population.*

The demand for land, the growing shortage of food, was not confined to England; it was noticeable throughout western and southern Europe. Of course, these trends were not immediately apparent to contemporaries. They could not, as we can, with the benefit of hindsight, disentangle the long-term upward trend of prices from the year-to-year variations due to the quality of the harvest. Men naturally drew long-term conclusion from immediate situations, and they were often wrong; in the same way as modern political writers are given to speculating about long-term electoral trends, usually erroneously, on the basis of a single general election result.

The rise in food prices proceeded in a series of spurts, the result of two or three years of bad harvest, often followed by a relatively easier period as the weather became less malignant.

* See now E. A. Wrigley and R. S. Schofield *The Population History of England 1541–1871* (Edward Arnold, 1981). They invoke a long time-lag between changes of living standard and changes in the age of marriage to explain high fertility in a period of declining real wages; and see the death-rate as determined more by epidemics than by living standards.

PEACE, PRINT AND PROTESTANTISM

There was a bad patch, for instance, in the early twenties, (the harvests of 1520 and 1521) and again from 1527–30.* There were other individual bad years, but nothing spectacular until the early forties (1543–6), and again the years 1550–2. Worst of all were the middle years of Mary's reign, best shown in tabular form –

Year	General Average price of wheat, shillings per quarter	General quality of harvest
1553–4	11·14	Good
1554–5	16·01	Average
1555–6	22·47	Dearth
1556–7	31·15	Dearth
1557–8	11·06	Good
1558–9	9·49	Abundant

The story behind the two years of dearth is one of sheer horror. A Suffolk rector wrote that 'the scarcity of bread that year was so great, in so much that the plain poor people did make much of acorns and a sickness of strong fever did sore molest them'. The death rate shot up. At St Margaret's Westminster, sixteen burials were baldly described as due to famine. In 1558 there was a killing epidemic, possibly influenza, which was probably helped on its way by a population weakened by two years of malnutrition. About a fifth of the entire population may have died between 1555–60.†

The result of this mid-Tudor crisis was to ease, temporarily, the pressure of population on resources. Elizabethan England could enjoy a period of relative freedom from continued subsistence crisis until the late eighties. Then the fearful pattern of hunger and epidemic reasserted itself, to produce in 1596–8 a crisis as bad as that of 1555–7; the low points, on Professor Phelps Brown's calculations, for the wage-earner's standard of living over the whole of English history since the Black Death.‡

When men tried to explain the general distress (which they did

* Adapted from W. G. Hoskins, 'Harvest Fluctuations and English Economic History, 1480–1619' in W. E. Minchinton (ed.), *Essays in Agrarian History* (Newton Abbott, 1968) vol. 1.

† F. J. Fisher, 'Influenza and Inflation in Tudor England' (*Econ. Hist. Rev.*, 2nd ser., vol. 28, 1965).

‡ Phelps Brown and Hopkins, *art. cit.* (above, p. 243).

endlessly in pamphlets, sermons and memoranda to the government), they had, for the most part, little concept of rising population. The first clear statement of the over-population argument dates from the 1570s. The usual assumption was of a declining population; the basic trouble was thought to be greed, 'covetousness', 'an inordinate desire to have that they had not'. Through greed, landlords expropriated tenants, enclosed land and converted it from arable to pasture. 'Where there have been a great many householders and inhabitants, there is now but a shepherd and his dog.' And this explained the widespread unemployment, the plagues of beggars haunting the insalubrious cities, the vagabonds terrorizing honest citizens on country roads.

In addition, the enclosing landlord was thought to be responsible for the rising cost of grain; and, since ploughmen were believed to make the best soldiers, he was also harming the country's military potential. 'As long as the sheep masters be suffered thus to encroach and gather ground in their hands and lay all to sheep pasture, you shall have neither victual cheap, the realm well inhabited, nor the common people able to help the king's majesty in his wars.'

As we have seen (above, pp. 94, 129), these problems had worried governments in the 1480s, and again around 1517, when commissioners had sought out those responsible for 'conversion' of land use. The campaign soon lost momentum (this was the common fate of attempts at state control of the economy) and a new tack was tried in 1534. Under Cromwell's aegis an act was passed forbidding men to keep over 2,400 sheep; the original bill seems to have been much more drastic (it would, for instance, have restricted the amount of land a man could lease) but came to grief on the vested interest of landowners in both houses of Parliament.* Prosecutions were spasmodic. Conversion of land use, or 'enclosure' in its various forms continued; though possibly without the acts the rate might have been much faster.

Broadly speaking, two issues were involved in 'enclosure'; the occupancy of land; and the use to which it might be put.

The first might involve nothing more than a peasant accumulating, by agreement or exchange with his neighbours, a solid

* G. R. Elton, *Reform and Renewal* (Cambridge, 1972) pp. 103-5.

block of land instead of a scattered holding of strips. This was obviously more efficient, but it had some repercussions on village life, since it prevented the common grazing of all the village animals, normally turned loose on to the stubble in the common field after the harvest. It might involve a landlord claiming that common land was rightly his own property, and enclosing it. This might be disastrous for the villagers, since they depended on the common land to graze their animals. 'They must have sheep to dung their ground for bearing of corn,' commented Hugh Latimer, yeoman's son turned bishop. Lastly, and most spectacularly, some landlords took over the holdings of the villagers; sometimes by buying out the tenants; sometimes by morally dubious but legally justifiable means, such as setting 'entry fines' at an impossibly high level, so that the tenant had to surrender his land; occasionally, by sheer force. Amalgamation of several holdings, known as 'engrossment', was reckoned a peculiarly heinous offence.

Conversion from arable to pasture decreased the supply of grain and the opportunities for rural employment. The classic wicked enclosure involved both engrossment and conversion. The enclosure commissioners tried to define it in 1548.

> It is not taken where a man doth enclose and hedge in his own proper ground where no man hath commons. For such enclosure is very beneficial to the commonwealth. It is a cause of great increase of wood. But it is meant thereby, where any man hath taken away and enclosed any other men's commons, or hath pulled down houses of husbandry, and converted the lands from tillage to pasture. This is the meaning of the word, and so we pray you to remember it.

A good deal of the country was hardly affected. Essex, Hertford, Kent and parts of Suffolk, Cornwall, Devon and Somerset, Shropshire, Worcester and Hereford, had all been enclosed centuries before. They had small, individually cultivated fields, and there was very little common pasture or waste, so that there was not much scope for change. The highland areas of the north and in Wales, might have their difficulties, especially over grazing rights or the waste; but the tension was less than in areas in which there was a conflict between a traditional, established, arable farming and the introduction of large flocks of sheep.

The classic enclosure country was the clay vales of the east Midlands: Leicester, Warwick, parts of Northampton, Oxford and Buckingham. It was this area which bulked largest in the returns to Wolsey's commissioners, and supplied stories like that of the Spencer family, of Wormleighton, in Warwick, which raised itself from tenant-farming to a peerage in just over a century, and ran a vast ranch with over fourteen thousand sheep. This area too was to see the only major rebellion exclusively concerned with enclosure, in 1607. One other county saw a major conflict between pasture and arable, and that was Norfolk. But there it did not involve enclosure, as much as attempts by landlords to disrupt a traditional balanced economy, in which sheep and corn complemented each other, by overstocking the commons with their own sheep (at the expense of those of the tenants), altering the dates at which the landlord's sheep were traditionally allowed to graze on the tenants' arable, and so on. Norfolk exploded into a spectacular peasant rebellion in 1549.

It would be wrong, then, to make enclosure the catch-all explanation of sixteenth-century distress, as some contemporary writers were inclined to do. Even where evidence exists (in court cases, the returns of the commissioners and so on), it is difficult to interpret. Wolsey's commissioners were unable to distinguish between permanent conversion to pasture, and the growing practice of convertible husbandry, that is temporary conversion of arable land to grass with an eye to eventual reconversion once fertility had been restored. The complaints of tenants in legal cases are often quoted by historians as if they are the unvarnished truth. In cases where the landlord's reply survives, the original complaints often seem much less convincing. But replies tend not to survive, and we very rarely know the court's verdict. So in most cases we have only a one-sided presentation of the disputed facts. Nevertheless, enclosure could not have become a universal scapegoat unless it represented a real evil. Such statistics as are available suggest a serious problem, though not a cataclysm. Leicestershire, one of the worst affected counties, saw eleven thousand acres enclosed in the period 1485–1517, about two per cent of the entire acreage of the county.

It might seem odd that landowners were tempted to convert to sheep-farming at all, since grain prices were rising faster than wool. But we come back to the difficulties that contemporaries had in calculating long-term trends, especially in grain prices; and, with increasing cloth exports, and possibly increased demand for wool and meat at home sheep-farming was certainly doing well in the first half of the sixteenth century. In any case for the country at large, average prices misrepresent the local situation. The Leicester, Warwick, Northampton region, for instance, was badly sited for water communication with London; and so transport costs would tend to tip the balance to sheep, since wool was so much lighter than grain, and sheep could go on the hoof to the London butchers. And so this area continued to convert to pasture even in the last years of Queen Elizabeth when, in general terms, the balance of advantage in the country had shifted towards grain production.

Enclosure was the most spectacular rural grievance. Hedges and fences offered tempting targets to rioting peasants, and smashing them was a tangible way of releasing frustration, however the frustration had been caused (although enclosure did not feature in the programme of the 1549 Norfolk rebels, the rebellion had its immediate origin in hedge-burning riots). Rents and dues probably caused more widespread grievances; especially as the complexity of the land laws might have been devised (as in a sense it had been) to give employment to lawyers, whose numbers were increasing dramatically.

The basic problem stemmed from rising prices and the attempts of landlords to adjust their incomes. With two classes of tenant there was no problem. Freeholders owed certain dues, but these were fixed and unchangeable. Leaseholders, farming the manorial demesnes which landlords had stopped cultivating directly in the previous two centuries, faced higher rents when their leases fell in; and although landlords at times might suffer from having granted imprudently long leases, this became less common as the century progressed and men woke up to the facts of inflation; short leases, seven years, even annual ones, became common.

The difficulty arose with the intermediate case of customary tenures, which comprised the great majority of holdings. Most of these tenures were by 'copyhold' (the tenant had a copy of the entry in the manorial court roll), and historians have got themselves entangled in the endless complexities of a tenure which varied from manor to manor. Some were almost as well placed as freeholders: their dues and 'entry fines' (payable when a tenant entered into his holding) were fixed, and the tenancy was inheritable. Others, 'tenants at will', were liable to eviction without legal redress, and were therefore easily forced to pay a higher rent. Between these, were two classes: those copyholders by inheritance who, though their annual dues were fixed, were liable to have to pay an 'arbitrary' entry fine at each change of tenant; and copyholders for 'lives' (a tenancy generally for a man, his wife and his son) who were likewise liable to arbitrary entry fines.

The prevailing tradition among modern historians, stemming mainly from the influential work of R. H. Tawney, has been that the copyholders' position was weak as against his lord's.* It was argued that the liability of the tenant, in so many cases, to an arbitrary entry fine weighted the balance in favour of the lord; either he could increase the entry fine to compensate for the loss he suffered if the annual rent was fixed; or, conceivably, he might deliberately raise the fine to an impossible level to force the copyholder to surrender his tenancy and take out a lease instead. Over and beyond this, it was believed that in practice the copyholder had little security of tenure at law; his first resort was to the manorial court which, it was held, was hardly likely to stand up to the lord whose court it was; the common-law courts would not protect the copyholder before the seventeenth century; the only way of seeking justice was to appeal to the king's prerogative courts, especially the court of chancery, and that was beset by numerous difficulties for the would-be peasant litigant.

These allegations that the system was heavily weighted against the peasant have recently been vigorously challenged.† 'Arbitrary' entry fines, it is asserted, had none the less to be 'reasonable'; no more than two or three years of the market-value rent. They had, too, to be agreed by the manorial court, consisting of .

* *The Agrarian Problem in the Sixteenth Century* (1912; repr. Harper Torchbooks, 1967).

† Eric Kerridge, *Agrarian Problems in the Sixteenth Century and After* (Allen & Unwin, 1969).

tenants who, if they leaned too far in favour of the lord, might find themselves hoist with their own petard. Moreover, the protection of the common-law courts *was* available to the copyholder, and Chief Justice Coke's triumphant paean was as justified in the sixteenth as in the seventeenth century.

> Now copyholders stand upon a sure ground, now they weigh not their lord's displeasure, they shake not at every sudden blast of wind, they eat, they drink and sleep securely, only having a special care of the mainchance, viz. to perform carefully what duties and services soever their tenure doth exact and custom doth require; then let lord frown, the copyholder cares not . . . for if the lord's anger grow to expulsion, the law hath provided several weapons of remedy . . . Time hath dealt very favourably with copyholders in divers respects.

All this is perhaps to take an unrealistic view of the way the law actually worked. Even though tenants could invoke the central lawcourts, they were obviously at a disadvantage compared to their wealthier lord when it came to hiring counsel or dragging out cases until one's opponents were crushed by unbearable expense; even when, as often happened, the men of a village combined together to fight their case. And it is naïve to generalize about the independence of manorial courts from a few examples. Nevertheless, it is difficult to sustain a picture of the peasantry systematically exploited by ruthless landlords. The truth is much more complicated.

Landlords did sooner or later manage to raise their rents. On the whole they were less successful at this in the sixteenth century than in the early seventeenth. It now seems generally accepted that rents tended to lag behind agricultural prices until about 1570 or 1580, and then overtook them. This is less gloomy for landlords than it might seem; their main expenditure was not on agricultural products (they produced a good deal of their own), but on building, manufactured goods and wages; and the cost of all these rose less than agricultural prices, probably less than rents. Clearly this should have been a good time for tenants; there was huge demand for their products, their rents did not rise in proportion, and neither did their other expenditure.

Many peasants in fact did very well for themselves; especially those with large holdings. Houses were rebuilt, windows inserted, comfortable furniture replaced the few sparse wooden forms of the fifteenth century, and men began to sleep between linen sheets rather than on straw. The movement gathered momentum in the later years of Elizabeth. But William Harrison could already in 1577 draw a picture of a yeoman with large savings, a 'fair garnish of pewter in his cupboard . . . three or four feather beds, so many coverlets and carpets of tapestry, a silver salt, a bowl of wine . . . and a dozen of spoons'. Harrison was an Essex rector, and his picture would not be true of the country at large; the south-east did well from the London food-market. But the increase in solid, modest comfort among the yeomen generally is well attested by the inventories drawn up after their death. The vast majority of peasants lived on a much lower level than this. Nevertheless, even small tenants were insulated from the major effects of the price rise by producing their own food. Their existence, of course, was precarious; it depended on the luck of the harvest, the health of animal or man, the thriftiness or otherwise of the family. But these were the normal hazards of peasant life, and not peculiar to this century. Provided that a man had land he should, with luck, have been all right. Those who stood to lose dramatically were the growing army of landless or near-landless rural labourers.

Even so, there was a good deal of peasant discontent. Because of the obstacles to adjusting some rents, others might be put higher to compensate. *New* lettings on the Herbert and Seymour estates in the first half of the sixteenth century were well above the general price level.* Moreover, rents were traditionally re- garded as fixed, and attempts to change them were resented. In the *Discourse of the Common Weal* (a discussion of economic problems written, probably, about 1549) the husbandman is challenged to explain why he thinks it unreasonable to pay more rent even though his profits have increased. He retorts 'My bargain was but to pay for my taking £6 13s. 4d. yearly . . . You can re- quire no more.' The Norfolk rebels in 1549 demanded a reduction of rents to 1485 levels; they said nothing about prices.

Another unsettling factor was the upheaval in landownership

* Eric Kerridge, 'The movement of Rent, 1540–1640' (*Econ. Hist. Rev.*, 2nd ser., vol. 6, 1953; reprinted in E. M. Carus-Wilson (ed.) *Essays in Economic History*, vol. 2 (1962)).

following the dissolution of the monasteries. As we saw with the Pilgrimage of Grace the takeover of monastic lands by the crown aroused widespread fears about the future. They were reinforced when the military expenditure of the 1540s led to large-scale sales (*see above*, p. 217). The long-term effects of the dissolution were, then, to increase the property of the nobility and gentry, not the crown.

This has sometimes been represented as a drastic change in the social balance, the emergence of a new-type of landed proprietor. The sale of the monastic lands appears to be a huge bonanza, in which lawyers, merchants and officials bought land cheap and then exploited it for maximum profit, regardless of social consequence, jacking up rents, converting good arable land to pasture and so on; in implied contrast to the moderation of monks and old-established families, inhibited from ruthlessness by tradition, local sentiment and ethics. There were in fact some spectacular examples of capitalist purchasers, like William Stumpe, who bought the site of Malmesbury Abbey, installed a clothing factory there, and built up a large country estate from monastic land. But most purchasers were already members of the landowning classes who were taking the opportunity to increase their estates; or the sort of successful businessmen and lawyers, often themselves of landed origin (younger sons and so on), and so intent on gaining acceptance as gentlemen that they hastened to conform to the social ethics of the countryside. New owners were not as ruthless, or their predecessors as naïve, as is sometimes implied. Even so, the exceptional scale of changes in the twenty years after the dissolution was likely to be unsettling. There was bound to be some element of new broom about a new owner. Any changes, any increase in rent, would be blamed on him, and the past would acquire an aura of nostalgia. By Elizabeth's reign preachers had to put up with men who thought

> When we had the old law
> A merry world was then –

especially as

> Before the friars went hence
> A bushel of the best wheat
> Was sold for fourteen pence.

There was no sudden transition from 'feudal' to 'capitalist' agriculture in the early sixteenth century. The replacement of copyhold by leasehold, the transformation from a society of smallholding peasants to one dominated by large tenant-farmers, was a gradual affair, extending over many centuries. Nevertheless, rising prices clearly accelerated the rate of change and produced exceptional tensions.

On the industrial side, the early sixteenth century saw some expansion, though not enough to soak up the surplus labour produced by rising population. Production of coal in Tyneside and its regular shipping to London began. Iron-making, previously a minuscule affair, was stimulated by Henry VIII's demand for guns; and grew so fast in the Sussex Weald that some men worried about blast-furnaces exhausting timber supplies. The expansion of the royal navy, which had relied on a single dock at Portsmouth (founded in 1496), led to the establishment of docks and supply yards in the Thames Estuary. Some two hundred and sixty shipwrights were brought to Woolwich to build the *Henry Grace à Dieu* in 1514, and by 1559 six hundred shipwrights and labourers were permanently employed in the naval dockyards. Most shipbuilding was still done on a small-scale basis at small ports round the coast; and most ships were very small, fifty to a hundred tons only, designed for the coasting trade or the London–Antwerp run.

Although much less spectacular, cloth-working was the country's major industry. How fast was this expanding? As far as exports were concerned, the peak figures of the end of Henry VII's reign (*see above*, p. 129) were not much surpassed until 1532–3, when for the first time the 100,000 mark was reached. Then began a steady expansion (though still at a slower rate than the middle year of Henry VII's reign) to 147,000 cloths in 1549–50. The debasement of the English coinage from 1542 is traditionally held to have helped on this expansion; like a modern devaluation its effect was to make English goods temporarily cheaper to foreigners and so encourage them to buy more of them. But the satisfying neatness of this theory has been challenged on technical grounds, and it looks as if real factors affecting the level of European demand are a better explanation than monetary ones.* After 1549–50 the figures are very defective, but it looks as if there was a sharp fall to about 100,000 cloths in 1550–1, before settling down to about 120,000–130,000 a year for the rest of the decade; back, that is, to the normal level of the mid-thirties.

Historians have been bemused by these figures; and have talked about a dizzy boom followed by a disastrous slump which produced widespread unemployment and distress among cloth-workers. But export figures are not the whole story; we know hardly anything about home consumption.† It seems a reasonable assumption that this also expanded in the years up to 1550, and it is possible that, like foreign demand, it declined in the 1550s, since bad harvests often had the effect of reducing demand for industrial goods. But the scale of the expansion and depression is beyond our knowledge.

The bulk of exported cloth was sent across the North Sea, from London to Antwerp, where it was re-shipped for the buoyant German market. This trade was largely in the hands of the Merchant Adventurers, an organization which included all Englishmen trading with the Netherlands. As their historian points out, the Adventurers 'belied their name; so far from adventuring . . . they pursued a safety-first policy of easy profits in an assured market . . .'‡ The Netherlands authorities, like other governments, preferred foreign merchants to be corporately organized, so that the group could be held responsible for the misdemeanours of individuals. A group of London merchants had, towards the end of the fifteenth century taken advantage of these arrangements to establish a cartel, controlling all English traders. The merchants of the outports complained about their monopoly to the 1497 Parliament citing 'every Englishman's liberty'; but the subsequent act gave *de facto* recognition to the Adventurers' monopoly

* J. D. Gould, *The Great Debasement* (Oxford, 1970).
† P. J. Bowden, *The Wool Trade in Tudor and Stuart England* (Macmillan, 1962) p. 37, estimates home consumption at about 33 per cent of the total. This may be too low – a contemporary estimate for 1618, when exports had grown still further puts it at 66 per cent of the total. (B. E. Supple, *Commercial Crisis & Change in England 1600–1642*, Cambridge, 1959, p. 16.) Either way home consumption was not as insignificant as historians, dazzled by the apparent certainty of the export figures, have implicitly assumed.
‡ Peter Ramsey, *Tudor Economic Problems* (Gollancz, 1963) p. 63.

though attempting to regulate the admission fee for the sake of the provincial merchants. The Adventurers were a regulated company; each merchant traded on his own account, but within a general framework of rules designed to minimize competition, to the annoyance of excluded merchants, and of the clothiers who complained that the Adventurers acted together to keep down the price they paid for cloth.

The monopoly had its advantages for the government. In Edward vi's reign Sir Thomas Gresham, the royal agent in the Netherlands, hit on a scheme to control the cloth sales in the interest of the crown. By taking personal charge of the shipments to Antwerp he was able to use his monopoly position to force up the exchange rate of the pound sterling, so that the crown could pay back its foreign debts on favourable terms. This sort of manipulation was only possible because the great bulk of English exports was very narrowly concentrated on the Adventurers' London–Antwerp axis. In return the Merchant Adventurers demanded the suppression of the extraordinary privileges which the German Hanseatic League had gained for its part in restoring Edward iv in 1471. The Hanse merchants handled about a quarter of English exports. It was fortunate for English clothmakers that the Adventurers' schemes were frustrated because the crown could not ditch the Hanse merchants. They were too important as the source of naval supplies and it was not until 1578–9 (by which time a considerable number of Englishmen were trading in the Baltic) that their privileges were reduced.

The dominance of Antwerp disturbed well-established patterns of European trade. Direct trade with Spain and the Mediterranean, which had flourished about the turn of the century, began to dry up from about 1530. Instead cloths for Italy and for the Eastern Mediterranean went to Antwerp, then up the Rhine and finally over land to Venice. Even Bristol was losing ground to London, while Southampton, which had been a useful base for the southern trades, decayed. The only port to escape was Hull, secure in its export of Yorkshire woollens to north Germany and the Baltic. This concentration on one route had its dangers. It discouraged the building of large ships, which could usefully double as warships. It also made England too dependent on one market.

Some attempt was made to guard against this. Voyages were made in the 1550s to the Morocco coast, some of them penetrating as far south as modern Ghana. (It was in 1555 that James Lock became the first Englishman to bring home black slaves from Africa.) Sebastian Cabot whom we last heard of in Henry VII's reign, engaged in hopeless exploration of Hudson's Bay, was enticed back from Spain to England in 1547, appointed *Pilot Mayor*, and set to work once more planning an English route to Asia. The result was the 1553 attempt by Hugh Willoughby and Richard Chancellor to find a north-east passage. Willoughby and two ships were lost *en route*, but Chancellor landed on the north coast of Russia and made his way to Moscow, where he secured trading privileges from Tsar Ivan IV (Ivan the Terrible). In 1555 the Muscovy Company was established.

Voyages to these exotic destinations laid the foundation for what would be, by the end of the century, the fastest-growing sectors of English trade; but in the short run they offered little in the way of markets for English products. The unhealthy concentration on Antwerp continued. There were no English commercial voyages to the Middle East between 1552 and the 1570s, and it is doubtful if English ships visited Italy in the same period. Trade remained firmly bound to its old ways, in spite of (perhaps because of) the slump of the 1550s. Not until Elizabeth's reign was English trade wrenched away from its well-established and comfortable dependence on the Netherlands; and then only because the market was disrupted by embargo and war.

At home, the cloth industry was already largely rural. Some attempt was made to curb this by legislation, in the interests of the towns, culminating in the 1563 Statute of Artificers, which extended the system of apprenticeship, previously administered by urban guilds, to the country at large. But it was impossible to reverse the drift to rural industry. The advantages of sweated rural labour were too great; and cheap labour was to be the basis of England's triumphant irruption into the Mediterranean market in the seventeenth century.

With industry increasingly centred in the countryside, and

with London swallowing the trade of provincial ports, many towns complained loudly of decay. Coventry was a striking example. 'That city was of much fame and antiquity, some times very wealthy, though now of late years brought into decay and poverty.' A few towns flourished: Newcastle which did well from the increase of the coal trade to London, Worcester which produced a quality cloth impervious to rural competition, Shrewsbury, from which the Welsh woollen industry was organized, and which still (developers permitting) has a splendid collection of Tudor merchants' houses to prove its prosperity. We should take the universal cries of disaster rather sceptically. But in general the development of provincial towns was not one of the more dynamic aspects of the economy. Their wealth increased modestly. Their population continued to rise, but often in unwelcome ways; the expulsion of destitute strangers featured large in municipal schemes for poor relief, and town by-laws generally prohibited citizens from taking lodgers. Attempts to hit out at rural industry or at London capitalists were generally ineffective; but slowly towns found that the social and commercial needs of the surrounding countryside could keep them going, as centres for service industries rather than manufactures.

Economic inertia is perhaps an explanation of urban political quiescence; increasingly control of the towns was confined to a small, self-perpetuating group of rich men, with very little apparent protest from the citizens themselves.

London, meanwhile, expanded fast. In 1501 its population was still roughly at the 1377 level; rather under thirty-five thousand. It doubled by 1548, and doubled again by the end of the century.* The unemployed were attracted by hope of work or of charity. In 1547 London introduced the country's first compulsory poor rate. Four of the medieval hospitals which had disappeared at the dissolution were refounded on a large scale, beginning with St Bartholomew's in 1544. A one-time royal palace at Bridewell became, in the 1550s, a 'house of correction' to cure the 'sturdy beggar' of his aversion from work; the forerunner

* S. L. Thrupp, *The Merchant Class of Medieval London* (Ann Arbor, 1948) pp. 41–52; J. C. Russell, *British Medieval Population* (Albuquerque, 1948). Both figures include the suburbs.

of what became after 1597 a national system of workhouses. But the ambitious and destitute continued to flock to London, as they do to modern Calcutta, swamping the available facilities, importuning, cheating and robbing respectable citizens, creating the myth of a highly organized alternative society, of a 'fraternity of vagabonds' with its 'twenty-five orders of knaves' in obscene parody of the god-given hierarchy of civil society.

Begging was a problem for the whole country. Although the dissolution had decreased the outlets for organized charity, this was soon countered by another effect of the Reformation; an increased tendency to bequeath money for secular charitable purposes, rather than religious ones. In simplified form, poor relief, bequests for hospitals, provision of capital (including dowries) for the deserving, and so on, in ten counties studied by Professor Jordan, rose as follows —

1521–30	£ 9,400
1531–40	24,800
1541–50	25,900
1551–60	104,200*

The last is an exceptional figure, swollen by £61,000 for the endowment of London hospitals. But even without this, charitable giving was keeping ahead of the general rise in prices. (The Phelps Brown index averages 151 for the 1520s and 289 for the 1550s.)

But private charity was not enough; legislation was needed as well. This took two forms; increased penalties for those who, it was believed, were workshy; and a very gradual move towards relief of the needy, and a better definition of the problem. For most of the fifteenth century vagabonds had been imprisoned. A deliberate attempt at a softer approach (three days in the stocks) under an act of 1495 failed. In 1531 an act ordered vagrants to be tied naked to a cart and whipped out of town; in 1536 mutilation was prescribed for a second offence, hanging for a third.

* W. K. Jordan, *Philanthropy in England* (1959) Appendix, pp. 368–9. Professor Jordan's counties include London, and are intended to be representative of the country as a whole. They include about a third of the total population. Not all historians accept Professor Jordan's claim to have uncovered almost all the charitable bequests made in these counties (p. 23).

In 1547 unemployed men refusing work offered them on any terms were to be enslaved by the affronted employer for two years; and set to work 'by beating, chaining or otherwise in . . . work . . . how vile soever it be'. This was too draconian to be effective, and was repealed in 1549; the penalty for vagrancy reverted to whipping.

Progress was slow on the positive side. An act of 1536 attempted to introduce method into the essentially haphazard scheme of private alms-giving; instead of alms being given direct to the needy, they were to be paid into a fund administered by local government officials. A further refinement was introduced in 1552, when municipal and parish authorities were to nominate officers to visit every man in the parish and ask for a contribution to the poor; those refusing were to be lectured on Christian charity by the parson and (fancifully) as a last resort by the bishop. This amounted to a compulsory poor-rate scheme; although a formal adoption by the state of compulsory poor rates had to wait until 1572. London as we have seen, had a compulsory rate in 1547, and some provincial towns followed suit, notably Norwich in 1549, and Ipswich and Colchester in 1557.

While the sick and old had always been considered worthy objects of charity, it had usually been assumed that if an able-bodied man was unemployed it was his own fault. This belief, which had never had much basis in fact, became increasingly preposterous in this period. The original government proposal for poor relief in 1536 (withdrawn because of Parliamentary opposition) had recognized that men were often unemployed because work was not available; but this distinction was not in fact recognized in law until 1576, and, rather more emphatically, 1597, when stocks of materials were provided 'to set the poor on work'. The problem of rising unemployment prompted a certain amount of initiative in the first half of the century, partly supported by voluntary gifts, and, tentatively, by compulsory rates; state provision hobbled rather uneasily behind.

The main cause of the worsening standard of living for the poorer part of the population was, then, the increase in numbers, with the resulting rise in the price of food, increase of unemployment and consequent fall in real wages. About this central problem the government, in contemporary terms, could do little. Yet, because of fear of riot or, still worse, rebellion (as well, perhaps, as a genuine conscience among rulers that their duty consisted in doing justice to their subjects), government had to act; and this explains enclosure legislation, the introduction in years of bad harvests of price controls, and fumbling attempts to deal with the problem of destitution. In various ways Wolsey (the Enclosure Commission of 1517–19) and Cromwell (the attempted rationalization of the poor law and the laws against keeping large flocks of sheep) had attempted to bring the situation under control, but to little effect. The 1540s saw two developments which aggravated the situation. On the one hand, as we have seen, there was an expansion of cloth exports which, by raising the price of wool increased the attractions of pasture. On the other hand, the debasement of the coinage was thought to be a cause of rising prices. While modern studies show that the correlation between the increase of the nominal value of coinage in circulation and the actual rise in prices was not very great, it is obvious that there was some connection. More important, contemporaries believed that there was, and held the new coinage in contempt. In this sense, then, attention was focused on causes which the government could, at least in principle, cure; it could prevent further change of land use by a more stringent application of the existing law, it could end inflation by restoring sound money. In addition many intellectuals believed that the Gospel would shine forth in full splendour in the new reign of Edward VI, and produce a just society; not by changing the social structure, but by banishing 'covetousness'. Each man would be content with his own, the landlord would not rack-rent the tenant, the tenant would lower the price of food, the worker would be content with his wages. This group, the 'Commonwealth Party' were influential with the head of the new government, Edward Seymour, by now Duke of Somerset. Real economic tensions combined with ideological conviction to push social issues for the first time into the forefront of politics. The result was to bring down Somerset's government within three years.

Chapter Nine

EDWARD VI AND MARY

EDWARD VI

'Woe to thee, O land, where the king is a child.' This passage from *Ecclesiastes* was quoted by Bishop Latimer, preaching before the boy-king in 1549. He passed rapidly to a more comfortable text, 'Blessed is the land where there is a noble king', and proceeded to apply it by listing Edward's virtues. Certainly Edward's piety, learning and – as far as we can judge from his schoolboy exercises – intellect were considerable. But all this was irrelevant for the moment. A minority inevitably meant struggles for control of the government, struggles which might escalate into war. Civil war was not a memory of the far-off fifteenth century for mid-Tudor Englishmen but an ever-present possibility. Latimer's re-assurance, delivered on the eve of the biggest social upheaval since the great Peasants' Revolt of 1381, was whistling in the dark.

The initial transition from the rule of the vigorous and domin-ant Henry to a regency for a small boy passed off surprisingly smoothly. Henry had entrusted power to a council named in his will; there was to be no individual regent. Within three days of his death, however, Edward's uncle Edward Seymour, Earl of Hertford, had become protector of the realm and governor of the king's person. This *coup* was engineered by Seymour himself, assisted by Sir William Paget, Henry's most intimate adviser in his last months and so the best authority on that most vital of matters, the interpretation of Henry's will. In particular Paget knew, or claimed to know, that Henry had been planning to distribute lands and titles to his most trusted councillors, and this was promptly done. Seymour himself became Duke of

Somerset. So mollified, the council acquiesced in Somerset's elevation.

Somerset's character has always aroused controversy. On the one hand, he is seen as a high-minded idealist and friend of the poor, and an opponent of religious persecution; both these points were held against him by contemporary politicians and have been counted in his favour by modern commentators. On the other hand he was undoubtedly self-seeking. No one indeed can have climbed so high without a good deal of ambition, and of application. Son of a Wiltshire knight, Somerset had risen through his sister Jane's marriage to Henry VIII. He had a distinguished career as a general, which included burning Edinburgh on Henry's orders in 1544. He was also involved in lending money, and was indeed a notably hard creditor; among his victims was Viscount Lisle, stepfather of the man who was to bring him to the block in 1552. He worked hard building up his own estate, forcing the Bishop of Bath and Wells to grant him large estates in Somerset, and pulling down a densely populated part of London to build his fashionable palace, Somerset House.* Among his sins in the eyes of contemporaries was the execution of his brother, Thomas Seymour, for treason in 1549. Thomas's offence had been to try and claim a higher position in the state: by marrying Henry's widow with rather indecent haste; by trying to win the boy-king away from Somerset (slipping him extra pocket money); and by trying to seduce or marry the Princess Elizabeth. But contemporaries thought it wrong to treat a brother like this, and in any case suspected that the plotting was not all on one side.

Somerset had an extraordinarily arrogant and tactless manner. Paget told of Sir Richard Lee who, when rebuked by Somerset 'came to my chamber weeping'. Most politicians were made of sterner stuff; but they would resent being treated by a mere protector in the way they accepted naturally from Henry VIII. It was possibly this arrogance and impatience which made Somerset rely much more on governing by royal proclamation

---

* M. L. Bush, 'The Lisle–Seymour Land Disputes' (*Hist. Journal*, 9, 1966, pp. 255–85); P. H. Hembry, *The Bishops of Bath and Wells, 1540-1640* (Athlone Press, 1967).

than Henry VIII had done. It could be that the repeal of Henry VIII's 1539 Proclamation Act in Edward's first Parliament, sometimes described as a liberal reaction against Henry's despotism, was merely designed to free Somerset from the necessity of getting the consent of twelve councillors to any proclamation.*

But although Somerset could be ambitious, grasping, and, at least as far as his colleagues were concerned, dictatorial, there was a conscious attempt to introduce a different political atmosphere to that of Henry VIII. 'Then all things were too straight [strict], and now they are too loose', thought Paget. Some of the repressive measures thought necessary to carry through the changes of the 1530s were now repealed; 'as in tempest or winter one course and garment is convenient, in calm or warm weather a more liberal ... or lighter garment may and ought to be followed', ran the preamble to an act repealing the treason laws of Henry VIII. The traditional definition of treason, based on the 1352 statute, was re-emphasized: plotting the death of the king, his consort or heir, waging war against the king, or serving his enemies. Denying the royal supremacy was still treason if it were in writing, but only for the third offence if it were in speech (with much more rigorous standards of proof required than under the 1534 act) so making 'treason by words' on the 1534 model a dead letter. More generally, methods of procedure in treason trials were to be tightened up, and two witnesses were now required to prove an offence. The same act swept away all repressive religious legislation, including the 1414 Act for the Burning of Heretics, and the 1539 Act of Six Articles. There were no religious martyrs on either side during Somerset's rule.

The Treason Act has to be seen in perspective. Henry VIII had made the same sort of bid for popularity in 1509 and Queen Mary was to do much the same in 1553. Even under the 1547 act the dice was still heavily loaded against the accused in treason trials; he had no right to confront the hostile witnesses (this was remedied by an act of 1552), he was denied counsel, and had little opportunity to prepare his case. As always, if a conviction could not be secured through the courts, there was always the possibility of

* G. R. Elton, *Studies in Tudor and Stuart Politics and Government* (Cambridge), vol. 1, p. 236.

an act of attainder – as used, for instance, in the case of Thomas Seymour and, eventually, of Somerset himself. Offences which were not treason might still be very severely punished. A proclamation of 1549 ordered men spreading rumours about military defeat to be made galley slaves in the royal navy. Less drastically, several Catholic-minded bishops, such as Gardiner of Winchester, Tunstall of Durham and Bonner of London were imprisoned for refusing to carry out the new religious programme, while on the other side an act of 1547 ordered imprisonment for those who disturbed the peace by speaking irreverently of the sacrament of the altar.

Somerset's successors tightened up the treason laws after his fall in 1549. It became treason for twelve or more persons to band together to kill or imprison a member of the Privy Council, or to forcibly alter the laws; it was also treason for forty or more persons to band together to break down enclosures. Radical religious opinions worried Protestant bishops who needed to distinguish their own beliefs from those of religious anarchists. Joan Bocher was burnt in 1550 for denying that Jesus was Mary's son; and a Dutchman, George van Parris, a year later for the opposite heresy, denying that Jesus was God. Even so, these two were the only executions for heresy in the whole of Edward's reign; a remarkable record, and an indication that belief in some form of toleration was not unique to Somerset, but was shared by several of his colleagues in the government. To some extent this may reflect the views of that group of Cambridge humanists who had educated Edward; Sir John Cheke, Sir Anthony Coke, Richard Cox and their allies Sir Thomas Smith and Sir William Cecil (both of them secretaries of state under Edward). Edward himself, presumably reflecting their views, was uncomfortable about the burning of Joan Bocher, and the group was to be influential in Elizabeth's government, with its reluctance to 'make windows into men's souls'.

In any case persecution was likely to be embarrassing in a period of rapid change. Cranmer was cautiously moving from a Lutheran to a Zwinglian view of the eucharist: that is, away from the view that Christ was in some sense 'really' present in the sacrament to a more symbolic view. This laid him open to Joan Bocher's taunt, that it was 'not long since you burnt Anne Askew for a piece of bread, and yet came yourselves to believe and propose the same doctrine'. The very precariousness of the Edwardian governments made it inadvisable to stir up more enemies than was absolutely necessary – though this, in fact, in other spheres is precisely what Somerset himself contrived to do.

We must also put Somerset's social policy, the most controversial of his actions, into perspective. We shall be considering this more fully later on. But it is worth making the point that what distinguished it from normal Tudor policy was not so much its aims – the prevention of economic change and social distress by a vigorous campaign against enclosures – as the zeal with which it was applied and the dangerous rhetoric which accompanied it; dangerous precisely because it aroused expectations which could not be fulfilled. In its essence, Somerset's view of the problem of poverty was thoroughly traditional. Its twin aims were to reduce the causes of poverty and to punish with increased penalties the allegedly workshy, a policy which reached the heights of absurdity in the act of 1547 which we have already mentioned (*see above*, p. 261): imposing slavery on those who refused to work; fortunately it seems to have been totally ineffective.

Somerset's contribution was, on one view, a pig-headed rashness and desire for popular adulation, combined with an impractical contempt for the conventions of his society; alternatively, a genuine paternalistic regard for the unfortunate. Paget's often despairing letters prove the protector's personal commitment.

The king's subjects are out of all discipline and of obedience . . . And what is the cause? Your own lenity, your softness, your opinion to be good to the poor: the opinion of such as say to your grace 'Oh! sir, there was never man had the hearts of the poor as you have. Oh! – the commons pray for you, sir, they say, God save your life.' I know your gentle heart right well, and that your meaning is good and godly, however some evil men list to prate here, that you have some greater enterprise in your head, that lean so much to the multitude, I know, I say, your meaning and honest virtue. But I say, sir, it is a great pity . . . in a warm summer, that ever warm weather should do harm.

(The climatic metaphor seems to have been a cliché in the Somerset circle.) As the letter hints, Somerset's rivals thought that there was a sinister motive in his concern for the 'multitude', and accused him in 1549 of stirring up the commons against his colleagues on the council. But it seems unlikely that a man who had climbed so high at Henry VIII's court could have believed that this was an effective political card, and it would be churlish to deny Somerset a genuine concern about social justice.

The immediate problem in 1547 was not social policy, but foreign affairs. For the moment England retained Boulogne, but it was due to be sold back to France in 1554, and there was a continual risk that the French might try to anticipate the day. Boulogne represented an expensive monument to Henry VIII's military ambitions.

More important was Scotland, where a series of English victories had achieved little. The chance of Edward's marrying Queen Mary was now remote, especially after the collapse, in March 1547, of the remnants of the pro-English Protestant party in Scotland. Among the prisoners shipped off to galley service in France was John Knox.

Somerset tried to retrieve the situation by a show of strength. He led a large army north in September 1547, and won a spectacular victory at Pinkie, only nine miles from Edinburgh. There was then the usual problem of what to do with victory. Burning Edinburgh had achieved nothing in 1544, and this time Somerset determined on the more scientific policy of leaving a string of garrisons through the Lowlands, presumably to wear down Scottish resistance until the French alliance finally collapsed.

It did not work out that way. The Scots decided that the French were less dangerous than the English, and arranged to marry their infant queen to the French dauphin. The question was now one of preventing that marriage taking place. The great fleet inherited from Henry VIII was powerful enough to keep the east coast supply routes open and so keep the English garrison going (no mean achievement), but not to seal off Scotland completely. In June 1548 a French fleet brought six thousand troops to Scotland, and took Mary away to Brest.

This was the moment to call off the war. The garrisons could now do nothing except keep up Scottish hostility. The best policy would be to make peace, and to hope that the attractions of the Gospel would combine with the Scots' dislike of being a French puppet to produce revolution. But the refusal to face facts was one facet of Somerset's arrogance; a policy which he had once begun had to be carried through. And so a large army was sent to relieve the garrisons, and they continued to be maintained, with awkward results for the royal finance. On top of this the French assaulted Boulogne in 1549, a blow to Somerset's prestige at a particularly awkward time. His successors recognized the inevitable by withdrawing the remaining garrisons from Scotland and making peace with France.

The fall of Gardiner and Norfolk at the end of Henry's reign had left the Catholics on the council leaderless, and unable to hold out against the Protestant inclinations of Somerset and Archbishop Cranmer. Cranmer began a lively correspondence with radical Swiss reformers, and welcomed some distinguished refugees from Germany, where Charles v's Catholic armies were carrying all before them. So we find Martin Bucer, from Strasbourg, a professor at Cambridge; an Italian Protestant, Peter Martyr, in the equivalent chair at Oxford; and a distinguished Polish Protestant, John à Lasco, superintending the refugee church in London. For the only time in its history England had become a major centre of theology. There was even John Knox, released from French galley service by Somerset's diplomacy. All seemed set fair for perfect reformation, provided only that the rival theologians did not tear each other apart first.

The first step was to press on with the unfinished work of Henry VIII; the delayed dissolution of the chantries was put into effect by Act of Parliament in 1547. It produced £610,000 for the crown, about a fifth as much as the monasteries had done, and made two thousand five hundred underpaid priests redundant; two thousand of them found benefices, the rest were pensioned. There was a certain amount of resistance in Parliament, not on theological grounds, but because the government was seen to be grabbing local assets for its own use; timely concessions to the ringleaders (Lynn and Coventry) eventually got the bill through.

Many of the chantry priests had eked out their stipends by teaching, and the effect of the dissolution on education has provoked a classic historical debate. A Victorian charity commissioner, A. F. Leach, calculated that many grammar schools disappeared, and that the numerous 'Edward VI' schools represent not new foundations but schools graciously allowed to continue. More recently Professor Jordan has calculated that the number of grammar schools increased from 217 to 272 in the course of the reign. There is a difficulty of definition here. Leach was rather inclined to ascribe continuous existence to any school he saw mentioned. Jordan, on the other hand, may have been too ready to admit certain schools into the category of grammar schools on rather dubious grounds. (Grammar schools were schools teaching Latin and therefore preparing pupils for the universities.) Even so, he appears to have the best of the argument. In itself the dissolution of the chantries reduced the number of schools. Most were re-founded, often with improved endowments; some were not. Moreover there was some delay, which led to allegations of bad faith on the government's part; notably by the sternly Protestant Thomas Lever, who thought the dissolution had resulted in 'the devilish drowning of youth in ignorance'. But any deficiency here was more than made up by new foundations by private citizens, even during Edward VI's reign; and the trend was to continue in Elizabeth's day.*

On the doctrinal front things moved forward cautiously at first. Royal injunctions of 1547 ordered weekly sermons (a book of homilies, or ready-made sermons, was thoughtfully provided), and the removal of images. In February 1549 an act of Parliament allowed priests to marry; a substantial minority (anything from a third to a tenth, depending on the diocese) did, so acquiring a vested interest in the Reformation. Experimental services began in 1548, using English instead of Latin. Eventually, in January 1549, Parliament, by the Act of Uniformity, ordered the use of a new Book of Common Prayer.

* A. F. Leach, *English Schools at the Reformation* (1896); W. K. Jordan, *Edward VI*, vol. 2 (1970). *See also* Joan Simon, *Education and Society in Tudor England* (Cambridge, 1966), and Nicholas Orme, *English Schools in the Middle Ages* (Methuen, 1973).

The new book was a remarkable achievement. Largely the work of Cranmer, it had been vetted by a theological commission and, with some hesitation, approved by the bishops. *Common* prayer was the point. The book embodied the concept of active congregational participation, that dialogue between priest and people, which is so characteristic of Anglican worship. The dialogue had in fact formed the basis of the worship of religious communities; its adaption to parochial use symbolized the Protestant stress on the priesthood of all believers, as opposed to the characteristically Catholic concept of a graded hierarchy of callings, of the essential distinction of layman and priest. No longer could a layman believe, as he was often induced to believe in the Catholic tradition, that the service was essentially a matter between the priest and God, to which he should give attention as a devout, prayerful onlooker. It was perhaps as much lay participation as the novelty of the new service which led the Cornish rebels of 1549 to call it a 'Christmas game'.

On the key matter of the eucharist, the new book was definitely Protestant. To a Catholic, Christ, corporally present in the host, underwent once more at each mass the sacrifice on behalf of his people. According to the 1549 Prayer Book, on the other hand Christ's passion at Calvary had been a 'full, perfect and sufficient sacrifice . . . for the sins of the whole world', which the communion service commemorated rather than re-enacted. Even so, Bishop Gardiner could claim that the book was acceptable, though not ideal. But appeasing Gardiner was not what the author had intended; for Gardiner, like Catholic-minded Anglicans since, had seized on ambiguities designed to fudge the issue between various Protestant factions, to interpret the service in a Catholic direction. He was helped by the fact that the form – as opposed to the theology – of the new book was traditional, presumably to win over the non-theologically minded to the new doctrines. Priests still wore the traditional vestments, and there was still a railed-off altar at the east end instead of more 'Protestant' communion table in the centre of the church. Protestants excused themselves to continental critics by the need for temporary expedients, 'lest the people, not having yet learned Christ, should be deterred by too extensive innovations from embracing his religion'.

Several Edwardian intellectuals found time to spare from theological debate for social questions. Somewhat unfortunately, they have become known as the 'Commonwealth party'; unfortunately, in that 'party' induces a misleading notion of organization. Unfortunate, too, in that they were not in any sense preaching a new doctrine. What they had to say had been a platitude of pre-Reformation sermons (in which the sufferings of the uncharitable and irresponsible rich in the next world had been a favourite subject); it was also the official ideology of the Tudor state, expressed at some length in the preambles to acts of Parliament. There was nothing revolutionary about what men like Latimer were preaching. 'The poorest ploughman is in Christ equal with the greatest prince that is'; the essential qualification lay in the words 'in Christ'. There was no question of social equality. Nevertheless, the commons ought to 'have sufficient to maintain them and find their necessaries', and this at the moment, they did not have. This was the fault of 'greedy cormorants', those who, in the words of Robert Crowley, had 'enclosed from the poor their due commons, levied greater fines than hertofore have been levied, put them from the liberties (and in a manner inheritance) that they held by custom and raised their rents'. Greed, human sin, not the social system, was the cause of evil; and while the preacher should denounce sin, the state, too, should apply its own laws and punish those who were disturbing the balance of society. Familiar as all this was, however, there was a degree of novelty in the urgency of its proclamation in Edward's reign. The belief in the new beginning which the Reformation had brought about, of the compelling effect of the rediscovered Gospel, of the opportunities now available for social as well as theological reform, had begun to influence policy in Cromwell's time; the reign of the young Josiah rekindled hopes. And when, later in the reign, those hopes had been frustrated, the preachers and pamphleteers took on instead a tone of bitter denunciation, a conscious imitation of the Old Testament prophet.

The best known of the group was Hugh Latimer. Latimer, a pioneer Cambridge Protestant in the twenties, had been made

Bishop of Worcester in 1535 under Cromwell's aegis; he resigned the bishopric in protest against the Act of Six Articles. In Edward's reign he concentrated on preaching, denouncing in earthy language the shortcomings of those in authority as 'lording loiterers', 'unpreaching prelates'.

> For ever since the prelates were made lords and nobles the plough standeth; there is no work done, the people starve. They hawk, they hunt, they card, they dice; they pastime in their prelacies with gallant gentlemen, with their dancing minions, and with their fresh companions, so that ploughing is set aside; and by their lording and loitering, preaching and ploughing is clean gone. And thus if the ploughmen of the country were as negligent in their office, as prelates be, we should not long live, for lack of sustenance.

Other 'Commonwealth' men included Nicholas Ridley, Bishop of London, who agitated for hospitals and workhouses for the London poor; Robert Crowley, a printer and popular propagandist, who modernized *Piers Plowman* for the better promotion of Protestantism and social justice; and John Hales, the somewhat tactless head of the 1549 enclosure commission.

Sir Thomas Smith once abused 'hotlings' who 'devise commonwealths as they like, and are angry that other men be not so hasty to run straight as their brains croweth'. Practical politicians had a good deal to put up with from the enthusiasts, but they did not differ in their essential analysis of the social problem. The keynote of the 'commonwealth' ideal was a static, well-ordered society, insulated from the horrors of economic change and of social mobility; eventually the same vision of society which guided the social policy of the Elizabethan government under the aegis of Cambridge intellectuals like Smith himself, William Cecil, Nicholas Bacon, men who had served their political apprenticeship under Edward. Both groups idealized the independent peasant and distrusted the industrial worker. Latimer spoke nostalgically of his father, who, renting £4 of land a year, managed to employ six labourers, kept a hundred sheep and thirty cows, turned out as a soldier on horseback for the king, and educated the future bishop 'or else I had not been able to preach before the king's majesty now'. Cecil could contemplate the decline of the cloth industry with equanimity; if the result was unemployment, he thought, 'the sturdier and stronger sort of the men' could be sent to colonize Ireland. What distinguished the 'Commonwealth' men, was not so much their analysis, but the depth of their concern, the violence of their denunciation, their real sympathy for the victims of economic change. What distinguished Somerset's government was its willingness to give them their head, without very much prudential regard to political reality.

Edward's reign was certainly a time of economic difficulty. We have already examined the long-term tensions. More immediately, rising prices were made worse by the continued debasement of the coinage to pay for the war. This was especially true of milk, butter and cheese, what Hales called the 'common and principal sustenance of the poor'. (Hales was as concerned with the dangers of sheep displacing cattle as he was with grain supplies.) The boom in cloth exports heightened the tendency to sheep-farming. The sale of ex-monastic and ex-chantry lands increased tenants' anxieties; and possibly landlords increased their pressure on tenants in the belief that a weak government would not be able to check them. One vital economic indicator, however, was favourable. Grain prices were low, down to some six shillings a quarter after topping 17·5 in 1545–6; and they remained low until the harvest of 1549. Two conclusions follow from this. First, that government concern about distress was not just a response to a crisis situation; it was as much the result of the intellectual climate as the economic. Secondly, that Somerset's critics may have been right in thinking that it was his measures, arousing unrealistic expectations (the classic dilemma of the liberal reformer), rather than desperation, which produced peasant rebellion in 1549. As Paget put it, 'Is victuals and other things so dear in England and nowhere else? ... If they ... have lived quietly above their sixty years, pastures being enclosed [they] ... have the least cause to complain ... What is the matter then ...? By my faith, Sir ... liberty, liberty.'

The first response by the government was the appointment of commissioners in 1548 to investigate breaches of the laws about enclosure and conversion. One set of commissioners, headed by John Hales, set out for the key area Oxford, Berkshire, Warwick

and Northampton. Hales was promptly accused of 'stirring ...
the commonalty against the nobility'. He denied the charge; but
not very convincingly. To compound their difficulties the commissioners lacked tact, as when they ordered Somerset's most
dangerous political rival, John Dudley, Earl of Warwick, to
plough up his park. There was widespread obstruction. Hales and
Latimer both complained of landlords packing and bullying
juries. The same sort of obstruction met Hales's attempts to
control sheep-farming by legislation. But Hales did manage to
get one bill through in 1549; a bill to raise revenue and encourage
arable farming by taxing sheep and cloth.

1548 saw a good deal of rioting. The crisis came in 1549.
On Whit Monday, the day after the statutory introduction of the
new prayer book, the villagers of Sampford Courtenay in Devon
forced their priest to say mass in the old style, and this sparked off
a dramatic rising. The Devon rebels were soon joined by Cornishmen, and proceeded to lay siege to Exeter. The protector hesi-
tated to send reinforcements to the hard-pressed sheriff of Devon,
in part because of riots and rumours of more dangerous risings
further east, in Somerset, Wiltshire and Hampshire. On 20 June
he issued a general pardon on condition that the rebels dispersed.

They did not. Instead they (or more probably their priests)
drew up a lengthy manifesto, demanding a return to the religion of
the last years of Henry VIII. The Act of Six Articles should be re-
introduced, and repressed ceremonies restored. In addition the
English Bible was to be suppressed (because otherwise the clergy
would be unable to 'confound the heretics'), and some monasteries re-established. Lurking rather uneasily among these ecclesiastical demands was one for severe restriction on the number of
gentlemen's servants. This produced a long reasoned reply from
Archbishop Cranmer, but little in the way of effective military
actions. It was not until 6 August, after a much smaller rebellion
in Oxfordshire and Buckinghamshire had been suppressed, that
government forces in the West Country were strong enough to
raise the siege of Exeter. Ten days later the rebel army was finally
defeated, oddly enough at Sampford Courtenay where the
rebellion had begun two months before.

While the western rebellion was taking place, another, equally dangerous, broke out in Norfolk. On 6 July some rioters tore down fences on the land of John Flowerdew, an unpopular lawyer turned country gentleman. There was nothing unusual about this sort of thing, nor about Flowerdew's response, which was to divert the rioters on to the land of his enemy, Robert Ket, a well-to-do tanner also well on his way to country gentleman status. Ket, however, for no very clear reason, set himself at the head of the rioters and marched them off to Norwich, where he eventually collected about sixteen thousand men, probably a third of the men of military age in Norfolk. The civic authorities, nervous of their own citizens (Norwich had an acute unemployment problem) cooperated, rather gingerly; the mayor joined Ket and peasant representatives in sending a petition to Somerset.

In contrast to the western rebels, this petition was concerned almost entirely with economic matters. Several clauses ask that the lords should not over-stock the commons with their beasts, nor try to twist to their own advantage the peculiar Norfolk rules, by which the tenants' arable land was manured for part of the year by the lord's sheep. Another major complaint was of increased rents and dues. One set of clauses was aimed against clerical abuses. Each parish was to have its resident clergyman, able to preach and educate poor men's children; clerical incomes were to be cut, and all tithe paid in cash, not kind. All this represents traditional anti-clericalism, the demand for spiritual value for money, now adapted to a Protestant mould, and influenced by the programme of the rebellious German peasants in 1525. So was a clause demanding freedom for the few serfs surviving in England, 'for God made all men free with his precious blood-letting'. Another clause demanded that commissioners chosen by the commons should reform the laws 'which hath been hidden by your justices of your peace ... from your poor commons', a reference probably stimulated by the belief that the landed gentry and the nobility had been obstructing the work of the enclosure commissioners. The only reference to enclosure in spite of the fence-breaking out of which the rebellion grew, was an odd demand that the anti-enclosure legislation should not apply to saffron fields; this is presumably because, as we have seen, the competition between sheep and grain took other forms than enclosure in Norfolk (*see above*). [The absence of any objection to the new service book is interesting; Robert Watson, a 'new preacher' from Norwich was influential with the rebels, and services at Mousehold Heath were conducted according to the Book of Common Prayer.*

All this happened in July, at a time when Somerset was fully occupied elsewhere. As with the western rebels, his first response was the offer of a pardon, and a sympathetic hearing of their grievances if only the rebels would return home. The herald sent to offer these terms was ripely insulted, and the rebels occupied Norwich. At the end of July a small army under the Marquis of Northampton (William Parr, brother of Queen Catherine Parr), was ignominiously beaten off. Almost a month later, on 23 August, a week after the final defeat of the western rebels, a more powerful royal army under John Dudley, Earl of Warwick, arrived in Norwich. Many of the rebels were by this time losing heart, and accepted a renewed offer of pardon. The remainder, after desperate fighting, left Norwich, and, on 27 August, were finally defeated at Dussindale, so fulfilling, it was said, an ancient prophecy:

> The country gruffs, Hob, Dick and Hick
> With clubs and clouted shoon,
> Shall fill up Dussindale with blood
> Of slaughtered bodies soon.

How had these rebellions happened? The general background of frustrated expectation of social reform was obviously important; as was, in many parts of the country outside East Anglia, the introduction of the new prayer book. Grumbling riot erupted into major revolt in the west and in East Anglia, probably for peculiar local reasons. The rebellions did not involve the whole of local society, in the way that the Pilgrimage of Grace had done. In the west only a few minor gentlemen were involved, in East Anglia none at all, except for the marginal case of Ket himself. But while the rebellions

---

* Watson had attracted Cromwell's favour in 1539 when he denounced the theology preached by the Bishop of Norwich; G. R. Elton, *Policy and Police* (Cambridge, 1972) pp. 138–9.

seem to be instigated from below, they were made possible by a certain vacuum of authority in the areas concerned. In the west, it seems clear that the new authority of Russell was not as great as that of Courtenay had been before 1538; and Russell spent a good deal of his time in London. But in Devon and Cornwall there was some attempt by the local gentry to organize resistance, and Exeter, in spite of the old-fashioned religious views of many of its citizens, held for the king.

Resistance in Norfolk, however, seems to have been almost non-existent. Norwich was, tactically, less defensible than Exeter and, as we have seen, there was probably a powerful 'fifth column' of disaffected citizens. More surprising is the passivity of the gentlemen, who apparently fled or hid themselves at the first signs of danger, only re-emerging when Warwick arrived with his army. It may be that the local gentry were unable to organize themselves in the absence of their leader, the Duke of Norfolk, who had been in the Tower since 1547; if so, it underlines the point that hewing down an 'over-mighty subject' might have to be paid for in terms of decreased security (a point borne out in Sussex, where another major rebellion was prevented by firm action on the part of the local magnate, the Earl of Arundel). But this apparent pusillanimity of the Norfolk gentry seems surprising, given the political independence and organization they had demonstrated in the previous century; it may just be possible that the gentlemen determined at first to let the rebellion run its course, in order to demonstrate to Somerset the dangers which his social policies were creating. It is also true that the rebellions were given impetus by the slowness of the government response; though whether this was due to lack of reliable forces, or to Somerset's preference for pardon if it would work, is not clear.

It may be that the distinction between a western rebellion dedicated to 'religious' ends, and the East Anglian one, concerned with economic issues and religiously 'advanced', is too clear cut. A good deal of supposition has to be made on the evidence of 'programmes', though it is difficult to tell how representative these are. Ket's programme was signed by two 'governors' from each hundred; nevertheless, the jumbled order of its arrangement, and the frequent erasures in the only surviving copy (apparently the one sent to Somerset) seem to indicate a list of demands thrashed out at a somewhat disorderly meeting, though clearly somebody there had a copy of the German demands of 1525. Its moderation may stem from its being the product of the early stages of the revolt, when it still seemed likely that the government would sympathize with the rebels. The Protestant tone of the religious demands may reflect the influence of a few advanced clergymen, and shows the way discontent could be channelled by circumstances. In 1537 Norfolk had come close to a conservative religious revolt on behalf of Walsingham Abbey. In the western rebellion the influence of priests on the programme was clearly paramount, and general discontent was mobilized against the new services, seen as the culmination of an attack by the state on the time-honoured practices of the parish. On the other hand, contemporaries did see certain economic grievances among the West Countrymen, including, ironically enough, the sheep tax, which, though designed to help the small farmer in arable areas, could only be a burden to his fellow small farmer in a pastoral region such as Devon and Cornwall. But there was an underlying resentment of religious innovation, on which priests could work; and as in the Pilgrimage of Grace, popular anti-clericalism was not so intense as to prevent peasants accepting priests as their leaders. Clerical leadership of this sort was not confined to remote areas; the Oxfordshire rioters tore down fences and killed sheep, but four of the thirteen ringleaders were priests.

The extent to which the normal social hierarchy was preserved in all these rebellions, even in the absence of gentry leadership, is remarkable. In Norwich, for instance, the great army of the unemployed never seems to have got out of hand, and a fair degree of order was preserved by an ex-mayor, Augustine Stiward. 'Trials' of captured gentry took place at Mousehold Heath, but none was put to death. Yet government propagandists like Sir John Cheke pointed out to the 'honest men' among the rebels the danger they ran from stirring up 'uproars of people, hurly-burlies of vagabonds, routs of robbers', and asked how, if they set a bad example, they could expect to be obeyed by their wives, children and servants. There was in fact some danger of total disintegration. The longer a rebellion went on, the less easy would it be for the 'respectable' elements of village society to keep control. Many of the rebels would slink away, back to the pressing needs of their neglected farms; those who were left would become more disorderly, more radical. A full-scale peasant rebellion was out of the question. All that could be done was to organize a large-scale demonstration, in the hope of persuading some powerful political figure to take up the grievances.

Could either of the main revolts have succeeded in these circumstances? The Norfolk revolt depended, obviously, on strengthening the hand of Somerset against his recalcitrant colleagues. Unfortunately the result was the opposite, damning Somerset and his policy of social appeasement for good. In the circumstances, that was probably inevitable. The westerners might have succeeded if their rebellion had persuaded some of the religiously more conservative councillors to overthrow Somerset. There was such a party, and at the end of 1549 it looked as if they were successful, but the net result was a regime more radical in religion than its predecessor. More generally, the rebellions increased class bitterness in the countryside. Many of the gentry, and indeed the other respectable classes, including some better-off peasants, had been frightened by the spectre of anarchy and lynch law, and the vivid if mistaken belief that their society was disintegrating. On the other hand, the mass of the commons cowed by defeat and repression (symbolized by the skeleton of Robert Ket, still hanging in chains over Norwich a year after the rebellion), now hated the gentry and only obeyed them 'so far forth as forced with fear'.

The rebellions shattered Somerset's reputation. He had, to all appearances, first stirred them up, and had allowed them to develop by being too ready to issue pardons (Paget compared them to Papal pardons 'which rather . . . gave men occasion and courage to sin, than to amend their faults'). He had played no part in their suppression; any credit here went to Russell and Warwick. In fact, Somerset's tactics in dealing with the rebellions were perfectly sensible; very similar, indeed, to those of Henry VIII in 1536. It was worth trying to solve the problem peacefully, by pardon; and it was right to stay in London, rather than to march off to Exeter or Norwich, when further rebellion might break out almost anywhere. (There were in fact isolated outbreaks all over the southern counties.) But while an established king could afford this sort of blow to his prestige, the position of a protector was much too vulnerable. By the end of September the majority of the council had decided on his removal.

It was then that Somerset tried to cash in on what he believed to be his general popularity. On 5 October he issued a proclamation; all loyal subjects were to rally to king and protector. The councillors issued counter-proclamations. Somerset reminded the people that 'the poor commons, being injured by the extortions of gentlemen, had our pardon this year by the mercy of the king and the goodness of the protector' and stigmatized his fellow councillors as 'come up of late from the dung-hill . . . more meet to keep swine than to occupy . . . offices'. The councillors, for their part, pointed out Somerset's pride, self-seeking and disregard of Henry VIII's will. The authorities of London (powerfully swayed by the presence of Warwick's troops) opted for the council. Russell's army from the west cut off any hope Somerset might have had of raising troops in his native Wiltshire. Without forces, he capitulated; and on 14 October entered the Tower as a prisoner.

After Somerset's fall the council as a whole exercised supreme power; there was no new protector. The lead in the *coup* however, had been taken by Warwick, and it was he who dominated the new government.

Warwick was the son of Edmund Dudley, Henry VII's unfortunate minister. Like Somerset, he had had a distinguished military career in the last years of Henry VIII. He is a mysterious figure – he has left no papers, and has eluded the biographer. Lawrence Humphrey summed him up as 'a man truly of a stout and haughty courage, and in war most valiant; but too much raging with ambition'. This was the standard Protestant view – Warwick as the scapegoat for the miseries of Edward's late years – and has a good deal of truth in it. But there is more to Warwick (created Duke of Northumberland in 1551) than that.* The source

* Although sometimes inaccurately, I shall from now on refer to him as 'Northumberland'. Pedantic accuracy would be too confusing.

of his dominance over his fellow councillors has never been explained, but undoubtedly he had great political ability. His rule was dogged by misfortune and ended in failure, but that was not entirely his fault. He did not have the personal qualities, for good or ill, which Somerset had; but it would be wrong to represent his rule merely as bleak reaction dominated by a set of men interested only in self-aggrandizement. Edwardian history has been written too glibly in terms of the contrast between the 'good' Duke of Somerset and the 'evil' Duke of Northumberland.

Northumberland had tried to bring together all factions against Somerset. He had managed to persuade the conservative Thomas Wriothesley, Earl of Southampton (a one-time protégé of Cromwell who had since moved rapidly to the right) and the Earl of Arundel that he meant to prevent further religious change, and possibly even go back on some of Somerset's reforms. But once Somerset was safely disposed of, Warwick could dispense with conservative support. By February 1550, both earls had been dismissed from the council, and the tiller was set for further religious innovation.

One of the first signs of this was the appointment of a keen reformer, Nicholas Ridley, to the see of London in April 1550. Almost immediately Ridley set about replacing altars by communion tables, placed in the centre of the church rather than at the east end to underline the Protestant interpretation of the eucharist. In July the much more extreme John Hooper was nominated to Gloucester. He caused considerable trouble by insisting on being consecrated without having to put on 'popish' vestments; Cranmer and Ridley refused to consecrate him on these conditions and, after a short spell in prison the new bishop gave way.

By this time a new prayer book was under discussion, the second Edwardian book, eventually introduced by Parliament in 1552. This broke the compromise of the 1549 book between Protestant doctrine and Catholic form. The order of the communion service was changed to erase any resemblance to the mass, vestments other than a plain surplice were abolished, altars became communion tables. The uncompromisingly Protestant nature of the new book was underlined by a rubric, inserted at the last moment, on the council's orders, that kneeling at communion did not imply 'any adoration ... either unto the Sacramental bread or wine ... or unto any real and essential presence there being of Christ's natural flesh and blood'. This time there were no armed protests; the failure of the 1549 revolts provided a powerful deterrent. Eventually in 1553, the doctrines of the reformed church were set out in the Forty-two Articles (better known, after Elizabethan revision, as the Thirty-nine) – an uncompromisingly Protestant formulation which has caused embarrassment to the 'Catholic' party in the Church of England ever since.

The form of ordination prescribed in 1552 described the office of the priest 'to minister the doctrine, and sacraments, and the discipline of Christ'. Doctrine and sacraments had been reformed; there remained 'discipline', the enforcement of the moral law. In fact, no reform of discipline was accomplished, though all pious Protestants were intent on modernizing the canon law, to make the enforcement of morality more effective. Cranmer drew up a revision of the canon law, but nothing came of it. This was partly because of lack of time; partly because of a fundamental contradiction within the Reformation. The reformers had attacked church discipline and church courts, not as evil in themselves, but as corrupt in their Catholic manifestation. In doing so, however, they had excited lay prejudice against the whole concept of ecclesiastical jurisdiction, of the notion that the church's preaching against sin (and especially sexual sin) should be backed up by a system of church courts. The religiously-inclined tore down in order to rebuild; the rest of the population was happy to preserve the debris. Richard Cox lamented the attitude of his compatriots. 'The severe institution of Christian discipline we most utterly abominate. We be sons and heirs, but we tremble at the rod.' No reform of church courts took place. They continued, largely in their old form, in the Elizabethan and early Stuart periods, still punishing moral offences such as adultery or slander. In doing so they annoyed the secular-minded who only wished to be left alone; but they also annoyed the zealots by relative ineffectiveness. 'The abuse of excommunication', its employment for trivial matters, and therefore its general ineffectiveness, was to be a major complaint of Elizabethan Puritans.

What the effect of religious changes had been on the people at large is very hard to gauge. One might guess that the short-term effect of any particular change would be negative; that, for instance, a change in church services would create a good deal of resentment, and gain few genuine converts. On the other hand, the long-term effect of officially inspired Protestantism was bound to be considerable. Catholicism was like an exposed cliff face, gradually sapped by the battering of the waves. The effects of the vernacular bible of Cromwell's time were now reinforced by the new services, gradually accustoming men to the notion that Protestant worship (whatever the Cornishmen might think) could be dignified, respectable, part of the natural order of things, not the anarchical practice of wild enthusiasts. The new services reinforced, too, the evangelical beliefs fostered by scripture reading. Vested interest in the new order was increasing; those who had benefited from the confiscation and sale of monastic lands were now joined by the many priests who had taken the opportunity to marry.

Mary's reign was to show that a dedicated minority of English people was prepared to suffer for the Protestant faith; some by exile, others (most of them non-intellectuals, craftsmen, housewives, apprentices) by being burnt to death. But it also showed that committed Protestantism was not yet sufficiently widespread to prevent the accession of a Catholic queen (as it might have done, fifty years later). It is probably true that the great majority of people were not committed irrevocably to either Protestantism or Catholicism – indeed they would have not thought in such hard-and-fast denominational terms. Political accident could yet determine the religious future of England.

On the secular side, Northumberland was mainly concerned to end the extravagances of Somerset's time. The expensive and pointless wars with Scotland and France were ended in 1550. Attempts were made to economize in government expenditure; it was hoped in 1552 to reduce it to the old peace-time footing, but that was now impossible; a large permanent navy, for instance, had come into being, and, although some reductions were made, it could not now be abolished. The rationalization of the separate revenue courts established in Cromwell's time was recommended; and the first stage of this was carried out in 1554, when two of the Cromwellian courts (augmentation and first fruits) were amalgamated with the exchequer.

Attempts were also made to reduce the crown's indebtedness at Antwerp. Gresham's expertise in exchange manipulation was put to good use in paying off the old debts and raising new ones on better terms. The internal crown debt was also reduced, although largely by sale of land, and so at the expense of capital. Northumberland, however, was too weak politically to be able to prevent the large-scale sale of crown lands. Indeed, on the record, noticeably weaker than Somerset had been – or less self-confident.

Year	Capital Value of Grants
1547	£108,000
1548	5,000
1549	8,000
1550	103,000
1551	55,000
1552	64,000
1553 (6 months only)	66,000
	£409,000

The total lands granted and sold (about £833,000 altogether) would bring in about £40,000 each year; about a fifth of what the crown did in fact get from its landed property in 1548.* It was in Edward's reign, as much as Henry's, that the foundations were laid for the 'new' aristocratic houses of Henrician politicians and soldiers; the Pagets, the Russells, the Wriothesleys, the Herberts and so on. Somerset and Northumberland both, of course, forfeited their lands on their downfall; but indulgent monarchs later restored considerable parts of them to the Seymour and Dudley families.

One result of the crown's financial desperation was continued monetary disorder. At first Northumberland continued Henry's and Somerset's policy of quick profits from the debasement of the coinage. Rightly or wrongly, this was blamed for rising

* W. K. Jordan, *Edward VI* (Allen & Unwin), vol. 1, pp. 118, 392.

prices; made worse because it now coincided with a run of bad harvests. Wheat rose from about 9 shillings a quarter in 1548-9, to 15 shillings in 1549-50, 18 shillings in 1550-1, and 19 shillings in 1551-2. This was mostly because of bad weather. But the net addition to the coins in circulation was considerably faster from 1549 onwards, and probably aggravated an already bad situation. An attempt was made to reverse the trend in June 1551. The coinage was 'called down'; coins with a face value of a shilling were to circulate at ninepence, and later at sixpence, and so on. Any hopes that this would eventually halve prices, however, were disappointed. Wages and rents which had risen during the inflation were not reduced. Food continued in short supply. And the only effect of 'calling down' was to make men afraid that the coins would be 'called down' yet again, and so rush to spend them.

If debasement had stimulated exports, then 'calling down' should have harmed them. Certainly cloth exports in the fifties were for the most part below the lead of the boom years of the late forties (see above, p. 129); but this was more likely to have been the result of a general depression of European trade, the result of a run of bad harvests and, possibly, of a monetary shortage due to a temporary diminution of silver imports from the Spanish New World, rather than of any specifically English currency problems. It seems likely, too, that bad harvests at home reduced domestic demand for cloth. How seriously total cloth production was affected we cannot know; but the heady days of expanding markets in the forties were definitely over.

It is against this background that social policy must be seen. The end of 1549 naturally saw a reaction against some of Somerset's policies. Hales's sheep tax was abolished. A statute asserted the right of lords of manors to appropriate wastes and commons, subject to certain safeguards. But the statutes against over-stocking with sheep, conversion of arable to pastures, and depopulation remained in force; and, although the enclosure commission disappeared, the total number of prosecutions for depopulation was rather higher in Northumberland's time than in Somerset's.

There was in fact a good deal of important social legislation in Northumberland's time. An act to protect arable farming was passed in 1552, with the important proviso that commissioners were to be appointed to enforce it (they never were). There was an act against 'forestallers' (dealers who, in modern terms, cornered the market in some vital commodity), an act to try to fix standards in the cloth industry. Usury, the lending of money at interest, had always been a major sin in the eye of the Edwardian preachers; it had been allowed, subject to conditions, in 1545, but was now once more prohibited, in language which Latimer doubtless approved. (Usurers were 'greedy, uncharitable and covetous persons', a prime cause of the 'terrible threatenings of God's wrath and vengeance that justly hangeth over the Realm'.) The 'extreme law' of 1547 on vagabonds (King Edward's description) was repealed in 1549, and in 1552 something like a compulsory poor rate was introduced (*see above*, p. 261). On whatever platform Northumberland had come to power in 1549, circumstances (particularly the economic situation, far worse than in Somerset's time) made it impractical to mount a campaign of black reaction. Tudor governments, if they were to avoid disorder, had necessarily to show some concern for social justice, and try to mitigate the effects of economic trends.

Northumberland's political position was extremely precarious. Somerset still had a considerable following, and attempts were made to patch up old enmities. Somerset was back in the council by April 1550, and a year later Northumberland's eldest son married Anne Seymour, Somerset's daughter. In October 1551, however, Somerset was once more in the Tower, and in January 1552, he was executed on a charge of planning an armed insurrection in London. In spite of a good deal of popular sympathy for the ex-protector, Northumberland seemed safe.

His position depended on the support of a group of great men – and on the life of the king. The council, once Somerset had been executed, acquiesced in Northumberland's rule. Councillors and other courtiers were given licences to recruit their own retainers; in Somerset's time only the protector himself had been allowed to do this. More important, some eight hundred professional cavalrymen, originally recruited for the Scottish war, were retained in service under the command of the leading councillors. (The government paid the troops' wages to their commanders –

so that the Earl of Pembroke for instance, got £2,000 a year to subsidize a private army.) Fortunately, these were disbanded, because of the crown's financial troubles, before the end of 1552. The system of lord lieutenancies, hitherto an emergency measure, was systematically extended, to cover the whole country. Groups of counties were placed under the military command of Northumberland's allies; Russell, now Earl of Bedford, in the West Country; Sir William Herbert, promoted Earl of Pembroke in 1551, in Wales; William Parr, Marquis of Northampton, in the counties between Cambridge and Oxford. But Northumberland could not dispense with the old nobility in some sensitive areas; the Earl of Shrewsbury was president of the council of the north and lord lieutenant of Yorkshire, and the Earl of Derby was lord lieutenant of Lancashire, although both had been suspected of plotting with Somerset in 1551 and preferred the old religion. On the other hand, the number of the old nobility who were in prison – the Duke of Norfolk, for instance, Edward Courtenay (in the Tower since 1538), the Earl of Arundel (for supporting Somerset) – reduced the chances of opposition, and in fact, after Somerset's removal, there was no overt challenge to Northumberland's authority. After all, even those who disliked him might as well profit from the opportunities of the moment – and look forward to the time when the king (fifteen at the end of 1552) might begin to assert himself and create a new pattern of political power.

But by February 1553 Edward was seriously ill, and the vital question was the succession. By Henry's will the crown should next pass to Mary – a prospect to which Edward himself was opposed, on conscientious grounds. If his father could leave the crown by will, why should Edward not do the same? One difficulty was that Henry VIII had parliamentary authority to do so, and Edward had not. Another was the obvious point that a will made by Henry was much more likely to be taken as representing the king's own wishes than one made by a fifteen-year-old boy in his last illness; especially when its provisions blatantly favoured the Duke of Northumberland's family.

Edward's first draft drawn up after he had become seriously ill seems to have been based on the assumption that a woman could transmit a claim to the throne, but not herself succeed to it. (Henry VII seems to have relied on the same principle, since his mother, through whom his claim was derived, was alive throughout his reign.) Having cut out his sisters Mary and Elizabeth, presumably because they were bastards, Edward followed his father in putting the descendants of Henry's younger sister Mary above those of his elder sister, Margaret, Queen of Scotland (*see table*, p. 356). Unless he had a son of his own, the throne was to descend to the *heirs male* of his cousin Frances, Duchess of Suffolk, if any, and then to the heirs male of Frances's daughters, Jane, Catherine and Mary. All this was somewhat unreal, since none of these ladies had a son as yet. Edward obviously had no sense of urgency. But by May or June, his health was worse and the draft was revised. The throne was now to pass, after the non-existent heirs male of Frances, to 'Lady Jane *and* her heirs male'; an odd arrangement, since if Jane could inherit the throne, and not merely transmit a claim to her son, so presumably could her mother. The sceptical could hardly be blamed for seeing the reason in Jane's marriage to Northumberland's son, Guilford Dudley, in May.

The judges, summoned by the king to draw up a formal will in these terms, at first refused, pleading the existing statutes. But at Edward's insistence they gave way; and the councillors swore to observe the succession according to Edward's settlement.

Edward died on 6 July 1553. Four days later Lady Jane was proclaimed queen. Mary, warned of what was happening, had refused to come to London, where she would certainly have been arrested. She had herself proclaimed queen at Bury St Edmunds, and set about raising troops. In the country there was widespread confusion, and in many places a reluctance to do anything decisive until it became clear which way the wind was blowing, though it seems fair to say that there was a good deal of sympathy for Mary, and none at all for Jane. Northumberland remained at first in London, rather than challenging Mary in the field, evidently because he did not trust his fellow councillors.

There was, however, no real alternative to the duke as commander, and eventually, on 14 July, he set out, ominously reminding the council before he went that they were as much involved as he was. As he rode out of London he noticed that, 'no one sayeth "God speed"'. News poured in from the country at large of gathering support for Mary. The resolution of the councillors in London began to crack. The Earl of Arundel (who had spent most of the last three years in prison for sympathizing with Somerset), lectured them at length on the principle of hereditary succession, a powerful argument among the landed class. The Earl of Pembroke, who had no axe to grind (Northumberland had got him his earldom, and his son was married to Queen Jane's sister Catherine), was briefer. 'If my lord of Arundel's persuasion cannot prevail with you, either this sword shall make Mary queen, or I'll lose my life.' With relief or reluctance, the council agreed. On 19 July Mary was proclaimed in London. Northumberland, deserted by his troops, surrendered peacefully, while his associates flocked to make their peace with the new queen.

Mary's accession was the only successful rebellion in Tudor England. To some extent, it seems to have been a popular rebellion; the sailors on board the royal ships at Yarmouth forced their captains to declare for Mary, and at Northampton Sir Nicholas Throckmorton, who had tried to prevent her proclamation, had to flee for his life (Throckmorton was playing both sides; he also claimed to have been the first to warn Mary of the intended *coup*, in spite of his fervent Protestantism, because 'that wicked notion right heirs for to displace I did detest.') The feelings of the mass of the Londoners were obvious and important. Mary's cause attracted, too, many nobles and leading gentlemen, who set about proclaiming her accession in the counties. Northumberland's allies, in spite of the attempt to build them up as the key figures in the provincial military system, were on the whole too recently established, too lacking in status, to swing the country into a course against the instincts of the landed classes. There seems in fact to have been little positive enthusiasm for Jane. Even the councillors hedged their bets, to judge from the behaviour of William Cecil's agent, Richard Troughton, who was busily rallying support for Mary in Lincolnshire while his master officially supported Jane in London.

Yet the triumph of Mary was not inevitable. Although there

was little support for Jane, there was a good deal of hesitation, or wait-and-see. If the council had managed to prevent Mary's flight into East Anglia, and had imprisoned her, her cause would not have had any credibility (Troughton's account of his work for Mary around Stamford shows how much he depended on news of her success in East Anglia), and her bandwagon would never have started to roll. All this underlines the fact that there was no long-term plot on Northumberland's part. Had there been, he could have done more to prepare the ground. Whatever the financial difficulties, the core of professional soldiers would not have been dismissed in 1552. A propaganda campaign could have been mounted, stressing Mary's Catholicism, bastardy and dependence upon the Habsburgs (the imperial ambassadors had been her advisers and protectors throughout Edward's reign) and preparing the people for the possibility of a Queen Jane. In fact, only in the last months of the reign did Northumberland try to bind several of the more powerful nobles to his cause. In May 1553 his daughter married the Earl of Huntingdon's son, and Jane Grey's sister married the Earl of Pembroke's son. At the same time the Earl of Arundel – the head of the most prestigious noble family in England – was forgiven a fine and readmitted to the council. But this was too late – and Arundel and Pembroke, as we have seen, took the lead in swinging the council for Mary.

Edward's reign had been an extraordinary tale of misfortune. England had been cheated by Scotland, and defeated by France. Government had been dogged by corruption and financial embarrassment. The country had been afflicted by currency manipulation, by uncertain foreign markets, and, from 1550, by a series of disastrous harvests. Above all the rebellions of 1549 had been a humiliation for the government, and had exacerbated class-bitterness in the countryside. The one positive achievement had been in religion; with the failure of Edward's succession scheme, that too, it seemed, had come to nothing.

MARY

The new reign had begun triumphantly. Mary had several assets. The greatest was probably the readiness of Englishmen to accept constituted authority; and the success of Mary's *coup* had shown that she represented constituted authority in the country. She was, of course, the first woman to occupy the English throne in her own right (Matilda, in the twelfth century, had managed to assert her claim only fitfully and for brief periods), and she was, legally at least, a bastard. Her way to the throne might have been more difficult if there had been a credible male rival. As for her bastardy, it is clear that there had always been a good deal of popular sympathy for Queen Catherine and for Mary. Cranmer's annulment of Henry VIII's marriage had been accepted as necessary for reasons of state; but nevertheless, it seems to have been considered a legalistic device. Mary was not *really* a bastard in the sense, say, that Henry's son, the Duke of Richmond, had been.

Her Catholicism was not necessarily a disadvantage. It is true that Protestantism had made considerable advances in the last twenty years; and that alongside a number of dedicated evangelicals there was also a considerable number of people whose instinctive scepticism and resentment at clerical pretensions had now found intellectual justification in official teaching; in the public discrediting of traditional cults, in the downfall of established institutions like the monasteries, in the equation of anti-Catholicism with a vigorous, xenophobic, nationalism. The distinction is a hazardous one; but it seems likely that anti-Catholicism was more widespread than positive Protestantism. These attitudes were undoubtedly important, a political fact which governments had to take account of; and especially in London.

But against this, we must reckon too on the great strength of conservatism, of a possibly unintellectual, instinctive, rather undemonstrative preference for the familiar which provided, at least, a prejudice in favour of Mary's religion (which, in 1553, might be thought of as a return to the situation under Henry VIII rather than to a fully-fledged Papal Catholicism); and which, in turn, had been fed by the juxtaposition of advanced Protestantism with faction, corruption and economic crisis in the last few years. 'It was a good world when the old Religion was, because all things were cheap' was still a sufficiently widespread opinion, even late in Elizabeth's reign, for earnest preachers to denounce it. Lastly that very feature about Catholicism which made it anathema to the serious-minded, its tolerance of superstition, was an advantage in a pre-scientific age.

Protestantism seemed in fact to be in retreat all over Europe. With England's return to the fold no major state was now officially Protestant. Charles v's great victory against the Protestant Germans in 1547 had resulted in the forced reconversion of a significant number of cities, especially in the south, and had created hopes of a Lutheran–Catholic compromise of an essentially conservative nature. Since then the military tide had turned against Charles, and hopes of a compromise had fallen through. But still, Protestantism was officially established, by and large, only in parts of northern and central Germany, in Scandinavia, in parts of Switzerland and in the independent city of Geneva. The fact that a new wave of Protestantism would soon spread from Geneva to cause civil war in France and the Netherlands and topple the government in Scotland was hidden from contemporaries. The first wave of the Protestant Reformation was over, a good deal of the initial freshness and attraction had vanished amidst inevitable institutionalization and doctrinal dispute; and Catholicism was slowly beginning to gird itself to win back, by spiritual means as well as by sword and stake, its straying sheep. Far from Marian Catholicism being a symptom of hopeless, anachronistic reaction, as it may seem to us, to contemporaries it represented the flow of the current.

Mary's personality promised well. She had borne the humiliations imposed on her by her father with dignity; and had sturdily resisted attempts in her brother's reign to make her change her religion. She had reacted vigorously to the crisis of 1553, and her judgement had been sound (as opposed to that of the imperial ambassador who thought she should recognize a *fait accompli*). Next year she showed her ability to rally her subjects once more, in terms which prefigure some of the speeches of Queen Elizabeth,

> And I say to you in the words of a Prince, I cannot tell how naturally the Mother loveth the Child, for I was never the mother of any; but certainly, if a Prince and Governor may as naturally and earnestly love her Subjects, as the Mother doth love the Child, then assure yourselves, that I, being your Lady and Mistress, do as earnestly and tenderly love and favour you . . .

From 1554, however, Mary lost that rapport with her subjects which was an essential part of good kingship. With her marriage, her duty as queen had to be reconciled with her duty as a wife to a foreign monarch; and while Mary saw no incompatibility, the harsh facts of international politics dictated otherwise. From 1555, cheated of the hoped-for child which she needed so desperately for political as well as emotional reasons, deserted by the husband for whom she had risked so much, Mary withdrew into a bitter brooding seclusion which only increased her subjects' fears and suspicions.

The reign began gently. Northumberland was promptly executed, after an edifying speech on the error of his ways and the truth of Catholicism. Other conspirators hastened to make their peace with the new regime. William Paulet, now Marquis of Winchester, and William Petre, old Henricians both, joined the council, in spite of their involvement with Queen Jane; so did William Paget, Somerset's candid friend, who became one of the leading figures of the new government. Space had also to be found for men like the old Duke of Norfolk and Bishop Gardiner, who had spent the last few years in prison, as well as for a host of lesser men who had earned the gratitude of the queen. The result of Mary's attempt to include as many politicians as possible was an unmanageable Privy Council of about fifty members.

With royal encouragement the mass was restored in parish churches (illegally, since the Edwardian legislation was still in force). This produced a riot at Paul's Cross, in London, and Bishop Gardiner had to have a bodyguard of a hundred men when he said mass at Greenwich, but there was little opposition – indeed a good deal of positive enthusiasm – in the country at large. Parliament met in October; it reversed all the Edwardian ecclesiastical legislation (except the Chantries Act, which would have involved awkward questions of property), so restoring the church to its position in the last year of Henry VIII. Nothing as yet was done about papal jurisdiction.

More pressing was the problem of the queen's marriage and the succession. Until she had a child of her own, the obvious heir was Elizabeth. Elizabeth was seventeen years younger and likely, if only by her birth, to favour Protestantism. Mary had to marry;

and since she was thirty-seven, she had to do so quickly if she was to produce a child. But marriage raised the problem which prejudiced contemporaries against women rulers. If she married an Englishman, she would stir up a hornet's nest of jealousies. If she married a foreign prince, she would be accused of subordinating English interests to those of her husband.

Her advisers were divided. Gardiner, now lord chancellor, urged the claims of Edward Courtenay, Earl of Devon; a young man of twenty-seven, who had been in prison since the execution of his father, the Marquis of Exeter in 1538. He was a somewhat colourless character, not surprisingly in the circumstances; Gardiner might have seen this as his major virtue. But Mary demanded more positive qualities; and did not approve of Courtenay's desperate attempt to compensate for lost youth in a round of debauchery. Why, she asked Gardiner, 'should she be forced to marry a man because a Bishop had made friends of him in prison'? Paget, on the other hand, advocated a Habsburg marriage; perhaps because he realized that this is what Mary herself wanted.

The House of Commons sided with Gardiner, petitioning the queen to marry an Englishman. Mary cut short the Speaker in mid-flow; 'Parliaments were not accustomed to use such language to the kings of England.' She had in fact already promised to marry Philip, the son of her cousin Charles V, and heir to Spain and the Netherlands. The marriage treaty was concluded in January 1554.

Rebellion broke out almost immediately. Some three thousand Kentishmen marched on London, including many leading gentlemen, and headed by Sir Thomas Wyatt, one of the largest Kentish landowners, an ex-sheriff, and son of another Thomas Wyatt, the Henrician poet and diplomat. Plans for rebellions elsewhere collapsed; Sir Peter Carew failed to raise Devon (he had helped to put down the last Devon rebellion in 1549), Lady Jane Grey's father, the Duke of Suffolk, was unable to raise Leicester, or Sir James Crofts the Welsh borders, possibly because the plot had been leaked to the government and the conspirators forced to premature action, but also because these areas were less politically sensitive than Kent. The intention seems to have been to force a Courtenay marriage, and the rallying cry was hatred of

Spain. Wyatt himself had Protestant sympathies, as had many of the leading conspirators; but he found it politic to conceal these and to concentrate on the nationalist issue. 'You may not so much as name religion, for that will withdraw from us the hearts of many.' Interestingly the government also assumed that it would harm the rebels to impute Protestantism to them. Mary told the Londoners that 'the marriage seemed to be but a Spanish cloak to cover their pretended purpose against our religion'.

In the event London rallied to the cause of order (spurred on by a personal appeal by the queen, which included a promise not to marry without parliamentary consent, and the news that the other rebellions had failed), and held out, though ambivalently, against Wyatt. An army, raised hastily by leading peers, and commanded by the Earl of Pembroke, crushed the remnant of Wyatt's followers in Fleet Street. All told, about a hundred people were executed; among them, naturally, Wyatt, Suffolk and Carew, but also Lady Jane Grey and her husband (totally innocent of any involvement in the Wyatt conspiracy, and as much victims of *raison d'état* as the Earl of Warwick fifty-five years before). Princess Elizabeth was also arrested; but spared by the refusal of Wyatt and others to incriminate her, and by the influence of Gardiner and of her uncle Lord William Howard.

A new Parliament met in April 1554. It confirmed the marriage treaty. Any child born of the marriage would inherit England and the Netherlands (if it had ever come about, a striking combination). If Philip's existing son, Don Carlos, were to die childless before his father, Mary's child would inherit the whole Spanish empire as well – including America, and the Spanish dominions in Italy. Philip was given the title of King of England, but his political role was severely restricted; he was to do no more than 'aid Her Highness . . . in the happy administration of her Grace's realms'. Specifically, all appointments were to be reserved for Englishmen, while England was not to be involved in the war then raging between Charles v and France.

English fears were obvious. Still, the treaty had been accepted; but in other respects this Parliament was unfortunate. The government was split between the Gardiner and Paget parties; Gardiner, scrambling back from supporting the wrong side over the marriage issue, and wanting to press ahead with the restoration of the old faith; Paget basking in his victory, but fearful of the effects of too rigid a line in religion, especially where former church lands were concerned. Paget thought that the need to include in the council representatives of Edward's government as well as old supporters of Mary meant that England 'was now governed by such a crowd that it was more like a republic' than a monarchy. Faction fights in government were of course nothing new; the deadly feuds of Henry VIII's last years are a case in point. But for the first time, probably, since Henry VI's reign, disagreements in the council were played out in Parliament. Gardiner seems to have had the greater influence in the Commons; Paget in the Lords. The result was that a bill to revive the heresy laws passed the Commons, but was rejected in the Lords; an unhappy foretaste of the trouble that was to come over religion. Parliament was promptly dissolved, and Paget disgraced. The Bishop of Norwich remarked that Henry VIII would have had him imprisoned.

Philip's arrival, in July 1554, was not a happy occasion. The imperial ambassador, Simon Renard, like his master Charles V, a French-speaking Burgundian, sent home shocked reports of the arrogance of Philip and his Spaniards. 'The people have never been known to be so licentious in word and deed, so eager to outrage foreigners; nor has it ever seemed more likely that the people would make common cause with the nobility.' Brawls in the streets of London were not the best preparation for yet another Parliament, the most important of the reign, called in November 1554 to reunite England with Rome.

Although directions had been given by the council that electors should choose 'of their inhabitants, as the old laws require (ie, not carpet-bagging gentlemen sitting for neighbouring boroughs, a habit now over a century old), 'and of the wise, grave, and catholic sort', the Parliament's composition seems to have been little different from its predecessor. Hard bargaining took place about the papal supremacy; the essential thing was to get a guarantee for all those church lands which had been sold off since 1536. Reginald Pole, twenty years an exile, and now appointed papal legate to reconcile his country to the Holy See, had to kick his heels at Brussels during the negotiations. He produced a papal dispensation to holders of church lands, solemnly promising that these were not to be disturbed. Parliament then humbly acknowledged the sins of its predecessors, and repealed the anti-papal legislation passed under Henry VIII, first writing Pole's dispensation into the act. Having secured the essential, Parliament went on to re-enact the laws against heresy, and affirmed Philip's right to be regent if his child became king while a minor. On the other hand, it refused to sanction war against France, or to allow Philip to be crowned as King of England. In all this the Paget–Gardiner feud continued. The Lords were more indulgent than the Commons to Philip's claims and to the possibility of war. The Commons, on the other hand, for reasons which are not clear (indeed, in the light of Henry VIII's Parliaments, surprising) were readier to do battle against heresy.

By 1555, then, the pattern of Mary's reign had been set. There was to be a struggle over English involvement in the Habsburg war with France; there was to be fierce persecution of heretics, coupled with sturdy defence of property rights; there was some attempt to convert mere reaction against Edwardian Protestantism into a more positive Catholic commitment. Fundamental to all this was the question of the succession.

We need to see these political problems against the background of the prolonged economic crisis which dogged Mary's reign, the worst in living memory in intensity and in effect. We have already described the disastrous harvests of 1555 and 1556, and the killing epidemic of 1558 (*see above*, p. 246). On top of this, industrial production was probably depressed; bad harvests tend to produce a lower demand for industrial goods, while there was a continued depression in the export market for cloth. An act of 1555, to restrict the activities of large-scale clothiers in rural districts, is a symptom of the concern about over-production. In 1556 the Merchant Adventurers had such a glut of cloth at Antwerp that the government prohibited any more exports until it was cleared. None of this could in any sense be blamed on the government. But disaster and economic crisis coloured men's reactions to government measures, and help to explain that air of gloom, dissatisfaction, riot and ultimate disillusion which overshadows Mary's brief reign. Influenza may have contributed more to this than the loss of Calais.

It was against this background that Mary worked to restore the old religion; and it was possibly this same influenza which killed her in November 1558 and so wrecked all she had worked for. It is all too easy to assume that Mary's plans were doomed to failure; that persecution could not be a success, that Englishmen were too inveterately anti-clerical or too far gone along the road to Protestantism for reconversion even if Mary had been given more time. Her task was a difficult one. In many ways it was clumsily executed; and, by associating the restoration of Catholicism with the Spanish marriage, Mary gave an additional boost to that sentiment Henry VIII had worked so hard to create, that opposition to Rome could be equated with a healthy patriotism (or perhaps, a less healthy xenophobia). But as against this, we must set those factors which predisposed men to obedience, to acceptance of authority, to restrict themselves to grumbling rather than rebellion; we must also set the ability of a long-sustained propaganda effort, in the right circumstances and skilfully directed, to work a radical change in men's outlook. History is never as straightforward as it seems in the comfortable perspective of hindsight.

Of course, more was needed than merely changes in the form of religion. The Venetian ambassador commented in 1555 that there were very few pious Catholics, and that all of these were over thirty-five; 'all the rest make this show of recantation [of Protestantism], yet do not effectually resume their Catholic faith.' He may have exaggerated; ambassadors only knew the south-east of the country, the most radical areas, and generalized far too easily from what they saw in London. But London's political importance was, of course, disproportionately large, and the situation in London was serious. Priests were mocked in the streets and church services were lampooned. A 'wretched and devilishly-disposed person' hanged a cat on the gallows at Cheapside, its head shaven like a priest's and its body enveloped in mock vestments. On Easter Day 1555 a priest was assaulted while saying mass at St Margaret's, Westminster, and a general massacre of foreigners was expected. Brawls in the streets escalated into political battles between Londoners and Spaniards. Rumours flew about that King Edward was still alive and would return to redeem his subjects from popery and Spanish domination. More significantly, there were continuous demonstrations in favour of the Princess Elizabeth, which made Mary's government think twice about depriving her of the right to succeed to the throne.

The ambassador's further comment, that Englishmen 'discharge their duty as subject to their prince by living as he lives, believing what he believes, and in short, doing whatever he commands, making use of it for external show . . . rather than from any internal zeal', may not have been very heartening from a Catholic point of view, but provided at least some hope of a base from which the task of more positive reconversion could be carried out.

Effective reconversion involved both the eradication of Protestantism and the forging of a new, more dynamic, Catholicism. The first, it was hoped, would be accomplished by terror. Some eight hundred Protestants fled abroad, to Frankfurt, to Strasburg and other German cities, but also to John Calvin's Geneva. Their experiences in exile, their quarrels over the liturgy, their discovery of purer forms of Protestantism than those of Edwardian England, were to help determine the form, and later the difficulties, of the Elizabethan church. More immediately the exiles constituted a 'remnant', a guarantee to men who identified their cause with that of the Jews of the Old Testament, that if God had punished them for the moment, he would not abandon their cause.

Mary's government did little to stop them going; at least, to judge by its failure to catch the Duchess of Suffolk, even though it took her a month from leaving her house in London (with six servants) to setting sail from Gravesend. The trouble was caused by those who stayed at home, most of them humbler men than the exiles. A large underground church flourished in London, meeting at various inns and houses with congregations up to two hundred. Smaller groups met elsewhere, always subject to the danger of government spies or to being given away by loose talk. A few bravely or rashly tried to preach the Gospel openly; like George

Eagles, alias 'Trudgeover' who tramped the woods of Essex and East Anglia until he was caught in 1556.

Altogether some 280 heretics were burnt in Mary's reign, the majority of them humble men like Thomas Hale, a Bristol shoemaker, or Cicely Ormes the wife of a Norwich weaver. Only twenty-one clergy were executed, though these included the three 'Oxford martyrs', Archbishop Cranmer, Bishop Ridley and Hugh Latimer. The great majority of these burnings were in the south-east. London provided 67 victims, Kent 58, Essex 39. Only two heretics were burnt north of the Trent, and, except for Gloucester (where the bishop, James Brooks, was a zealot and there were ten victims) very few in the west of England or in Wales. This may reflect on the spread of Protestantism in Edward's time; but it may also be due to the personalities of the bishops concerned (Pole at Canterbury, Bonner in London), and the greater effectiveness of government in the south-east. The burnings impinged very little, therefore, on the majority of the population; but disproportionately on those who could best make their hostility felt, and whose adhesion was likely to be decisive in a crisis.

The burnings caused a good deal of local popular resentment. The London authorities were told to prevent demonstrations of sympathy at executions and specifically to see that apprentices and servants were kept at home on execution days; and there is plenty of similar evidence for other places. The imperial ambassador described the scene at the burning of John Rogers.

> Some of the onlookers wept, others prayed to God to give him strength, perseverance and patience to bear the pain and not to recant, others gathered the ashes and bones and wrapped them in paper to preserve them, yet others threatening the bishops. The haste with which the bishops have proceeded in this matter may well cause a revolt.

(Renard preferred 'secret executions, banishment, and imprisonment' as less provocative.) Some of the bitterness was because the victims were humble men who maintained what had so recently been official doctrine. 'Who hath been thy schoolmaster,' Sir Anthony Browne asked Thomas Watts, a Billericay linen-draper. 'Forsooth ... even you, sir ... For in King Edward's day in open sessions you spoke against the religion now used, no preacher more.'

Whether resentment was such that it was bound, sooner or later to produce rebellion, is however much more difficult to judge. Burnings were not peculiar to Mary's reign, though their scale was. Protestant theologians did not, for the most part, disapprove of burning heretics, they merely disagreed about the definition of heresy, and many (like Cranmer) were themselves involved in persecution. More generally, capital punishment was common. After the northern rebellion of 1569, some seven hundred people were 'appointed for hanging';* while anything between 17 and 54 people were hanged each year in Elizabethan Essex, generally for small-scale theft, and this was not an untypical county. (The risk of being judicially executed in mid-Tudor Nottinghamshire was roughly equivalent to the risk of being killed in a road accident today.†) People then were hardened to brutal punishment; and, if not always approving, prepared to grumble but submit, to prefer obedience to disorder. We do not know if this was in fact the situation about Mary's burnings. But what we must do is to try to clear our minds of the retrospective view of the reign which was created by Elizabethan propaganda; and particularly by John Foxe's *Actes and Monuments* (better known as the Book of Martyrs) which became an Elizabethan best-seller.

Foxe was convinced of England's God-given mission to bear witness to the faith. God's purpose was writ large in history; and to prove that Protestantism was no new-fangled invention of the sixteenth century but the original Christian faith, it was necessary to establish some sort of continuity with the church of the apostles. As against the formal institutional continuity which the Catholics claimed, Foxe looked for a continuing underground tradition, which had preserved the true faith since the institutional church had entered on the path of increasing corruption

* Possibly less than half were actually hanged: *see* H. B. McCall in *Yorkshire Archaeological Journal*, vol. 18, 1904–5.

† P. E. H. Hair, 'Deaths from Violence in Britain: A Tentative Secular Study', *Population Studies*, vol. 25, 1971.

ın the fourth century. As far as his sources and the historical conventions of his day allowed, Foxe wrote good history; and for recent history, a checking of his account by such official records as survive, shows him to be substantially accurate about facts. Foxe's account was successful precisely because it invoked known truths, and because it evoked a response from his readers. But in doing so it also transformed that response, gave shape to something which may well have been an instinctive revulsion, but little more, and produced instead a concrete, articulate, passionate belief which could form the basis of a political attitude. In short, one can read back from Foxe that persecution was unpopular; one cannot deduce that it was so unpopular as to be necessarily self-defeating. One of the more unpalatable lessons of history is that persecution often works.

Where religious persecution did succeed in sixteenth-century Europe, however (in Austria and Bavaria, for instance), it did so in the context of a comprehensive programme of evangelization. The state and the pulpit worked together. This did not happen in Marian England. Although the old services were restored, the same clergy officiated as in the Edwardian period. Even those priests who had married were allowed to continue to officiate after they had put away their wives and done penance. The queen at her own expense restored monastic life at Westminster and Syon, founded two houses for nuns, and two for friars. But her subjects failed to follow her example (which may have been an advantage; religiously speaking, it could be maintained that a small number of dedicated monks might be more use than the inflated and arrogantly rich monastic establishment before the Dissolution). The wills of Mary's reign show that very little money was left for prayers for the dead, and there was no rush to restock churches with treasures after the Edwardian depredations. Marian Catholicism produced only one pamphleteer of any distinction, able to appeal to common sense and common prejudice in earthy language: Myles Huggarde, a London hosier. (By contrast Protestants abroad smuggled into England a mass of lively pamphlets – including, to the embarrassment of Lord Chancellor Gardiner, a translation of his defence of Henry VIII's supremacy.) Spiritual fervour was at a low ebb; to the despair of Cardinal

Pole who, with his usual lack of tact, preached to the Londoners about the superior spiritual virtues of Milan, Venice and Rome.

Mary and Pole have been criticized for not doing more to promote the more positive aspects of reconversion. In terms of achievement this is true. But the criticism seems largely beside the point. Mary's reign was too short to effect a large-scale transformation of spiritual values. Had she lived longer, however, something might have been done; and indeed, even as things were, there were the signs of a beginning of a real attempt at Catholic reform.

The most striking developments were on the episcopal bench. Naturally, many of Mary's bishops were old Henricians, men like Stephen Gardiner, Bonner of London, Tunstall of Durham, restored to their sees after deprivation under Edward. Some of the others, however, were rather strikingly representative of a new type of Catholic bishop, the enthusiast rather than the traditional judicious administrator. A number of them had been in exile abroad; including Bishop Pate of Worcester, a man who had been a diplomat in Henry VIII's service in the 1530s, but had then fled to Italy and attended the Council of Trent. Pole, Archbishop of Canterbury, had refused to return to England in 1534, had written against the royal supremacy, and had been a member of a group of influential liberal Catholics who had launched a successful programme of administrative reform at the Papal Curia. Most surprising of all was Goldwell, bishop of the obscure diocese of St Asaph, but evidently destined for much higher things. He had been a member of Pole's household in Italy, and in 1547 had joined the Theatines, one of the most dynamic of the new Italian religious orders. When he was deprived of his see in 1559 he managed to get back to Italy, refused a cardinal's hat and an Italian bishopric, and eventually in 1580 was taken ill while on his way to serve in England as an illegal missionary priest.

Goldwell was exceptional. But the transformation in the episcopal bench was remarkable, and was strikingly illustrated by the events of 1559, all the bishops except one (Kitchen of Llandaff) refused the new oath of supremacy and were deprived of their sees. As it happened, the Elizabethan government was wisely reluctant to make martyrs, and they suffered no worse fate than imprisonment, often in their own palaces. But they could not have foreseen this; and in opposing the new settlement they might well fear the same fate as Bishop Fisher in 1535. The contrast between their behaviour and that of their Henrician predecessors was striking; although one of them, Tunstall, was involved on both occasions, reluctantly submitting in 1534 and refusing in 1559.

On the other hand, signs of self-sacrifice among the lower clergy were few. They went on to serve Elizabeth, as they had served in turn Henry, Edward and Mary. The task of spreading a more uncompromising attitude to religious change had not yet penetrated very far down the clerical ranks. (Even so, many more of the clergy were involved in opposition to Elizabeth's regime than to Edward's.) The most promising development was in the reform of clerical education. Pole advocated the establishment of seminaries (a favourite demand of Catholic reformers in Europe, and one that bore good fruit), and in fact one was established at the cathedral school at York. He also wanted to found a college for the sons of the nobility at Rome to train leaders for the church (as a descendant of the Yorkist royal family, Pole had an aristocrat's belief that episcopal resistance to Henry VIII had crumbled so easily because the bishops were of low birth). But he ignored a suggestion by Ignatius Loyola that his newly founded Jesuit order should train young men for the English mission, and the first Jesuit arrived in England, ironically, only in November 1558.

Some thought, too, was given to the instruction of the laity – if only because the Protestant accent on the Bible and on preaching forced Catholics to adopt the same weapons. Edmund Bonner, the persecuting Bishop of London, and Thomas Watson, Bishop of Lincoln, one of the ablest of the Marian bishops (he had had a distinguished career at St John's, Cambridge, that nursery of Edwardian statesmen), both produced books of *Homilies*, lucid and effective expositions of Catholic doctrine. Pole's legatine synod of 1555 authorized production of a catechism, an official set of homilies, and a Catholic translation of the New Testament; though none of these appeared before the end of the reign.

These projected reforms were in tune with progressive Catholic opinion in Europe. In this connection, we need to remember how late was the timing of Catholic reform, of the Counter-Reformation, in Europe generally. The Jesuits were not founded until 1540. The Council of Trent had held its first meeting in 1545, but it had been suspended again two years later, and its second session, in 1551-2, had been very brief. Pole's proposals preceded the Council's decrees for the establishment of seminaries, which were not promulgated until the last session in 1562-3; and the first real attempt to provide systematic education for the priesthood was that of Cardinal Borromeo in Milan from 1565. The fumblings of the Marian church, the accent on repression rather than renewal, were not an indication of a peculiarly English spiritual lukewarmness. In the last third of the sixteenth century, a real movement of spiritual renewal took place in Catholic Europe, particularly on the parochial level. The historian who considers, for instance, the political behaviour of the people of Paris in the 1580s, can have little doubt of the ability of revived Catholicism to strike roots among the laity.

The heart of the matter was time; of how long Catholicism had to re-establish itself before facing the threat of a Protestant succession. Through the summer of 1555 Mary believed herself to be pregnant, and Philip, eager to be away, was kept waiting disconsolately for the delivery. On 30 April London's bells rang to celebrate the birth of a prince; but the news was false. Soon, other, uglier rumours spread: that the queen had given birth to a deformed child, or that the whole *accouchement* was a fraud, part of a plan to pass off another child as Mary's own. By August even Mary had recognized that her pregnancy was a delusion, and Philip was able to leave. In spite of renewed hopes at the beginning of 1558, Elizabeth's eventual succession was becoming increasingly likely.

There was for a start, no very obvious alternative; Mary's cousin, Mary Stuart, Queen of Scotland, who was to be the Catholic alternative in Elizabeth's reign, was the wife of the heir to the French throne, and her becoming Queen of England as well was obviously unacceptable to Philip. Parliament's wariness about crowning Philip and the unpopularity of the Spanish marriage scotched any notion that he might be allowed to succeed if his wife died. It is unlikely that any Parliament in the foreseeable future would agree to disinherit Elizabeth, while, as Mary had good cause to know, the reaction of the country at large was likely to be hostile and decisive if any attempt were made to tamper with the succession. On the other hand, Mary could not bring herself to recognize Elizabeth as her heir. If she had done so, a plan of Philip's, that Elizabeth should be safely married off to his staunch ally the Duke of Savoy, might have been feasible. But even that reckons without the likely refusal of consent by the council – or indeed, by Elizabeth herself. The only hope for Catholicism for the moment lay in Mary's life.

Mary might outlive her younger sister, though obviously the chances were against it. Even if she did not, she might live long enough to re-establish a real Catholicism in the country (she would not have been sixty till 1576), to the extent that a middle-aged Elizabeth succeeding to the throne might have judged it best to let well alone. Against this it might be suggested that even if Mary had lived, a national rebellion would in any case have foiled her plans. The sullen resentment of London, the endemic rioting, the demonstrations of hostility even when Mary herself rode through the streets show that a rebellion was possible, and the story of the revolt of the Netherlands (whose position as a component of the Habsburg conglomeration provides an obvious parallel to England) shows that it might well have been successful. It would be as foolish to conclude that England was bound to be reconverted successfully to Catholicism if Mary had lived, as it would be to assert that it was bound to evolve into Protestantism, whatever the dynastic circumstances. The imponderables on both sides are much too great for the sort of doctrinaire judgement commonly made by those who too readily invoke either 'national character' or sociological determinism.

Meanwhile foreign policy was causing trouble. Philip, on his first visit, had tried and failed to involve England in war with France. Shortly after he left again, in September 1555, he succeeded his father, first as ruler of the Netherlands, then as King of Spain; and by the end of 1556 he was at war, not only with France, but with the pope, Paul IV, an irascible Neapolitan who resented Spanish control of Italy. (One ironical result of this situation was that Cardinal Pole was deprived of his legateship and summoned to Rome on a charge of heresy, and Mary prevented his going, asserting that heresy cases should be tried in the realm.) The English government still held out against the war; partly because it was short of money (a suspicious Parliament in September 1555 had turned down most of its demands for taxation) and partly because the economic situation made war in any case too difficult. London was too dependent on French grain supplies in the famine conditions created by the harvests of 1555 and 1556; and disorder in the streets of London could easily spark off rebellion. Philip, reluctantly, came to England once more, in March 1557, but had no more success, until Henry II of France played into his hands; in April 1557 a certain Thomas Stafford, who since Wyatt's rebellion had been at the French court, arrived at Scarborough with two ships, seized the castle and proclaimed himself 'Protector of England'. This incident provided an unequivocally English reason for war, and the council was swayed at last; especially now that, with summer coming on, grain prices were tumbling as the next harvest promised to be a good one. Philip departed in July, reasonably pleased with his second (and last) visit.

The French war was not, then, merely a response by an English puppet-government to Spanish string-pulling. English interests since the days of Edward IV had involved preventing French expansion northwards into the Netherlands as Henry II was now threatening. War, too, offered the chance of healing some of the wounds which religious and political divisions had inflicted on the English ruling class. Military service enabled the Duke of Northumberland's three sons to purge the role they had played in their father's conspiracy; one of them, Henry Dudley, was killed on campaign, the other two, Ambrose and Robert, were to be leading (and very Protestant) members of Elizabeth's court. Another keen Protestant was Francis Russell, second Earl of Bedford. He had been imprisoned in 1553, was secretly involved in the Wyatt conspiracy, and then fled to Geneva; but returned home to join the army in 1557.

The war began well with a spectacular victory by Philip at St Quentin, some twenty miles inside the French frontier; England provided some seven thousand of the fifty thousand troops, commanded by the Earl of Pembroke. The main French army was away in Italy, and the way was open to Paris; but Philip, cautious as ever, preferred to take the town of St Quentin, and then dispersed his troops for the winter, with the usual assumption that there would be no serious military action. The French had different ideas, however. On New Year's Day 1558 an impressive army appeared before the gates of Calais and a fleet blockaded the port. The Calais garrison was short of food and ammunition and surrendered within a week. Calais had been lost to England after two hundred years.

Recriminations flew about. Philip was accused of delay in sending reinforcements. The governor of Calais, Lord Wentworth, was charged with surrendering too quickly; certainly his colleague Lord Grey of Wilton put up a much more spirited defence in the sister-fortress of Guisnes. Had Wentworth held out a day or two longer, the French king believed that his own troops would have had to withdraw because of the difficulties of winter campaigning. There was nothing new about Calais being badly supplied; what was new was the daring gamble of the French. Whatever the reasons, English pride was badly wounded. Parliament in January 1558 voted an immediate subsidy of £140,000, as much as had ever been voted to Henry VIII in a single sum. During the summer men stood by on the south coast expecting a French invasion. Philip was not able to reconquer Calais, and it was low on the list of priorities at the peace talks which started in August. The Spanish marriage had more than confirmed the worst fears of its opponents.

In all this tale of failure and frustration, some positive achievement can be found in the unglamorous world of government finance. The main credit here seems to be due to William Paulet, now Marquis of Winchester, the lord treasurer, the archetypal Tudor administrator, interested primarily in good government, whatever the theology of the moment. The findings of the 1552 commission were put into effect; the exchequer swallowed up the rival courts, except the relatively small Court of Wards and Duchy of Lancaster; so unifying administration, though at the expense of perpetuating some of the archaic bureaucratic procedures of that ancient body. (Fortunately some of the technical innovations of the new courts, in audit methods and so on, continued; if they had not, chaos might have ensued.) A drive against the corruption revealed in the Edwardian investigations achieved remarkable results. The net yield of the lands previously handled by the Court of Augmentations doubled in the course of the reign. Although Mary was generous to the church, this was balanced by a reduction in pensions and an end to the reckless sale and grant of lands which had characterized Edward's reign.

Even more important, a new book of rates was introduced for the customs in 1558, adjusting duties to the realities of half a century of inflation. As a result, customs revenues rose from £29,000 in Mary's last year to no less than £83,000 in Elizabeth's first. On this basis Mary's administration was more spectacularly successful than even those of Henry VII or Edward IV. But a good part of this reform came too late to help Mary's government. Faced with Parliament's reluctance to vote taxes, Mary's financial situation was always desperately tight. It was Elizabeth, not Mary, who benefited from the financial reforms; to such effect that in Elizabeth's reign little or no attempt was made to raise revenues to keep step with inflation. The customs rates were not raised again until 1604.

Vigorous reform took place, too, in the navy. Finances were rationalized from 1557 with a definite fixed annual allocation for the upkeep of ships. The building of warships began again in 1555, after a gap of five years, and reached an extraordinary height in 1558-9 (as much tonnage was built in a year as in the five years before the Armada). This was too late to save Calais, but it did provide the means for Elizabeth's intervention in Scotland in 1560 which, by helping a party of Scottish noblemen topple the pro-French government, removed the threat of attack on two fronts which had hung over England since 1548. The navy, in fact, was becoming a much more permanent, professional body; to take only one test, ships were put to sea in winter more frequently in Mary's reign than in the whole of Henry VIII's.

It was also in Mary's reign, in 1557, that the rebuilding of the fortifications at Berwick took place; the new long low walls, which still survive, were designed to give the smallest possible target to enemy artillery, while projecting bastions gave the defending guns a wide field of fire which could play havoc with any attacking force. Berwick is one of the earliest and most impressive applications in northern Europe of an art developed in war-torn Italy; and while it is tempting to attribute the initiative to Philip's Italian engineers, it seems to have been an Englishman, Sir Richard Lee, who was responsible. Lastly, in 1558, fear of invasion after the loss of Calais led to the passing of two acts to improve the militia and, especially, to modernize its arms. The foundatior of the Elizabethan military system had been laid under Mary.

Another sphere in which Mary's reign saw a positive policy and one which foreshadowed future developments was Ireland. As we have seen, from 1534 the English crown had been attempting to assert its authority; but it hoped to do this cheaply, by winning over the Anglo-Irish lords and the Gaelic chiefs. Disorder, however, had continued on a large scale, and especially in the lordships of Leix and Offaly (dangerously situated within fifty miles of Dublin). In 1550 these were confiscated by the crown, and the English Privy Council decided to introduce colonists there. It was not, however, till 1556 that the plantation policy really began. Settlers were to hold by military tenures; if they were Irish, they were to sever all connections with their fellows, wear English dress, use English law and bring up their children to speak English. As Queen's County and King's County, Leix and Offaly foreshadowed the bloody history of Ireland for the next century; a continual round of desperate rebellion, confiscation and colonization which was to reach its peak in that un-Marian figure Oliver Cromwell.

In England Mary could not afford to act so brusquely. Her position was too weak to offend the nobility to whom, in part, she owed her throne. Although she wished to abolish the system which had developed in Northumberland's time, of noble lords-lieutenants supervising the military forces of the counties, she was forced to continue it because of the danger of rebellion and invasion. Her lieutenants included both the 'old nobility' and the newer, ex-Henrician civil servants who had done so well for themselves in Edward's reign. So successive Russells, Earls of Bedford, continued to rule in the south-west, as they had done since 1540 (in spite of the second earl's vehement Protestantism), the Dukes of Norfolk in East Anglia, the Earl of Arundel in Sussex and the Earl of Pembroke in Wales. Like Northumberland, Mary issued licences to selected nobles to keep retainers, especially from 1556 onwards. Military necessity – defence against the Scots – involved the return of the earldom of Northumberland to the Percy family in 1557. (Not, as might be expected, blind gratitude on the queen's part for the Pilgrimage of Grace – if that were the case, why wait four years?) A forward policy against the nobility, on the lines of those of Henry VII or Henry VIII was only possible from a position of strength.

The weakness of the crown was rather reminiscent of the 1450s: in the tendency to opposition in Parliament; in the need to keep a wary eye on popular opinion, especially in London; in the need to calculate the attitudes of individual noblemen. But the situation was not really comparable. There has been little work on the impact of government on the localities in the mid-Tudor period; but while Tudor government in general was a good deal less effective than is sometimes implied, it does look as if law and order were rather better observed even in the 1550s than in the 1450s, if only because the drive to make decisions of the courts respected, by Edward IV and Henry VII, by Wolsey and by Cromwell, had achieved a certain momentum. Nor can one easily imagine the Marian financial reforms being put into effect a century earlier. There was not the same air of crisis in Mary's reign as in Henry VI's; Mary's council may have been torn by faction and rivalries may have been fought out in Parliament; but it did not escalate into armed warfare. Above all, where Mary may have had her deficiencies, there is no question of total incompetence as there had been with Henry VI; the danger in her case was of stirring up resentment, possibly eventually rebellion, by too inflexible a pursuit of policies she believed to be right.

Mary's weakness was partly the result of the continued uncertainties since 1547, which had increased both the wealth of the nobility (albeit largely Henry VIII's new nobles), and the importance of the military factor in politics. Mary's sex was a drawback, too. Although she clearly had a will of her own, her councillors allowed themselves a good deal more latitude than with Henry VIII;

it is difficult to imagine a councillor in Henry's time behaving like Paget in stirring up parliamentary opposition to government policy. We must remember, too, the very difficult economic background, the slump in the cloth trade, above all the series of disastrous harvests which go some way at least to explaining the apparently endemic tendency of Londoners to riot.

Beyond this, opposition to Mary's government was due, in part at least, to the very importance of the issues at stake. The problem of the queen's marriage, of the succession, of arrangements for a regency and so on, were obviously of vital concern to the country at large. So, too, the Henrician Reformation had introduced a whole new dimension into politics. On one level, the dissolution of monasteries and chantries and the sale of their lands meant that religious issues were inextricably entangled with issues of property. It was not merely greed and crass materialism that made the 1554 Parliament so keen on extracting guarantees before recognizing papal authority; if the issue of church lands had not been settled, the confusion in the country at large, not only among owners of ex-monastic estates (many of them now at third or fourth hand) but also among their tenants and their creditors, would have been intolerable. On another level, religious differences had introduced the possibility of ideological politics – of a continued opposition, based on clear-cut principles of a sort which had not existed since the great conflict of church and state in the twelfth century. Attitudes to government were bound to be radically affected if a number of its subjects considered it to be waging war against the forces of light. Of course, only a minority were so motivated, and in Mary's reign they could not come out into the open; they would not get far, in practical terms, by openly advocating Protestantism in Parliament, and, as we have seen, Wyatt thought it best to play down the Protestant element in his rebellion. Nevertheless, even in Mary's Parliaments, a small opposition group could manipulate the prejudices of their fellows (as for instance, on the property rights of exiles), or cause trouble by making use of divisions within the government. Elizabeth's reign was to show much more vividly the ability of a group of religious zealots to constitute something like a real parliamentary opposition.

It is tempting to contrast the weakness of Mary's government with the success of her sister's. Yet, in fact, many of the same traits persisted. In 1559 Elizabeth was swept into a religious settlement she was not yet ready for, by the pressure of her council and her Parliament. Throughout her reign, on issues like the succession, harsher treatment of Catholics, a more committedly, ideological, Protestant, foreign policy, a more conciliatory attitude to Puritans, and so on, an opposition group in the Commons could take heart from the fact that some councillors were urging exactly the same policies on the queen as they were. Elizabeth's council at various times was as violently split as was Mary's – though on the whole, it seems to have been slightly more discreet about parading its differences than Paget and Gardiner had been. Elizabeth undoubtedly handled the problem of faction more successfully than Mary did. In part this was the result of superior skill. In part, though, it was because Mary had a harder task, the implementation of positive policies, the reconversion of her people, aligning England in war on the side of Spain; whereas Elizabeth had no missionary zeal, and usually preferred to do nothing while waiting on events. It is easier to beat off demands for action, than to act in the teeth of opposition.

Mary was dangerously ill through the summer of 1558. She got much worse in October, and the question of the succession, which she had been so reluctant to face, was now urgent. Eventually, on 9 November her council got her to acknowledge Elizabeth as her successor, although she had little confidence in her sister's designs. Already, an alternative government was taking shape around Elizabeth at Hatfield, largely through the efforts of the circumspect Sir William Cecil, one-time secretary in Edward's reign. Philip's ambassador was beginning to take discreet soundings, reminding Elizabeth of past favours from her brother-in-law, and suggesting that Philip, after a decent interval, would need a new wife. In the morning of 17 November Mary died, at St James. Across the river at Lambeth her kinsman and *confidant*, Reginald Pole, was also seriously ill. He died before the day was out.

The world at large assumed that a decisive break had occurred; most obviously, of course, in religion. Elizabeth might flirt with the Spanish ambassador, might have mass said in her private chapel and order that no change was to be made in religious observance, but neither the Londoners who rang their bells nor Bishop White who preached at Mary's funeral against the wolves of heresy had much doubt about the future. From Frankfurt and Geneva, Emden and Strasburg, English Protestants were hastening home 'for the walls of Jerusalem to be built again in that kingdom'; and in London and elsewhere, Edwardian or more radical forms of service were openly performed.

Elizabeth was not the dedicated Protestant which her birth suggested. Neither was she a Catholic. Even in the sixteenth century there were a considerable number of people in all churches who believed that religion was essentially a private matter between man and God, who viewed sceptically the claims of zealots that their system represented God's will to be forced on the world at large. The finer points of religion could with advantage be left conservatively ambiguous, in the spirit of the attitude Elizabeth reputedly took on Christ's presence in the eucharist:

> 'Twas God the word that spake it,
> He took the bread and brake it,
> And what the word did make it,
> That I believe and take it.

This attitude understandably annoyed her more militant subjects. But it had the advantage of flexibility. Elizabeth had been prepared to conform under Mary (as Mary most decidedly, had not been prepared to conform under Edward) and seems now to have favoured something like the Henrician, non-papal Catholicism; whether because she thought it dangerous to hurry her subjects, or because this represented her own position, is impossible to tell.

Nevertheless, what emerged from the 1559 Parliament was a decidedly Protestant prayer book, modelled, though with tactful amendments, on the more radical of the two Edwardian books, that of 1552. Her change of mind seems to have been due, in part, to pressure by a Parliament which included a vigorous minority of dedicated Protestants, many of them returned exiles; partly to the pressure of her advisers, most notably William Cecil, a decided if cautious Protestant; and partly, perhaps to the conclusion of peace with France which made her less dependent on Philip. But what was also significant was the near-unanimous opposition as we have seen, of the surviving Marian bishops to the new Supremacy Act. Their refusal to accept the queen as 'Supreme Governor' of the Church of England meant that she had to rely on Protestants, for leadership in the church; and so made the 'Henrician Catholic' solution impractical.* Edward's and Mary's reigns had polarized religious opinions among the theologically learned, if not yet in the country at large; and had reduced that air of confusion and incomprehension which had been a vital ingredient in the success of Henry's Reformation.

If Mary, not Elizabeth, had reigned in England in the 1560s, we cannot tell what might have been the outcome. But, whether a restored Catholicism had successfully taken root, or whether Protestantism had asserted itself by bloody revolution, opinion would have polarized even further, and the result would hardly have been that moderate, humane, rational, rather lukewarm Anglicanism which was, in fact, the long-term result of the 1559 settlement. For good or ill the timing of Mary's death was decisive; not only for England's religion, but for that vague but real entity, national character, which Anglicanism has done so much to mould.

---

* J. E. Neale's thesis that Elizabeth preferred a conservative settlement is now being challenged; see Winthrop S. Hudson, *The Cambridge Connection and the Elizabethan Settlement of 1559* (Duke Univ. Press, North Carolina, 1980), and Norman L. Jones, *Faith by Statute: Parliament and the Settlement of Religion, 1559* (Royal Hist. Soc., Studies in History, 32, 1982).

CONCLUSION

How far had England changed in this hundred years? At one level, of course, very little. The majority of men were still scratching a living from the soil, in much the same way as they had been for centuries past. The impact of the various changes we have described, expansion of foreign trade, the growth of manufacturing industry, even the enclosure movement, was relatively small as far as the average peasant-farmer was concerned. Far more important were the changes in the population level, and the resulting redistribution of income between classes; the increased prosperity of the yeoman, or the small gentleman, the increased numbers of the destitute, of vagabonds and beggars, was probably the most striking change in the country at large. Society was still intensely hierarchical, men's relationships were still regulated by an elaborate code of patronage and deference; the social order was still a matter of different groups, each with their specific functions and states. But individual social mobility had increased dramatically, it was now easier for a man to climb higher (or, indeed, to slip downward) than ever before. The shrill insistence on 'order' and 'degree' by Elizabethan writers is probably a deliberate reaction to this new fluidity rather than a true reflection of the world about them.

The government now intervened in many more aspects of national life; most strikingly, in religion, but also in its attempts to deal with social problems: the slow evolution of a national system for dealing with poverty; the various attempts to regulate the change of land-use from arable to pasture, and so on. This was an obvious response to a rapidly deteriorating social situation; but the appetite grows with eating, and the schemes of the 'Commonwealth Party', even if some of them were impractical, show how the concept of an 'interventionist' state had grown. At the start of the period almost the only important piece of 'national' economic legislation (as opposed to parliamentary interference in, for instance, competing claims to privilege in various towns, or competing guilds in a particular town) was the attempt to regulate wages through the fourteenth-century Statutes of Labourers. By 1563 the Statute of Artificers could attempt, with some success, to apply on a national basis the sort of regulation of labour conditions which guilds and municipalities had provided locally; and could even specify the hours of work (5 am to 7 or 8 pm in summer, dawn to dusk in winter) for wage-earners.

The crown was far stronger than it had been. The royal navy, for instance, had been transformed from a handful of ships to a powerful and permanent fleet, complete with large dockyards to service it. On the other hand the dangers from abroad were far greater; a France which by acquiring Brittany and pushing north the Netherlands frontier, was now strategically placed for a possible large-scale invasion of England; and that unreliable English ally, Burgundy, now transformed into a world-wide Spanish Habsburg empire, still inconveniently able to strangle England's trade by its control of the Netherlands. A Franco-Spanish Catholic alliance could never be ruled out, though the logic of power politics made it unlikely; the 1559 Peace of Câteau-Cambrésis was concluded with much rhetoric about the need to extirpate heresy. A good deal had been done to build up a native armaments industry, but the first years of Elizabeth were to see feverish attempts by Thomas Gresham to bring in huge stocks of arms and gunpowder from Europe. There was no sort of professional army; and while there had been some shift from the practice of relying on noblemen to provide troops for foreign service, to a more 'national' system, the quality of the troops so provided was, as Elizabeth's reign was to show, dismally low.

The crown was also now a good deal richer than in the fifteenth century, though much less so than it had been in, say, 1540. But about a quarter of the monastic lands still remained in its possession; there had been other pickings at the Reformation (forced, and, from the crown's point of view, highly profitable exchanges of land with bishops, for instance), and the customs had benefited from increased trade and revised rates. Very roughly total income, excluding parliamentary taxation, was about £160,000 at the beginning of Elizabeth's reign; it had been about £35,000 in the 1450s. Even allowing for inflation, the latter figure would hardly be worth more than £100,000 at 1559 values, so the increase was substantial.*

The richest peer in 1450 had been the Duke of York, with at least £3,500, roughly a tenth of the crown's income. In 1559 the richest peer was the Duke of Norfolk, with about £6,000, so that the crown had 26 times as much. In general the sixteenth century had not seen noblemen accumulating land through marriage on the fifteenth-century scale; partly because of closer royal control over the disposal of heiresses. The largest fifteenth-century estates had come into crown ownership, either by inheritance, or by confiscation for political reasons; and in that sense the day of the 'over-mighty subject' was over. The ratio of royal income to that of the average peer had changed from 50:1 to 90:1. (The average peer had £768 in 1436, £1,780 in 1559.†) More generally, the period had seen a successful attack on noble privilege and local particularism, in the north, in Wales, even in Ireland; and systematic repression by Henry VII, by Wolsey, and by Thomas Cromwell had done a good deal to curb the militaristic, assertive tendencies of the great nobility.

Even so, 1569 was to see an important rebellion by the northern earls (Neville of Westmorland and Percy of Northumberland), encouraged from the wings by Thomas Howard, Duke of Norfolk (grandson of that familiar figure of the same name in the reign of Henry VIII). As Professor Stone has shown the propensity of the peerage to resort to violence in their feuds with neighbours and rivals persisted at a high level well into Elizabeth's reign; to take one example, the Earl of Sussex complained in 1565 that he was set upon at court by 'great bands of men with swords and bucklers' in the service of the Earl of Leicester.‡ The attraction of gentlemen and others – often in liveries – into a great man's

* *See above*, p. 68 for the 1450s, p. 310 for the customs in 1559, and G. Batho, in Thirsk (ed.), *Agrarian History, 1500–1640* pp. 265–6 for other revenues in 1559.

† *See above*, pp. 50, 63: L. Stone, *The Crisis of the Aristocracy, 1558–1641* (Oxford, 1965) p. 760.

‡ *Ibid.*, chap. 5.

service also continued into Elizabeth's reign, though formal retaining (except by royal licence) had died out. It was in fact the long period of internal peace, after 1569, which gradually reduced the military tendencies of the nobility; so much so that when civil war broke out in 1642, noblemen, by and large, showed themselves incompetent leaders, and the victorious parliamentary forces were eventually led by two gentlemen, Thomas Fairfax and Oliver Cromwell.* That would not have been possible in the fifteenth century; the concept would still have seemed far-fetched in the early Tudor period.

Elizabeth's success in demilitarizing the nobility was partly the result of policy, her attempt (and Cecil's) to 'freeze' society. She insisted on the importance of hierarchy, and of birth (whereas in the 1530s, especially, there had been much more talk of merit); was remarkably indulgent to noble debtors, and leased crown land to them on extraordinarily favourable terms. She also ended that division between the 'old' and the 'new' (Henrician, Edwardian) nobility which persisted into the 1560s; by strategic inter-marriages, arranged by Cecil as Master of the Court of Wards, and by a notable niggardliness in creating new peerages, so giving time for the social order, so badly shaken in the 1530s and 1540s, to settle down once more. It was in these conditions that the humanist ideals of courtliness, of education, of a civilized, 'gentlemanly' life were able at long last to take hold of the English aristocracy.

That long internal peace depended on two related factors Elizabeth's longevity (she was the longest-lived English monarch since the Conquest), and the undisputed accession of James I. Had she died, say, in the sixties or seventies (smallpox nearly killed her in 1562), civil war would almost certainly have followed. There would have been strong opposition to the accession of Mary Stuart, the Scottish queen; and even if Mary had succeeded peacefully, there would have been the same fight between rival factions to control the queen and her policies which took place

* Even so, the local influence of great men in raising troops was still important, and the crown could not neglect it even after 1660; *see* J. R. Western, *Monarchy and Revolution, the English State in the 1680s* (Blandford, 1972) pp. 48-54.

during her disastrous reign in Scotland. Worse, any civil war would in these circumstances have become a religious war; and the injection of the religious factor into the usual play of noble faction would have made the Wars of the Roses innocuous by comparison.

This excursus into Elizabethan history, or even the might-have-beens of Elizabethan history, has its relevance for our subject, since it affects the perspective in which we see the period 1547–58. As it happened, this constituted a brief interruption in the march of Tudor monarchy towards a stable society. Had things turned out differently in the sixties, the mid-Tudor years would have looked like the beginnings of the English Wars of Religion. Historians would talk about the resurrection of noble political power, and the constructive work of Wolsey and Cromwell, even of Edward IV and Henry VII, would have been wasted. The gradual decline of violence which is a definite feature of sixteenth-century development depended on luck as well as statesmanship.

Parliament in our period had been for the most part relatively quiescent. It was a useful, indeed indispensable political institution as far as legislation and the voting of taxes were concerned. prepared to resist the crown on matters of property (benevolences under Richard III, taxes in Wolsey's times, the Statute of Uses, the security of ex-monastic lands). But previous Parliaments had from time to time (notably in the years around 1400, and again during the crisis of 1449–50) claimed a more positive role. The last impeachment of a minister by the Commons before the procedure was revived in 1621 for Francis Bacon, was that of the Duke of Suffolk in 1450. Parliament in 1450 appointed, as previous parliaments had occasionally done, special treasurers to oversee the spending of taxes. This was not done again until 1624. There was no question during Edward VI's minority of his council being 'named' in Parliament, as had happened in the minority of Henry VI and during his breakdown in 1453; Henry IV, indeed, had had to accede to such demands during the years 1401–11, even though he was an adult in control of his faculties. The demand was not made again until 1641, on the eve of the Civil War.

Of course, Elizabethan Parliaments were voluble in their opposition on certain issues; and on one occasion, as we have seen, the making of the religious settlement of 1559, they had their way against the initial hesitations of the queen. There can be no doubt that the Reformation Parliament had enormously increased the prestige of Parliament; while the events of Mary's reign had shown the nuisance value of skilfully conducted opposition. Nevertheless, Mary's Parliaments were so troublesome because of the divisions in the council, the use of Parliament by the Paget and Gardiner factions for their own ends. The same was true of most of the parliamentary opposition in at least the first thirty years of Elizabeth's reign. The issues which produced the dramatic clashes so vividly described by Professor Neale, were issues on which either the whole council was urging the queen to act (to settle the succession in 1563 and 1566, to have Mary Stuart executed in 1587), or on which a substantial group of councillors disagreed with royal policy, urging, for instance, a more active committedly Protestant foreign policy or further reform in the church; and such 'Puritan' councillors as Sir Walter Mildmay or Sir Francis Knollys, or even the Earl of Leicester, were not averse to stimulating opposition to royal policy when it suited their book.*

Elizabethan Parliaments were stormy precisely because prompting from above, by councillors, or by powerful noble patrons like the Earl of Bedford, found a ready response in a small but nationally-organized, ideologically committed 'party' of Puritan gentry; between them they were able to manipulate the reasonable anxieties of many members about important aspects of Elizabethan policy. The doctrine of parliamentary free speech, so vigorously espoused by the Wentworth brothers, rose directly out of the urgent need to settle the succession lest the country be involved in civil war on the queen's death.

These clashes in Parliament had an important long-term result. From the end of Elizabeth's reign the Commons were prepared to attack the government about issues like monopolies or purveyance which represented a general 'country' grievance against the 'court' as a whole, rather than taking part in a disagreement about policy between different factions in the government. And,

* J. E. Neale, *Elizabeth I and her Parliaments* (Jonathan Cape, 2 vols., 1953–7).

of course, in the seventeenth century, the 'initiative' fell to the Commons; the lead in political agitation was taken by members of the gentry class in the lower house, rather than by peers or by disgruntled members of the government (though there were still important instances of this, especially in the 1620s). The contrast here between the fifteenth and the seventeenth centuries is not absolute; as we have seen, the gentry interest had to be considered, in certain circumstances at least, in Henry VI's reign. Nevertheless, there had been a definite shift of emphasis, a change in the balance of political forces between the nobility and the gentry; and it is this change which the controversy over the 'rise of the gentry' seeks to explain.

Once again, this is largely outside our period. Certainly it is not a matter, as has been thought, of a sudden invasion of the burgess seats in the Commons by gentry, better born and more inclined to assert themselves than mere townsfolk; this development was well under way in the fifteenth century. Better education played its part in increasing the self-confidence of Members of Parliament (see below, p. 326). So too did the very importance of the issues dealt with in the sixteenth century, and particularly the religious issue. Perhaps the indispensable condition was, once more, internal peace and stability; a nobleman's trump card, his ability to raise troops, lost a good deal of its value in this situation, and the gentry were the obvious beneficiaries.

Further down the social scale, there seems to have been, from the mid-sixteenth century, rather less influence by the people at large on politics than there had been earlier. 1549 saw the last large-scale popular revolt. (The 1569 northern revolt was much more straightforwardly noble-led than that of 1536; the 1607 anti-enclosure revolt in the Rugby area was on a smaller scale than Ket's rebellion had been, as were various other disturbances of the early Stuart period; while the surprising thing about the Civil War is the absence of large-scale peasant revolt.) Here again, general political stability is important; for many popular revolts from Cade onwards, as we have seen, may have been surreptitiously inspired by dissident nobles. The revolts of 1549 seem to have had a traumatic effect on the propertied classes, leading them to greater vigilance and reducing the temptation to stir the flames (1381 may have had a similar effect; the next sixty years were fairly untroubled). And certainly the Elizabethan policy of closing ranks and restricting social mobility was justified by its authors in terms of reducing the risk of disorder.

On the other hand, the residual role of the people, or some of them, in times of crisis was still important; the reaction of the Londoners determined the downfall of Somerset in October 1549, and popular reaction in the country at large made Mary queen in 1553. Popular opinion, at least in London, was still worth cultivating as a factor in politics; in preventing, for instance, the implementation of plans to disinherit Elizabeth during Mary's reign. In 1601 agitation in the city strengthened the Commons in their fight against monopolies; a foretaste of 1641 when rioting Londoners assembled to intimidate the peers as they discussed the fate of the Earl of Strafford.

In one sense, then, our period saw the beginnings of a change from factional politics to ideological politics. Faction, of course, continued; politics was, as always, concerned with the often cynical pursuit of office and profit. Nevertheless, the injection of the religious issue helped to change the tone of events. During the fifteenth century there had been no fundamental cleavage in the ruling class about the methods or the ends of government; controversy was about the inefficiencies and failings of particular rulers. As soon as the immediate problem was settled any political grouping tended to fall apart. This was very much apparent in the political oscillations of the 1450s. The only, minor, 'ideological' element in events was the existence of some sort of Lancastrian legitimist opposition in the 1460s; and even that was unimpressive. Protestantism in Mary's reign, 'Puritanism' in Elizabeth's and later, did provide, as we have seen, some sort of basis for a continuing party, did help eventually to bring to birth the self-conscious, detached, critical 'country' attitude to politics which was an essential element in early Stuart history.

Not of course, that England was overwhelmingly, or even predominantly 'Protestant' in 1559, whatever may have been true of London. A habitual, conventional Catholicism took a generation to die out, and in some parishes mass was said more or less openly in defiance of the law for ten years or so. Only a small core of men were prepared, however, to take the much more positive step of refusal to attend their parish church, once the generation of Marian priests had died away, and maintaining Catholic practice had come to involve harbouring illegal, foreign-trained, priests. Elizabeth's reign saw the development of a virulent popular anti-Catholicism, whose seeds we have already seen in early sixteenth-century London, and which was further fostered by increasingly strained relations with Spain. Even so, pockets of Catholicism survived in what the Puritans called the 'dark corners of the realm'. Even more annoying to the zealots was the continuing indifference of many people to religious matters; the poor, it was complained, 'seldom repairing to their parish church to hear and learn their duties better', while many of those who did attend had a comfortable, minimal, commonsense view of religion; 'that it is safest to do in religion as most do', or 'that drinking in the alehouse is good fellowship and shows a kind nature and maintains neighbourhood'. Not all Elizabethans were obsessed by sin and salvation; although those who were were disproportionately influential.

One curious result of the Reformation stemmed from Protestantism's inferiority to Catholicism as a folk religion. It set, as it were, its standards too high for many people. Protestantism demanded a high level of commitment if it were to mean anything at all. Catholicism, on the other hand, was very much more adaptable to different levels of spiritual sophistication. As we have seen, it was in fact popular pressure which had imported into Catholicism a good deal of that magical, superstitious element, against which Protestants reacted. A naïve Catholic survivalism persisted for generations; as late as 1721 the Welsh were said to still bathe and 'leave some small oblations behind them' at certain springs which had been dedicated to saints. The belief that for certain purposes Catholic priests had exceptional magic powers persisted far longer. Another unintended result of Protestantism was the growth of all sorts of non-Christian magical practices; white magic, sorcery, and witchcraft, which seem to have been far more widespread around 1600 than they had been a century earlier.*

* K. V. Thomas, *Religion and the Decline of Magic* (Weidenfeld & Nicolson, 1971, Penguin 1973).

It would be ludicrous to under-estimate the importance of Protestantism in English history. The contribution of 'Puritanism' to forming the attitudes of men of all classes in the seventeenth century, to go no further, is undeniable. Nevertheless, Protestantism in England was to be dogged by the muddied circumstances of its early days; by the alliance which we have described with secularism and anti-clericalism, useful in pulling down the temples of the idolaters, a continuing embarrassment in the task of building a pure new church. The conflict between laicism and clericalism (albeit a new Protestant clericism) or rather between secularism and theocracy, was to be the dominant theme in the religious history of the next century.

It is hard to say how far education had expanded. We have seen how difficult it is to establish reliable statistics for endowed schools when we were discussing the dissolution of the chantries (*see above*, p. 270). But a good deal of secondary education, including preparation for the universities was done in small fee-paying schools, or by clergymen taking on a few pupils and so on. Scattered statistics about the proportion of people able to sign their names vary so much from place to place as to make it impossible, on present evidence at least, to guess at the trend in basic literacy. At the other end of the scale, there was an expansion of colleges at the universities. But it must be remembered that fifteenth-century Oxford and Cambridge were *not* essentially collegiate universities, and the foundation of colleges represents as much a change in educational methods and social ideals (arguably to establish greater control over a somewhat unorganized and unruly student body) as expansion of numbers.

But even so, the interest shown by a substantial number of the laity in university education was new; and this was to increase. At least 15 per cent of MPs in 1563 had been to university (67 out of 420); by 1593 this had risen to about 35 per cent (161 out of 462). During the same period the number of members who had attended the Inns of Court had also increased dramatically.*

This interest in education derived partly from Protestantism, partly from the newly fashionable humanism. It may also have

* J. E. Neale, *The Elizabethan House of Commons* (Jonathan Cape, 1949) pp. 140, 303.

been stimulated by the apparent success of clever humanist-trained graduates in royal service. Sir Thomas Smith, a farmer's son, rose via an academic career at Cambridge (Regius Professor of Civil Law at the age of twenty-six, vice-chancellor at thirty), to be secretary under Edward VI, and again under Elizabeth. This sort of career was wholly exceptional; Smith's friend and colleague, William Cecil, had a better start in life as the son of a minor royal official. And it was not unprecedented; the church had traditionally provided a ladder for the ambitious young man of humble origins. Nevertheless, the degree of upward mobility in the 1530s and 1540s was striking, and was underlined by the peerages and lands given to royal officials. (The saving grace of the old-fashioned clerical statesman, after all, was that he could not found a landed family.) To some extent, then, the new upper-class interest in education may have been a defensive reaction against this sort of social threat by the educated outsider, 'new men', likely to 'forget their duty . . . and subvert the noble houses'.

One unusual feature of the early Tudor court was the provision of a humanist education for girls: in the royal family, for instance, or in that of Sir Thomas More, of Protector Somerset, of Anthony Coke (tutor to Edward VI and father-in-law of William Cecil and Nicholas Bacon), and of Henry Grey, Duke of Suffolk, father of Lady Jane Grey, The fashion was very much that of a court group (Catherine of Aragon's influence seems to have been important here) and did not become general; paradoxically, it seems to have died out in the reign of Queen Elizabeth, herself one of its most distinguished products; perhaps because of the absence of a royal nursery to set the tone for upper-class society; perhaps because the queen preferred to shine alone in an essentially masculine society.

Hugh Latimer complained that the influx of gentleman-students was squeezing out the traditional poor scholar, with his way to make in the church. This may have been true in the short run. In the long term, however, the sons of 'plebeians' seem to have attended universities in much the same numbers as they had done before; the influx of gentlemen being accommodated, in the Elizabethan period at least, by an increased number of places, not by squeezing out the poor. Indeed, one result of

Protestant insistence on a 'learned ministry', able to expound the Scriptures and instruct the people, was to be the formation of a largely graduate clerical profession; the proportion of graduate clergymen in Worcester diocese, for instance, rose from 19 per cent in 1560 to 84 per cent in 1640.* More generally, Protestantism may have encouraged a greater provision of schools, if only because a religion based on Scripture inevitably put a premium on the ability to read. Our period, whatever its own achievements, laid the foundation for what was almost certainly an unprecedented expansion in the next century.

The sermon, the learned and instructive (in theory at least) Protestant sermon, was to do a good deal in the way of popular education; not merely in theology, but in related spheres like political theory. This and the growth of the printed book were probably far more important in the spread of ideas than was the provision of schools and colleges. We have already suggested some of the consequences (*see above*, p. 132). One other may be mentioned here. Printed books and pamphlets were an important means of subversion, as Mary's reign showed. The government fought back in two ways. An all-embracing censorship was introduced in 1538; and government also organized its own propaganda. Part of Thomas Cromwell's genius lay in his realization of the need to publicize Henry's case. Perhaps the most influential book produced in sixteenth-century England, next to the English Bible, was Cranmer's *Book of Homilies*; appointed to be read in parish churches Sunday by Sunday; its views on authority and degree underlie that whole hierarchic attitude to society which Shakespeare was to exemplify. Nevertheless, the fact that issues of this sort, and at times rather complicated issues of theology, were now discussed from pulpits where previously there had been little else but exhortations to personal morality backed by stories of the saints, must have stimulated thought, and at times dissent; the soldiers in Shakespeare's *Henry V* have some bloody minded if simplistic views on political authority.

Caxton had discovered that English was too blunt, too clumsy to express easily the niceties of philosophic arguments or scholarly distinction; his own translation of Boethius is a very laboured

* C. Hill, *Economic Problems of the Church* (Oxford, 1956) p. 207.

affair. But an increasing number of books began to be translated, or even written, in English, and the language became more flexible. More's *Utopia* was written in Latin; but a translation was published in 1551. Sir Thomas Elyot's *The boke named the gouernor*, a treatise on the proper (humanist) education of the aristocracy, was written in English and published in 1531. Authors experimented with words, adapting new ones from Latin and Greek, paying attention to rhythm and alliteration (eg, Sir John Cheke's 'uproars of people, hurly-burlies of vagabonds, routs of robbers', the body, so he thought of the 1549 rebellion). The result was sometimes ridiculous extravagance; at its best it produced the Edwardian prayer books, anonymous and collective enterprises, whose haunting cadences were to become, with the Bible, the most influential of English prose.

The best poet of the period was probably John Skelton, a roistering cleric and master of invective, used with devastating effect against Wolsey. In spite of his literary pretensions (he was 'poet laureate' of both Oxford and Cambridge) he fits far better into the tradition of anonymous popular verse than into the humanist camp, and had little time for Italianate views on poetic form. More up to date were Sir Thomas Wyatt and Henry Howard, Earl of Surrey, the ill-fated son of Henry VIII's Duke of Norfolk. Both of these wrote sonnets on the Italian model, and Surrey was the first Englishman to write blank verse. But these foreshadowings of the age of Shakespeare were unrepresentative and short lived. The Edwardian and Marian courts had little appreciation of imaginative literature, and it was not until the 1570s, with Philip Sidney and Edmund Spenser, that England again produced poets of European reputation.

England, according to John Major, a Scotsman who had lived in France, was pre-eminent for music; elsewhere 'you may meet with some musicians of such absolute accomplishment, yet not in such numbers'. A strong tradition of church music persisted, in the cathedrals and chapel royal, in spite of the dissolution of the monasteries. Thomas Tallis, organist of Waltham Abbey, afterwards became a gentleman of the chapel royal until his death in 1585; he produced with William Byrd a musical setting of Latin sacred texts, the *Cantiones Sacrae*, which acquired a European reputation for English musicians for the first time since the days of John Dunstable.

The Puritans complained of cathedrals as 'dens of thieves' where divine service was 'most filthily abused in piping of organs, in singing, ringing and trouling from one side of the choir to another'; and this emphasizes how odd it was that a great tradition of church choral music should flourish during a Protestant Reformation. This was partly because the Reformation first came to England in its Lutheran, rather than Calvinist, form; partly because Cranmer minimized objections by adapting the liturgy to music in such a way that the words would still be understood.

Erasmus, who seems to have had a virulent dislike of all music, made the uncharacteristic observation that there was none in St Paul's time and 'if they want music, let them sing psalms, like rational beings, and not too many of them'. In fact metrical versions of the psalms were far more influential than cathedral anthems. Verse translations were common; even Surrey tried his elegant hand. But the most successful was the collection produced by Thomas Sternhold, a courtier of Henry VIII's, and John Hopkins, a Suffolk cleric. This was one of the great best-sellers; no fewer than six hundred editions of Sternhold and Hopkins were published by 1828. They were despised, with some justification, by those with literary or musical sensibilities.

> Like a cracked saints bell jarring the steeple.
> Tom Sternhold's wretched prick song for the people.

wrote Milton's nephew. But their influence was widespread and profound. They provided, in effect, the only hymn book in use for almost three centuries; and it was to Sternhold and Hopkins's battle-songs that Cromwell's armies marched.

Henry VIII's court provided the setting for important developments in the visual arts. Foreign craftsmen of all sorts, gunmakers and armourers, engineers and builders, sculptors, painters and musicians, were attracted to England in large numbers. There was not much difference between the artificer and the artist. Men were respected for their skills as craftsmen and there was none of that modern mystique of 'the artist' as somebody singled out by a special quality of spiritual insight. So the German painter Hans Holbein came to Henry's notice through his acquaintance with Thomas More, and produced the magnificent, revealing portraits which immortalized Henry's courtiers; he duly appears in the accounts of the royal household, along with armourers, surgeons, book-binders and keepers of the royal dogs. French craftsmen were busy at the huge palace at Nonsuch, begun in 1538. (It involved, incidentally the total destruction of a village, its church, and some 1,200 acres of good farm land.) Had it survived, instead of being demolished in 1682, the comparison between Henry's court and that of Francis I might have appeared less one-sided than it does to those dazzled by Fontainebleau and Chambord; though Henry never pulled off a *coup* equivalent to Francis's attracting Leonardo da Vinci and Benvenuto Cellini to his court.

Nonsuch with its soaring towers and pinnacles (as, indeed Chambord), its air of strain, of extravagance, of striving after the fantastic, seems a world apart from that cool, ordered classicism which was the vogue in Italy; classicism at Nonsuch was a matter of decoration, rather than of overall planning, which still bears witness to its descent from the Gothic castle. There was in fact a brief breakthrough to a rather more thorough-going classicism in the academic, humanist-inspired court of Edward VI. Protector Somerset's many houses, including Somerset House in the Strand (another great building long since demolished), was in the new style; while it was Northumberland who sent the architect John Shute to Italy to provide correct classical patterns. But, in spite of Longleat (the work, in its various incarnations, of Somerset's steward John Thynne) classicism did not take real hold in England until the days of Inigo Jones, over fifty years later. The great Elizabethan houses with their dramatic skylines and their great square windows ('Hardwick Hall, more glass than wall') are a direct adaption of late perpendicular church architecture; 'the domestic counterpart of King's Chapel'.*

It is not easy to provide a balance sheet of changes in the quality of life in our period. As we saw when looking at economic develop-

* M. Girouard, 'Elizabethan Architecture and the Gothic Tradition' (*Architectural History*, vol. 6, 1963, p. 30).

ments 'averages', even if they were possible, are distinctly mis-leading. Cultural life shows something of the same shift towards greater polarization – not so much between the very rich and the rest, but between the comfortably off and those who lived precariously on subsistence level – as does the economy; in this case, roughly speaking, between the literate and the illiterate. To some extent culture had become less open, more private, more dependent on the great man's purse.

The great focus of artistic activity in the fifteenth century had been the church; and while much of the best surviving church furnishings come from private chapels or from monastic build-ings, considerable communal pride was invested in the parish church, and bore fruit not only in the architecture that we can still enjoy, but in works of craftsmanship: stained glass, images of the saints, communion vessels, embroidered vestments. The transfer of resources to private individuals which is one aspect of the Reformation, along with the greater cult of privacy (apparent in the provision of extra rooms in the houses of the yeomanry, as well as the increasing tendency to abandon 'hall dinner' to servants and dependants in the houses of the great), necessarily impoverished the parish church. Almost the only expenditure in parish churches in the Elizabethan period was on the provision of gaudy and arrogant tombs for the nobility and gentry: tan-gible examples of that victory of secularism which was one aspect of the Reformation. At the same time town pageants of popular drama and miracle plays gradually disappeared. They were too plainly idolatrous or at least conducive to idolatry; the elaborate, civic ceremonies at Coventry, for instance, fell gradually into disuse between 1535 and 1591.*

All this can be seen as the falling apart of a communal ideal. We must not exaggerate the change, and represent the world which emerged from the Reformation as one of naked individual-ism which had freed itself from the constraints of a corporate view of society. Nor should we suggest that a period of intellectual stultification gave way to one of lively debate. Nevertheless, Peace, Printing and Protestantism between them combined to

* C. Phythian-Adams, in P. Clark and P. Slack (eds.), *Crisis and Order in English Towns 1500–1700* (Routledge, 1972).

foster a more private spirit of critical introspection which could involve a fundamental re-examination of accepted ideas. Our century had seen the birth of this new force; the next was to see its fruition.

PRICES AND WAGES

Graph A is Professor Phelps Brown's and Miss Hopkins's attempt to chart the long-term course of real wages in England. This was done by comparing the money wages of a builder's labourer with the cost of a 'composite unit of consumables'. Eighty per cent of this 'composite unit' is made up of food, and over half of that represents grain products. The chart therefore tends to reflect, in modified form, the general trend of grain prices.

It must be emphasized that this represents the purchasing power of wage-earners, a minority of the working population at this time; that the notion of a 'composite unit' is necessarily rather arbitrary; that it takes no account of an important element, rent; and the prices on which it is based are the prices of raw materials, eg, grain, not the finished product, eg, flour or bread, which the wage-earner would buy. Nor, of course, can it allow for the yield of smallholdings and so on. Nevertheless, provided that these limitations are borne in mind, the chart is useful as a rough guide. It shows very clearly (perhaps too clearly) the relative prosperity of the mid-fifteenth century; and the rapid decline of wage-earner's living standards beginning round about 1500.

Graph B shows annual wheat prices in our period. It is based on the information supplied by P. J. Bowden in J. Thirsk (ed.), *The Agrarian History of England and Wales*, vol. 4 (1500–1640), (Cambridge, 1967). Again, its limitations must be kept in mind. Wheat is the grain of the better-off; and while cheaper grains generally moved in sympathy with wheat prices, they did not always do so in the same proportion. Wheat prices could also vary considerably in different parts of the country; though not to the extent of producing abundance in one area when there was a bad harvest in another. Nevertheless, the graph is useful as an

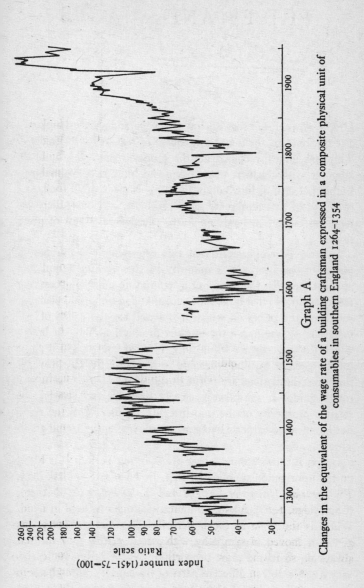

Graph A

Changes in the equivalent of the wage rate of a building craftsman expressed in a composite physical unit of consumables in southern England 1264-1354

335

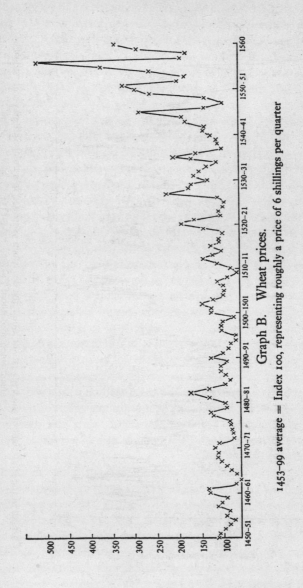

Graph B. Wheat prices.

1453–99 average = Index 100, representing roughly a price of 6 shillings per quarter

indication of the general trend in grain prices and provides some indication of annual variations and their magnitude.

It should be noted that, unlike Graph A, Graph B is not plotted on a 'logarithmetic' or 'ratio' scale. (That is, a scale intended to show differences in proportion, as opposed to absolute increases; such a graph gives the same value to a 100 per cent increase, representing a movement from 5 to 10, as to one representing a movement of 20 to 40.) A logarithmic scale would make it more difficult for most readers to read off the figure for a given year. But one result is that, as it stands, the graph exaggerates year-to-year fluctuations in the later years of our period. The increase in the index from 94 to 177 in 1482–3 was very close in proportionate terms to that from 267 in 1554–5 to 528 in 1556–7. Doubling over two years represents disaster, in whatever context. Nevertheless, the latter rise looks far more dramatic on the graph.

The years quoted are 'harvest years', eg, '1477–8' represents the period from Michaelmas (29 September) 1477 to Michaelmas 1478, since this conforms to the agricultural year. This point is often overlooked. The 1549 rebellions, for instance, broke out in the early summer, and therefore took place in the economic climate governed by the harvest of 1548, not that (yet to be gathered) of 1549.

About one year in six saw average wheat prices rise more than 25 per cent above the norm (calculated on a '31-year moving average' to take account of the upward movement of the trend), Professor Hoskins's threshold for a 'bad' year. Five years in our period saw the even more horrendous 'dearth' level of 50 per cent above the norm.

Individual 'bad' years might be bearable; two or more in succession a disaster. I have singled out such sequences below. Different results are obtained by using the *Agrarian History* figures as Dr C. J. Harrison does, and the 'London' series used by Professor Hoskins. I have erred on the side of including marginal cases. Professor Hoskins's figures start in 1475; Dr Harrison, using the *Agrarian History* figures, begins his 'moving averages' in 1465. I have done my own calculations, based on the Thorold Rogers figures, for the earlier years. Interestingly, all the 'dearth' years are included within the sequences; they are marked with an asterisk.

1460–1,	1461–2	
1481–2,	1482–3,*	1483–4
1501–2,	1502–3,	1503 4 (and 1500–1 only marginally fails to qualify)
1520–1,*	1521–2	
1527–8,*	1528–9	
1550–1,	1551–2	
1555–6,	1556–7*	

The Phelps Brown and Hopkins article was first published in *Economica*, n.s. vol. 23, 1955; it has been reprinted in E. M. Carus-Wilson, ed., *Essays in Economic History*, vol. 2 (1962); and in P. H. Ramsey, *The Price of Revolution in Sixteenth Century England* (1971). For Bowden, *see above*. W. G. Hoskins, 'Harvest Fluctuations and English Economic History, 1480–1619' originally published in *Agricultural Hist. Rev.*, vol. 12, 1964, was reprinted in W. E. Minchinton, ed. *Essays in Agrarian History*, vol. 1 (Newton Abbot, 1968). *See*, too, C. J. Harrison in *Agricultural Hist. Rev.*, vol. 19, 1971. J. E. Thorold Rogers compiled the pioneering *History of Agriculture and Prices in England* (7 vols., Oxford, 1866–1900).

CHRONOLOGY

1477	Death of Charles, Duke of Burgundy
1478	Execution of Clarence
1481-2	Scottish war
1483	Death of Edward IV
	Proclamation of Edward V and then Richard III
	Buckingham rebellion
	Charles VIII, King of France
1485	Bosworth
	Accession of Henry VII
1487	Simnel rebellion defeated at Stoke
1488	James IV, King of Scotland
1492	Invasion of France
	Treaty of Étaples
	Spanish conquest of Granada
	Columbus to West Indies
1494	French invasion of Italy
1495	Poynings' law in Ireland
1497	Cornish rebellion
1498	Louis XII, King of France
1501	Prince Arthur–Catherine of Aragon marriage
1502	Death of Prince Arthur
1503	Margaret Tudor–James IV marriage
1509	Accession of Henry VIII
1512	Attempted invasion of Gascony
1513	Scots defeated at Flodden, French at 'Battle of the Spurs'
	James V, King of Scotland
1514	Peace with France
1515	Francis I, King of France
1516	Death of Ferdinand of Aragon
	Archduke Charles, ruler of the Netherlands, becomes King of Spain
1517	Depopulation commission
	Luther's protest at Wittenberg
1518	Treaty of London
1519	Death of Emperor Maximilian
	Election of Charles V
1520	Field of Cloth of Gold
1521	Trial of Buckingham
1522	Surrey's invasion of France
1523	Suffolk's invasion of France
1525	Francis I taken prisoner at Pavia

English victory over Scots at Solway Moss
Death of James v
Beginning of coinage debasement
1543 'King's Book'
Catherine Parr marriage
Treaty of Greenwich with Scotland
1544 Sack of Edinburgh
Capture of Boulogne
1545 French invasion threat
1546 Peace with France
Fall of the Howards
1547 Henry viii's death
Somerset Protector
Henry ii, King of France
Battle of Pinkie
Dissolution of Chantries
1548 Queen Mary of Scotland taken to France
1549 First Prayer Book
Western and Norfolk rebellions
French besiege Boulogne
Fall of Somerset
1550 Peace with France and Scotland
1551 'Calling down' of the coinage
1552 Execution of Somerset
Second Prayer Book
1553 Willoughby–Chancellor voyage
Death of Edward vi
Jane Grey episode
Accession of Mary
Restoration of Catholic liturgy
1554 Wyatt rebellion
Mary marries Philip
Papal Supremacy restored
1555 Philip, ruler of the Netherlands, and (January 1556) King of
Spain
1557 French war
Victory at St Quentin
1558 Loss of Calais
Death of Mary and of Pole
Accession of Elizabeth
1559 Acts of Supremacy and Uniformity

FURTHER READING

General

Very few books straddle the 'medieval-modern' divide. One recent example is D. M. Loades, *Politics and the Nation, 1450–1660* (Harvester and Fontana, 1974). Maurice Keen, *England in the Later Middle Ages, a Political History* (Methuen, 1973) is a lively account. G. R. Elton, *England Under the Tudors* (Methuen, 1955; rev. ed. 1974) has become a classic; it is best treated as a lively and argumentative statement of a case rather than, as too often, as holy writ. Conrad Russell, *The Crisis of Parliaments, 1509–1660* (Oxford University Press, 1971) is a thoughtful, discursive work.

Chapter One

A. R. Myers, *English Historical Documents, 1327–1485* (vol. 4 of *English Historical Documents*, ed. D. C. Douglas, Eyre and Spottiswoode, 1969) provides an excellently chosen selection of contemporary sources, linked by skilful editorial comment which constitutes an important work in its own right. Joan Thirsk's geographical introduction to the *Agrarian History of England and Wales, 1500–1640* (Cambridge University Press, 1967, ed. Thirsk; it constitutes vol. 4 of the *Agrarian History of England and Wales*, ed. H. P. R. Finberg) is fundamental. A useful general survey of the economy is provided by A. R. H. Baker in H. C. Darby (ed.), *A New Historical Geography of England* (Cambridge University Press, 1973). For an excellent essay in the interpretation of how people thought, felt and reacted, see F. R. H. du Boulay, *An Age of Ambition: English Society in the Later Middle Ages* (Nelson, 1970). It is conventional to refer readers to the Paston Letters, available both in large scholarly editions (by J. Gairdner, 1872–5, several new eds., now being superseded by Norman Davis's ed. Oxford University Press 1971–) and in more popular 'selections'; it is best to dip and browse after a lead in from H. S. Bennett, *The Pastons and their England* (Cambridge University Press, 1932).

Chapter Two

J. R. Lander, *Conflict and Stability in Fifteenth-Century England*

(Hutchinson, 1969) is succinct, sane and stimulating. K. B. McFarlane, *The Nobility of Later Medieval England* (Oxford University Press, 1973) is unfortunately a posthumous publication put together from notes and drafts; McFarlane was always very reluctant to publish. His 'Wars of the Roses', in his *England in the Fifteenth Century* (Hambledon Press, 1981) includes more matter than most books.

Chapter Three
In addition to the above, see the skilfully linked contemporary accounts in J. R. Lander, *The Wars of the Roses* (Putnam, 1967). For an interesting view of Henry VI see B. P. Wolffe, in S. B. Chrimes, C. D. Ross and R. A. Griffiths (eds.), *Fifteenth Century England* (Manchester University Press, 1972), a foretaste of his *Henry VI* (Methuen, 1981).

Chapter Four
See Pugh (on Magnates), Ross (on Edward IV), and Chrimes (on Henry VII) in Chrimes, Ross and Griffiths, *op. cit.* A good general account of Henry VII is that by R. L. Storey (Blandford, 1968). Charles Ross has written excellent studies of *Edward IV* and *Richard III* (Methuen, 1974 and 1981).

Chapter Five
du Boulay, as above, is a good introduction to religious attitudes; so, too, the early chapters of Keith Thomas, *Religion and the Decline of Magic* (Weidenfeld, 1971; Penguin, 1973). R. W. Southern provides a stimulating account of *Western Society and the Church in the Middle Ages* (Penguin, 1970). A. G. Dickens, *The English Reformation* (Batsford, 1964) has a good introduction to these problems. Peter Heath deals with a key subject in his *English Parish Clergy on the Eve of the Reformation* (Routledge, 1969).

Chapters Six and Seven
The general works of Elton and Dickens, already mentioned, constitute the best introduction. For the early period, A. F. Pollard, *Wolsey* (Longmans, 1929) is still worth reading. J. J. Scarisbrick, *Henry VIII* (Eyre Methuen, 1968; Penguin, 1971) is a masterly study, and G. R. Elton, *Policy and Police* (Cambridge University Press, 1972) is a closely argued book on the 'enforcement' of the Henrician Reformation. The editorial material in Elton's *The Tudor Constitution* (Cambridge University Press, 2nd ed, 1982), an indispensable collection of documents, will guide the student through difficult terrain.

Chapter Eight
Peter Ramsey, *Tudor Economic Problems* (Gollancz, 1963) is a useful brief introduction. The *Agrarian History* (above) is an enormous quarry; the non-specialist will find useful Joan Thirsk's study of enclosure and related problems. There is good succinct survey of *Inflation in Tudor and Stuart England* by R. B. Outhwaite (Macmillan, for Economic History Society, rev. ed, 1982); and of *Poverty and Vagrancy in Tudor England* by John Pound (Longmans, 1971).

Chapter Nine
There is relatively little work on the mid-Tudor period which is not unmanageably unwieldy. Whitney R. D. Jones, *The Mid-Tudor Crisis, 1539–63* (Macmillan, 1973) is a useful general survey. S. T. Bindoff has written a miniature masterpiece on *Ket's Rebellion* (reprinted in J. Hurstfield, ed. *The Tudors*, Sidgwick and Jackson, 1973). Hugh Latimer's *Sermons* (Everyman, n.d.) will provide an insight into the outlook of the 'Commonwealth Party'.

Conclusion
Lawrence Stone, *The Crisis of the Aristocracy* (Oxford University Press, 1965; abbreviated ed. 1967) provides evidence of the survival of 'bastard-feudal' habits well into the Elizabethan period. J. Simon, *Education in Tudor England* (Cambridge University Press, 1966) and K. Charlton, *Education in Renaissance England* (Routledge, 1965) both provide an admirable account of their subject, Charlton being rather more sceptical of the efficacy of education than Simon. Thomas, *Religion and the Decline of Magic* (above) investigates the teeming world of superstition.

Postscript (1984)
D. C. Coleman, *The Economy of England 1450–1750* (Oxford University Press, 1977) is an excellent introduction to the quantitative approach to the economy. Two volumes in the 'New History of England' (Edward Arnold), J. R. Lander, *Government and Community, 1450–1509*, and G. R. Elton, *Reform and Reformation, 1509–58* interpret recent research and qualify the authors' earlier views. The essays edited by Jennifer Loach and Robert Tittler, *The Mid-Tudor Polity, c. 1540–1560* (Macmillan, 1980) furthers the re-interpretation of that period. Penry Williams, *The Tudor Regime* (Oxford University Press, 1979, paperback 1981) is an excellent study of government in action. J. J. Scarisbrick, *The Reformation and the English People* (Blackwell, Oxford, 1984) argues for the sustained popularity of Catholic devotions up to (and beyond) the Henrician Reformation.

BIOGRAPHICAL INDEX

ABERGAVENNY: *see* Neville.

BEAUFORT (*see* Table I): descendants of John of Gaunt by his mistress, later wife, Catherine Swynford. Henry, Bishop of Winchester and cardinal (d 1447), leading statesman, enemy of Humphrey of Gloucester. His nephews John (d 1444) and Edmund (killed in battle 1455); dukes of Somerset, commanded in France; Edmund was the main opponent of Richard of York. John's daughter Margaret (1443–1509) married Edmund Tudor, and was mother to the future Henry VII; she later married Henry Stafford, and then Thomas Stanley; latter part of her life devoted to piety and promotion of learning; died in 1509, shortly after Henry VII.

BONNER, Edmund: diplomat, and Henrician Catholic churchman; Bishop of London 1540–9 (deprived), and 1553–9; reputation as a persecutor; imprisoned 1559; died 1569.

BRANDON, Charles: son of Henry VII's standard-bearer; friend of Henry VIII; created Duke of Suffolk 1514; married Henry's sister Mary, widowed Queen of France 1515; commanded French invasion 1523; died 1545.

BUCKINGHAM, dukes of: *see* Stafford.

CABOT, John: Genoese sailor in English service; claimed discovery of Newfoundland 1497; killed at sea 1498. His son Sebastian also involved in American exploration; transferred to Spanish service 1512; returned to England 1547; helped to inspire North-East passage exploration; died 1557.

CAXTON, William: English merchant at Bruges; translator; established Westminster printing press 1476; died 1491.

CECIL, William (1520–98): son of royal household official; educated St John's, Cambridge; personal secretary to Somerset; royal secretary 1550–3; secretary and lord treasurer under Elizabeth.

CHARLES, Duke of Burgundy from 1467; usually called 'the Bold' (le Téméraire); ally and brother-in-law of Edward IV; killed in battle 1477.

CHEKE, John (1514–57): fellow of St John's, Cambridge, and professor of Greek; tutor to Prince Edward; abducted from Flanders, and forced to recant Protestantism 1556.

CLARENCE, George, Duke of (1449–78): younger brother of Edward IV; supported his father-in-law Warwick in restoration of Henry VI: reconciled to Edward before battle of Barnet 1471; executed.

COURTENAY, Henry: Earl of Devon, favourite of Henry VIII, who created him Marquis of Exeter 1525; through his mother a grandson of Edward IV; executed 1538. His son Edward, imprisoned 1538–53; considered a possible husband for Queen Mary; died abroad 1556.

CRANMER, Thomas (1489–1556): Cambridge theologian, supporter of Henry VIII's divorce case; Archbishop of Canterbury 1533; discreet leader of Protestantizing party under Henry; chief compiler of Edwardian prayer books; imprisoned 1553; burned.

CROMWELL, Thomas (1485?–1540): *See above*, p. 189 for early career; secretary 1534; vice-gerent in spirituals 1535; lord privy seal 1536; in practice, chief minister from late 1532; Earl of Essex 17 April 1540; executed 28 July 1540.

DEVON, earls of: *see* Courtenay.

DORSET: *see* Grey.

DUDLEY, Edmund: lawyer, minister to Henry VII; executed 1510. His son John (1502–53) had distinguished military career; created Earl of Warwick 1547; suppressed Ket rebellion, and displaced Somerset as leading member of the council (though never protector) 1549; created Duke of Northumberland 1551; executed.

EMPSON, Richard: lawyer and minister to Henry VII; executed 1510.

EXETER, Marquis of: *see* Courtenay.

FISHER, John: Cambridge theologian; confessor to Lady Margaret Beaufort; patron of Greek and Hebrew studies; opponent of Luther; Bishop of Rochester 1504; champion of Catherine of Aragon; encouraged Nun of Kent; refused succession oath 1534; and executed for refusal of royal supremacy 1535.

FITZGERALD: Earls of Kildare, greatest of the Anglo-Irish lords; successive lords deputy of Ireland with brief intervals 1455–1534. Gerald, eighth earl, (succeeded 1477) almost independent ruler of Ireland; deposed 1494; reinstated 1496; died 1513. Wolsey attempted to curb power of Gerald, ninth earl, (d 1534). His son, Thomas, rebelled 1534; executed 1537. Fitzgerald was also the family name of the Earls of Desmond.

FORTESCUE, John: chief justice of King's Bench 1443; exile 1460s; reconciled to Edward IV 1471; author of *De Laudibus Legum Angliae* ('In Praise of the Laws of England') and *The Governance of England*. Died 1476 or later.

GARDINER, Stephen (1497?–1555): canon lawyer; secretary of Wolsey, negotiating at Rome, 1528 and 1529; Bishop of Winchester, 1531; defends royal supremacy; leads 'Catholic party' among Henrician bishops; dropped from privy council 1547; imprisoned 1548–53; deprived of bishopric 1551; restored and created lord chancellor, 1553; opposed Spanish marriage; acknowledged Roman supremacy, and urged persecution of heretics.

GLOUCESTER, Humphrey, Duke of: youngest brother of Henry V; leader of anti-Beaufort faction; bibliophile and benefactor of Oxford university; died, believed murdered, 1447.

GRESHAM, Richard (1485?–1549): London merchant and financier. His son Thomas (c. 1519–79) merchant, and king's agent for finance and supplies in the Netherlands from 1551.

GREY: family descended from Queen Elizabeth Woodville by her first marriage. Thomas Grey (1451–1501): created Marquis of Dorset 1475; fled to Brittany 1483; and supported Henry VII 1485; early patron of Wolsey. His grandson Henry, third marquis, married Frances Brandon, daughter of Henry VIII's sister Mary (*see* table 2); promoted Duke of Suffolk 1551; father of Lady Jane Grey; executed after unsuccessfully trying to raise rebellion 1554.

HALES, John: government official (clerk of the hanaper); and keen opponent of enclosure for sheep-farming during Somerset's rule; died 1571.

HASTINGS, William: servant of Richard of York, friend and loyal supporter of Edward IV; created baron 1461; summarily executed shortly before Richard III proclaimed king 1483 (*see above*, p. 93).

HERBERT, William: steward of Duke of York's estates in South Wales; baron 1461; Earl of Pembroke 1468; executed after battle of Edgecote 1469. His son succeeded as Earl of Pembroke, exchanged for earldom of Huntingdon 1479. Sir William Herbert (1501–70) was a grandson of the first earl, through a bastard son; married Anne Parr, sister of Queen Catherine Parr; granted considerable landed estates by Henry VIII, including Wilton nunnery; president of Council of Wales 1550; Earl of Pembroke 1551; acquiesced in Jane Grey coup, but then rallied the council to Mary; commanded troops against Wyatt rebels, and English troops at St Quentin 1557.

HOOPER, John: returned from Zurich 1549 as convinced Zwinglian; consecrated Bishop of Gloucester, after hesitation over vestments etc. 1551; keen and radical diocesan reformer; from 1552 also Bishop of Worcester; burned 1555.

HOWARD, John: Norfolk landowner, and connection of the Mowbray Dukes of Norfolk; supporter of Richard III; created Duke of Norfolk 1483; killed at Bosworth 1485. His son Thomas (1443–1524); Earl of Surrey 1483; imprisoned 1485; title restored 1489; lord treasurer to Henry VII; victor of Flodden and Duke of Norfolk 1513. Thomas II (1473–1554): general; statesman; uncle of Queens Anne Boleyn and Catherine Howard; in charge of troops against Pilgrimage of Grace 1536; leader of anti-Cromwellian party; imprisoned 1546; released 1553. His son Henry: Earl of Surrey, poet, executed 1547.

KILDARE: *see* Fitzgerald.

KNOX, John: Scottish preacher; rebel 1547; galley slave in France 1547-9; refused bishopric of Rochester; Geneva 1554; Edinburgh 1559; leader of Scottish reformers; died 1572.

LATIMER, Hugh: son of Leicestershire yeoman; Cambridge Protestant: Bishop of Worcester 1535-9; court-preacher denouncing corruption and social injustice during the reign of Edward VI; arrested 1553; burned 1555.

MORE, Thomas (1478-1535): son of a London lawyer, and himself a barrister; author of *Utopia* 1516; friend of Erasmus, Colet; entered royal service; speaker of House of Commons 1523; lord chancellor 1529, in spite of reservation about the divorce; keen persecutor of heretics; resigned 1532; executed for refusing royal supremacy.

MORTON, John: ecclesiastical lawyer and diplomat; Bishop of Ely 1479; arrested 1483 before Richard III's accession; helped to instigate Buckingham rebellion; Archbishop of Canterbury 1486; lord chancellor 1487; cardinal 1493; died 1500.

MOWBRAY, John (1415-61): Duke of Norfolk; enemy of Suffolk 1450; equivocal supporter of York. His son John, the last of the Mowbray dukes of Norfolk; died 1476.

NEVILLE: an old baronial family with extensive lands in Durham, Yorkshire and Cumberland. Ralph (d 1425) acquired the earldom of Westmorland which remained in the main line of the family; the later earls of Westmorland, played little part in national affairs, until the sixth earl joined in the 1569 rising. Ralph's son by his second marriage, Richard, acquired the lands and title of the Montacute earls of Salisbury through his wife. Family feuds with Edmund Beaufort, Earl of Somerset, made him the political ally of his brother-in-law, Richard of York, from 1453. Salisbury was killed after the battle of Wakefield 1460. His son Richard had become a great nobleman when his wife inherited the lands of the Beauchamp earls of Warwick in 1449; Richard became earl; won a military reputation as captain of Calais from 1456, and was one of the handful of peers who proclaimed his cousin Edward king in 1461. The subsequent differences with Edward, Warwick's restoration of Henry VI, and death at the battle of Barnet, 1471, are dealt with at length above. Richard's younger brother John was Earl of

Northumberland, 1464–70, then Marquis Montagu; he, too, killed at Barnet 1471. Another brother George was chancellor 1460–7, and again during Henry VI's re-adeption; and Archbishop of York 1460–76. The Neville lords of Abergavenny (Burgavenny) were descended from Edward, younger son of Ralph Earl of Westmorland; he, too, married an heiress. His grandson George, fined £70,000 for retaining, 1507; died 1535.

NORFOLK: see Mowbray, Howard.

NORTHUMBERLAND: see Percy, Dudley.

OLDHALL, William: soldier, chamberlain and political adviser to Richard of York; Speaker, Parliament of 1450–1; attainted 1453; died 1460.

PAGET, William (1505?–63): of London artisan origins; via St Paul's School and Cambridge, to the service of Bishop Gardiner; diplomatic service and, from 1543, secretary of state; helped to engineer 1547 coup; baron after Dudley's coup 1549, but fell out of favour with Dudley until just before the Jane Grey episode, which he supported, but rapidly changed sides, and proclaimed Mary; proponent of Spanish marriage; headed the opposition to Gardiner in the council; lord privy seal 1555; excluded from government on death of Mary.

PAULET, William: administrator; from a gentry family; made a career in the royal administration, notably as lord treasurer from 1550–72, in spite of successive changes of regime; 'made of willow, not oak'; successively Lord St John, Earl of Wiltshire and Marquis of Winchester. Died 1572.

PEMBROKE: see Herbert.

PERCY: an ancient northern family; its influence centred in Yorkshire and Northumberland. Henry Percy was created Earl of Northumberland 1377; he helped to make Henry IV king 1399; but with his son Henry ('Hotspur'), rose in revolt 1403. The second earl, son of Hotspur, was in feud with the Nevilles in 1453; his son supported Henry VI; forfeited the earldom 1461. Edward IV's attempt to restore a balance against the Nevilles led, in 1470, to restoration of another Percy as fourth earl, whose deliberate failure to oppose Edward in 1471 helped the Yorkist restoration. The fourth earl also held back at Bosworth; killed in a tax riot in 1489. Henry VII used the minority of the fifth earl to undermine Percy influence; and Henry VIII forced the sixth earl (d 1537) to disinherit his brothers Thomas and Ingram, who took part in the Pilgrimage of Grace. Thomas's son, also Thomas, was restored to the earldom in 1557; subsequently led the 1569 rebellion; executed 1572.

DE LA POLE: descendants of William; financier in reign of Edward III. His son Michael Earl of Suffolk 1385. William (1396–1450), first duke; impeached 1449; murdered. His son, John, second duke, married a daughter of his father's enemy York. John, Earl of Lincoln, son of the last was therefore nephew to Richard III and heir to throne 1485; made his peace with Henry VII, but supported Simnel invasion 1487; killed at Stoke. Lincoln's brothers Edmund Earl of Suffolk (executed 1513) and Richard (killed at Pavia 1525), potential Yorkist claimants, and so used by European rulers.

POLE: (Not to be confused with the above.) Sir Geoffrey, married Margaret, daughter of Duke of Clarence; she was created Countess of Salisbury 1513. Her son Reginald opposed Henry's divorce; refused to return from Italy 1534; cardinal 1536. Her sons Geoffrey and Henry (Lord Montague) accused of treason 1538; Margaret executed 1541. Reginald championed moderate reform in Rome; nearly elected pope 1549; papal legate 1553; Archbishop of Canterbury 1556; died 17 November 1558.

RIDLEY, Nicholas (1503–55): Protestant Bishop of London 1550; a zealous reformer, though irritated by Hooper's scruples (*q.v.*); burned at Oxford.

RUSSELL, John: of a Dorset gentry family; diplomat, and soldier; created baron 1539, with generous grant of land and offices, and president of Council of the West; put down Western Rebellion of 1549; refused to support Somerset; became Earl of Bedford 1550. His son Francis, second earl; religious exile in Mary's reign; returned to serve in 1557–8; important Puritan patron under Elizabeth.

RYVERS: *see* Woodville.

BIOGRAPHICAL INDEX

SALISBURY: *see* Neville, Pole.

SEYMOUR, Edward: brother of Queen Jane Seymour; military commander (as Earl of Hertford) in last years of Henry VIII; protector 1547, and Duke of Somerset; deposed as protector 1549; reinstated in the council 1550; arrested 1551; executed January 1552. His brother Thomas, married Queen Catherine Parr 1547; accused of treason; executed 1549.

SOMERSET: *see* Beaufort, Seymour.

STAFFORD, Humphrey: grandson of Thomas, Duke of Gloucester, youngest son of Edward III; created Duke of Buckingham 1444; reputedly richest man in England. With his brother Thomas Bourchier, Archbishop of Canterbury, played balancing role in politics of 1450s; killed battle of Northampton 1460. Henry, second duke, supported Richard III 1483; then rebelled and executed. Edward, third duke, executed on treason charge 1521.

STANLEY: the family had extensive lands in north Wales, Cheshire and Lancashire. Thomas Stanley married Margaret Beaufort, Henry VII's mother; by prevarication he and his brother William helped Henry's victory at Bosworth, for which he was created Earl of Derby. William executed on treason charge 1495.

SUFFOLK: *see* Grey, de la Pole.

TUNSTALL, Cuthbert (1474–1559): Bishop of London, 1522–30, Durham from 1530; hesitant acceptance of royal supremacy; privy councillor in Edward's reign until accused of treason 1550; composed defence of Catholic eucharistic doctrine; deprived of bishopric 1552; restored in Mary's reign; deprived again in 1559 for opposing the Elizabethan settlement.

TUDOR: Anglesey gentry family. Owen Tudor secretly married Queen Catherine, widow of Henry V, about 1430. Their sons Edmund and Jasper were therefore Henry VI's half-brothers. Edmund was created Earl of Richmond 1453; and married to Margaret Beaufort in 1456; died before the birth of his son, the future Henry VII. Jasper, created Earl of Pembroke in 1453, was a loyal Lancastrian; with his nephew in exile, he then became Duke of Bedford 1485; died, without legitimate issue, 1495.

TYNDALE, William: Oxford scholar, early Lutheran; in Germany from 1524; translated New Testament; burned as heretic in Netherlands 1536.

WARHAM, William: Archbishop of Canterbury from 1504 until death in 1532.

WARWICK: *see* Neville, Dudley.

WOLSEY, Thomas (1475?–1530): born at Ipswich, allegedly butcher's son; Oxford academic; tutor to family of Marquis of Dorset; almoner to Henry VII; Henry VIII's chief minister from 1512; Bishop of Lincoln, then Archbishop of York 1514; held in plurality with York, bishopric of Bath and Wells 1518–23, Durham 1523–9, Winchester 1529–30; cardinal 1515; lord chancellor 1515; papal legate from 1518; dismissed from political office 1529.

WOODVILLE, Richard: brought the family to prominence in 1436 by marrying Jacquetta of Luxemburg, widow of Henry v's brother John, Duke of Bedford. Richard became a baron in 1448, and was created Earl Ryvers in 1466 after his daughter Elizabeth married Edward IV; executed 1469. His son **Anthony**, second earl, was guardian of the future Edward V; executed 1483. Anthony's brother **Lionel**, Bishop of Salisbury from 1482, took part in the Buckingham rebellion of 1483; died in exile 1484.

WYATT, Thomas: courtier, diplomat, and poet; one-time lover of Anne Boleyn; gave evidence against Anne 1536; died 1542. His son, also **Thomas**, led the Kentish rebellion of 1554, for which he was executed.

YORK, Richard, Duke of (1411–60): doubly descended from Edward III; considered heir to Henry VI until birth of Henry's son 1453; (*see* chapter 3 *passim*) claimed throne; and killed at Wakefield 1460.

YORK, Margaret of (1446–1503): sister of Edward IV; married Charles, Duke of Burgundy (*q.v*), 1468; widowed 1477; supported Simnel and Warbeck.

The Crown and its Claimants 1399–1485

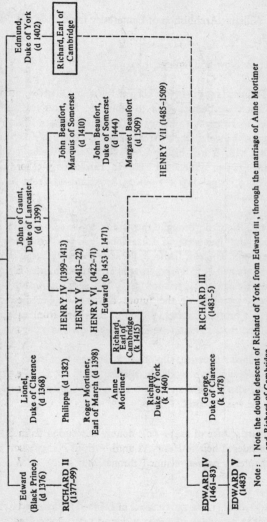

Note: 1 Note the double descent of Richard of York from Edward III, through the marriage of Anne Mortimer and Richard of Cambridge.

2 Note the difficulties of Henry VII's claim; it depended on his mother being able to transmit a claim to the throne – yet on that principle the Yorkist claim was clearly superior. In addition, his great-grandfather John Beaufort was born a bastard, and, though he was later legitimated, this probably barred a claim to the throne.

3 Henry VIII, on the other hand, had a good claim to the throne, on Yorkist grounds – his mother, Elizabeth, being the eldest daughter of Edward IV.

Table 2
The Crown 1485–1603

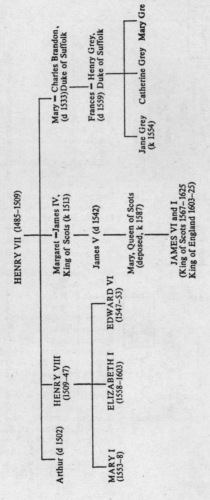

Note: 1 That Henry VIII's will gave priority to descendants of his youngest sister Mary over those of Margaret.

2 That, even if Edward VI's sisters Mary and Elizabeth were excluded as bastards, and Henry's provisions for the further descent followed, the natural claimant would be Frances Grey, not her daughter Jane.

INDEX

INDEX